Projections of Education Statistics to 2024

43rd Edition

National Center for Education Statistics

The National Center for Education Statistics (NCES) is the primary federal entity for collecting, analyzing, and reporting data related to education in the United States and other nations. It fulfills a congressional mandate to collect, collate, analyze, and report full and complete statistics on the condition of education in the United States; conduct and publish reports and specialized analyses of the meaning and significance of such statistics; assist state and local education agencies in improving their statistical systems; and review and report on education activities in foreign countries.

NCES activities are designed to address high-priority education data needs; provide consistent, reliable, complete, and accurate indicators of education status and trends; and report timely, useful, and high-quality data to the U.S. Department of Education, the Congress, the states, other education policymakers, practitioners, data users, and the general public. Unless specifically noted, all information contained herein is in the public domain.

We strive to make our products available in a variety of formats and in language that is appropriate to a variety of audiences. You, as our customer, are the best judge of our success in communicating information effectively. If you have any comments or suggestions about this or any other NCES product or report, we would like to hear from you. Please direct your comments to

NCES, IES, U.S. Department of Education Potomac Center Plaza 550 12th Street, SW Washington, DC 20202

The NCES Home Page address is http://nces.ed.gov. The NCES Publications and Products address is http://nces.ed.gov/pubsearch.

This report was prepared in part under Contract No. ED-IES-14-O-5005 with IHS Global Inc. Mention of trade names, commercial products, or organizations does not imply endorsement by the U.S. Government.

Suggested Citation
Hussar, W.J., and Bailey, T.M. (2016). *Projections of Education Statistics to 2024* (NCES 2016-013). U.S. Department of Education, National Center for Education Statistics. Washington, DC: U.S. Government Printing Office.

Content Contact
(202) 245-6389

william.hussar@ed.gov

ISBN: 978-1-59888-847-8

Foreword

Projections of Education Statistics to 2024 is the 43rd report in a series begun in 1964. It includes statistics on elementary and secondary schools and degree-granting postsecondary institutions. This report provides revisions of projections shown in *Projections of Education Statistics to 2023* and projections of enrollment, graduates, teachers, and expenditures to the year 2024.

In addition to projections at the national level, the report includes projections of public elementary and secondary school enrollment and public high school graduates to the year 2024 at the state level. The projections in this report were produced by the National Center for Education Statistics (NCES) to provide researchers, policy analysts, and others with state-level projections developed using a consistent methodology. They are not intended to supplant detailed projections prepared for individual states.

Assumptions regarding the population and the economy are the key factors underlying the projections of education statistics. NCES projections do not reflect changes in national, state, or local education policies that may affect education statistics.

Appendix A of this report outlines the projection methodology and describes the models and assumptions used to develop the national and state projections. The enrollment models use enrollment data and population estimates and projections from NCES and the U.S. Census Bureau. The models are based on the mathematical projection of past data patterns into the future. The models also use projections of economic variables from IHS Global Inc., an economic forecasting service.

The projections presented in this report are based on the 2010 census and assumptions for the fertility rate, internal migration, net immigration, and mortality rate from the Census Bureau. For further information, see appendix A.

Thomas D. Snyder, Supervisor
Annual Reports and Information Staff
National Center for Education Statistics

This page intentionally left blank.

Contents

List of Tables

Appendix A. Introduction to Projection Methodology

Appendix B. Supplementary Tables

List of Figures

About This Report

PROJECTIONS

This edition of *Projections of Education Statistics* provides projections for key education statistics, including enrollment, graduates, teachers, and expenditures in elementary and secondary public and private schools, as well as enrollment and degrees conferred at degree-granting postsecondary institutions. Included are national data on enrollment and graduates for at least the past 15 years and projections to the year 2024. Also included are state-level data on enrollment in public elementary and secondary schools and public high schools beginning in 1990, with projections to 2024. This report is organized by the level of schooling with sections 1, 2, 3, and 4 covering aspects of elementary and secondary education and sections 5 and 6 covering aspects of postsecondary education.

There are a number of limitations in projecting some statistics. Because of this, state-level data on enrollment and graduates in private elementary and secondary schools and on enrollment and degrees conferred in degree-granting postsecondary institutions are not included. Neither the actual numbers nor the projections of public and private elementary and secondary school enrollment include homeschooled students. Projections of elementary and secondary school enrollment and public high school graduates by age, state, and race/ethnicity are not included as the projections of the population by age, state, and race/ethnicity are not presently available. While there were enough years of data to produce projections of public elementary and secondary enrollment separately for Asians and Pacific Islanders, there were not enough years of data to produce separate projections for Asians and Pacific Islanders for either public high school graduates or enrollment in degree-granting postsecondary institutions.

Similar methodologies were used to obtain a uniform set of projections for each of the 50 states and the District of Columbia. These projections are further adjusted to agree with the national projections of public elementary and secondary school enrollment and public high school graduates contained in this report.

The summary of projections provides highlights of the national and state data, while the reference tables and figures present more detail. All calculations within *Projections of Education Statistics* are based on unrounded estimates. Therefore, the reader may find that a calculation, such as a difference or percentage change, cited in the text or figure may not be identical to the calculation obtained by using the rounded values shown in the accompanying tables. Most figures in this report present historical and forecasted data from 1999 through 2024. The shaded area of these figures highlights the projected data and begins at the last year of actual data and ends in 2024. As the last year of historical data differs by survey, the year in which the shaded area begins also differs.

Most statements in sections 1 through 6 examine a single statistic over a period of time. In each case, a trend test using linear regression was conducted to test for structure in the data over that time period. If the p value for the trend variable was less than 0.05, the text states that the statistic has either increased or decreased. If the p value of the trend variable was greater than 0.05, different procedures were followed, depending on the sources of the data of the first and last years of the time period. If the data for at least one of the two years came from a sample survey, a two-tailed t test at the .05 level was conducted to determine if any apparent difference between the data for the two years is not reliably measurable due to the uncertainty around the data. Depending on the results of the test, the text either includes a comparison of the two numbers or says that there was no measurable difference between the two numbers. However, if both the first and last years of the time period came from a universe sample and/or were projections, then the text compares the first and last years in the time period.

Appendix A describes the methodology and assumptions used to develop the projections; appendix B presents supplementary tables; appendix C describes data sources; appendix D is a list of the references; appendix E presents a list of abbreviations; and appendix F is a glossary of terms.

LIMITATIONS OF PROJECTIONS

Projections of a time series usually differ from the final reported data due to errors from many sources, such as the properties of the projection methodologies, which depend on the validity of many assumptions.

The mean absolute percentage error is one way to express the forecast accuracy of past projections. This measure expresses the average of the absolute values of errors in percentage terms, where errors are the differences between past projections and actual data. For example, based on past editions of *Projections of Education Statistics*, the mean absolute percentage errors of public school enrollment in grades prekindergarten through 12 for lead times of 1, 2, 5, and 10 years were 0.3, 0.5, 1.3, and 2.4 percent, respectively. In contrast, mean absolute percentage errors of private school enrollment in grades prekindergarten through 8 for lead times of 1, 2, 5, and 10 years were 2.6, 5.8, 10.0, and 17.9 percent, respectively. For more information on mean absolute percentage errors, see table A-2 in appendix A.

This page intentionally left blank.

Section 1
Elementary and Secondary Enrollment

INTRODUCTION

Total public and private elementary and secondary school enrollment was 55 million in fall 2012, representing a 4 percent increase since fall 1999 (table 1). Between fall 2012, the last year of actual public school data, and fall 2024, a further increase of 5 percent is expected. Public school enrollment is projected to be higher in 2024 than in 2012 while private school enrollment is projected to be lower. Public school enrollments are projected to be to be higher in 2024 than in 2012 for Hispanics, Asians/Pacific Islanders, and students of Two or more races. Enrollment is projected to be lower for Whites, American Indians/Alaska Natives, and about the same for Blacks (table 6). Public school enrollments are projected to be higher in 2024 than in 2012 for the South and West, and about the same in the Northeast and Midwest (table 3).

Factors affecting the projections

The grade progression rate method was used to project school enrollments. This method assumes that future trends in factors affecting enrollments will be consistent with past patterns. It implicitly includes the net effect of factors such as dropouts, deaths, nonpromotion, transfers to and from public schools, and, at the state level, migration. See appendixes A.0 and A.1 for more details.

Factors that were not considered

The projections do not assume changes in policies or attitudes that may affect enrollment levels. For example, they do not account for changing state and local policies on prekindergarten (preK) and kindergarten programs. Continued expansion of these programs could lead to higher enrollments at the elementary school level. Projections exclude the number of students who are homeschooled.

Students of Two or more races

This is the fourth edition of *Projections of Education Statistics* to include actual and projected numbers for enrollment in public elementary and secondary school for students of Two or more races. Collection of enrollment data for this racial/ethnic group began in 2008. The actual values from 2008 through 2012 and all the projected values for enrollments of the other racial/ethnic groups are lower than they would have been if this racial/ethnic category had not been added.

Accuracy of Projections

An analysis of projection errors from the past 31 editions of *Projections of Education Statistics* indicates that the mean absolute percentage errors (MAPEs) for lead times of 1, 2, 5, and 10 years out for projections of public school enrollment in grades preK–12 were 0.3, 0.5, 1.3, and 2.4 percent, respectively. For the 1-year-out prediction, this means that the methodology used by the National Center for Education Statistics (NCES) has produced projections that have, on average, deviated from actual observed values by 0.3 percent. For projections of public school enrollment in grades preK–8, the MAPEs for lead times of 1, 2, 5, and 10 years out were 0.3, 0.6, 1.5, and 3.0 percent, respectively, while the MAPEs for projections of public school enrollment in grades 9–12 were 0.4, 0.6, 1.2, and 2.5 percent, respectively, for the same lead times. An analysis of projection errors from the past 13 editions of *Projections of Education Statistics* indicates that the mean absolute percentage errors (MAPEs) for lead times of 1, 2, 5, and 10 years out for projections of private school enrollment in grades preK–12 were 2.2, 5.5, 8.3, and 15.2 percent, respectively. For projections of private school enrollment in grades preK–8, the MAPEs for lead times of 1, 2, 5, and 10 years out were 2.6, 5.8, 10.0, and 17.9 percent, respectively, while the MAPEs for projections of private school enrollment in grades 9–12 were 2.7, 4.2, 2.6, and 6.6 percent, respectively, for the same lead times. For more information, see table A-2 in appendix A.

Total elementary and secondary enrollment

▲ increased 4 percent between 1999 and 2012; and

▲ is projected to increase 5 percent between 2012 and 2024.

Enrollment in prekindergarten through grade 8

■ was not measurably different in 2012 than in 1999; and

▲ is projected to increase 7 percent between 2012 and 2024.

Enrollment in grades 9–12

▲ increased 10 percent between 1999 and 2012; and

▲ is projected to increase 2 percent between 2012 and 2024.

For more information:
Table 1

Figure 1. **Actual and projected numbers for enrollment in elementary and secondary schools, by grade level: Fall 1999 through fall 2024**

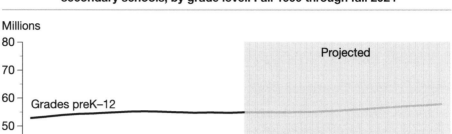

NOTE: PreK = prekindergarten. Enrollment numbers for prekindergarten through 12th grade and prekindergarten through 8th grade include private nursery and prekindergarten enrollment in schools that offer kindergarten or higher grades. Since the biennial Private School Universe Survey (PSS) is collected in the fall of odd-numbered years, private school numbers for alternate years are estimated based on data from the PSS. Some data have been revised from previously published figures. Mean absolute percentage errors of selected education statistics can be found in table A-2, appendix A.
SOURCE: U.S. Department of Education, National Center for Education Statistics, Common Core of Data (CCD), "State Nonfiscal Survey of Public Elementary/Secondary Education," 1999–2000 through 2012–13; Private School Universe Survey (PSS), selected years 1999–2000 through 2011–12; and National Elementary and Secondary Enrollment Projection Model, 1972 through 2024. (This figure was prepared May 2015.)

Figure 2. Actual and projected numbers for enrollment in elementary and secondary schools, by control of school: Fall 1999 through fall 2024

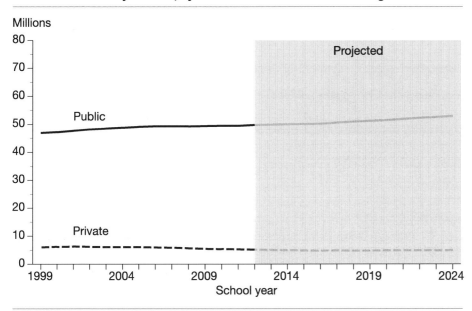

NOTE: Private school numbers include private nursery and prekindergarten enrollment in schools that offer kindergarten or higher grades. Since the biennial Private School Universe Survey (PSS) is collected in the fall of odd-numbered years, private school numbers for alternate years are estimated based on data from the PSS. Some data have been revised from previously published figures. Mean absolute percentage errors of selected education statistics can be found in table A-2, appendix A.
SOURCE: U.S. Department of Education, National Center for Education Statistics, Common Core of Data (CCD), "State Nonfiscal Survey of Public Elementary/Secondary Education," 1999–2000 through 2012–13; Private School Universe Survey (PSS), selected years 1999–2000 through 2011–12; and National Elementary and Secondary Enrollment Projection Model, 1972 through 2024. (This figure was prepared May 2015.)

Enrollment by control of school

Enrollment in public elementary and secondary schools

▲ increased 6 percent between 1999 and 2012; and

▲ is projected to increase 6 percent between 2012 and 2024.

Enrollment in private elementary and secondary schools

▼ decreased 14 percent between 1999 and 2012; and

▼ is projected to be 4 percent lower in 2024 than in 2012.

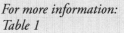

For more information:
Table 1

Enrollment by state

The expected 6 percent national increase in public school enrollment between 2012 and 2024 plays out differently among the states.

▲ Enrollments are projected to be higher in 2024 than in 2012 for 36 states and the District of Columbia, with projected enrollments

  • 5 percent or more higher in 23 states; and

  • less than 5 percent higher in 13 states and the District of Columbia.

▼ Enrollments are projected to be lower in 2024 than in 2012 for 14 states, with projected enrollments

  • 5 percent or more lower in 3 states; and

  • less than 5 percent lower in 11 states.

For more information:
Tables 3 through 5

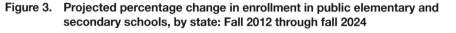

Figure 3. Projected percentage change in enrollment in public elementary and secondary schools, by state: Fall 2012 through fall 2024

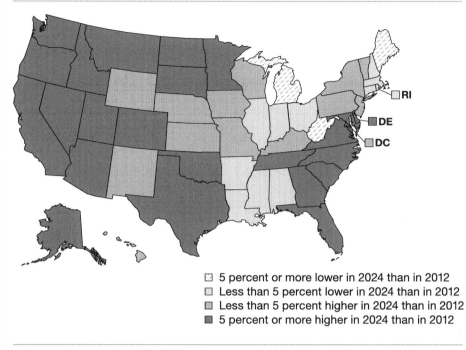

☐ 5 percent or more lower in 2024 than in 2012
☐ Less than 5 percent lower in 2024 than in 2012
☐ Less than 5 percent higher in 2024 than in 2012
■ 5 percent or more higher in 2024 than in 2012

NOTE: Calculations are based on unrounded numbers. Mean absolute percentage errors of enrollment in public elementary and secondary schools by state and region can be found in table A-7, appendix A. The states comprising each geographic region can be found in appendix F.
SOURCE: U.S. Department of Education, National Center for Education Statistics, Common Core of Data (CCD), "State Nonfiscal Survey of Public Elementary/Secondary Education," 2012–13; and State Public Elementary and Secondary Enrollment Projection Model, 1980 through 2024. (This figure was prepared May 2015.)

Figure 4.   Actual and projected numbers for enrollment in public elementary and secondary schools, by region: Fall 2006, fall 2012, and fall 2024

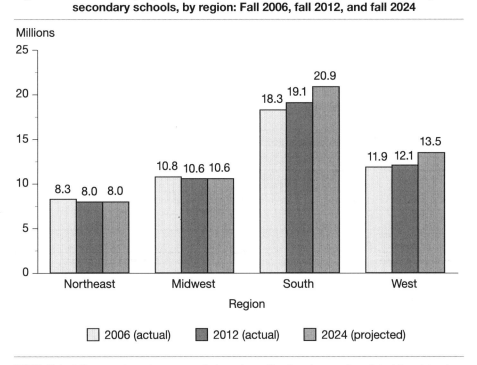

Millions

Region	2006 (actual)	2012 (actual)	2024 (projected)
Northeast	8.3	8.0	8.0
Midwest	10.8	10.6	10.6
South	18.3	19.1	20.9
West	11.9	12.1	13.5

☐ 2006 (actual)   ▨ 2012 (actual)   ☐ 2024 (projected)

NOTE: Calculations are based on unrounded numbers. See the glossary for a list of the states in each region. Mean absolute percentage errors of enrollment in public elementary and secondary schools by state and region can be found in table A-7, appendix A. Some data have been revised from previously published figures. The states comprising each geographic region can be found in appendix F.

SOURCE: U.S. Department of Education, National Center for Education Statistics, Common Core of Data (CCD), "State Nonfiscal Survey of Public Elementary/Secondary Education," 2006–07 and 2012–13; and State Public Elementary and Secondary Enrollment Projection Model, 1980 through 2024. (This figure was prepared May 2015.)

Enrollment by region

Public elementary and secondary enrollment is projected to

■ be about the same number in 2012 and 2024 for students in the Northeast;

■ be about the same number in 2012 and 2024 for students in the Midwest;

▲ increase 9 percent between 2012 and 2024 in the South; and

▲ increase 11 percent between 2012 and 2024 in the West.

For more information:
Tables 3 through 5

RACE/ETHNICITY (PUBLIC SCHOOL DATA)

Enrollment by race/ethnicity

Enrollment in public elementary and secondary schools is projected to

▼ decrease 5 percent between 2012 and 2024 for students who are White;

■ be about the same number in 2012 and 2024 for students who are Black;

▲ increase 28 percent between 2012 and 2024 for students who are Hispanic;

▲ increase 18 percent between 2012 and 2024 for students who are Asian/Pacific Islander;

▼ decrease 8 percent between 2012 and 2024 for students who are American Indian/Alaska Native; and

▲ increase 38 percent between 2012 and 2024 for students who are of Two or more races. (The line for this racial/ethnic group in figure 5 begins in 2010 when data for that group is available for all 50 states and the District of Columbia.)

For more information:
Tables 6 and 7

Figure 5. Actual and projected numbers for enrollment in public elementary and secondary schools, by race/ethnicity: Fall 1999 through fall 2024

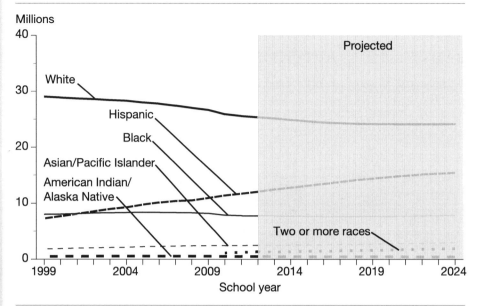

NOTE: Race categories exclude persons of Hispanic ethnicity. Enrollment data for students not reported by race/ethnicity were prorated by state and grade to match state totals. Data on students of Two or more races were not collected separately prior to 2008 and data on students of Two or more races from 2008 and 2009 were not reported by all states. Only in 2010 and later years were those data available for all 50 states. Total counts of ungraded students were prorated to prekindergarten through grade 8 and grades 9 through 12 based on prior reports. Some data have been revised from previously published figures. Detail may not sum to totals because of rounding. Mean absolute percentage errors of selected education statistics can be found in table A-2, appendix A.
SOURCE: U.S. Department of Education, National Center for Education Statistics, Common Core of Data (CCD), "State Nonfiscal Survey of Public Elementary/Secondary Education," 1998–99 through 2012–13; and National Public Elementary and Secondary Enrollment by Race/Ethnicity Projection Model, 1994 through 2024. (This figure was prepared May 2015.)

Section 2
Elementary and Secondary Teachers

INTRODUCTION

Between fall 2012, the last year of actual public school data, and fall 2024, the number of teachers in elementary and secondary schools is projected to rise (table 8). The increase is projected to occur in public schools. The number of teachers in private schools in 2024 is projected to be about the same number as in 2012. Both public and private schools are projected to experience a decline in pupil/teacher ratios. The annual number of new teacher hires is projected to be higher in 2024 than in 2012 in both public and private schools.

Factors affecting the projections

The projections of the number of elementary and secondary teachers are related to projected levels of enrollments and education revenue receipts from state sources per capita. For more details, see appendixes A.0 and A.3.

Factors that were not considered

The projections do not take into account possible changes in the number of teachers due to the effects of government policies.

About pupil/teacher ratios

The overall elementary and secondary pupil/teacher ratio and pupil/teacher ratios for public and private schools were computed based on elementary and secondary enrollment and the number of classroom teachers by control of school.

About new teacher hires

A teacher is considered to be a new teacher hire for a certain control of school (public or private) for a given year if the teacher teaches in that control that year but had not taught in that control in the previous year. A teacher who moves from teaching in one control of school to the other control is considered a new teacher hire, but a teacher who moves from one school to another school in the same control is not considered a new teacher hire.

Accuracy of Projections

An analysis of projection errors from the past 24 editions of *Projections of Education Statistics* indicates that the mean absolute percentage errors (MAPEs) for projections of classroom teachers in public elementary and secondary schools were 0.8 percent for 1 years out, 1.6 percent for 2 years out, 3.0 percent for 5 years out, and 5.4 percent for 10 years out. For the 1-year-out prediction, this means that one would expect the projection to be within 0.8 percent of the actual value, on average. For more information on the MAPEs of different National Center for Education Statistics (NCES) projection series, see table A-2 in appendix A.

Number of teachers

The total number of elementary and secondary teachers

▲ increased 6 percent between 1999 and 2012, a period of 13 years; and

▲ is projected to increase 10 percent between 2012 and 2024, a period of 12 years.

The number of teachers in public elementary and secondary schools

▲ increased 7 percent between 1999 and 2012; and

▲ is projected to increase 11 percent between 2012 and 2024.

The number of teachers in private elementary and secondary schools

■ was not measurably different in 2012 than in 1999; and

■ is projected to be about the same number in 2024 as in 2012.

For more information:
Table 8

Figure 6. Actual and projected numbers for elementary and secondary teachers, by control of school: Fall 1999 through fall 2024

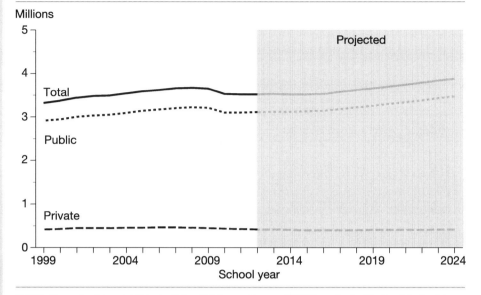

NOTE: Since the biennial Private School Universe Survey (PSS) is collected in the fall of odd-numbered years, private school numbers for alternate years are estimated based on data from the PSS. Data for teachers are expressed in full-time equivalents (FTE). Counts of private school teachers include prekindergarten through grade 12 in schools offering kindergarten or higher grades. Counts of public school teachers include prekindergarten through grade 12. Some data have been revised from previously published figures. Mean absolute percentage errors of selected education statistics can be found in table A-2, appendix A.
SOURCE: U.S. Department of Education, National Center for Education Statistics, Common Core of Data (CCD), "State Nonfiscal Survey of Public Elementary/Secondary Education," 1999–2000 through 2012–13; Private School Universe Survey (PSS), selected years, 1999–2000 through 2011–12; Elementary and Secondary Teacher Projection Model, 1973 through 2024. (This figure was prepared May 2015.)

Figure 7. **Actual and projected numbers for the pupil/teacher ratios in elementary and secondary schools, by control of school: Fall 1999 through fall 2024**

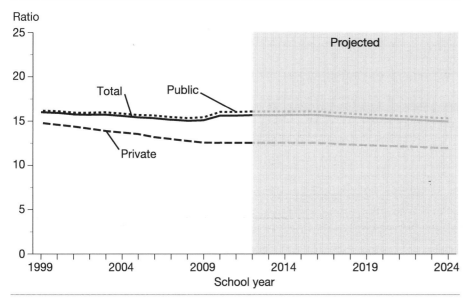

NOTE: Since the biennial Private School Universe Survey (PSS) is collected in the fall of odd-numbered years, private school numbers for alternate years are estimated based on data from the PSS. Data for teachers are expressed in full-time equivalents (FTE). Counts of private school teachers and enrollment include prekindergarten through grade 12 in schools offering kindergarten or higher grades. Counts of public school teachers and enrollment include prekindergarten through grade 12. Some data have been revised from previously published figures. Mean absolute percentage errors of selected education statistics can be found in table A-2, appendix A.
SOURCE: U.S. Department of Education, National Center for Education Statistics, Common Core of Data (CCD), "State Nonfiscal Survey of Public Elementary/Secondary Education," 1999–2000 through 2012–13; Private School Universe Survey (PSS), selected years, 1999–2000 through 2011–12; National Elementary and Secondary Enrollment Projection Model, 1972 through 2024; and Elementary and Secondary Teacher Projection Model, 1973 through 2024. (This figure was prepared May 2015.)

Pupil/teacher ratios

The pupil/teacher ratio in elementary and secondary schools

▼ decreased from 15.9 to 15.6 between 1999 and 2012; and

▼ is projected to decrease to 14.9 in 2024.

The pupil/teacher ratio in public elementary and secondary schools

▼ decreased from 16.1 to 16.0 between 1999 and 2012; and

▼ is projected to decrease to 15.3 in 2024.

The pupil/teacher ratio in private elementary and secondary schools

▼ decreased from 14.7 to 12.5 between 1999 and 2012; and

▼ is projected to decrease to 11.9 in 2024.

For more information:
Table 8

New teacher hires

The total number of new teacher hires

▲ was 5 percent higher in 2012 than in 1999 (321,000 versus 305,000); and

▲ is projected to increase 17 percent between 2012 and 2024, to 375,000.

The number of new teacher hires in public schools

▲ was 11 percent higher in 2012 than in 1999 (247,000 versus 222,000); and

▲ is projected to increase 19 percent between 2012 and 2024, to 293,000.

The number of new teacher hires in private schools

▼ was 11 percent lower in 2012 than in 1999 (74,000 versus 83,000); and

▲ is projected to increase 10 percent between 2012 and 2024, to 81,000.

For more information:
Table 8

Figure 8. Actual and projected numbers for elementary and secondary new teacher hires, by control of school: Fall 1999, fall 2012, and fall 2024

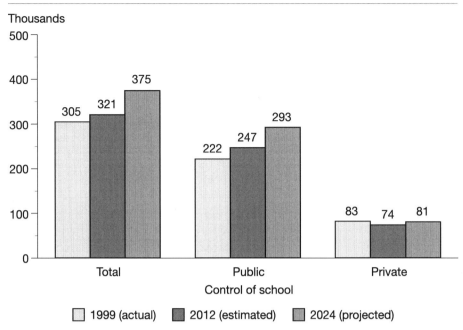

NOTE: Data for teachers are expressed in full-time equivalents (FTE). A teacher is considered to be a new hire for a public or private school if the teacher had not taught in that control of school in the previous year. A teacher who moves from a public to private or a private to public school is considered a new teacher hire, but a teacher who moves from one public school to another public school or one private school to another private school is not considered a new teacher hire. For more information about the New Teacher Hires Model, see appendix A.3. Calculations are based on unrounded numbers. Some data have been revised from previously published figures.

SOURCE: U.S. Department of Education, National Center for Education Statistics, Common Core of Data (CCD), "State Nonfiscal Survey of Public Elementary/Secondary Education," 1999–2000 and 2012–13; Private School Universe Survey (PSS), 1999–2000 and 2011–12; Schools and Staffing Survey (SASS), "Public School Teacher Data File," and "Private School Teacher Data File," 1999–2000 and 2011–12; Elementary and Secondary Teacher Projection Model, 1973 through 2024 and New Teacher Hires Projection Model, 1988 through 2024. (This figure was prepared May 2015.)

Section 3
High School Graduates

INTRODUCTION

The number of high school graduates increased nationally by 22 percent between 1999–2000 and 2011–12, the last year of actual data for public schools (table 9). The number of high school graduates is projected to be 3 percent higher in 2024–25 than in 2011–12. The number of public high school graduates is projected to be higher in 2024–25 than in 2011–12 while the number of private high school graduates is projected to be lower. The numbers of high school graduates are projected to be higher in 2024–25 than in 2011–12 in the South and West, lower in the Northeast, and about the same in the Midwest (table 10).

Factors affecting the projections

The projections of high school graduates are related to projections of 12th-graders and the historical relationship between the number of 12th-graders and the number of high school graduates. The methodology implicitly includes the net effect of factors such as dropouts, transfers to and from public schools, and, at the state level, migration. For more details, see appendixes A.0 and A.3.

About high school graduates

A high school graduate is defined as an individual who has received formal recognition from school authorities, by the granting of a diploma, for completing a prescribed course of study. This definition does not include other high school completers or high school equivalency recipients. Projections of graduates could be affected by changes in policies influencing graduation requirements.

High school graduates of Two or more races

This is the second edition of *Projections of Education Statistics* to include actual and projected numbers for high school graduates of Two or more races. Collection of high school graduate data for this racial/ethnic group began in 2008–09. The actual values from 2008–09 through 2011–12 and all the projected values for high school graduates of the other racial/ethnic groups are lower than they would have been if this racial/ethnic category had not been added.

Accuracy of Projections

For National Center for Education Statistics (NCES) projections of public high school graduates produced over the last 23 years, the mean absolute percentage errors (MAPEs) for lead times of 1, 2, 5, and 10 years out were 1.0, 1.1, 2.2, and 5.0, respectively. For the 1-year-out prediction, this means that one would expect the projection to be within 1.0 percent of the actual value, on average. For NCES projections of private high school graduates produced over the last 11 years, the MAPEs for lead times of 1, 2, 5, and 10 years out were 0.9, 1.2, 4.1, and 4.9 percent, respectively. For more information, see table A-2 in appendix A.

The total number of high school graduates

▲ increased 22 percent between 1999–2000 and 2011–12, a period of 12 years; and

▲ is projected to increase 3 percent between 2011–12 and 2024–25.

The number of public high school graduates

▲ increased 23 percent between 1999–2000 and 2011–12; and

▲ is projected to increase 6 percent between 2011–12 and 2024–25.

The number of private high school graduates

▲ increased 10 percent between 1999–2000 and 2011–12; and

▼ is projected to decrease 25 percent between 2011–12 and 2024–25.

For more information:
Table 9

Figure 9. Actual and projected numbers for high school graduates, by control of school: School years 1999–2000 through 2024–25

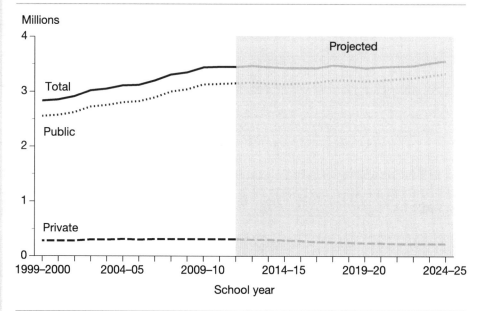

NOTE: Since the biennial Private School Universe Survey (PSS) is collected in the fall of odd-numbered years and the numbers collected for high school graduates are for the preceding year, private school numbers for odd years are estimated based on data from the PSS. Includes graduates of regular day school programs. Excludes graduates of other programs, when separately reported, and recipients of high school equivalency certificates. Some data have been revised from previously published figures. Mean absolute percentage errors of selected education statistics can be found in table A-2, appendix A.
SOURCE: U.S. Department of Education, National Center for Education Statistics, Common Core of Data (CCD), "State Nonfiscal Survey of Public Elementary/Secondary Education," 2000–01 through 2009–10; "State Dropout and Completion Data File," 2010–11 and 2011–12; Private School Universe Survey (PSS), selected years, 1999–2000 through 2011–12; and National High School Graduates Projection Model, 1972–73 through 2024–25. (This figure was prepared May 2015.)

Figure 10. Projected percentage change in the number of public high school graduates, by state: School years 2011–12 through 2024–25

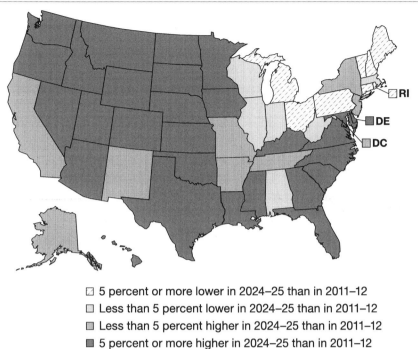

☐ 5 percent or more lower in 2024–25 than in 2011–12
☐ Less than 5 percent lower in 2024–25 than in 2011–12
▨ Less than 5 percent higher in 2024–25 than in 2011–12
▨ 5 percent or more higher in 2024–25 than in 2011–12

NOTE: Includes graduates of regular day school programs. Excludes graduates of other programs, when separately reported, and recipients of high school equivalency certificates. Calculations are based on unrounded numbers. Mean absolute percentage errors of public high school graduates by state and region can be found in table A-14, appendix A.
SOURCE: U.S. Department of Education, National Center for Education Statistics, Common Core of Data (CCD), "State Dropout and Completion Data File," 2011–12; and State Public High School Graduates Projection Model, 1980–81 through 2024–25. (This figure was prepared May 2015.)

High school graduates by state

The number of public high school graduates is projected to be higher in 2024–25 than in 2011–12. This plays out differently among the states.

▲ High school graduates are projected to be higher in 2024–25 than in 2011–12 for 36 states and the District of Columbia, with projected high school graduates

- 5 percent or more higher in 28 states; and

- less than 5 percent higher in 8 states and the District of Columbia.

▼ High school graduates are projected to be lower in 2024–25 than in 2011–12 for 14 states, with projected high school graduates

- 5 percent or more lower in 8 states; and

- less than 5 percent lower in 6 states.

For more information:
Table 10

High school graduates by region

The number of public high school graduates is projected to

▼ decrease 4 percent between 2011–12 and 2024–25 in the Northeast;

▼ be 1 percent lower in 2024–25 than in 2011–12 in the Midwest;

▲ increase 13 percent between 2011–12 and 2024–25 in the South; and

▲ increase 8 percent between 2011–12 and 2024–25 in the West.

For more information:
Table 10

Figure 11. Actual and projected numbers for public high school graduates, by region: School years 2006–07, 2011–12, and 2024–25

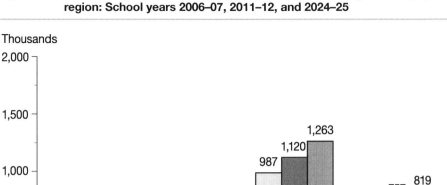

NOTE: Includes graduates of regular day school programs. Excludes graduates of other programs, when separately reported, and recipients of high school equivalency certificates. See the glossary for a list of states in each region. Mean absolute percentage errors of public high school graduates by state and region can be found in table A-14, appendix A. Calculations are based on unrounded numbers. Some data have been revised from previously published figures.
SOURCE: U.S. Department of Education, National Center for Education Statistics, Common Core of Data (CCD), "State Nonfiscal Survey of Public Elementary/Secondary Education," 2007–08; "State Dropout and Completion Data," 2011–12; and State Public High School Graduates Projection Model, 1980–81 through 2024–25. (This figure was prepared May 2015.)

Figure 12.   Actual and projected numbers for public high school graduates, by race/ethnicity: School years 1999–2000 through 2024–25

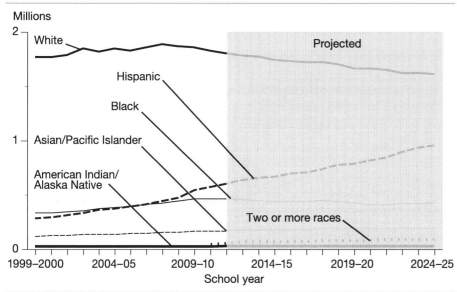

NOTE: Race categories exclude persons of Hispanic ethnicity. Data on students of Two or more races were not collected separately prior to 2007–08 and data on students of Two or more races from 2007–08 through 2009–10 were not reported by all states. Therefore, the data are not comparable to figures for 2010–11 and later years. Detail may not sum to totals because of rounding. Mean absolute percentage errors of selected education statistics can be found in table A-2, appendix A. Some data have been revised from previously published figures.
SOURCE: U.S. Department of Education, National Center for Education Statistics, Common Core of Data (CCD), "State Nonfiscal Survey of Public Elementary/Secondary Education," 1999–2000 through 2009–10; "State Dropout and Completion Data File," 2010–11 and 2011–12; and National Public High School Graduates by Race/Ethnicity Projection Model, 1995–96 through 2024–25. (This figure was prepared May 2015.)

High school graduates by race/ethnicity

The number of public high school graduates is projected to

▼   decrease 10 percent between 2011–12 and 2024–25 for students who are White;

▼   decrease 8 percent between 2011–12 and 2024–25 for students who are Black;

▲   increase 59 percent between 2011–12 and 2024–25 for students who are Hispanic;

▲   increase 8 percent between 2011–12 and 2024–25 for students who are Asian/Pacific Islander;

▼   decrease 15 percent between 2011–12 and 2024–25 for students who are American Indian/Alaska Native; and

▲   increase 52 percent between 2011–12 and 2024–25 for students who are of Two or more races.

For more information:
Table 11

This page intentionally left blank.

Section 4
Expenditures for Public Elementary and Secondary Education

INTRODUCTION

Current expenditures (e.g., instruction and support services) for public elementary and secondary education are projected to increase 21 percent in constant dollars (adjusted for inflation) between school years 2011–12, the last year of actual data, and 2024–25 (table 12).

Factors affecting the projections

The projections of current expenditures are related to projections of economic growth as measured by disposable income per capita and assistance by state governments to local governments. For more details, see appendixes A.0 and A.4.

Factors that were not considered

Many factors that may affect future school expenditures were not considered in the production of these projections. Such factors include policy initiatives as well as potential changes in the age distribution of elementary and secondary teachers as older teachers retire and are replaced by younger teachers, or as older teachers put off retirement for various reasons.

About constant dollars and current dollars

Throughout this section, projections of current expenditures are presented in constant 2013–14 dollars. The reference tables, later in this report, present these data both in constant 2013–14 dollars and in current dollars. The projections were developed in constant dollars and then placed in current dollars using projections for the Consumer Price Index (CPI) (table B-6 in appendix B). Projections of current expenditures in current dollars are not shown after 2016–17 due to the uncertain behavior of inflation over time.

Accuracy of Projections

An analysis of projection errors from similar models used in the past 24 editions of *Projections of Education Statistics* that contained expenditure projections indicates that mean absolute percentage errors (MAPEs) for total current expenditures in constant dollars were 1.6 percent for 1 year out, 2.4 percent for 2 years out, 2.5 percent for 5 years out, and 5.0 percent for 10 years out. For the 1-year-out prediction, this means that one would expect the projection to be within 1.4 percent of the actual value, on average. MAPEs for current expenditures per pupil in fall enrollment in constant dollars were 1.6 percent for 1 year out, 2.3 percent for 2 years out, 2.6 percent for 5 years out, and 5.7 percent for 10 years out. See appendix A for further discussion of the accuracy of recent projections of current expenditures, and see table A-2 in appendix A for the mean absolute percentage errors (MAPEs) of these projections.

Current expenditures

Current expenditures in constant 2013–14 dollars

▲ increased 21 percent from 1999–2000 to 2011–12, a period of 12 years; and

▲ are projected to increase 21 percent, to $659 billion, from 2011–12 to 2024–25, a period of 13 years.

For more information:
Table 12

Figure 13. Actual and projected current expenditures for public elementary and secondary schools (in constant 2013–14 dollars): School years 1999–2000 through 2024–25

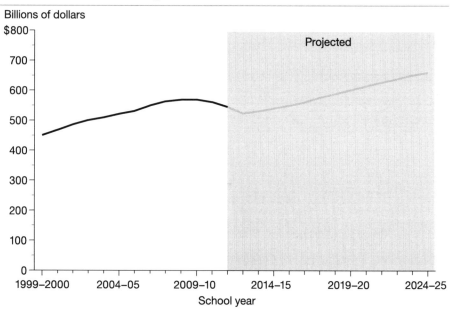

NOTE: Numbers were placed in constant dollars using the Consumer Price Index (CPI) for all urban consumers, Bureau of Labor Statistics, U.S. Department of Labor. For more detail about CPI, see table B-6 in appendix B. Current expenditures include instruction, support services, food services, and enterprise operations. Some data have been revised from previously published figures. Mean absolute percentage errors of selected education statistics can be found in table A-2, appendix A.
SOURCE: U.S. Department of Education, National Center for Education Statistics, Common Core of Data (CCD), "National Public Education Financial Survey," 1999–2000 through 2011–12; Public Elementary and Secondary School Current Expenditures Projection Model, 1969–70 through 2024–25. (This figure was prepared May 2015.)

Figure 14. Actual and projected current expenditures per pupil in fall enrollment in public elementary and secondary schools (in constant 2013–14 dollars): School years 1999–2000 through 2024–25

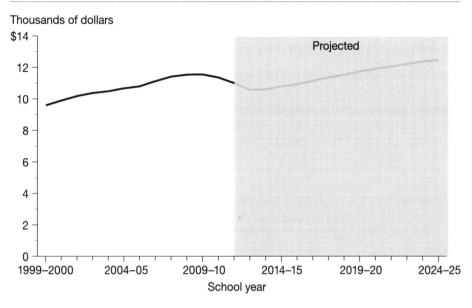

Thousands of dollars

NOTE: Numbers were placed in constant dollars using the Consumer Price Index (CPI) for all urban consumers, Bureau of Labor Statistics, U.S. Department of Labor. For more detail about CPI, see table B-6 in appendix B. Current expenditures include instruction, support services, food services, and enterprise operations. Some data have been revised from previously published figures. Mean absolute percentage errors of selected education statistics can be found in table A-2, appendix A. Fall enrollment pertains only to students for whom finance data were collected. This enrollment count differs slightly from enrollment counts reported on some tables.
SOURCE: U.S. Department of Education, National Center for Education Statistics, Common Core of Data (CCD), "State Nonfiscal Survey of Public Elementary/Secondary Education," 1999–2000 through 2012–13; "National Public Education Financial Survey," 1999–2000 through 2011–12; National Elementary and Secondary Enrollment Projection Model, 1972 through 2024; and Elementary and Secondary School Current Expenditures Projection Model, 1969–70 through 2024–25. (This figure was prepared May 2015.)

Current expenditures per pupil

Current expenditures per pupil in fall enrollment in constant 2013–14 dollars

▲ increased 15 percent from 1999–2000 to 2011–12; and

▲ are projected to increase 13 percent, to $12,500, from 2011–12 to 2024–25.

For more information:
Table 12

This page intentionally left blank.

Section 5
Enrollment in Degree-Granting Postsecondary Institutions

INTRODUCTION

Total enrollment in degree-granting postsecondary institutions is expected to increase 14 percent between fall 2013, the last year of actual data, and fall 2024 (table 13). Degree-granting institutions are postsecondary institutions that provide study beyond secondary school and offer programs terminating in an associate's, baccalaureate, or higher degree and participate in federal financial aid programs. Differential growth is expected by student characteristics such as age, sex, and attendance status (part-time or full-time). Enrollment is expected to increase in both public and private degree-granting postsecondary institutions.

Factors affecting the projections

The projections of enrollment levels are related to projections of college-age populations, disposable income, and unemployment rates. For more details, see appendixes A.0 and A.5. An important factor in the enrollment projections is the expected change in the population of 18- to 29-year-olds from 1999 through 2024 (table B-4 in appendix B).

Factors that were not considered

The enrollment projections do not take into account such factors as the cost of a college education, the economic value of an education, and the impact of distance learning due to technological changes. These factors may produce changes in enrollment levels. The racial/ethnic backgrounds of nonresident aliens are not known.

Figure 15. Actual and projected population numbers for 18- to 24-year-olds and 25- to 29-year-olds: 1999 through 2024

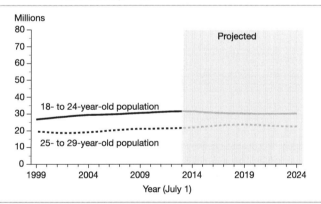

NOTE: Some data have been revised from previously published figures. Projections are from the U.S. Census Bureau's 2012 National Population Projections, ratio-adjusted to line up with the most recent historical estimate. SOURCE: U.S. Department of Commerce, Census Bureau, Population Estimates, retrieved January 5, 2015 from http://www.census.gov/popest/data/index.html; and Population Projections, retrieved January 5, 2015, from http://www.census.gov/population/projections/data/national/2012.html; and IHS Global Inc., "U.S. Quarterly Macroeconomic Model, 1st Quarter 2015 Short-Term Baseline Projections." (This table was prepared March 2015.)

Accuracy of Projections

For projections of total enrollment in degree-granting postsecondary institutions, an analysis of projection errors based on the past 17 editions of *Projections of Education Statistics* indicates that the mean absolute percentage errors (MAPEs) for lead times of 1, 2, 5, and 10 years out were 1.6, 2.6, 5.4, and 12.4 percent, respectively. For the 1-year-out prediction, this means that one would expect the projection to be within 1.6 percent of the actual value, on average. For more information, see table A-2 in appendix A.

TOTAL ENROLLMENT

Total enrollment in degree-granting postsecondary institutions

▲ increased 37 percent from 1999 to 2013, a period of 14 years; and

▲ is projected to increase 14 percent, to 23 million, from 2013 to 2024, a period of 11 years.

For more information:
Table 13

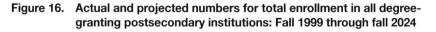

Figure 16.   Actual and projected numbers for total enrollment in all degree-granting postsecondary institutions: Fall 1999 through fall 2024

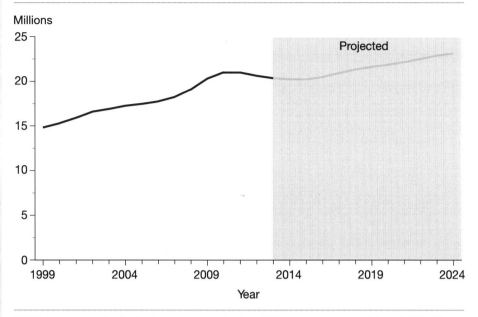

NOTE: Degree-granting institutions grant associate's or higher degrees and participate in Title IV federal financial aid programs. Some data have been revised from previously published figures. Mean absolute percentage errors of selected education statistics can be found in table A-2, appendix A. SOURCE: U.S. Department of Education, National Center for Education Statistics, Integrated Postsecondary Education Data System (IPEDS) "Fall Enrollment Survey" (IPEDS-EF:99); IPEDS Spring 2001 through Spring 2014, Enrollment component; and Enrollment in Degree-Granting Institutions Projection Model, 1980 through 2024. (This figure was prepared May 2015.)

Figure 17. Actual and projected numbers for total enrollment in all degree-granting postsecondary institutions, by age group: Fall 1999, fall 2013, and fall 2024

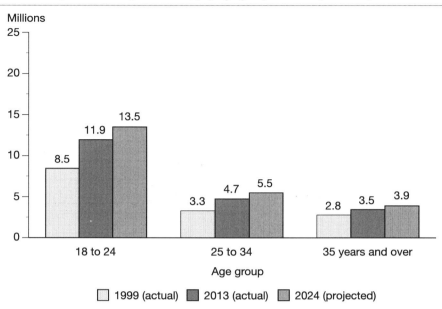

NOTE: Degree-granting institutions grant associate's or higher degrees and participate in Title IV federal financial aid programs. Distributions by age are estimates based on samples of the civilian noninstitutional population from the U.S. Census Bureau's Current Population Survey. Mean absolute percentage errors of selected education statistics can be found in table A-2, appendix A. Calculations are based on unrounded numbers.
SOURCE: U.S. Department of Education, National Center for Education Statistics, Integrated Postsecondary Education Data System (IPEDS) "Fall Enrollment Survey" (IPEDS-EF:99); IPEDS Spring 2014, Enrollment component; Enrollment in Degree-Granting Institutions Projection Model, 1980 through 2024; and U.S. Department of Commerce, Census Bureau, Current Population Reports, "Social and Economic Characteristics of Students," various years. (This figure was prepared May 2015.)

Enrollment by age of student

Enrollment in degree-granting postsecondary institutions of students who are 18 to 24 years old

▲ increased 40 percent between 1999 and 2013; and

▲ is projected to increase 13 percent between 2013 and 2024.

Enrollment in degree-granting postsecondary institutions of students who are 25 to 34 years old

▲ increased 41 percent between 1999 and 2013; and

▲ is projected to increase 17 percent between 2013 and 2024.

Enrollment in degree-granting postsecondary institutions of students who are 35 years old and over

▲ increased 25 percent between 1999 and 2013; and

▲ is projected to increase 10 percent between 2013 and 2024.

For more information:
Table 15

Figure 18. Actual and projected numbers for enrollment in all degree-granting postsecondary institutions, by sex: Fall 1999 through fall 2024

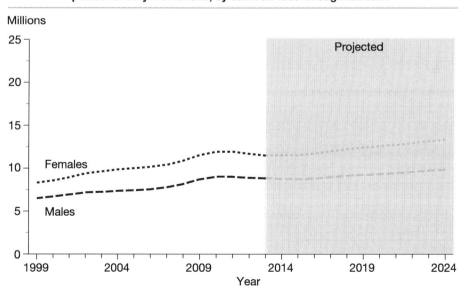

NOTE: Degree-granting institutions grant associate's or higher degrees and participate in Title IV federal financial aid programs. Some data have been revised from previously published figures. Mean absolute percentage errors of selected education statistics can be found in table A-2, appendix A.
SOURCE: U.S. Department of Education, National Center for Education Statistics, Integrated Postsecondary Education Data System (IPEDS) "Fall Enrollment Survey" (IPEDS-EF:99); IPEDS Spring 2001 through Spring 2014, Enrollment component; and Enrollment in Degree-Granting Institutions Projection Model, 1980 through 2024. (This figure was prepared May 2015.)

Enrollment by sex of student

Enrollment of males in degree-granting postsecondary institutions

▲ increased 36 percent between 1999 and 2013; and

▲ is projected to increase 11 percent between 2013 and 2024.

Enrollment of females in degree-granting postsecondary institutions

▲ increased 38 percent between 1999 and 2013; and

▲ is projected to increase 16 percent between 2013 and 2024.

For more information:
Tables 13 and 15

Enrollment by attendance status

Enrollment of full-time students in degree-granting postsecondary institutions

▲ increased 43 percent between 1999 and 2013; and

▲ is projected to increase 14 percent between 2013 and 2024.

Enrollment of part-time students in degree-granting postsecondary institutions

▲ increased 29 percent between 1999 and 2013; and

▲ is projected to increase 13 percent between 2013 and 2024.

For more information:
Tables 13–15

Figure 19.   Actual and projected numbers for enrollment in all degree-granting postsecondary institutions, by attendance status: Fall 1999 through fall 2024

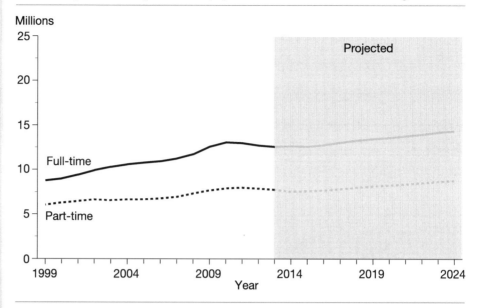

NOTE: Degree-granting institutions grant associate's or higher degrees and participate in Title IV federal financial aid programs. Some data have been revised from previously published figures. Mean absolute percentage errors of selected education statistics can be found in table A-2, appendix A. SOURCE: U.S. Department of Education, National Center for Education Statistics, Integrated Postsecondary Education Data System (IPEDS) "Fall Enrollment Survey" (IPEDS-EF:99); IPEDS Spring 2001 through Spring 2014, Enrollment component; and Enrollment in Degree-Granting Institutions Projection Model, 1980 through 2024. (This figure was prepared May 2015.)

Enrollment by level of student

Enrollment of undergraduate students in degree-granting postsecondary institutions

▲ increased 37 percent between 1999 and 2013; and

▲ is projected to increase 12 percent between 2013 and 2024.

Enrollment of postbaccalaureate students in degree-granting postsecondary institutions

▲ increased 37 percent between 1999 and 2013; and

▲ is projected to increase 20 percent between 2013 and 2024.

For more information:
Tables 16–17

Figure 20.   Actual and projected numbers for enrollment in all degree-granting postsecondary institutions, by level of degree: Fall 1999 through fall 2024

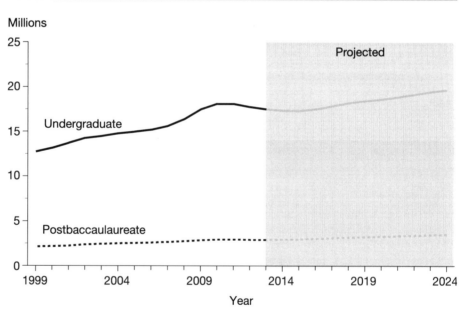

NOTE: Degree-granting institutions grant associate's or higher degrees and participate in Title IV federal financial aid programs. Some data have been revised from previously published figures. Mean absolute percentage errors of selected education statistics can be found in table A-2, appendix A. SOURCE: U.S. Department of Education, National Center for Education Statistics, Integrated Postsecondary Education Data System (IPEDS) "Fall Enrollment Survey" (IPEDS-EF:99); IPEDS Spring 2001 through Spring 2014, Enrollment component; and Enrollment in Degree-Granting Institutions Projection Model, 1980 through 2024. (This figure was prepared May 2015.)

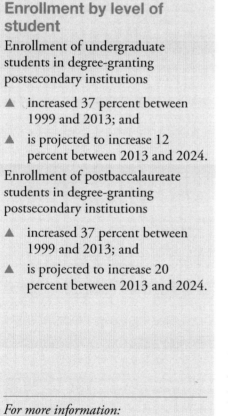

Figure 21. Actual and projected numbers for enrollment of U.S. residents in all degree-granting postsecondary institutions, by race/ethnicity: Fall 1999 through fall 2024

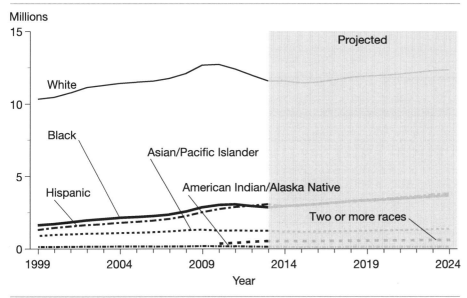

NOTE: Race categories exclude persons of Hispanic ethnicity. Because of underreporting and nonreporting of racial/ethnic data and nonresident aliens, some estimates are slightly lower than corresponding data in other published tables. Enrollment data in the "race/ethnicity unknown" (all years) and "Two or more races" (2008 and 2009 only) categories of the IPEDS "Enrollment component" have been prorated to the other racial/ethnic categories at the institutional level. Mean absolute percentage errors of selected education statistics can be found in table A-2, appendix A. Some data have been revised from previously published figures.
SOURCE: U.S. Department of Education, National Center for Education Statistics, Integrated Postsecondary Education Data System (IPEDS) "Fall Enrollment Survey" (IPEDS-EF:99); IPEDS Spring 2001 through Spring 2014, Enrollment component; and Enrollment in Degree-Granting Institutions by Race/Ethnicity Institutions Projection Model, 1980 through 2024. (This figure was prepared May 2015.)

Enrollment by race/ethnicity

Enrollment of U.S. residents is projected to

▲ increase 7 percent for students who are White between 2013 and 2024;

▲ increase 28 percent for students who are Black between 2013 and 2024;

▲ increase 25 percent for students who are Hispanic between 2013 and 2024;

▲ increase 10 percent for students who are Asian/Pacific Islander between 2013 and 2024;

■ be about the same number in 2013 and 2024 for students who are American Indian/Alaska Native; and

▲ increase 13 percent for students who are of Two or more races between 2013 and 2024.

For more information:
Table 19

Figure 22. Actual and projected numbers for enrollment in all degree-granting postsecondary institutions, by control of institution: Fall 1999 through fall 2024

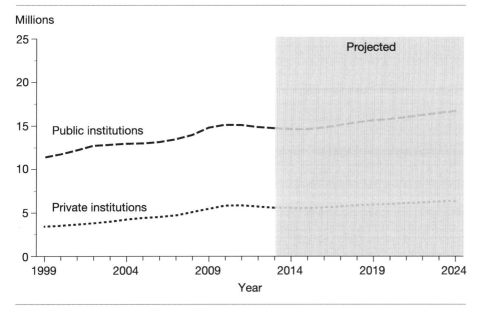

NOTE: Degree-granting institutions grant associate's or higher degrees and participate in Title IV federal financial aid programs. Some data have been revised from previously published figures. Mean absolute percentage errors of selected education statistics can be found in table A-2, appendix A.
SOURCE: U.S. Department of Education, National Center for Education Statistics, Integrated Postsecondary Education Data System (IPEDS) "Fall Enrollment Survey" (IPEDS-EF:99); IPEDS Spring 2001 through Spring 2014, Enrollment component; Enrollment in Degree-Granting Institutions Projection Model, 1980 through 2024. (This figure was prepared May 2015.)

Enrollment in public and private institutions

Enrollment in public degree-granting postsecondary institutions

▲ increased 30 percent between 1999 and 2013; and

▲ is projected to increase 13 percent between 2013 and 2024.

Enrollment in private degree-granting postsecondary institutions

▲ increased 62 percent between 1999 and 2013; and

▲ is projected to increase 14 percent between 2013 and 2024.

For more information:
Table 13

FIRST-TIME FRESHMEN ENROLLMENT

First-time freshmen fall enrollment

Total first-time freshmen fall enrollment in all degree-granting postsecondary institutions

▲ increased 27 percent from 1999 to 2013; and

▲ is projected to increase 12 percent between 2013 and 2024.

First-time freshmen fall enrollment of males in all degree-granting postsecondary institutions

▲ increased 26 percent from 1999 to 2013; and

▲ is projected to increase 9 percent between 2013 and 2024.

Total first-time freshmen fall enrollment of females in all degree-granting postsecondary institutions

▲ increased 27 percent from 1999 to 2013; and

▲ is projected to increase 15 percent between 2013 and 2024.

For more information:
Table 18

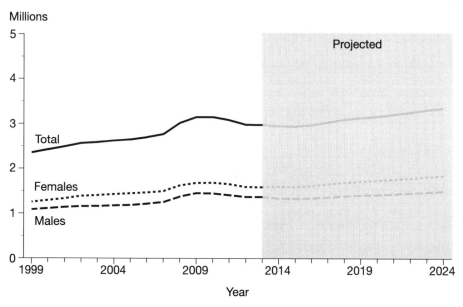

Figure 23. Actual and projected numbers for total first-time freshmen fall enrollment in all degree-granting postsecondary institutions, by sex: Fall 1999 through fall 2024

NOTE: Degree-granting institutions grant associate's or higher degrees and participate in Title IV federal financial aid programs. Some data have been revised from previously published figures. Mean absolute percentage errors of selected education statistics can be found in table A-2, appendix A. SOURCE: U.S. Department of Education, National Center for Education Statistics, Integrated Postsecondary Education Data System (IPEDS) "Fall Enrollment Survey" (IPEDS-EF:99); IPEDS Spring 2001 through Spring 2014, Enrollment component; Enrollment in Degree-Granting Institutions Projection Model, 1980 through 2024; and First-Time Freshmen Projection Model, 1975 through 2024. (This figure was prepared May 2015.)

Section 6
Postsecondary Degrees Conferred

INTRODUCTION

Long-term growth in enrollment in degree-granting postsecondary institutions has been reflected by increases in the numbers of associate's, bachelor's, master's and doctor's degrees conferred (tables 13 and 21). Increases in the number of degrees conferred are expected to continue between academic year 2012–13, the last year of actual data, and academic year 2024–25.

Factors affecting the projections

The projections of the number of degrees conferred are related to projections of the college-age populations developed by the Census Bureau and college enrollments from this report. For more details, see appendixes A.0 and A.6.

Factors that were not considered

Some factors that may affect future numbers of degrees, such as choice of degree and labor force requirements, were not included in the projection models.

Changes in degree classifications

The National Center for Education Statistics (NCES) no longer uses the first-professional degree classification. Most degrees formerly classified as first-professional—such as M.D., D.D.S., and law degrees—are now classified as doctor's degrees. However, master's of divinity degrees are now classified as master's degrees. This is the fourth edition of *Projections of Education Statistics* to use these new classifications. With this change, the actual numbers of master's and doctor's and degrees conferred are higher than the actual numbers in *Projections of Education Statistics to 2020* and earlier editions of this report. The revisions of actual numbers are reflected in the projections.

Accuracy of Projections

An analysis of projection errors from the past 6 editions of *Projections of Education Statistics* indicates that the mean absolute percentage errors (MAPEs) for lead times of 1, 2, and 5 years out for projections of associate's degrees conferred were 2.7, 6.1, and 18.3 percent, respectively. For the 1-year-out prediction, this means that the methodology used by the National Center for Education Statistics (NCES) has produced projections that have, on average, deviated from actual observed values by 2.7 percent. For projections of bachelor's degrees conferred, the MAPEs for lead times of 1, 2, and 5 years out were 0.7, 0.4, and 5.5 percent. No MAPEs were calculated for master's and doctor's degrees as only three other editions of *Projections of Education Statistics* used the current model for producing their projections due to the changes in classifications described above. For more information, see table A-2 in appendix A.

Associate's degrees

The total number of associate's degrees

▲ increased 78 percent between 1999–2000 and 2012–13; and

▲ is projected to increase 14 percent between 2012–13 and 2024–25.

The number of associate's degrees awarded to males

▲ increased 73 percent between 1999–2000 and 2012–13; and

▲ is projected to increase 10 percent between 2012–13 and 2024–25.

The number of associate's degrees awarded to females

▲ increased 82 percent between 1999–2000 and 2012–13; and

▲ is projected to increase 17 percent between 2012–13 and 2024–25.

For more information:
Table 21

Figure 24. Actual and projected numbers for associate's degrees conferred by degree-granting postsecondary institutions, by sex of recipient: Academic years 1999–2000 through 2024–25

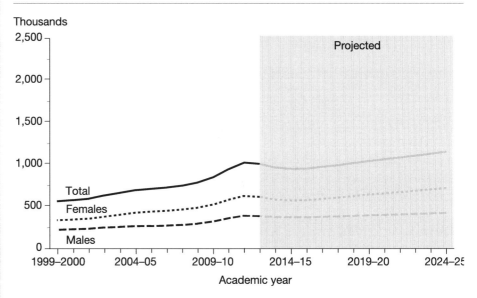

NOTE: Some data have been revised from previously published figures. Mean absolute percentage errors of selected education statistics can be found in table A-2, appendix A. SOURCE: U.S. Department of Education, National Center for Education Statistics, Integrated Postsecondary Education Data System (IPEDS); IPEDS Fall 2000 through Fall 2013 Completions component; and Degrees Conferred Projection Model, 1980–81 through 2024–25. (This figure was prepared May 2015.)

Bachelor's degrees

The total number of bachelor's degrees

▲ increased 49 percent between 1999–2000 and 2012–13; and

▲ is projected to increase 10 percent between 2012–13 and 2024–25.

The number of bachelor's degrees awarded to males

▲ increased 48 percent between 1999–2000 and 2012–13; and

▲ is projected to increase 7 percent between 2012–13 and 2024–25.

The number of bachelor's degrees awarded to females

▲ increased 49 percent between 1999–2000 and 2012–13; and

▲ is projected to increase 13 percent between 2012–13 and 2024–25.

For more information:
Table 21

Figure 25. Actual and projected numbers for bachelor's degrees conferred by degree-granting postsecondary institutions, by sex of recipient: Academic years 1999–2000 through 2024–25

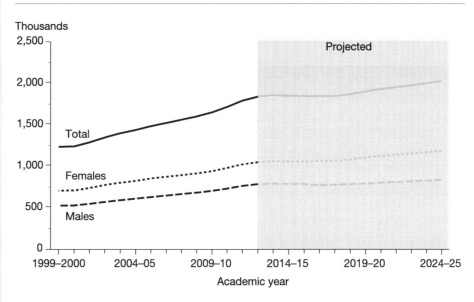

NOTE: Some data have been revised from previously published figures. Mean absolute percentage errors of selected education statistics can be found in table A-2, appendix A. SOURCE: U.S. Department of Education, National Center for Education Statistics, Integrated Postsecondary Education Data System (IPEDS); IPEDS Fall 2000 through Fall 2013 Completions component; and Degrees Conferred Projection Model, 1980–81 through 2024–25. (This figure was prepared May 2015.)

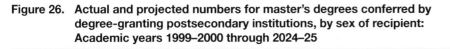

Figure 26. Actual and projected numbers for master's degrees conferred by degree-granting postsecondary institutions, by sex of recipient: Academic years 1999–2000 through 2024–25

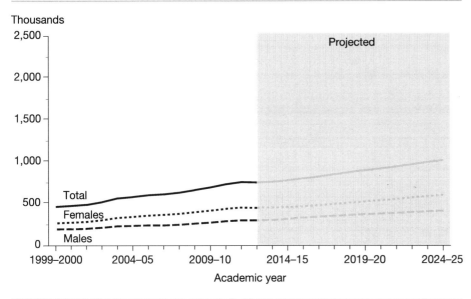

NOTE: Includes some degrees formerly classified as first professional such as divinity degrees (M.Div. and M.H.L./Rav). Some data have been revised from previously published figures. SOURCE: U.S. Department of Education, National Center for Education Statistics, Integrated Postsecondary Education Data System (IPEDS); IPEDS Fall 2000 through Fall 2013 Completions component; and Degrees Conferred Projection Model, 1980–81 through 2024–25. (This figure was prepared May 2015.)

Master's degrees

The total number of master's degrees

▲ increased 62 percent between 1999–2000 and 2012–13; and

▲ is projected to increase 36 percent between 2012–13 and 2024–25.

The number of master's degrees awarded to males

▲ increased 54 percent between 1999–2000 and 2012–13; and

▲ is projected to increase 38 percent between 2012–13 and 2024–25.

The number of master's degrees awarded to females

▲ increased 69 percent between 1999–2000 and 2012–13; and

▲ is projected to increase 34 percent between 2012–13 and 2024–25.

For more information:
Table 21

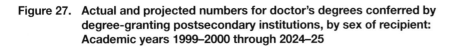

Figure 27. Actual and projected numbers for doctor's degrees conferred by degree-granting postsecondary institutions, by sex of recipient: Academic years 1999–2000 through 2024–25

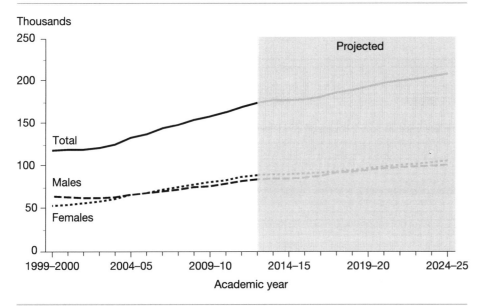

NOTE: Doctor's degrees include Ph.D., Ed.D., and comparable degrees at the doctoral level. Includes most degrees formerly classified as first-professional, such as M.D., D.D.S., and law degrees. Some data have been revised from previously published figures. Mean absolute percentage errors of selected education statistics can be found in table A-2, appendix A. SOURCE: U.S. Department of Education, National Center for Education Statistics, Integrated Postsecondary Education Data System (IPEDS); IPEDS Fall 2000 through Fall 2013 Completions component; and Degrees Conferred Projection Model, 1980–81 through 2024–25. (This figure was prepared May 2015.)

Doctor's degrees

The total number of doctor's degrees

▲ increased 47 percent between 1999–2000 and 2012–13; and

▲ is projected to increase 19 percent between 2012–13 and 2024–25.

The number of doctor's degrees awarded to males

▲ increased 31 percent between 1999–2000 and 2012–13; and

▲ is projected to increase 20 percent between 2012–13 and 2024–25.

The number of doctor's degrees awarded to females

▲ increased 67 percent between 1999–2000 and 2012–13; and

▲ is projected to increase 18 percent between 2012–13 and 2024–25.

For more information:
Table 21

This page intentionally left blank.

Reference Tables

This page intentionally left blank.

Table 1.
Table 1. Enrollment in elementary, secondary, and degree-granting postsecondary institutions, by level and control of institution: Selected years, 1869–70 through fall 2024

[In thousands]

Year	Total enrollment, all levels	Elementary and secondary, total	Public elementary and secondary schools			Private elementary and secondary schools[1]			Degree-granting postsecondary institutions[2]		
			Total	Prekindergarten through grade 8	Grades 9 through 12	Total	Prekindergarten through grade 8	Grades 9 through 12	Total	Public	Private
1	2	3	4	5	6	7	8	9	10	11	12
1869–70	—	—	6,872	6,792	80	—	—	—	52	—	—
1879–80	—	—	9,868	9,757	110	—	—	—	116	—	—
1889–90	14,491	14,334	12,723	12,520	203	1,611	1,516	95	157	—	—
1899–1900	17,092	16,855	15,503	14,984	519	1,352	1,241	111	238	—	—
1909–10	19,728	19,372	17,814	16,899	915	1,558	1,441	117	355	—	—
1919–20	23,876	23,278	21,578	19,378	2,200	1,699	1,486	214	598	—	—
1929–30	29,430	28,329	25,678	21,279	4,399	2,651	2,310	341	1,101	—	—
1939–40	29,539	28,045	25,434	18,832	6,601	2,611	2,153	458	1,494	797	698
1949–50	31,151	28,492	25,111	19,387	5,725	3,380	2,708	672	2,659	1,355	1,304
Fall 1959	44,497	40,857	35,182	26,911	8,271	5,675	4,640	1,035	3,640	2,181	1,459
Fall 1969	59,055	51,050	45,550	32,513	13,037	5,500[3]	4,200[3]	1,300[3]	8,005	5,897	2,108
Fall 1979	58,221	46,651	41,651	28,034	13,616	5,000[3]	3,700[3]	1,300[3]	11,570	9,037	2,533
Fall 1985	57,226	44,979	39,422	27,034	12,388	5,557	4,195	1,362	12,247	9,479	2,768
Fall 1990	60,683	46,864	41,217	29,876	11,341	5,648[3]	4,512[3]	1,136[3]	13,819	10,845	2,974
Fall 1991	62,087	47,728	42,047	30,503	11,544	5,681	4,550	1,131	14,359	11,310	3,049
Fall 1992	63,181	48,694	42,823	31,086	11,737	5,870[3]	4,746[3]	1,125[3]	14,487	11,385	3,103
Fall 1993	63,837	49,532	43,465	31,502	11,963	6,067	4,950	1,118	14,305	11,189	3,116
Fall 1994	64,385	50,106	44,111	31,896	12,215	5,994[3]	4,856[3]	1,138[3]	14,279	11,134	3,145
Fall 1995	65,020	50,759	44,840	32,338	12,502	5,918	4,756	1,163	14,262	11,092	3,169
Fall 1996	65,911	51,544	45,611	32,762	12,849	5,933[3]	4,755[3]	1,178[3]	14,368	11,120	3,247
Fall 1997	66,574	52,071	46,127	33,071	13,056	5,944	4,759	1,185	14,502	11,196	3,306
Fall 1998	67,033	52,526	46,539	33,344	13,195	5,988[3]	4,776[3]	1,212[3]	14,507	11,138	3,369
Fall 1999	67,725	52,875	46,857	33,486	13,371	6,018	4,789	1,229	14,850	11,376	3,474
Fall 2000	68,685	53,373	47,204	33,686	13,517	6,169[3]	4,906[3]	1,264[3]	15,312	11,753	3,560
Fall 2001	69,920	53,992	47,672	33,936	13,736	6,320	5,023	1,296	15,928	12,233	3,695
Fall 2002	71,015	54,403	48,183	34,114	14,069	6,220[3]	4,915[3]	1,306[3]	16,612	12,752	3,860
Fall 2003	71,551	54,639	48,540	34,201	14,339	6,099	4,788	1,311	16,911	12,859	4,053
Fall 2004	72,154	54,882	48,795	34,178	14,618	6,087[3]	4,756[3]	1,331[3]	17,272	12,980	4,292
Fall 2005	72,674	55,187	49,113	34,204	14,909	6,073	4,724	1,349	17,487	13,022	4,466
Fall 2006	73,066	55,307	49,316	34,235	15,081	5,991[3]	4,631[3]	1,360[3]	17,759	13,180	4,579
Fall 2007	73,449	55,201	49,291	34,204	15,086	5,910	4,546	1,364	18,248	13,491	4,757
Fall 2008	74,076	54,973	49,266	34,286	14,980	5,707[3]	4,365[3]	1,342[3]	19,103	13,972	5,131
Fall 2009	75,163	54,849	49,361	34,409	14,952	5,488	4,179	1,309	20,314	14,811	5,503
Fall 2010	75,886	54,867	49,484	34,625	14,860	5,382[3]	4,084[3]	1,299[3]	21,019	15,142	5,877
Fall 2011	75,800	54,790	49,522	34,773	14,749	5,268	3,977	1,291	21,011	15,116	5,894
Fall 2012	75,595	54,952	49,771	35,018	14,753	5,181[4]	3,906[4]	1,275[4]	20,643	14,880	5,762
Fall 2013[4]	75,412	55,036	49,942	35,188	14,754	5,094	3,858	1,236	20,376	14,746	5,630
Fall 2014[4]	75,219	54,965	49,986	35,159	14,826	4,979	3,779	1,200	20,255	14,660	5,595
Fall 2015[4]	75,227	54,994	50,094	35,182	14,912	4,899	3,744	1,155	20,234	14,646	5,588
Fall 2016[4]	75,563	55,077	50,229	35,282	14,947	4,848	3,728	1,120	20,486	14,820	5,666
Fall 2017[4]	76,372	55,447	50,584	35,595	14,989	4,863	3,768	1,095	20,925	15,129	5,796
Fall 2018[4]	77,049	55,719	50,871	35,856	15,015	4,848	3,786	1,063	21,330	15,421	5,909
Fall 2019[4]	77,661	56,031	51,183	36,125	15,058	4,848	3,813	1,035	21,630	15,639	5,991
Fall 2020[4]	78,263	56,404	51,547	36,366	15,182	4,856	3,839	1,017	21,859	15,802	6,057
Fall 2021[4]	78,948	56,779	51,910	36,587	15,324	4,869	3,863	1,006	22,168	16,022	6,146
Fall 2022[4]	79,662	57,151	52,260	36,839	15,421	4,891	3,889	1,003	22,511	16,267	6,243
Fall 2023[4]	80,405	57,524	52,601	37,223	15,378	4,922	3,924	998	22,881	16,531	6,350
Fall 2024[4]	81,007	57,872	52,920	37,615	15,304	4,952	3,959	994	23,135	16,716	6,419

—Not available.

[1]Beginning in fall 1985, data include estimates for an expanded universe of private schools. Therefore, direct comparisons with earlier years should be avoided.

[2]Data for 1869–70 through 1949–50 include resident degree-credit students enrolled at any time during the academic year. Beginning in 1959, data include all resident and extension students enrolled at the beginning of the fall term.

[3]Estimated.

[4]Projected data. Fall 2013 data for degree-granting postsecondary institutions are actual.

NOTE: Data for 1869–70 through 1949–50 reflect enrollment for the entire school year. Elementary and secondary enrollment includes students in local public school systems and in most private schools (religiously affiliated and nonsectarian), but generally excludes homeschooled children and students in subcollegiate departments of colleges and in federal schools. Excludes preprimary pupils in private schools that do not offer kindergarten or above. Postsecondary data through 1995 are for institutions of higher education, while later data are for degree-granting institutions. Degree-granting institutions grant associate's or higher degrees and participate in Title IV federal financial aid programs. The degree-granting classification is very similar to the earlier higher education classification, but it includes more 2-year colleges and excludes a few higher education institutions that did not grant degrees. Some data have been revised from previously published figures. Detail may not sum to totals because of rounding.

SOURCE: U.S. Department of Education, National Center for Education Statistics, *Annual Report of the Commissioner of Education*, 1870 to 1910; *Biennial Survey of Education in the United States*, 1919–20 through 1949–50; *Statistics of Public Elementary and Secondary School Systems*, 1959 through 1979; Common Core of Data (CCD), "State Nonfiscal Survey of Public Elementary and Secondary Education," 1989–90 through 2012–13; Private School Universe Survey (PSS), 1991–92 through 2011–12; National Elementary and Secondary Enrollment Projection Model, 1972 through 2024; Opening (Fall) Enrollment in Higher Education, 1959; Higher Education General Information Survey (HEGIS), "Fall Enrollment in Institutions of Higher Education" surveys, 1969, 1979, and 1985; Integrated Postsecondary Education Data System (IPEDS), "Fall Enrollment Survey" (IPEDS-EF:90–99); IPEDS Spring 2001 through Spring 2014, Enrollment component; and Enrollment in Degree-Granting Institutions Projection Model, 1980 through 2024. (This table was prepared March 2015.)

Table 2. Enrollment in public elementary and secondary schools, by level and grade: Selected years, fall 1980 through fall 2024

[In thousands]

Year	All grades	Elementary													Secondary					
		Total	Pre-kinder-garten	Kinder-garten	1st grade	2nd grade	3rd grade	4th grade	5th grade	6th grade	7th grade	8th grade	Un-graded	Total	9th grade	10th grade	11th grade	12th grade	Un-graded
1	2	3	4	5	6	7	8	9	10	11	12	13	14	15	16	17	18	19	20
1980	40,877	27,647	96	2,593	2,894	2,800	2,893	3,107	3,130	3,038	3,085	3,086	924	13,231	3,377	3,368	3,195	2,925	366
1985	39,422	27,034	151	3,041	3,239	2,941	2,895	2,771	2,776	2,789	2,938	2,982	511	12,388	3,439	3,230	2,866	2,550	303
1990	41,217	29,876	303	3,306	3,499	3,327	3,297	3,248	3,197	3,110	3,067	2,979	541	11,341	3,169	2,896	2,612	2,381	284
1991	42,047	30,503	375	3,311	3,556	3,360	3,334	3,315	3,268	3,239	3,181	3,020	542	11,544	3,313	2,915	2,645	2,392	278
1992	42,823	31,086	505	3,313	3,542	3,431	3,361	3,342	3,325	3,303	3,299	3,129	536	11,737	3,352	3,027	2,656	2,431	272
1993	43,465	31,502	545	3,377	3,529	3,429	3,437	3,361	3,350	3,356	3,355	3,249	513	11,963	3,487	3,050	2,751	2,424	250
1994	44,111	31,896	603	3,444	3,593	3,440	3,439	3,426	3,372	3,381	3,404	3,302	492	12,215	3,604	3,131	2,748	2,488	244
1995	44,840	32,338	637	3,536	3,671	3,507	3,445	3,431	3,438	3,395	3,422	3,356	500	12,502	3,704	3,237	2,826	2,487	247
1996	45,611	32,762	670	3,532	3,770	3,600	3,524	3,454	3,453	3,494	3,464	3,403	399	12,849	3,801	3,323	2,930	2,586	208
1997	46,127	33,071	695	3,503	3,755	3,689	3,597	3,507	3,458	3,492	3,520	3,415	440	13,056	3,819	3,376	2,972	2,673	216
1998	46,539	33,344	729	3,443	3,727	3,681	3,696	3,592	3,520	3,497	3,530	3,480	449	13,195	3,856	3,382	3,021	2,722	214
1999	46,857	33,486	751	3,397	3,684	3,656	3,691	3,686	3,604	3,564	3,541	3,497	415	13,371	3,935	3,415	3,034	2,782	205
2000	47,204	33,686	776	3,382	3,636	3,634	3,676	3,711	3,707	3,663	3,629	3,538	334	13,517	3,963	3,491	3,083	2,803	177
2001	47,672	33,936	865	3,379	3,614	3,593	3,653	3,695	3,727	3,769	3,720	3,616	304	13,736	4,012	3,528	3,174	2,863	159
2002	48,183	34,114	915	3,434	3,594	3,565	3,623	3,669	3,711	3,788	3,821	3,709	285	14,069	4,105	3,584	3,229	2,990	161
2003	48,540	34,201	950	3,503	3,613	3,544	3,611	3,619	3,685	3,772	3,841	3,809	255	14,339	4,190	3,675	3,277	3,046	150
2004	48,795	34,178	990	3,544	3,663	3,560	3,580	3,612	3,635	3,735	3,818	3,825	215	14,618	4,281	3,750	3,369	3,094	122
2005	49,113	34,204	1,036	3,619	3,691	3,606	3,586	3,578	3,633	3,670	3,777	3,802	205	14,909	4,287	3,866	3,454	3,180	121
2006	49,316	34,235	1,084	3,631	3,751	3,641	3,627	3,586	3,602	3,660	3,716	3,766	170	15,081	4,260	3,882	3,551	3,277	110
2007	49,291	34,204	1,081	3,609	3,750	3,704	3,659	3,624	3,600	3,628	3,700	3,709	139	15,086	4,200	3,863	3,557	3,375	92
2008	49,266	34,286	1,180	3,640	3,708	3,699	3,708	3,647	3,629	3,614	3,653	3,692	117	14,980	4,123	3,822	3,548	3,400	87
2009	49,361	34,409	1,223	3,678	3,729	3,665	3,707	3,701	3,652	3,644	3,641	3,651	119	14,952	4,080	3,809	3,541	3,432	90
2010	49,484	34,625	1,279	3,682	3,754	3,701	3,686	3,711	3,718	3,682	3,676	3,659	77	14,860	4,008	3,800	3,538	3,472	42
2011	49,522	34,773	1,291	3,746	3,773	3,713	3,703	3,672	3,699	3,724	3,696	3,679	77	14,749	3,957	3,751	3,546	3,452	43
2012	49,771	35,018	1,307	3,831	3,824	3,729	3,719	3,690	3,673	3,746	3,746	3,699	76	14,753	3,975	3,730	3,528	3,477	43
Projected																			
2013	49,942	35,188	1,304	3,822	3,865	3,780	3,736	3,719	3,696	3,694	3,745	3,750	76	14,754	3,997	3,747	3,508	3,460	42
2014	49,986	35,159	1,266	3,711	3,855	3,821	3,787	3,736	3,725	3,717	3,715	3,749	76	14,826	4,052	3,767	3,524	3,440	42
2015	50,094	35,182	1,269	3,720	3,744	3,811	3,828	3,787	3,743	3,746	3,739	3,719	75	14,912	4,051	3,820	3,543	3,456	42
2016	50,229	35,282	1,281	3,756	3,753	3,701	3,818	3,828	3,793	3,764	3,768	3,743	75	14,947	4,019	3,819	3,593	3,475	42
2017	50,584	35,595	1,344	3,940	3,790	3,711	3,708	3,818	3,834	3,815	3,786	3,772	76	14,989	4,044	3,788	3,591	3,523	42
2018	50,871	35,856	1,354	3,970	3,976	3,747	3,717	3,708	3,825	3,856	3,837	3,790	76	15,015	4,076	3,812	3,563	3,522	42
2019	51,183	36,125	1,364	3,997	4,006	3,930	3,754	3,717	3,714	3,846	3,879	3,841	77	15,058	4,095	3,842	3,585	3,494	42
2020	51,547	36,366	1,372	4,022	4,033	3,960	3,938	3,754	3,724	3,735	3,869	3,883	77	15,182	4,150	3,860	3,614	3,516	42
2021	51,910	36,587	1,380	4,044	4,058	3,987	3,967	3,938	3,760	3,744	3,757	3,873	78	15,324	4,195	3,912	3,630	3,543	42
2022	52,260	36,839	1,387	4,065	4,081	4,012	3,994	3,967	3,944	3,781	3,767	3,761	78	15,421	4,185	3,955	3,680	3,560	43
2023	52,601	37,223	1,394	4,085	4,103	4,035	4,019	3,995	3,974	3,966	3,803	3,771	79	15,378	4,064	3,944	3,719	3,608	42
2024	52,920	37,615	1,399	4,102	4,122	4,056	4,042	4,019	4,001	3,996	3,990	3,807	80	15,304	4,074	3,831	3,710	3,647	42

NOTE: Due to changes in reporting and imputation practices, prekindergarten enrollment for years prior to 1992 represent an undercount compared to later years. The total ungraded counts of students were prorated to the elementary and secondary levels based on prior reports. Detail may not sum to totals because of rounding.

SOURCE: U.S. Department of Education, National Center for Education Statistics, *Statistics of Public Elementary and Secondary School Systems, 1980–81*; Common Core of Data (CCD), "State Nonfiscal Survey of Public Elementary/Secondary Education," 1985–86 through 2012–13; and National Elementary and Secondary Enrollment Projection Model, 1972 through 2024. (This table was prepared March 2015.)

This page intentionally left blank.

Table 3. Enrollment in public elementary and secondary schools, by region, state, and jurisdiction: Selected years, fall 1990 through fall 2024

Region, state, and jurisdiction	Actual total enrollment												
	Fall 1990	Fall 2000	Fall 2002	Fall 2003	Fall 2004	Fall 2005	Fall 2006	Fall 2007	Fall 2008	Fall 2009	Fall 2010	Fall 2011	Fall 2012
1	2	3	4	5	6	7	8	9	10	11	12	13	14
United States..........	41,216,683	47,203,539	48,183,086	48,540,215	48,795,465	49,113,298	49,315,842	49,290,559	49,265,572	49,360,982	49,484,181	49,521,669	49,771,118
Region													
Northeast	7,281,763	8,222,127	8,296,621	8,292,315	8,271,259	8,240,160	8,257,889	8,122,022	8,052,985	8,092,029	8,071,335	7,953,981	7,959,128
Midwest	9,943,761	10,729,987	10,818,970	10,808,977	10,775,409	10,818,815	10,819,248	10,770,210	10,742,973	10,672,171	10,609,604	10,573,792	10,559,230
South	14,807,016	17,007,261	17,471,440	17,672,745	17,891,987	18,103,166	18,293,633	18,422,773	18,490,770	18,651,889	18,805,000	18,955,932	19,128,376
West	9,184,143	11,244,164	11,596,055	11,766,178	11,856,810	11,951,157	11,945,072	11,975,554	11,978,844	11,944,893	11,998,242	12,037,964	12,124,384
State													
Alabama.........................	721,806	739,992	739,366	731,220	730,140	741,761	743,632	742,919	745,668	748,889	755,552	744,621	744,637
Alaska............................	113,903	133,356	134,364	133,933	132,970	133,288	132,608	131,029	130,662	131,661	132,104	131,167	131,489
Arizona	639,853	877,696	937,755	1,012,068	1,043,298	1,094,454	1,068,249	1,087,447	1,087,817	1,077,831	1,071,751	1,080,319	1,089,384
Arkansas........................	436,286	449,959	450,985	454,523	463,115	474,206	476,409	479,016	478,965	480,559	482,114	483,114	486,157
California........................	4,950,474	6,140,814	6,353,667	6,413,867	6,441,557	6,437,202	6,406,750	6,343,471	6,322,528	6,263,438	6,289,578	6,287,834	6,299,451
Colorado.........................	574,213	724,508	751,862	757,693	765,976	779,826	794,026	801,867	818,443	832,368	843,316	854,265	863,561
Connecticut....................	469,123	562,179	570,023	577,203	577,390	575,059	575,100	570,626	567,198	563,968	560,546	554,437	550,954
Delaware........................	99,658	114,676	116,342	117,668	119,091	120,937	122,254	122,574	125,430	126,801	129,403	128,946	129,026
District of Columbia.........	80,694	68,925	76,166	78,057	76,714	76,876	72,850	78,422	68,681	69,433	71,284	73,911	76,140
Florida............................	1,861,592	2,434,821	2,539,929	2,587,628	2,639,336	2,675,024	2,671,513	2,666,811	2,631,020	2,634,522	2,643,347	2,668,156	2,692,162
Georgia	1,151,687	1,444,937	1,496,012	1,522,611	1,553,437	1,598,461	1,629,157	1,649,589	1,655,792	1,667,685	1,677,067	1,685,016	1,703,332
Hawaii............................	171,708	184,360	183,829	183,609	183,185	182,818	180,728	179,897	179,478	180,196	179,601	182,706	184,760
Idaho..............................	220,840	245,117	248,604	252,120	256,084	261,982	267,380	272,119	275,051	276,299	275,859	279,873	284,834
Illinois............................	1,821,407	2,048,792	2,084,187	2,100,961	2,097,503	2,111,706	2,118,276	2,112,805	2,119,707	2,104,175	2,091,654	2,083,097	2,072,880
Indiana...........................	954,525	989,267	1,003,875	1,011,130	1,021,348	1,035,074	1,045,940	1,046,764	1,046,147	1,046,661	1,047,232	1,040,765	1,041,369
Iowa...............................	483,652	495,080	482,210	481,226	478,319	483,482	483,122	485,115	487,559	491,842	495,775	495,870	499,825
Kansas...........................	437,034	470,610	470,957	470,490	469,136	467,525	469,506	468,295	471,060	474,489	483,701	486,108	489,043
Kentucky.........................	636,401	665,850	660,782	663,369	674,796	679,878	683,152	666,225	670,030	680,089	673,128	681,987	685,167
Louisiana........................	784,757	743,089	730,464	727,709	724,281	654,526	675,851	681,038	684,873	690,915	696,558	703,390	710,903
Maine.............................	215,149	207,037	204,337	202,084	198,820	195,498	193,986	196,245	192,935	189,225	189,077	188,969	185,739
Maryland.........................	715,176	852,920	866,743	869,113	865,561	860,020	851,640	845,700	843,861	848,412	852,211	854,086	859,638
Massachusetts.................	834,314	975,150	982,989	980,459	975,574	971,909	968,661	962,958	958,910	957,053	955,563	953,369	954,773
Michigan.........................	1,584,431	1,720,626	1,785,160	1,757,604	1,751,290	1,742,282	1,722,656	1,692,739	1,659,921	1,649,082	1,587,067	1,573,537	1,555,370
Minnesota.......................	756,374	854,340	846,891	842,854	838,503	839,243	840,565	837,578	836,048	837,053	838,037	839,738	845,404
Mississippi......................	502,417	497,871	492,645	493,540	495,376	494,954	495,026	494,122	491,962	492,481	490,526	490,619	493,650
Missouri..........................	816,558	912,744	906,499	905,941	905,449	917,705	920,353	917,188	917,871	917,982	918,710	916,584	917,900
Montana..........................	152,974	154,875	149,995	148,356	146,705	145,416	144,418	142,823	141,899	141,807	141,693	142,349	142,908
Nebraska.........................	274,081	286,199	285,402	285,542	285,761	286,646	287,580	291,244	292,590	295,368	298,500	301,296	303,505
Nevada...........................	201,316	340,706	369,498	385,401	400,083	412,395	424,766	429,362	433,371	428,947	437,149	439,634	445,707
New Hampshire	172,785	208,461	207,671	207,417	206,852	205,767	203,572	200,772	197,934	197,140	194,711	191,900	188,974
New Jersey	1,089,646	1,313,405	1,367,438	1,380,753	1,393,347	1,395,602	1,388,850	1,382,348	1,381,420	1,396,029	1,402,548	1,356,431	1,372,203
New Mexico.....................	301,881	320,306	320,234	323,066	326,102	326,758	328,220	329,040	330,245	334,419	338,122	337,225	338,220
New York.........................	2,598,337	2,882,188	2,888,233	2,864,775	2,836,337	2,815,581	2,809,649	2,765,435	2,740,592	2,766,052	2,734,955	2,704,718	2,710,703
North Carolina.................	1,086,871	1,293,638	1,335,954	1,360,209	1,385,754	1,416,436	1,444,481	1,489,492	1,488,645	1,483,397	1,490,605	1,507,864	1,518,465
North Dakota...................	117,825	109,201	104,225	102,233	100,513	98,283	96,670	95,059	94,728	95,073	96,323	97,646	101,111
Ohio...............................	1,771,089	1,835,049	1,838,285	1,845,428	1,840,032	1,839,683	1,836,722	1,827,184	1,817,163	1,764,297	1,754,191	1,740,030	1,729,916
Oklahoma.......................	579,087	623,110	624,548	626,160	629,476	634,739	639,391	642,065	645,108	654,802	659,911	666,120	673,483
Oregon...........................	472,394	546,231	554,071	551,273	552,505	552,194	562,574	565,586	575,393	582,839	570,720	568,208	587,564
Pennsylvania...................	1,667,834	1,814,311	1,816,747	1,821,146	1,828,089	1,830,684	1,871,060	1,801,971	1,775,029	1,785,993	1,793,284	1,771,395	1,763,677
Rhode Island...................	138,813	157,347	159,205	159,375	156,498	153,422	151,612	147,629	145,342	145,118	143,793	142,854	142,481
South Carolina................	622,112	677,411	694,389	699,198	703,736	701,544	708,021	712,317	718,113	723,143	725,838	727,186	735,998
South Dakota..................	129,164	128,603	130,048	125,537	122,798	122,012	121,158	121,606	126,429	123,713	126,128	128,016	130,471
Tennessee......................	824,595	909,161	927,608	936,682	941,091	953,928	978,368	964,259	971,950	972,549	987,422	999,693	993,496
Texas.............................	3,382,887	4,059,619	4,259,823	4,331,751	4,405,215	4,525,394	4,599,509	4,674,832	4,752,148	4,850,210	4,935,715	5,000,470	5,077,659
Utah...............................	446,652	481,485	489,262	495,981	503,607	508,430	523,386	576,244	559,778	571,586	585,552	598,832	613,279
Vermont..........................	95,762	102,049	99,978	99,103	98,352	96,638	95,399	94,038	93,625	91,451	96,858	89,908	89,624
Virginia	998,601	1,144,915	1,177,229	1,192,092	1,204,739	1,213,616	1,220,440	1,230,857	1,235,795	1,245,340	1,251,440	1,257,883	1,265,419
Washington.....................	839,709	1,004,770	1,014,798	1,021,349	1,020,005	1,031,985	1,026,774	1,030,247	1,037,018	1,035,347	1,043,788	1,045,453	1,051,694
West Virginia...................	322,389	286,367	282,455	281,215	280,129	280,866	281,939	282,535	282,729	282,662	282,879	282,870	283,044
Wisconsin.......................	797,621	879,476	881,231	880,031	864,757	875,174	876,700	874,633	873,750	872,436	872,436	871,105	872,436
Wyoming	98,226	89,940	88,116	87,462	84,733	84,409	85,193	86,422	87,161	88,155	89,009	90,099	91,533
Jurisdiction													
Bureau of Indian Education	—	46,938	46,126	45,828	45,828	50,938	—	—	40,927	41,351	41,962	—	—
DoD, overseas.................	—	73,581	72,889	71,053	68,327	62,543	60,891	57,247	56,768	—	—	—	—
DoD, domestic.................	—	34,174	32,115	30,603	29,151	28,329	26,631	27,548	28,013	—	—	—	—
Other jurisdictions													
American Samoa.........	12,463	15,702	15,984	15,893	16,126	16,438	16,400	—	—	—	—	—	—
Guam	26,391	32,473		31,572	30,605	30,986	—	—	—	—	31,618	31,243	31,186
Northern Marianas	6,449	10,004	11,251	11,244	11,601	11,718	11,695	11,299	10,913	10,961	11,105	11,011	10,646
Puerto Rico.................	644,734	612,725	596,502	584,916	575,648	563,490	544,138	526,565	503,635	493,393	473,735	452,740	434,609
U.S. Virgin Islands........	21,750	19,459	18,333	17,716	16,429	16,750	16,284	15,903	15,768	15,493	15,495	15,711	15,192

See notes at end of table.

Table 3. Enrollment in public elementary and secondary schools, by region, state, and jurisdiction: Selected years, fall 1990 through fall 2024—Continued

Region, state, and jurisdiction	Percent change in total enrollment, 2007 to 2012	Projected total enrollment Fall 2013	Fall 2014	Fall 2015	Fall 2016	Fall 2020	Fall 2024	Percent change in total enrollment, 2012 to 2024
1	15	16	17	18	19	20	21	22
United States...........	1.0	49,941,900	49,985,600	50,094,400	50,229,000	51,547,400	52,919,600	6.3
Region								
Northeast........................	-2.0	7,928,100	7,887,700	7,861,000	7,839,300	7,899,500	7,958,400	#
Midwest...........................	-2.0	10,549,500	10,512,200	10,493,800	10,479,700	10,536,700	10,553,800	-0.1
South..............................	3.8	19,283,200	19,359,300	19,449,800	19,542,100	20,187,900	20,899,600	9.3
West...............................	1.2	12,181,100	12,226,400	12,289,800	12,367,900	12,923,300	13,507,900	11.4
State								
Alabama..........................	0.2	743,500	739,500	735,000	731,000	724,100	723,900	-2.8
Alaska.............................	0.4	131,800	132,700	133,900	135,400	144,500	153,800	17.0
Arizona...........................	0.2	1,097,600	1,105,700	1,116,900	1,132,900	1,222,300	1,320,000	21.2
Arkansas.........................	1.5	486,300	484,100	481,600	479,600	478,800	482,800	-0.7
California.........................	-0.7	6,311,800	6,314,700	6,328,400	6,351,400	6,586,000	6,833,200	8.5
Colorado..........................	7.7	873,100	879,900	887,600	894,400	929,300	961,200	11.3
Connecticut......................	-3.4	543,500	535,900	530,300	525,300	521,000	524,400	-4.8
Delaware.........................	5.3	129,800	130,200	130,800	131,700	136,500	138,300	7.2
District of Columbia..........	-2.9	77,700	77,800	78,200	78,400	80,100	78,300	2.8
Florida	1.0	2,707,400	2,717,000	2,727,000	2,742,300	2,868,200	3,040,900	13.0
Georgia	3.3	1,716,100	1,722,100	1,729,500	1,735,600	1,788,600	1,858,300	9.1
Hawaii..............................	2.7	186,500	187,000	187,400	188,000	190,900	189,300	2.5
Idaho...............................	4.7	288,300	290,400	293,000	295,400	305,900	313,000	9.9
Illinois..............................	-1.9	2,069,800	2,059,400	2,055,500	2,052,800	2,052,200	2,037,000	-1.7
Indiana.............................	-0.5	1,039,100	1,032,900	1,028,500	1,023,600	1,017,400	1,029,800	-1.1
Iowa.................................	3.0	502,800	502,800	503,600	504,400	510,300	506,400	1.3
Kansas............................	4.4	491,000	490,900	492,000	492,500	498,800	499,800	2.2
Kentucky..........................	2.8	687,700	686,500	686,700	686,300	689,400	689,200	0.6
Louisiana.........................	4.4	714,800	714,400	714,700	714,900	715,700	707,400	-0.5
Maine...............................	-5.4	183,300	181,100	179,400	177,700	175,700	173,100	-6.8
Maryland..........................	1.6	864,600	869,100	875,900	884,800	941,100	989,800	15.1
Massachusetts.................	-0.8	952,800	947,000	941,900	936,900	936,000	944,000	-1.1
Michigan..........................	-8.1	1,542,100	1,527,100	1,513,600	1,502,800	1,483,100	1,474,600	-5.2
Minnesota........................	0.9	854,600	861,300	868,800	877,900	925,100	961,600	13.7
Mississippi.......................	-0.1	494,000	493,200	492,000	490,400	485,900	478,900	-3.0
Missouri...........................	0.1	916,500	912,800	910,400	908,000	914,700	919,000	0.1
Montana...........................	0.1	144,400	145,300	146,400	147,400	152,700	154,100	7.8
Nebraska..........................	4.2	307,000	307,800	309,100	310,700	317,000	316,400	4.2
Nevada............................	3.8	447,900	452,900	458,600	464,900	505,300	560,900	25.8
New Hampshire................	-5.9	185,900	183,600	181,500	180,000	180,300	185,000	-2.1
New Jersey......................	-0.7	1,367,500	1,362,200	1,357,400	1,353,200	1,361,200	1,374,200	0.1
New Mexico......................	2.8	339,900	340,500	341,300	341,900	344,800	340,800	0.8
New York..........................	-2.0	2,710,500	2,704,900	2,702,000	2,701,100	2,741,800	2,762,300	1.9
North Carolina..................	1.9	1,530,600	1,538,600	1,546,800	1,555,100	1,617,500	1,717,900	13.1
North Dakota....................	6.4	104,300	106,600	109,100	111,300	121,100	124,200	22.9
Ohio.................................	-5.3	1,719,600	1,708,800	1,699,600	1,690,100	1,671,500	1,651,900	-4.5
Oklahoma.........................	4.9	679,600	682,400	685,600	688,100	703,600	711,500	5.6
Oregon	3.9	583,000	584,300	587,200	590,200	616,900	649,900	10.6
Pennsylvania....................	-2.1	1,754,900	1,745,600	1,742,400	1,739,900	1,755,200	1,764,700	0.1
Rhode Island....................	-3.5	140,700	139,200	138,100	137,400	137,900	137,800	-3.3
South Carolina.................	3.3	743,600	749,100	754,700	759,500	784,600	805,400	9.4
South Dakota...................	7.3	131,100	132,000	133,100	134,300	139,500	140,600	7.8
Tennessee........................	3.0	998,000	999,100	1,001,800	1,004,800	1,034,400	1,071,900	7.9
Texas...............................	8.6	5,154,100	5,200,200	5,250,300	5,297,300	5,540,000	5,766,300	13.6
Utah.................................	6.4	626,100	636,400	646,000	654,100	688,800	719,400	17.3
Vermont...........................	-4.7	89,000	88,300	88,000	87,900	90,400	92,900	3.6
Virginia............................	2.8	1,273,200	1,277,200	1,283,000	1,289,100	1,336,600	1,388,100	9.7
Washington......................	2.1	1,057,500	1,062,300	1,068,200	1,076,100	1,138,100	1,216,900	15.7
West Virginia....................	0.2	282,000	279,000	276,100	273,100	262,800	250,700	-11.4
Wisconsin.........................	-0.3	871,700	869,800	870,500	871,400	885,900	892,300	2.3
Wyoming..........................	5.9	93,400	94,400	95,200	95,800	97,800	95,300	4.1
Jurisdiction								
Bureau of Indian Education	—	—	—	—	—	—	—	—
DoD, overseas.................	—	—	—	—	—	—	—	—
DoD, domestic.................	—	—	—	—	—	—	—	—
Other jurisdictions								
American Samoa.........	—	—	—	—	—	—	—	—
Guam	—	—	—	—	—	—	—	—
Northern Marianas.......	-5.8	—	—	—	—	—	—	—
Puerto Rico.................	-17.5	—	—	—	—	—	—	—
U.S. Virgin Islands	-4.5	—	—	—	—	—	—	—

—Not available.
#Rounds to zero.
NOTE: DoD = Department of Defense. The states comprising each geographic region can be found in appendix F. Detail may not sum to totals because of rounding. Some data have been revised from previously published figures.

SOURCE: U.S. Department of Education, National Center for Education Statistics, Common Core of Data (CCD), "State Nonfiscal Survey of Public Elementary/Secondary Education," 1990–91 through 2012–13; and State Public Elementary and Secondary Enrollment Projection Model, 1980 through 2024. (This table was prepared August 2015.)

Table 4. Public school enrollment in prekindergarten through grade 8, by region, state, and jurisdiction: Selected years, fall 1990 through fall 2024

Region, state, and jurisdiction	Actual enrollment												
	Fall 1990	Fall 2000	Fall 2002	Fall 2003	Fall 2004	Fall 2005	Fall 2006	Fall 2007	Fall 2008	Fall 2009	Fall 2010	Fall 2011	Fall 2012
1	2	3	4	5	6	7	8	9	10	11	12	13	14
United States............	29,875,914	33,686,421	34,114,245	34,200,741	34,177,565	34,203,962	34,234,751	34,204,081	34,285,564	34,409,260	34,624,530	34,772,751	35,017,893
Region													
Northeast	5,188,795	5,839,970	5,809,545	5,751,561	5,689,094	5,622,955	5,573,729	5,504,400	5,476,224	5,494,080	5,540,276	5,479,174	5,493,308
Midwest	7,129,501	7,523,246	7,534,620	7,501,579	7,438,674	7,425,308	7,404,578	7,359,028	7,373,391	7,361,959	7,349,334	7,358,792	7,368,484
South	10,858,800	12,314,176	12,573,054	12,675,179	12,780,160	12,881,836	12,989,696	13,085,045	13,166,980	13,300,643	13,434,553	13,578,211	13,711,284
West	6,698,818	8,009,029	8,197,026	8,272,422	8,269,637	8,273,863	8,266,748	8,255,608	8,268,969	8,252,578	8,300,367	8,356,574	8,444,817
State													
Alabama........................	527,097	538,634	533,207	525,313	521,757	529,347	528,664	525,978	528,078	529,394	533,612	527,006	527,434
Alaska...........................	85,297	94,442	94,380	93,695	91,981	91,225	90,167	88,980	89,263	90,824	91,990	92,057	93,069
Arizona.........................	479,046	640,564	660,359	704,322	722,203	739,535	759,656	771,056	771,749	760,420	751,992	759,494	767,734
Arkansas......................	313,505	318,023	318,826	321,508	328,187	335,746	336,552	339,920	341,603	344,209	345,808	346,022	347,631
California......................	3,613,734	4,407,035	4,525,385	4,539,777	4,507,355	4,465,615	4,410,105	4,328,968	4,306,258	4,264,020	4,293,968	4,308,441	4,331,807
Colorado.......................	419,910	516,566	534,465	536,325	540,695	549,875	559,041	565,726	580,304	591,378	601,077	610,854	617,510
Connecticut..................	347,396	406,445	405,998	407,794	404,169	399,705	398,063	394,034	392,218	389,964	387,475	383,377	380,709
Delaware.......................	72,606	80,801	82,221	82,898	83,599	84,639	84,996	85,019	86,811	87,710	90,279	90,624	91,004
District of Columbia.........	61,282	53,692	58,802	59,489	57,118	55,646	52,391	55,836	50,779	51,656	53,548	56,195	58,273
Florida..........................	1,369,934	1,759,902	1,809,279	1,832,376	1,857,798	1,873,395	1,866,562	1,855,859	1,849,295	1,850,901	1,858,498	1,876,102	1,892,560
Georgia.........................	849,082	1,059,983	1,088,561	1,103,181	1,118,379	1,145,446	1,166,508	1,178,577	1,185,684	1,194,751	1,202,479	1,211,250	1,222,289
Hawaii...........................	122,840	132,293	130,862	130,054	128,788	127,472	126,008	125,556	125,910	127,477	127,525	131,005	133,590
Idaho............................	160,091	170,421	173,249	175,424	178,221	182,829	187,005	191,171	193,554	194,728	194,144	198,064	202,203
Illinois..........................	1,309,516	1,473,933	1,487,650	1,492,725	1,483,644	1,480,320	1,477,679	1,472,909	1,479,195	1,463,713	1,454,793	1,453,156	1,448,201
Indiana.........................	675,804	703,261	714,003	716,819	720,006	724,467	730,108	729,550	730,021	730,599	729,414	724,605	725,040
Iowa.............................	344,804	333,750	325,843	326,831	324,169	326,160	326,218	329,504	335,566	341,333	348,112	350,152	355,041
Kansas	319,648	323,157	321,795	322,491	321,176	320,513	326,201	326,771	331,079	332,997	342,927	347,129	349,695
Kentucky.......................	459,200	471,429	476,751	478,254	485,794	487,429	487,165	469,373	472,204	484,466	480,334	488,456	491,065
Louisiana......................	586,202	546,579	536,882	536,390	533,751	482,082	492,116	499,549	504,213	509,883	512,266	518,802	524,792
Maine............................	155,203	145,701	141,776	139,420	136,275	133,491	132,338	130,742	129,324	128,646	128,929	130,046	127,924
Maryland.......................	526,744	609,043	610,337	605,862	597,417	588,571	579,065	576,479	576,473	581,785	588,156	594,216	602,802
Massachusetts.................	604,234	702,575	701,050	692,130	682,175	675,398	670,628	666,926	666,538	666,551	666,402	666,314	667,267
Michigan.......................	1,144,878	1,222,482	1,253,811	1,229,121	1,211,698	1,191,397	1,170,558	1,136,823	1,118,569	1,114,611	1,075,584	1,070,873	1,061,930
Minnesota.....................	545,556	577,766	567,701	564,049	558,447	557,757	558,445	558,180	560,184	564,661	569,963	575,544	583,363
Mississippi....................	371,641	363,873	360,254	360,881	361,057	358,030	356,382	353,512	351,807	351,652	350,885	352,999	356,364
Missouri........................	588,070	644,766	634,667	632,227	628,667	635,142	634,275	631,746	635,411	638,082	642,991	645,376	647,530
Montana........................	111,169	105,226	101,177	100,160	98,673	97,770	97,021	96,354	96,869	97,868	98,491	99,725	100,819
Nebraska.......................	198,080	195,486	195,113	195,417	194,816	195,055	195,769	200,095	202,912	206,860	210,292	213,504	215,432
Nevada.........................	149,881	250,720	270,940	280,734	288,753	295,989	302,953	307,573	308,328	305,512	307,297	309,360	313,730
New Hampshire	126,301	147,121	143,616	142,031	140,241	138,584	136,188	134,359	132,995	132,768	131,576	129,632	128,169
New Jersey	783,422	967,533	978,609	978,440	975,856	970,592	963,418	954,418	956,765	968,332	981,255	947,576	956,070
New Mexico....................	208,087	224,879	224,497	226,032	227,900	229,552	230,091	229,718	231,415	235,343	239,345	239,481	240,978
New York.......................	1,827,418	2,028,906	2,016,282	1,978,181	1,942,575	1,909,028	1,887,284	1,856,315	1,843,080	1,847,003	1,869,150	1,857,574	1,868,561
North Carolina................	783,132	945,470	963,967	974,019	985,740	1,003,118	1,027,067	1,072,324	1,058,926	1,053,801	1,058,409	1,074,063	1,080,090
North Dakota..................	84,943	72,421	69,089	67,870	67,122	65,638	64,395	63,492	63,955	64,576	66,035	67,888	70,995
Ohio..............................	1,257,580	1,293,646	1,283,795	1,278,202	1,267,088	1,261,331	1,253,193	1,241,322	1,239,494	1,225,346	1,222,808	1,217,226	1,211,299
Oklahoma......................	424,899	445,402	449,030	450,310	452,942	456,954	459,944	462,629	467,960	476,962	483,464	490,196	496,144
Oregon..........................	340,243	379,264	381,988	378,052	376,933	379,680	380,576	383,598	395,421	404,451	392,601	391,310	409,325
Pennsylvania..................	1,172,164	1,257,824	1,241,636	1,235,624	1,234,828	1,227,625	1,220,074	1,205,351	1,194,327	1,200,446	1,209,766	1,204,850	1,204,732
Rhode Island.................	101,797	113,545	112,544	111,209	107,040	103,870	101,996	99,159	97,983	98,184	97,734	97,659	97,809
South Carolina	452,033	493,226	500,427	500,743	504,264	498,030	501,273	504,566	507,602	512,124	515,581	519,389	527,350
South Dakota.................	95,165	87,838	89,450	86,015	83,891	83,530	83,137	83,424	87,477	85,745	87,936	90,529	93,204
Tennessee.....................	598,111	668,123	673,337	675,277	670,880	676,576	691,971	681,751	684,549	686,668	701,707	712,749	711,525
Texas	2,510,955	2,943,047	3,079,665	3,132,584	3,184,235	3,268,339	3,319,782	3,374,684	3,446,511	3,520,348	3,586,609	3,636,852	3,690,146
Utah..............................	324,982	333,104	342,607	348,840	355,445	357,644	371,272	410,258	404,469	413,343	424,979	434,536	444,202
Vermont........................	70,860	70,320	68,034	66,732	65,935	64,662	63,740	63,096	62,994	62,186	67,989	62,146	62,067
Virginia.........................	728,280	815,748	831,504	837,258	839,687	841,299	841,685	850,444	855,008	864,020	871,446	881,225	889,444
Washington	612,597	694,367	697,191	699,248	695,405	699,482	694,858	697,407	704,794	705,387	714,172	718,184	724,560
West Virginia..................	224,097	201,201	200,004	198,836	197,555	197,189	197,573	198,545	199,477	200,313	201,472	202,065	202,371
Wisconsin......................	565,457	594,740	591,703	589,812	577,950	583,998	584,600	585,212	589,528	593,436	598,479	602,810	606,754
Wyoming.......................	70,941	60,148	59,926	59,759	57,285	57,195	57,995	59,243	60,635	61,825	62,786	64,057	65,290
Jurisdiction													
Bureau of Indian Education	—	35,746	34,392	33,671	33,671	36,133	—	—	30,612	31,381	31,985	—	—
DoD, overseas.................	—	59,299	58,214	56,226	53,720	48,691	47,589	44,418	43,931	—	—	—	—
DoD, domestic..................	—	30,697	28,759	27,500	26,195	25,558	24,052	24,807	25,255	—	—	—	—
Other jurisdictions													
American Samoa..........	9,390	11,895	11,838	11,772	11,873	11,766	11,763	—	—	—	—	—	—
Guam	19,276	23,698	—	22,551	21,686	21,946	—	—	—	—	21,561	21,223	21,166
Northern Marianas	4,918	7,809	8,379	8,192	8,416	8,427	8,504	8,140	7,816	7,743	7,688	7,703	7,396
Puerto Rico	480,356	445,524	429,413	418,649	408,671	399,447	382,647	372,514	355,115	347,638	334,613	318,924	305,048
U.S. Virgin Islands	16,249	13,910	12,933	12,738	11,650	11,728	11,237	10,770	10,567	10,409	10,518	10,576	10,302

See notes at end of table.

Table 4. Public school enrollment in prekindergarten through grade 8, by region, state, and jurisdiction: Selected years, fall 1990 through fall 2024—Continued

Region, state, and jurisdiction	Percent change in enrollment, 2007 to 2012	Projected enrollment						Percent change in enrollment, 2012 to 2024
		Fall 2013	Fall 2014	Fall 2015	Fall 2016	Fall 2020	Fall 2024	
1	15	16	17	18	19	20	21	22
United States...........	2.4	35,187,700	35,159,200	35,181,900	35,282,300	36,365,600	37,615,400	7.4
Region								
Northeast......................	-0.2	5,487,900	5,458,400	5,436,900	5,427,600	5,485,000	5,587,800	1.7
Midwest.........................	0.1	7,371,200	7,330,100	7,299,400	7,284,100	7,335,700	7,405,800	0.5
South.............................	4.8	13,821,000	13,827,800	13,852,400	13,914,300	14,450,200	15,048,400	9.8
West..............................	2.3	8,507,600	8,542,900	8,593,300	8,656,300	9,094,600	9,573,500	13.4
State								
Alabama.........................	0.3	526,400	521,400	517,100	514,300	514,600	516,800	-2.0
Alaska............................	4.6	93,800	94,600	95,700	97,300	104,900	112,100	20.5
Arizona..........................	-0.4	778,800	789,500	800,300	812,400	876,600	957,400	24.7
Arkansas........................	2.3	346,500	343,600	340,900	338,800	339,900	347,700	#
California........................	0.1	4,355,900	4,361,500	4,379,200	4,402,600	4,602,600	4,809,500	11.0
Colorado.........................	9.2	623,900	626,100	628,300	630,700	651,900	682,200	10.5
Connecticut.....................	-3.4	375,500	370,400	366,300	363,700	365,200	377,300	-0.9
Delaware........................	7.0	92,000	92,400	93,100	93,700	95,700	97,500	7.2
District of Columbia.........	4.4	60,300	60,300	60,700	61,300	62,300	58,600	0.6
Florida...........................	2.0	1,903,500	1,907,300	1,914,400	1,931,200	2,055,200	2,194,200	15.9
Georgia..........................	3.7	1,228,400	1,227,300	1,227,900	1,232,600	1,282,000	1,343,900	9.9
Hawaii............................	6.4	135,400	135,300	135,800	135,700	136,100	134,700	0.9
Idaho.............................	5.8	204,200	205,500	206,400	207,400	213,700	219,500	8.6
Illinois............................	-1.7	1,448,300	1,436,600	1,428,700	1,421,200	1,412,900	1,427,000	-1.5
Indiana...........................	-0.6	722,500	716,100	708,100	704,100	712,300	728,000	0.4
Iowa..............................	7.8	357,700	356,900	356,900	357,200	358,600	353,600	-0.4
Kansas...........................	7.0	351,500	350,600	350,000	350,100	353,500	355,100	1.5
Kentucky.........................	4.6	493,600	491,300	488,700	487,600	488,500	490,300	-0.2
Louisiana........................	5.1	528,800	526,100	524,300	522,500	522,000	512,700	-2.3
Maine.............................	-2.2	126,600	125,200	124,200	123,500	122,800	122,500	-4.2
Maryland.........................	4.6	611,200	616,400	624,200	631,100	671,500	708,900	17.6
Massachusetts.................	0.1	665,800	660,000	654,800	651,100	653,200	671,500	0.6
Michigan.........................	-6.6	1,053,300	1,040,900	1,031,000	1,024,200	1,024,600	1,030,700	-2.9
Minnesota.......................	4.5	591,700	596,600	601,600	608,100	637,700	666,800	14.3
Mississippi......................	0.8	357,000	354,400	352,600	351,300	349,500	341,000	-4.3
Missouri..........................	2.5	646,600	643,100	641,000	640,400	646,700	654,000	1.0
Montana.........................	4.6	102,200	103,400	104,200	105,100	108,200	107,100	6.3
Nebraska........................	7.7	218,900	219,200	219,400	219,400	220,100	220,300	2.3
Nevada...........................	2.0	316,900	320,300	324,400	329,400	365,600	410,700	30.9
New Hampshire...............	-4.6	126,400	125,000	124,000	123,200	126,200	132,700	3.5
New Jersey.....................	0.2	953,100	947,300	942,500	939,900	949,400	971,200	1.6
New Mexico.....................	4.9	242,100	242,100	241,700	241,600	242,600	238,900	-0.8
New York........................	0.7	1,876,300	1,872,100	1,871,200	1,872,700	1,898,500	1,921,000	2.8
North Carolina.................	0.7	1,086,100	1,086,500	1,087,600	1,093,000	1,157,300	1,243,600	15.1
North Dakota...................	11.8	73,900	76,100	78,100	79,900	84,200	82,800	16.6
Ohio...............................	-2.4	1,206,500	1,195,500	1,185,400	1,178,200	1,169,700	1,165,200	-3.8
Oklahoma.......................	7.2	500,100	499,800	500,400	501,300	509,300	515,100	3.8
Oregon...........................	6.7	404,700	406,000	408,300	411,800	435,900	462,200	12.9
Pennsylvania...................	-0.1	1,204,500	1,199,400	1,195,700	1,195,800	1,209,600	1,226,600	1.8
Rhode Island...................	-1.4	97,600	97,100	96,100	95,300	95,000	97,900	0.1
South Carolina.................	4.5	532,500	534,100	536,100	539,400	559,000	570,600	8.2
South Dakota..................	11.7	93,800	94,700	95,700	96,600	98,600	98,100	5.2
Tennessee......................	4.4	716,100	715,700	716,400	719,100	744,600	778,300	9.4
Texas.............................	9.3	3,740,000	3,755,100	3,772,200	3,799,500	3,972,300	4,164,100	12.8
Utah...............................	8.3	452,200	456,600	460,700	464,700	483,700	507,600	14.3
Vermont..........................	-1.6	62,000	61,800	62,000	62,300	65,100	67,200	8.3
Virginia...........................	4.6	896,600	897,500	900,000	904,700	942,000	988,500	11.1
Washington.....................	3.9	731,000	734,800	740,400	749,400	805,200	867,200	19.7
West Virginia...................	1.9	201,900	198,600	195,900	192,900	184,500	176,700	-12.7
Wisconsin........................	3.7	606,400	603,800	603,500	604,600	616,800	624,100	2.9
Wyoming.........................	10.2	66,700	67,300	67,800	68,200	67,700	64,300	-1.5
Jurisdiction								
Bureau of Indian Education..................	—	—	—	—	—	—	—	—
DoD, overseas.................	—	—	—	—	—	—	—	—
DoD, domestic.................	—	—	—	—	—	—	—	—
Other jurisdictions								
American Samoa.........	—	—	—	—	—	—	—	—
Guam........................	—	—	—	—	—	—	—	—
Northern Marianas.......	-9.1	—	—	—	—	—	—	—
Puerto Rico.................	-18.1	—	—	—	—	—	—	—
U.S. Virgin Islands........	-4.3	—	—	—	—	—	—	—

—Not available.
#Rounds to zero.
NOTE: DoD = Department of Defense. The states comprising each geographic region can be found in appendix F. Detail may not sum to totals because of rounding. Some data have been revised from previously published figures.

SOURCE: U.S. Department of Education, National Center for Education Statistics, Common Core of Data (CCD), State Nonfiscal Survey of Public Elementary/Secondary Education, 1990–91 through 2012–13; and State Public Elementary and Secondary Enrollment Projection Model, 1980 through 2024. (This table was prepared August 2015.)

Table 5. Public school enrollment in grades 9 through 12, by region, state, and jurisdiction: Selected years, fall 1990 through fall 2024

Region, state, and jurisdiction	Actual enrollment												
	Fall 1990	Fall 2000	Fall 2002	Fall 2003	Fall 2004	Fall 2005	Fall 2006	Fall 2007	Fall 2008	Fall 2009	Fall 2010	Fall 2011	Fall 2012
1	2	3	4	5	6	7	8	9	10	11	12	13	14
United States..........	11,340,769	13,517,118	14,068,841	14,339,474	14,617,900	14,909,336	15,081,091	15,086,478	14,980,008	14,951,722	14,859,651	14,748,918	14,753,225
Region													
Northeast	2,092,968	2,382,157	2,487,076	2,540,754	2,582,165	2,617,205	2,684,160	2,617,622	2,576,761	2,597,949	2,531,059	2,474,807	2,465,820
Midwest........................	2,814,260	3,206,741	3,284,350	3,307,398	3,336,735	3,393,507	3,414,670	3,411,182	3,369,582	3,310,212	3,260,470	3,215,000	3,190,746
South...........................	3,948,216	4,693,085	4,898,386	4,997,566	5,111,827	5,221,330	5,303,937	5,337,728	5,323,790	5,351,246	5,370,447	5,377,721	5,417,092
West.............................	2,485,325	3,235,135	3,399,029	3,493,756	3,587,173	3,677,294	3,678,324	3,719,946	3,709,875	3,692,315	3,697,875	3,681,390	3,679,567
State													
Alabama	194,709	201,358	206,159	205,907	208,383	212,414	214,968	216,941	217,590	219,495	221,940	217,615	217,203
Alaska.........................	28,606	38,914	39,984	40,238	40,989	42,063	42,441	42,049	41,399	40,837	40,114	39,110	38,420
Arizona........................	160,807	237,132	277,396	307,746	321,095	354,919	308,593	316,391	316,068	317,411	319,759	320,825	321,650
Arkansas......................	122,781	131,936	132,159	133,015	134,928	138,460	139,857	139,096	137,362	136,350	136,306	137,092	138,526
California......................	1,336,740	1,733,779	1,828,282	1,874,090	1,934,202	1,971,587	1,996,645	2,014,503	2,016,270	1,999,416	1,995,610	1,979,387	1,967,644
Colorado......................	154,303	207,942	217,397	221,368	225,281	229,951	234,985	236,141	238,139	240,990	242,239	243,411	246,051
Connecticut..................	121,727	155,734	164,025	169,409	173,221	175,354	177,037	176,592	174,980	174,004	173,071	171,060	170,245
Delaware......................	27,052	33,875	34,121	34,770	35,492	36,298	37,258	37,555	38,619	39,091	39,124	38,322	38,022
District of Columbia........	19,412	15,233	17,364	18,568	19,596	21,230	20,459	22,586	17,902	17,777	17,736	17,716	17,867
Florida.........................	491,658	674,919	730,650	755,252	781,538	801,629	804,951	810,952	781,725	783,621	784,849	792,054	799,602
Georgia	302,605	384,954	407,451	419,430	435,058	453,015	462,649	471,012	470,108	472,934	474,588	473,766	481,043
Hawaii.........................	48,868	52,067	52,967	53,555	54,397	55,346	54,720	54,341	53,568	52,719	52,076	51,701	51,170
Idaho	60,749	74,696	75,355	76,696	77,863	79,153	80,375	80,948	81,497	81,571	81,715	81,809	82,631
Illinois.........................	511,891	574,859	596,537	608,236	613,859	631,386	640,597	639,896	640,512	640,462	636,861	629,941	624,679
Indiana........................	278,721	286,006	289,872	294,311	301,342	310,607	315,832	317,214	316,126	316,062	316,188	316,160	316,329
Iowa............................	138,848	161,330	156,367	154,395	154,150	157,322	156,904	155,611	151,993	150,509	147,663	145,718	144,784
Kansas........................	117,386	147,453	149,162	147,999	147,960	147,012	143,305	141,524	139,981	141,492	140,774	138,979	139,348
Kentucky......................	177,201	194,421	184,031	185,115	189,002	192,449	195,987	196,852	197,826	195,623	192,794	193,531	194,102
Louisiana.....................	198,555	196,510	193,582	191,319	190,530	172,444	183,735	181,489	180,660	181,032	184,292	184,588	186,111
Maine..........................	59,946	61,336	62,561	62,664	62,545	62,007	61,648	65,503	63,611	60,579	60,148	58,923	57,815
Maryland	188,432	243,877	256,406	263,251	268,144	271,449	272,575	269,221	267,388	266,627	264,055	259,870	256,836
Massachusetts..............	230,080	272,575	281,939	288,329	293,399	296,511	298,033	296,032	292,372	290,502	289,161	287,055	287,506
Michigan......................	439,553	498,144	531,349	528,483	539,592	550,885	552,098	555,916	541,352	534,471	511,483	502,664	493,440
Minnesota....................	210,818	276,574	279,190	278,805	280,056	281,486	282,120	279,398	275,864	272,392	268,074	264,194	262,041
Mississippi...................	130,776	133,998	132,391	132,659	134,319	136,924	138,644	140,610	140,155	140,829	139,641	137,620	137,286
Missouri.......................	228,488	267,978	271,832	273,714	276,782	282,563	286,078	285,442	282,460	279,900	275,719	271,208	270,370
Montana.......................	41,805	49,649	48,818	48,196	48,032	47,646	47,397	46,469	45,030	43,939	43,202	42,624	42,089
Nebraska......................	76,001	90,713	90,289	90,125	90,945	91,591	91,591	91,811	91,149	89,678	88,508	87,792	88,073
Nevada........................	51,435	89,986	98,558	104,667	111,330	116,406	121,813	121,789	125,043	123,435	129,852	130,274	131,977
New Hampshire	46,484	61,340	64,055	65,386	66,611	67,183	67,384	66,413	64,939	64,372	63,135	62,268	60,805
New Jersey	306,224	345,872	388,829	402,313	417,491	425,010	425,432	427,930	424,655	427,697	421,293	408,855	416,133
New Mexico...................	93,794	95,427	95,737	97,034	98,202	97,206	98,129	99,322	98,830	99,076	98,777	97,744	97,242
New York......................	770,919	853,282	871,951	886,594	893,762	906,553	922,365	909,120	897,512	919,049	865,805	847,144	842,142
North Carolina...............	303,739	348,168	371,987	386,190	400,014	413,318	417,414	417,168	429,719	429,596	432,196	433,801	438,375
North Dakota.................	32,882	36,780	35,136	34,363	33,391	32,645	32,275	31,567	30,773	30,497	30,288	29,758	30,116
Ohio............................	513,509	541,403	554,490	567,226	572,944	578,352	583,529	585,862	577,669	538,951	531,383	522,804	518,617
Oklahoma.....................	154,188	177,708	175,518	175,850	176,534	177,785	179,447	179,436	177,148	177,840	176,447	175,924	177,339
Oregon.........................	132,151	166,967	172,083	173,221	175,572	172,514	181,998	181,988	179,972	178,388	178,119	176,898	178,239
Pennsylvania.................	495,670	556,487	575,111	585,522	593,261	603,059	650,986	596,620	580,702	585,547	583,518	566,545	558,945
Rhode Island.................	37,016	43,802	46,661	48,166	49,458	49,552	49,616	48,470	47,359	46,934	46,059	45,195	44,672
South Carolina..............	170,079	184,185	193,962	198,455	199,472	203,514	206,748	207,751	210,511	211,019	210,257	207,797	208,648
South Dakota................	33,999	40,765	40,598	39,522	38,907	38,482	38,021	38,182	38,952	37,968	38,192	37,487	37,267
Tennessee....................	226,484	241,038	254,271	261,405	270,211	277,352	286,397	282,508	287,401	285,881	285,715	286,944	281,971
Texas	871,932	1,116,572	1,180,158	1,199,167	1,220,980	1,257,055	1,279,727	1,300,148	1,305,637	1,329,862	1,349,106	1,363,618	1,387,513
Utah............................	121,670	148,381	146,655	147,141	148,162	150,786	152,114	165,986	155,309	158,243	160,573	164,296	169,077
Vermont.......................	24,902	31,729	31,944	32,371	32,417	31,976	31,659	30,942	30,631	29,265	28,869	27,762	27,557
Virginia........................	270,321	329,167	345,725	354,834	365,052	372,317	378,755	380,413	380,787	381,320	379,994	376,658	375,975
Washington	227,112	310,403	317,607	322,101	324,600	332,503	331,916	332,840	332,224	329,960	329,616	327,269	327,134
West Virginia.................	98,292	85,166	82,451	82,379	82,574	83,677	84,366	83,990	83,252	82,349	81,407	80,805	80,673
Wisconsin.....................	232,164	284,736	289,528	290,219	286,807	291,176	292,100	289,421	284,222	279,000	273,807	268,295	265,682
Wyoming......................	27,285	29,792	28,190	27,703	27,448	27,214	27,198	27,179	26,526	26,330	26,223	26,042	26,243
Jurisdiction													
Bureau of Indian Education	—	11,192	11,734	12,157	12,157	14,805	—	—	10,315	9,970	9,977	—	—
DoD, overseas...............	—	14,282	14,675	14,827	14,607	13,852	13,302	12,829	12,837	—	—	—	—
DoD, domestic...............	—	3,477	3,356	3,103	2,956	2,771	2,579	2,741	2,758	—	—	—	—
Other jurisdictions													
American Samoa.........	3,073	3,807	4,146	4,121	4,253	4,672	4,637	—	—	—	—	—	—
Guam.........................	7,115	8,775	—	9,021	8,919	9,040	—	—	—	—	10,057	10,020	10,020
Northern Marianas	1,531	2,195	2,872	3,052	3,185	3,291	3,191	3,159	3,097	3,218	3,417	3,308	3,250
Puerto Rico.................	164,378	167,201	167,089	166,267	166,977	164,043	161,491	154,051	148,520	145,755	139,122	133,816	129,561
U.S. Virgin Islands	5,501	5,549	5,400	4,978	4,779	5,022	5,047	5,133	5,201	5,084	4,977	5,135	4,890

See notes at end of table.

Region, state, and jurisdiction	Percent change in enrollment, 2007 to 2012	Projected enrollment						Percent change in enrollment, 2012 to 2024
		Fall 2013	Fall 2014	Fall 2015	Fall 2016	Fall 2020	Fall 2024	
1	15	16	17	18	19	20	21	22
United States...........	-2.2	14,754,200	14,826,400	14,912,500	14,946,700	15,181,900	15,304,200	3.7
Region								
Northeast	-5.8	2,440,300	2,429,300	2,424,200	2,411,700	2,414,500	2,370,600	-3.9
Midwest......................	-6.5	3,178,300	3,182,100	3,194,400	3,195,600	3,201,000	3,148,000	-1.3
South	1.5	5,462,200	5,531,500	5,597,400	5,627,700	5,737,700	5,851,200	8.0
West	-1.1	3,673,400	3,683,500	3,696,600	3,711,600	3,828,700	3,934,400	6.9
State								
Alabama.....................	0.1	217,000	218,100	218,000	216,700	209,500	207,100	-4.7
Alaska.........................	-8.6	38,000	38,100	38,100	38,100	39,700	41,700	8.6
Arizona.......................	1.7	318,800	316,200	316,600	320,500	345,700	362,700	12.8
Arkansas.....................	-0.4	139,800	140,500	140,700	140,900	138,900	135,100	-2.5
California.....................	-2.3	1,955,800	1,953,200	1,949,100	1,948,900	1,983,500	2,023,700	2.8
Colorado.....................	4.2	249,100	253,700	259,300	263,800	277,400	279,100	13.4
Connecticut.................	-3.6	168,000	165,500	163,900	161,500	155,800	147,100	-13.6
Delaware.....................	1.2	37,800	37,700	37,700	38,000	40,800	40,800	7.3
District of Columbia.........	-20.9	17,500	17,500	17,500	17,100	17,800	19,700	10.1
Florida........................	-1.4	803,900	809,700	812,600	811,000	813,000	846,700	5.9
Georgia.......................	2.1	487,800	494,800	501,600	503,000	506,600	514,400	6.9
Hawaii........................	-5.8	51,100	51,700	51,600	52,300	54,800	54,600	6.7
Idaho	2.1	84,100	84,900	86,500	87,900	92,100	93,500	13.2
Illinois........................	-2.4	621,500	622,800	626,800	631,600	639,400	610,000	-2.4
Indiana.......................	-0.3	316,600	316,700	320,500	319,400	305,100	301,800	-4.6
Iowa...........................	-7.0	145,100	145,900	146,700	147,200	151,700	152,800	5.6
Kansas	-1.5	139,500	140,400	142,000	142,300	145,400	144,700	3.9
Kentucky.....................	-1.4	194,100	195,200	198,000	198,700	200,900	198,900	2.5
Louisiana.....................	2.5	186,100	188,400	190,400	192,500	193,800	194,700	4.6
Maine..........................	-11.7	56,800	55,900	55,200	54,100	52,900	50,600	-12.5
Maryland.....................	-4.6	253,400	252,600	251,800	253,600	269,600	280,900	9.4
Massachusetts................	-2.9	287,000	287,000	287,100	285,800	282,700	272,500	-5.2
Michigan.....................	-11.2	488,800	486,200	482,600	478,600	458,500	443,900	-10.0
Minnesota....................	-6.2	262,800	264,600	267,200	269,800	287,400	294,800	12.5
Mississippi...................	-2.4	137,000	138,700	139,400	139,200	136,400	137,900	0.5
Missouri......................	-5.3	269,900	269,700	269,500	267,700	268,000	265,000	-2.0
Montana	-9.4	42,200	41,900	42,100	42,300	44,500	47,000	11.6
Nebraska.....................	-3.4	88,000	88,600	89,700	91,300	96,900	96,000	9.0
Nevada	8.4	131,100	132,600	134,200	135,500	139,700	150,200	13.8
New Hampshire...............	-8.4	59,500	58,600	57,600	56,800	54,200	52,300	-14.0
New Jersey	-2.8	414,300	414,800	414,900	413,200	411,800	403,000	-3.1
New Mexico...................	-2.1	97,700	98,400	99,600	100,300	102,200	101,800	4.7
New York.....................	-7.4	834,200	832,800	830,700	828,400	843,300	841,400	-0.1
North Carolina................	5.1	444,600	452,100	459,100	462,100	460,300	474,400	8.2
North Dakota.................	-4.6	30,400	30,500	31,000	31,400	36,900	41,500	37.7
Ohio...........................	-11.5	513,100	513,300	514,100	511,900	501,900	486,700	-6.2
Oklahoma....................	-1.2	179,500	182,700	185,200	186,800	194,300	196,500	10.8
Oregon	-2.1	178,300	178,300	178,900	178,400	181,000	187,600	5.3
Pennsylvania.................	-6.3	550,400	546,100	546,700	544,100	545,600	538,100	-3.7
Rhode Island.................	-7.8	43,100	42,100	42,000	42,100	42,900	39,900	-10.6
South Carolina	0.4	211,100	215,000	218,700	220,000	225,500	234,800	12.6
South Dakota.................	-2.4	37,200	37,300	37,400	37,800	40,900	42,500	14.1
Tennessee....................	-0.2	281,900	283,400	285,300	285,700	289,800	293,600	4.1
Texas	6.7	1,414,100	1,445,100	1,478,100	1,497,900	1,567,700	1,602,200	15.5
Utah...........................	1.9	173,900	179,800	185,300	189,400	205,100	211,800	25.3
Vermont......................	-10.9	27,000	26,500	26,000	25,600	25,300	25,700	-6.9
Virginia	-1.2	376,600	379,800	383,000	384,400	394,500	399,600	6.3
Washington..................	-1.7	326,500	327,500	327,800	326,700	332,900	349,700	6.9
West Virginia.................	-3.9	80,100	80,400	80,300	80,100	78,300	73,900	-8.3
Wisconsin....................	-8.2	265,300	266,000	267,000	266,800	269,000	268,200	1.0
Wyoming.....................	-3.4	26,700	27,100	27,400	27,600	30,100	31,000	18.0
Jurisdiction								
Bureau of Indian Education.............	—	—	—	—	—	—	—	—
DoD, overseas.................	—	—	—	—	—	—	—	—
DoD, domestic.................	—	—	—	—	—	—	—	—
Other jurisdictions								
American Samoa.........	—	—	—	—	—	—	—	—
Guam	—	—	—	—	—	—	—	—
Northern Marianas	2.9	—	—	—	—	—	—	—
Puerto Rico.................	-15.9	—	—	—	—	—	—	—
U.S. Virgin Islands	-4.7	—	—	—	—	—	—	—

—Not available.

NOTE: DoD = Department of Defense. The states comprising each geographic region can be found in appendix F. Detail may not sum to totals because of rounding. Some data have been revised from previously published figures.

SOURCE: U.S. Department of Education, National Center for Education Statistics, Common Core of Data (CCD), "State Nonfiscal Survey of Public Elementary/Secondary Education," 1990–91 through 2012–13; and State Public Elementary and Secondary Enrollment Projection Model, 1980 through 2024. (This table was prepared August 2015.)

Table 6. Enrollment and percentage distribution of enrollment in public elementary and secondary schools, by race/ethnicity and region: Selected years, fall 1995 through fall 2024

	Enrollment (in thousands)							Percentage distribution						
Region and year	Total	White	Black	Hispanic	Asian/ Pacific Islander	American Indian/ Alaska Native	Two or more races	Total	White	Black	Hispanic	Asian/ Pacific Islander	American Indian/ Alaska Native	Two or more races
1	2	3	4	5	6	7	8	9	10	11	12	13	14	15
United States														
1995	44,840	29,044	7,551	6,072	1,668	505	—	100.0	64.8	16.8	13.5	3.7	1.1	†
2000	47,204	28,878	8,100	7,726	1,950	550	—	100.0	61.2	17.2	16.4	4.1	1.2	†
2001	47,672	28,735	8,177	8,169	2,028	564	—	100.0	60.3	17.2	17.1	4.3	1.2	†
2002	48,183	28,618	8,299	8,594	2,088	583	—	100.0	59.4	17.2	17.8	4.3	1.2	†
2003	48,540	28,442	8,349	9,011	2,145	593	—	100.0	58.6	17.2	18.6	4.4	1.2	†
2004	48,795	28,318	8,386	9,317	2,183	591	—	100.0	58.0	17.2	19.1	4.5	1.2	†
2005	49,113	28,005	8,445	9,787	2,279	598	—	100.0	57.0	17.2	19.9	4.6	1.2	†
2006	49,316	27,801	8,422	10,166	2,332	595	—	100.0	56.4	17.1	20.6	4.7	1.2	†
2007	49,291	27,454	8,392	10,454	2,396	594	—	100.0	55.7	17.0	21.2	4.9	1.2	†
2008	49,266	27,057	8,358	10,563	2,451	589	247 [1]	100.0	54.9	17.0	21.4	5.0	1.2	0.5 [1]
2009	49,361	26,702	8,245	10,991	2,484	601	338 [1]	100.0	54.1	16.7	22.3	5.0	1.2	0.7 [1]
2010	49,484	25,933	7,917	11,439	2,466	566	1,164	100.0	52.4	16.0	23.1	5.0	1.1	2.4
2011	49,522	25,602	7,827	11,759	2,513	547	1,272	100.0	51.7	15.8	23.7	5.1	1.1	2.6
2012	49,771	25,386	7,803	12,104	2,552	534	1,393	100.0	51.0	15.7	24.3	5.1	1.1	2.8
2013[2]	49,942	25,194	7,787	12,497	2,571	530	1,362	100.0	50.4	15.6	25.0	5.1	1.1	2.7
2014[2]	49,986	24,913	7,740	12,812	2,585	524	1,412	100.0	49.8	15.5	25.6	5.2	1.0	2.8
2015[2]	50,094	24,665	7,700	13,150	2,604	520	1,456	100.0	49.2	15.4	26.2	5.2	1.0	2.9
2016[2]	50,229	24,437	7,671	13,476	2,630	516	1,499	100.0	48.7	15.3	26.8	5.2	1.0	3.0
2017[2]	50,584	24,326	7,679	13,845	2,672	513	1,549	100.0	48.1	15.2	27.4	5.3	1.0	3.1
2018[2]	50,871	24,214	7,678	14,176	2,699	510	1,594	100.0	47.6	15.1	27.9	5.3	1.0	3.1
2019[2]	51,183	24,179	7,673	14,438	2,745	503	1,645	100.0	47.2	15.0	28.2	5.4	1.0	3.2
2020[2]	51,547	24,158	7,694	14,702	2,791	498	1,705	100.0	46.9	14.9	28.5	5.4	1.0	3.3
2021[2]	51,910	24,142	7,734	14,939	2,837	495	1,763	100.0	46.5	14.9	28.8	5.5	1.0	3.4
2022[2]	52,260	24,131	7,778	15,152	2,887	492	1,819	100.0	46.2	14.9	29.0	5.5	0.9	3.5
2023[2]	52,601	24,142	7,821	15,328	2,944	491	1,875	100.0	45.9	14.9	29.1	5.6	0.9	3.6
2024[2]	52,920	24,157	7,862	15,473	3,010	489	1,929	100.0	45.6	14.9	29.2	5.7	0.9	3.6
Northeast														
1995	7,894	5,497	1,202	878	295	21	—	100.0	69.6	15.2	11.1	3.7	0.3	†
2000	8,222	5,545	1,270	1,023	361	24	—	100.0	67.4	15.4	12.4	4.4	0.3	†
2002	8,297	5,503	1,287	1,091	390	26	—	100.0	66.3	15.5	13.2	4.7	0.3	†
2005	8,240	5,317	1,282	1,189	425	27	—	100.0	64.5	15.6	14.4	5.2	0.3	†
2006	8,258	5,281	1,279	1,230	440	28	—	100.0	64.0	15.5	14.9	5.3	0.3	†
2007	8,122	5,148	1,250	1,246	451	27	—	100.0	63.4	15.4	15.3	5.6	0.3	†
2008	8,053	5,041	1,226	1,267	467	27	25 [1]	100.0	62.6	15.2	15.7	5.8	0.3	0.3 [1]
2009	8,092	5,010	1,230	1,308	487	27	30 [1]	100.0	61.9	15.2	16.2	6.0	0.3	0.4 [1]
2010	8,071	4,876	1,208	1,364	500	27	96	100.0	60.4	15.0	16.9	6.2	0.3	1.2
2011	7,954	4,745	1,166	1,394	510	27	113	100.0	59.7	14.7	17.5	6.4	0.3	1.4
2012	7,959	4,665	1,161	1,444	523	27	138	100.0	58.6	14.6	18.1	6.6	0.3	1.7
Midwest														
1995	10,512	8,335	1,450	438	197	92	—	100.0	79.3	13.8	4.2	1.9	0.9	†
2000	10,730	8,208	1,581	610	239	92	—	100.0	76.5	14.7	5.7	2.2	0.9	†
2002	10,819	8,118	1,638	704	255	104	—	100.0	75.0	15.1	6.5	2.4	1.0	†
2005	10,819	7,950	1,654	836	283	96	—	100.0	73.5	15.3	7.7	2.6	0.9	†
2006	10,819	7,894	1,655	883	290	97	—	100.0	73.0	15.3	8.2	2.7	0.9	†
2007	10,770	7,808	1,642	922	300	99	—	100.0	72.5	15.2	8.6	2.8	0.9	†
2008	10,743	7,734	1,632	963	314	99	—	100.0	72.0	15.2	9.0	2.9	0.9	†
2009	10,672	7,622	1,606	1,000	318	98	29 [1]	100.0	71.4	15.0	9.4	3.0	0.9	0.3 [1]
2010	10,610	7,327	1,505	1,077	312	94	294	100.0	69.1	14.2	10.2	2.9	0.9	2.8
2011	10,574	7,240	1,485	1,127	321	90	311	100.0	68.5	14.0	10.7	3.0	0.9	2.9
2012	10,559	7,175	1,464	1,167	330	89	334	100.0	68.0	13.9	11.1	3.1	0.8	3.2
South														
1995	16,118	9,565	4,236	1,890	280	148	—	100.0	59.3	26.3	11.7	1.7	0.9	†
2000	17,007	9,501	4,516	2,468	352	170	—	100.0	55.9	26.6	14.5	2.1	1.0	†
2002	17,471	9,457	4,617	2,822	394	180	—	100.0	54.1	26.4	16.2	2.3	1.0	†
2005	18,103	9,381	4,738	3,334	456	194	—	100.0	51.8	26.2	18.4	2.5	1.1	†
2006	18,294	9,358	4,729	3,522	485	200	—	100.0	51.2	25.9	19.3	2.6	1.1	†
2007	18,423	9,286	4,750	3,674	511	201	—	100.0	50.4	25.8	19.9	2.8	1.1	†
2008	18,491	9,190	4,771	3,790	537	203	—	100.0	49.7	25.8	20.5	2.9	1.1	†
2009	18,652	9,074	4,710	4,039	555	219	55 [1]	100.0	48.6	25.3	21.7	3.0	1.2	0.3 [1]
2010	18,805	8,869	4,545	4,206	555	207	424	100.0	47.2	24.2	22.4	3.0	1.1	2.3
2011	18,956	8,830	4,535	4,353	577	198	463	100.0	46.6	23.9	23.0	3.0	1.0	2.4
2012	19,128	8,780	4,545	4,513	595	191	504	100.0	45.9	23.8	23.6	3.1	1.0	2.6
West														
1995	10,316	5,648	662	2,866	896	244	—	100.0	54.7	6.4	27.8	8.7	2.4	†
2000	11,244	5,624	733	3,625	998	264	—	100.0	50.0	6.5	32.2	8.9	2.4	†
2002	11,596	5,541	757	3,976	1,049	273	—	100.0	47.8	6.5	34.3	9.0	2.4	†
2005	11,951	5,356	771	4,428	1,115	281	—	100.0	44.8	6.5	37.1	9.3	2.4	†
2006	11,945	5,268	759	4,531	1,117	270	—	100.0	44.1	6.4	37.9	9.4	2.3	†
2007	11,976	5,213	750	4,611	1,134	267	—	100.0	43.5	6.3	38.5	9.5	2.2	†
2008	11,979	5,092	728	4,543	1,133	261	222 [1]	100.0	42.5	6.1	37.9	9.5	2.2	1.9 [1]
2009	11,945	4,997	699	4,645	1,124	256	223 [1]	100.0	41.8	5.9	38.9	9.4	2.1	1.9 [1]
2010	11,998	4,861	659	4,792	1,100	237	349	100.0	40.5	5.5	39.9	9.2	2.0	2.9
2011	12,038	4,787	642	4,886	1,105	233	385	100.0	39.8	5.3	40.6	9.2	1.9	3.2
2012	12,124	4,766	632	4,978	1,104	227	417	100.0	39.3	5.2	41.1	9.1	1.9	3.4

—Not available.

†Not applicable.

[1]For this year, data on students of Two or more races were reported by only a small number of states. Therefore, the data are not comparable to figures for 2010 and later years.

[2]Projected.

NOTE: Race categories exclude persons of Hispanic ethnicity. Enrollment data for students not reported by race/ethnicity were prorated by state and grade to match state totals. Prior to 2008, data on students of Two or more races were not collected. Some data have been revised from previously published figures. The states comprising each geographic region can be found in appendix F. Detail may not sum to totals because of rounding.

SOURCE: U.S. Department of Education, National Center for Education Statistics, Common Core of Data (CCD), "State Nonfiscal Survey of Public Elementary and Secondary Education," 1995–96 through 2012–13; and National Elementary and Secondary Enrollment by Race/Ethnicity Projection Model, 1972 through 2024. (This table was prepared March 2015.)

This page intentionally left blank.

Table 7. Enrollment and percentage distribution of enrollment in public elementary and secondary schools, by race/ethnicity and level of education: Fall 1999 through fall 2024

Level of education and year	Enrollment (in thousands) Total	White	Black	His-panic	Asian/Pacific Islander Total	Asian	Pacific Islander	American Indian/ Alaska Native	Two or more races	Percentage distribution Total	White	Black	His-panic	Asian/Pacific Islander Total	Asian	Pacific Islander	American Indian/ Alaska Native	Two or more races
1	2	3	4	5	6	7	8	9	10	11	12	13	14	15	16	17	18	19
Total																		
1999	46,857	29,035	8,066	7,327	1,887	—	—	542	—	100.0	62.0	17.2	15.6	4.0	†	†	1.2	†
2000	47,204	28,878	8,100	7,726	1,950	—	—	550	—	100.0	61.2	17.2	16.4	4.1	†	†	1.2	†
2001	47,672	28,735	8,177	8,169	2,028	—	—	564	—	100.0	60.3	17.2	17.1	4.3	†	†	1.2	†
2002	48,183	28,618	8,299	8,594	2,088	—	—	583	—	100.0	59.4	17.2	17.8	4.3	†	†	1.2	†
2003	48,540	28,442	8,349	9,011	2,145	—	—	593	—	100.0	58.6	17.2	18.6	4.4	†	†	1.2	†
2004	48,795	28,318	8,386	9,317	2,183	—	—	591	—	100.0	58.0	17.2	19.1	4.5	†	†	1.2	†
2005	49,113	28,005	8,445	9,787	2,279	—	—	598	—	100.0	57.0	17.2	19.9	4.6	†	†	1.2	†
2006	49,316	27,801	8,422	10,166	2,332	—	—	595	—	100.0	56.4	17.1	20.6	4.7	†	†	1.2	†
2007	49,291	27,454	8,392	10,454	2,396	—	—	594	—	100.0	55.7	17.0	21.2	4.9	†	†	1.2	†
2008	49,266	27,057	8,358	10,563	2,451	2,405	46	589	247[1]	100.0	54.9	17.0	21.4	5.0	4.9	0.1	1.2	0.5[1]
2009	49,361	26,702	8,245	10,991	2,484	2,435	49	601	338[1]	100.0	54.1	16.7	22.3	5.0	4.9	0.1	1.2	0.7[1]
2010	49,484	25,933	7,917	11,439	2,466	2,296	171	566	1,164	100.0	52.4	16.0	23.1	5.0	4.6	0.3	1.1	2.4
2011	49,522	25,602	7,827	11,759	2,513	2,334	179	547	1,272	100.0	51.7	15.8	23.7	5.1	4.7	0.4	1.1	2.6
2012	49,771	25,386	7,803	12,104	2,552	2,372	180	534	1,393	100.0	51.0	15.7	24.3	5.1	4.8	0.4	1.1	2.8
2013[2]	49,942	25,194	7,787	12,497	2,571	2,388	183	530	1,362	100.0	50.4	15.6	25.0	5.1	4.8	0.4	1.1	2.7
2014[2]	49,986	24,913	7,740	12,812	2,585	2,399	186	524	1,412	100.0	49.8	15.5	25.6	5.2	4.8	0.4	1.0	2.8
2015[2]	50,094	24,665	7,700	13,150	2,604	2,416	188	520	1,456	100.0	49.2	15.4	26.2	5.2	4.8	0.4	1.0	2.9
2016[2]	50,229	24,437	7,671	13,476	2,630	2,440	190	516	1,499	100.0	48.7	15.3	26.8	5.2	4.9	0.4	1.0	3.0
2017[2]	50,584	24,326	7,679	13,845	2,672	2,479	193	513	1,549	100.0	48.1	15.2	27.4	5.3	4.9	0.4	1.0	3.1
2018[2]	50,871	24,214	7,678	14,176	2,699	2,503	195	510	1,594	100.0	47.6	15.1	27.9	5.3	4.9	0.4	1.0	3.1
2019[2]	51,183	24,179	7,673	14,438	2,745	2,548	196	503	1,645	100.0	47.2	15.0	28.2	5.4	5.0	0.4	1.0	3.2
2020[2]	51,547	24,158	7,694	14,702	2,791	2,594	197	498	1,705	100.0	46.9	14.9	28.5	5.4	5.0	0.4	1.0	3.3
2021[2]	51,910	24,142	7,734	14,939	2,837	2,639	198	495	1,763	100.0	46.5	14.9	28.8	5.5	5.1	0.4	1.0	3.4
2022[2]	52,260	24,131	7,778	15,152	2,887	2,689	198	492	1,819	100.0	46.2	14.9	29.0	5.5	5.1	0.4	0.9	3.5
2023[2]	52,601	24,142	7,821	15,328	2,944	2,746	198	491	1,875	100.0	45.9	14.9	29.1	5.6	5.2	0.4	0.9	3.6
2024[2]	52,920	24,157	7,862	15,473	3,010	2,810	200	489	1,929	100.0	45.6	14.9	29.2	5.7	5.3	0.4	0.9	3.6
Prekindergarten through grade 8																		
1999	33,486	20,327	5,952	5,512	1,303	—	—	391	—	100.0	60.7	17.8	16.5	3.9	†	†	1.2	†
2000	33,686	20,130	5,981	5,830	1,349	—	—	397	—	100.0	59.8	17.8	17.3	4.0	†	†	1.2	†
2001	33,936	19,960	6,004	6,159	1,409	—	—	405	—	100.0	58.8	17.7	18.1	4.2	†	†	1.2	†
2002	34,114	19,764	6,042	6,446	1,447	—	—	415	—	100.0	57.9	17.7	18.9	4.2	†	†	1.2	†
2003	34,201	19,558	6,015	6,729	1,483	—	—	415	—	100.0	57.2	17.6	19.7	4.3	†	†	1.2	†
2004	34,178	19,368	5,983	6,909	1,504	—	—	413	—	100.0	56.7	17.5	20.2	4.4	†	†	1.2	†
2005	34,204	19,051	5,954	7,216	1,569	—	—	412	—	100.0	55.7	17.4	21.1	4.6	†	†	1.2	†
2006	34,235	18,863	5,882	7,465	1,611	—	—	414	—	100.0	55.1	17.2	21.8	4.7	†	†	1.2	†
2007	34,204	18,679	5,821	7,632	1,660	—	—	412	—	100.0	54.6	17.0	22.3	4.9	†	†	1.2	†
2008	34,286	18,501	5,793	7,689	1,705	1,674	31	410	187[1]	100.0	54.0	16.9	22.4	5.0	4.9	0.1	1.2	0.5[1]
2009	34,409	18,316	5,713	7,977	1,730	1,697	33	419	254[1]	100.0	53.2	16.6	23.2	5.0	4.9	0.1	1.2	0.7[1]
2010	34,625	17,823	5,495	8,314	1,711	1,589	122	394	887	100.0	51.5	15.9	24.0	4.9	4.6	0.4	1.1	2.6
2011	34,773	17,654	5,470	8,558	1,744	1,616	128	384	963	100.0	50.8	15.7	24.6	5.0	4.6	0.4	1.1	2.8
2012	35,018	17,535	5,473	8,804	1,773	1,644	129	375	1,057	100.0	50.1	15.6	25.1	5.1	4.7	0.4	1.1	3.0
2013[2]	35,188	17,409	5,475	9,103	1,796	1,665	131	373	1,032	100.0	49.5	15.6	25.9	5.1	4.7	0.4	1.1	2.9
2014[2]	35,159	17,182	5,432	9,309	1,800	1,668	132	368	1,069	100.0	48.9	15.4	26.5	5.1	4.7	0.4	1.0	3.0
2015[2]	35,182	16,987	5,398	9,521	1,813	1,680	133	364	1,100	100.0	48.3	15.3	27.1	5.2	4.8	0.4	1.0	3.1
2016[2]	35,282	16,839	5,392	9,729	1,829	1,695	134	360	1,133	100.0	47.7	15.3	27.6	5.2	4.8	0.4	1.0	3.2
2017[2]	35,595	16,803	5,442	9,961	1,854	1,718	136	360	1,174	100.0	47.2	15.3	28.0	5.2	4.8	0.4	1.0	3.3
2018[2]	35,856	16,771	5,480	10,158	1,876	1,740	137	360	1,211	100.0	46.8	15.3	28.3	5.2	4.9	0.4	1.0	3.4
2019[2]	36,125	16,825	5,503	10,275	1,919	1,783	136	355	1,248	100.0	46.6	15.2	28.4	5.3	4.9	0.4	1.0	3.5
2020[2]	36,366	16,864	5,528	10,362	1,967	1,831	136	353	1,292	100.0	46.4	15.2	28.5	5.4	5.0	0.4	1.0	3.6
2021[2]	36,587	16,903	5,546	10,437	2,017	1,880	137	350	1,334	100.0	46.2	15.2	28.5	5.5	5.1	0.4	1.0	3.6
2022[2]	36,839	16,963	5,567	10,523	2,064	1,926	137	347	1,374	100.0	46.0	15.1	28.6	5.6	5.2	0.4	0.9	3.7
2023[2]	37,223	17,074	5,613	10,655	2,120	1,982	138	347	1,414	100.0	45.9	15.1	28.6	5.7	5.3	0.4	0.9	3.8
2024[2]	37,615	17,188	5,667	10,783	2,175	2,035	139	346	1,457	100.0	45.7	15.1	28.7	5.8	5.4	0.4	0.9	3.9

See notes at end of table.

Table 7. Enrollment and percentage distribution of enrollment in public elementary and secondary schools, by race/ethnicity and level of education: Fall 1999 through fall 2024—Continued

Level of education and year	Enrollment (in thousands)									Percentage distribution								
					Asian/Pacific Islander			American Indian/ Alaska Native	Two or more races					Asian/Pacific Islander			American Indian/ Alaska Native	Two or more races
	Total	White	Black	His-panic	Total	Asian	Pacific Islander			Total	White	Black	His-panic	Total	Asian	Pacific Islander		
1	2	3	4	5	6	7	8	9	10	11	12	13	14	15	16	17	18	19
Grades 9 through 12																		
1999	13,371	8,708	2,114	1,815	584	—	—	151	—	100.0	65.1	15.8	13.6	4.4	†	†	1.1	†
2000	13,517	8,747	2,119	1,896	601	—	—	153	—	100.0	64.7	15.7	14.0	4.4	†	†	1.1	†
2001	13,736	8,774	2,173	2,011	619	—	—	159	—	100.0	63.9	15.8	14.6	4.5	†	†	1.2	†
2002	14,069	8,854	2,257	2,148	642	—	—	168	—	100.0	62.9	16.0	15.3	4.6	†	†	1.2	†
2003	14,339	8,884	2,334	2,282	663	—	—	177	—	100.0	62.0	16.3	15.9	4.6	†	†	1.2	†
2004	14,618	8,950	2,403	2,408	679	—	—	178	—	100.0	61.2	16.4	16.5	4.6	†	†	1.2	†
2005	14,909	8,954	2,490	2,570	709	—	—	186	—	100.0	60.1	16.7	17.2	4.8	†	†	1.2	†
2006	15,081	8,938	2,540	2,701	720	—	—	181	—	100.0	59.3	16.8	17.9	4.8	†	†	1.2	†
2007	15,086	8,775	2,571	2,821	736	—	—	183	—	100.0	58.2	17.0	18.7	4.9	†	†	1.2	†
2008	14,980	8,556	2,565	2,874	746	731	15	179	59 [1]	100.0	57.1	17.1	19.2	5.0	4.9	0.1	1.2	0.4 [1]
2009	14,952	8,385	2,532	3,014	754	738	16	182	84 [1]	100.0	56.1	16.9	20.2	5.0	4.9	0.1	1.2	0.6 [1]
2010	14,860	8,109	2,422	3,125	755	707	49	171	277	100.0	54.6	16.3	21.0	5.1	4.8	0.3	1.2	1.9
2011	14,749	7,948	2,357	3,202	769	719	50	163	309	100.0	53.9	16.0	21.7	5.2	4.9	0.3	1.1	2.1
2012	14,753	7,851	2,330	3,300	779	727	51	158	335	100.0	53.2	15.8	22.4	5.3	4.9	0.3	1.1	2.3
2013 [2]	14,754	7,786	2,312	3,394	776	723	53	157	329	100.0	52.8	15.7	23.0	5.3	4.9	0.4	1.1	2.2
2014 [2]	14,826	7,731	2,308	3,503	785	731	54	156	343	100.0	52.1	15.6	23.6	5.3	4.9	0.4	1.1	2.3
2015 [2]	14,912	7,678	2,302	3,629	791	736	55	156	356	100.0	51.5	15.4	24.3	5.3	4.9	0.4	1.0	2.4
2016 [2]	14,947	7,598	2,279	3,747	801	745	56	156	366	100.0	50.8	15.2	25.1	5.4	5.0	0.4	1.0	2.5
2017 [2]	14,989	7,523	2,237	3,883	818	760	57	154	374	100.0	50.2	14.9	25.9	5.5	5.1	0.4	1.0	2.5
2018 [2]	15,015	7,443	2,198	4,018	822	764	59	151	383	100.0	49.6	14.6	26.8	5.5	5.1	0.4	1.0	2.6
2019 [2]	15,058	7,354	2,170	4,163	826	765	61	148	397	100.0	48.8	14.4	27.6	5.5	5.1	0.4	1.0	2.6
2020 [2]	15,182	7,294	2,166	4,339	824	763	61	146	413	100.0	48.0	14.3	28.6	5.4	5.0	0.4	1.0	2.7
2021 [2]	15,324	7,238	2,189	4,502	820	759	61	145	429	100.0	47.2	14.3	29.4	5.4	5.0	0.4	0.9	2.8
2022 [2]	15,421	7,168	2,211	4,629	823	762	61	145	445	100.0	46.5	14.3	30.0	5.3	4.9	0.4	0.9	2.9
2023 [2]	15,378	7,069	2,208	4,672	824	764	60	144	461	100.0	46.0	14.4	30.4	5.4	5.0	0.4	0.9	3.0
2024 [2]	15,304	6,969	2,195	4,690	836	775	61	143	472	100.0	45.5	14.3	30.6	5.5	5.1	0.4	0.9	3.1

—Not available.

†Not applicable.

[1] For this year, data on students of Two or more races were reported by only a small number of states. Therefore, the data are not comparable to figures for 2010 and later years.

[2] Projected.

NOTE: Race categories exclude persons of Hispanic ethnicity. Enrollment data for students not reported by race/ethnicity were prorated by state and grade to match state totals. Prior to 2008, data on students of Two or more races were not collected separately. Total counts of ungraded students were prorated to prekindergarten through grade 8 and grades 9 through 12 based on prior reports. Some data have been revised from previously published figures. Detail may not sum to totals because of rounding.

SOURCE: U.S. Department of Education, National Center for Education Statistics, Common Core of Data (CCD), "State Nonfiscal Survey of Public Elementary and Secondary Education," 1998–99 through 2012–13; and National Elementary and Secondary Enrollment by Race/Ethnicity Projection Model, 1972 through 2024. (This table was prepared March 2015.)

Table 8. Public and private elementary and secondary teachers, enrollment, pupil/teacher ratios, and new teacher hires: Selected years, fall 1955 through fall 2024

Year	Teachers (in thousands)			Enrollment (in thousands)			Pupil/teacher ratio			Number of new teacher hires (in thousands)[1]		
	Total	Public	Private	Total	Public	Private	Total	Public	Private	Total	Public	Private
1	2	3	4	5	6	7	8	9	10	11	12	13
1955	1,286	1,141	145[2]	35,280	30,680	4,600[2]	27.4	26.9	31.7[2]	—	—	—
1960	1,600	1,408	192[2]	42,181	36,281	5,900[2]	26.4	25.8	30.7[2]	—	—	—
1965	1,933	1,710	223	48,473	42,173	6,300	25.1	24.7	28.3	—	—	—
1970	2,292	2,059	233	51,257	45,894	5,363	22.4	22.3	23.0	—	—	—
1971	2,293	2,063	230[2]	51,271	46,071	5,200[2]	22.4	22.3	22.6[2]	—	—	—
1972	2,337	2,106	231[2]	50,726	45,726	5,000[2]	21.7	21.7	21.6[2]	—	—	—
1973	2,372	2,136	236[2]	50,445	45,445	5,000[2]	21.3	21.3	21.2[2]	—	—	—
1974	2,410	2,165	245[2]	50,073	45,073	5,000[2]	20.8	20.8	20.4[2]	—	—	—
1975	2,453	2,198	255[2]	49,819	44,819	5,000[2]	20.3	20.4	19.6[2]	—	—	—
1976	2,457	2,189	268	49,478	44,311	5,167	20.1	20.2	19.3	—	—	—
1977	2,488	2,209	279	48,717	43,577	5,140	19.6	19.7	18.4	—	—	—
1978	2,479	2,207	272	47,637	42,551	5,086	19.2	19.3	18.7	—	—	—
1979	2,461	2,185	276[2]	46,651	41,651	5,000[2]	19.0	19.1	18.1[2]	—	—	—
1980	2,485	2,184	301	46,208	40,877	5,331	18.6	18.7	17.7	—	—	—
1981	2,440	2,127	313[2]	45,544	40,044	5,500[2]	18.7	18.8	17.6[2]	—	—	—
1982	2,458	2,133	325[2]	45,166	39,566	5,600[2]	18.4	18.6	17.2[2]	—	—	—
1983	2,476	2,139	337	44,967	39,252	5,715	18.2	18.4	17.0	—	—	—
1984	2,508	2,168	340[2]	44,908	39,208	5,700[2]	17.9	18.1	16.8[2]	—	—	—
1985	2,549	2,206	343	44,979	39,422	5,557	17.6	17.9	16.2	—	—	—
1986	2,592	2,244	348[2]	45,205	39,753	5,452[2]	17.4	17.7	15.7[2]	—	—	—
1987	2,631	2,279	352	45,488	40,008	5,479	17.3	17.6	15.6	—	—	—
1988	2,668	2,323	345[2]	45,430	40,189	5,242[2]	17.0	17.3	15.2[2]	—	—	—
1989	2,713	2,357	356	46,141	40,543	5,599	17.0	17.2	15.7	—	—	—
1990	2,759	2,398	361[2]	46,864	41,217	5,648[2]	17.0	17.2	15.6[2]	—	—	—
1991	2,797	2,432	365	47,728	42,047	5,681	17.1	17.3	15.6	—	—	—
1992	2,823	2,459	364[2]	48,694	42,823	5,870[2]	17.2	17.4	16.1[2]	—	—	—
1993	2,868	2,504	364	49,532	43,465	6,067	17.3	17.4	16.7	—	—	—
1994	2,922	2,552	370[2]	50,106	44,111	5,994[2]	17.1	17.3	16.2[2]	—	—	—
1995	2,974	2,598	376	50,759	44,840	5,918	17.1	17.3	15.7	—	—	—
1996	3,051	2,667	384[2]	51,544	45,611	5,933[2]	16.9	17.1	15.5[2]	—	—	—
1997	3,138	2,746	391	52,071	46,127	5,944	16.6	16.8	15.2	—	—	—
1998	3,230	2,830	400[2]	52,526	46,539	5,988[2]	16.3	16.4	15.0[2]	—	—	—
1999	3,319	2,911	408	52,875	46,857	6,018	15.9	16.1	14.7	305	222	83
2000	3,366	2,941	424[2]	53,373	47,204	6,169[2]	15.9	16.0	14.5[2]	—	—	—
2001	3,440	3,000	441	53,992	47,672	6,320	15.7	15.9	14.3	—	—	—
2002	3,476	3,034	442[2]	54,403	48,183	6,220[2]	15.7	15.9	14.1[2]	—	—	—
2003	3,490	3,049	441	54,639	48,540	6,099	15.7	15.9	13.8	311	236	74
2004	3,536	3,091	445[2]	54,882	48,795	6,087[2]	15.5	15.8	13.7[2]	—	—	—
2005	3,593	3,143	450	55,187	49,113	6,073	15.4	15.6	13.5	—	—	—
2006	3,622	3,166	456[2]	55,307	49,316	5,991[2]	15.3	15.6	13.2[2]	—	—	—
2007	3,656	3,200	456	55,201	49,291	5,910	15.1	15.4	13.0	327	246	80
2008	3,670	3,222	448[2]	54,973	49,266	5,707[2]	15.0	15.3	12.8[2]	—	—	—
2009	3,647	3,210	437	54,849	49,361	5,488	15.0	15.4	12.5	—	—	—
2010	3,529	3,099	429[2]	54,867	49,484	5,382[2]	15.5	16.0	12.5[2]	—	—	—
2011	3,524	3,103	421	54,790	49,522	5,268	15.5	16.0	12.5	241	173	68
2012	3,523	3,109	414[3]	54,952	49,771	5,181[3]	15.6	16.0	12.5[3]	321	247	74
2013[3]	3,527	3,120	407	55,036	49,942	5,094	15.6	16.0	12.5	319	250	69
2014[3]	3,520	3,122	398	54,965	49,986	4,979	15.6	16.0	12.5	310	244	66
2015[3]	3,521	3,129	391	54,994	50,094	4,899	15.6	16.0	12.5	316	249	67
2016[3]	3,525	3,138	387	55,077	50,229	4,848	15.6	16.0	12.5	318	250	68
2017[3]	3,577	3,185	392	55,447	50,584	4,863	15.5	15.9	12.4	364	288	76
2018[3]	3,617	3,224	393	55,719	50,871	4,848	15.4	15.8	12.3	358	283	74
2019[3]	3,660	3,264	395	56,031	51,183	4,848	15.3	15.7	12.3	361	286	76
2020[3]	3,700	3,302	398	56,404	51,547	4,856	15.2	15.6	12.2	362	285	76
2021[3]	3,743	3,342	401	56,779	51,910	4,869	15.2	15.5	12.1	367	289	77
2022[3]	3,788	3,383	405	57,151	52,260	4,891	15.1	15.4	12.1	371	292	79
2023[3]	3,840	3,429	410	57,524	52,601	4,922	15.0	15.3	12.0	381	300	81
2024[3]	3,881	3,466	415	57,872	52,920	4,952	14.9	15.3	11.9	375	293	81

—Not available.

[1] A teacher is considered to be a new hire for a public or private school if the teacher had not taught in that control of school in the previous year. A teacher who moves from a public to private or a private to public school is considered a new teacher hire, but a teacher who moves from one public school to another public school or one private school to another private school is not considered a new teacher hire.

[2] Estimated.

[3] Projected.

NOTE: Data for teachers are expressed in full-time equivalents (FTE). Counts of private school teachers and enrollment include prekindergarten through grade 12 in schools offering kindergarten or higher grades. Counts of public school teachers and enrollment include prekindergarten through grade 12. The pupil/teacher ratio includes teachers for students with disabilities and other special teachers, while these teachers are generally excluded from class size calculations. Ratios for public schools reflect totals reported by states and differ from totals reported for schools or school districts. Some data have been revised from previously published figures. Detail may not sum to totals because of rounding.

SOURCE: U.S. Department of Education, National Center for Education Statistics, *Statistics of Public Elementary and Secondary Day Schools*, 1955–56 through 1980–81; Common Core of Data (CCD), "State Nonfiscal Survey of Public Elementary/Secondary Education," 1981–82 through 2012–13; Private School Universe Survey (PSS), 1989–90 through 2011–12; Schools and Staffing Survey (SASS), "Public School Teacher Data File" and "Private School Teacher Data File," 1999–2000 through 2011–12; Elementary and Secondary Teacher Projection Model, 1973 through 2024; and New Teacher Hires Projection Model, 1988 through 2024. (This table was prepared March 2015.)

School year	High school graduates							Averaged freshman graduation rate for public schools[3]	Population 17 years old[4]	Graduates as a ratio of 17-year-old population
	Total[1]	Sex		Control						
				Public[2]			Private			
		Males	Females	Total	Males	Females				
1	2	3	4	5	6	7	8	9	10	11
1869–70	16,000	7,064	8,936	—	—	—	—	—	815,000	2.0
1879–80	23,634	10,605	13,029	—	—	—	—	—	946,026	2.5
1889–90	43,731	18,549	25,182	21,882	—	—	21,849 [5]	—	1,259,177	3.5
1899–1900	94,883	38,075	56,808	61,737	—	—	33,146 [5]	—	1,489,146	6.4
1909–10	156,429	63,676	92,753	111,363	—	—	45,066 [5]	—	1,786,240	8.8
1919–20	311,266	123,684	187,582	230,902	—	—	80,364 [5]	—	1,855,173	16.8
1929–30	666,904	300,376	366,528	591,719	—	—	75,185 [5]	—	2,295,822	29.0
1939–40	1,221,475	578,718	642,757	1,143,246	538,273	604,973	78,229 [5]	—	2,403,074	50.8
1949–50	1,199,700	570,700	629,000	1,063,444	505,394	558,050	136,256 [5]	—	2,034,450	59.0
1959–60	1,858,023	895,000	963,000	1,627,050	791,426	835,624	230,973	—	2,672,000	69.5
1969–70	2,888,639	1,430,000	1,459,000	2,588,639	1,285,895	1,302,744	300,000 [5]	78.7	3,757,000	76.9
1974–75	3,132,502	1,542,000	1,591,000	2,822,502	1,391,519	1,430,983	310,000 [5]	74.9	4,256,000	73.6
1975–76	3,142,120	1,552,000	1,590,000	2,837,129	1,401,064	1,436,065	304,991	74.9	4,272,000	73.6
1976–77	3,139,536	1,551,000	1,589,000	2,837,340	—	—	302,196	74.4	4,272,000	73.5
1977–78	3,128,824	1,546,000	1,583,000	2,824,636	—	—	304,188	73.2	4,286,000	73.0
1978–79	3,101,152	1,532,000	1,569,000	2,801,152	—	—	300,000 [5]	71.9	4,327,000	71.7
1979–80	3,042,214	1,503,000	1,539,000	2,747,678	—	—	294,536	71.5	4,262,000	71.4
1980–81	3,020,285	1,492,000	1,528,000	2,725,285	—	—	295,000 [5]	72.2	4,212,000	71.7
1981–82	2,994,758	1,479,000	1,515,000	2,704,758	—	—	290,000 [5]	72.9	4,134,000	72.4
1982–83	2,887,604	1,426,000	1,461,000	2,597,604	—	—	290,000 [5]	73.8	3,962,000	72.9
1983–84	2,766,797	—	—	2,494,797	—	—	272,000 [5]	74.5	3,784,000	73.1
1984–85	2,676,917	—	—	2,413,917	—	—	263,000 [5]	74.2	3,699,000	72.4
1985–86	2,642,616	—	—	2,382,616	—	—	260,000 [5]	74.3	3,670,000	72.0
1986–87	2,693,803	—	—	2,428,803	—	—	265,000 [5]	74.3	3,754,000	71.8
1987–88	2,773,020	—	—	2,500,020	—	—	273,000 [5]	74.2	3,849,000	72.0
1988–89	2,743,743	—	—	2,458,800	—	—	284,943	73.4	3,842,000	71.4
1989–90[6]	2,574,162	—	—	2,320,337	—	—	253,825 [7]	73.6	3,505,000	73.4
1990–91	2,492,988	—	—	2,234,893	—	—	258,095 [7]	73.7	3,417,913	72.9
1991–92	2,480,399	—	—	2,226,016	—	—	254,383 [7]	74.2	3,398,884	73.0
1992–93	2,480,519	—	—	2,233,241	—	—	247,278	73.8	3,449,143	71.9
1993–94	2,463,849	—	—	2,220,849	—	—	243,000 [5]	73.1	3,442,521	71.6
1994–95	2,519,084	—	—	2,273,541	—	—	245,543	71.8	3,635,803	69.3
1995–96	2,518,109	—	—	2,273,109	—	—	245,000 [5]	71.0	3,640,132	69.2
1996–97	2,611,988	—	—	2,358,403	—	—	253,585	71.3	3,792,207	68.9
1997–98	2,704,050	—	—	2,439,050	1,187,647	1,251,403	265,000 [5]	71.3	4,008,416	67.5
1998–99	2,758,655	—	—	2,485,630	1,212,924	1,272,706	273,025	71.1	3,917,885	70.4
1999–2000	2,832,844	—	—	2,553,844	1,241,631	1,312,213	279,000 [5]	71.7	4,056,639	69.8
2000–01	2,847,973	—	—	2,569,200	1,251,931	1,317,269	278,773	71.7	4,023,686	70.8
2001–02	2,906,534	—	—	2,621,534	1,275,813	1,345,721	285,000 [5]	72.6	4,023,968	72.2
2002–03	3,015,735	—	—	2,719,947	1,330,973	1,388,974	295,788	73.9	4,125,087	73.1
2003–04[6,8]	3,054,438	—	—	2,753,438	1,347,800	1,405,638	301,000 [5]	74.3	4,113,074	74.3
2004–05	3,106,499	—	—	2,799,250	1,369,749	1,429,501	307,249	74.7	4,120,073	75.4
2005–06[6]	3,122,544	—	—	2,815,544	1,376,458	1,439,086	307,000 [5]	73.4	4,200,554	74.3
2006–07	3,199,650	—	—	2,893,045	1,414,069	1,478,976	306,605	73.9	4,297,239	74.5
2007–08	3,312,337	—	—	3,001,337	1,467,180	1,534,157	311,000 [5]	74.7	4,436,955	74.7
2008–09[6]	3,347,828	—	—	3,039,015	1,490,317	1,548,698	308,813	75.5	4,336,950	77.2
2009–10	3,439,102	—	—	3,128,022	1,542,684 [9]	1,585,338 [9]	311,080 [5]	78.2	4,311,831	79.8
2010–11	3,449,719	—	—	3,143,879	—	—	305,840	79.6	4,368,154	79.0
2011–12	3,454,010	—	—	3,147,790	—	—	306,220 [5]	80.8	4,294,956	80.4
2012–13[10]	3,470,660	—	—	3,170,700	—	—	299,960	—	—	—
2013–14[10]	3,451,590	—	—	3,154,960	—	—	296,630	—	—	—
2014–15[10]	3,429,770	—	—	3,136,920	—	—	292,850	—	—	—
2015–16[10]	3,427,660	—	—	3,151,390	—	—	276,270	—	—	—
2016–17[10]	3,432,890	—	—	3,168,410	—	—	264,490	—	—	—
2017–18[10]	3,475,330	—	—	3,212,490	—	—	262,840	—	—	—
2018–19[10]	3,462,200	—	—	3,211,480	—	—	250,720	—	—	—
2019–20[10]	3,429,870	—	—	3,185,810	—	—	244,060	—	—	—
2020–21[10]	3,446,760	—	—	3,206,080	—	—	240,680	—	—	—
2021–22[10]	3,464,070	—	—	3,231,310	—	—	232,760	—	—	—
2022–23[10]	3,471,880	—	—	3,246,200	—	—	225,690	—	—	—
2023–24[10]	3,517,300	—	—	3,290,220	—	—	227,070	—	—	—
2024–25[10]	3,555,400	—	—	3,325,870	—	—	229,530	—	—	—

—Not available.

[1] Includes graduates of public and private schools.

[2] Data for 1929–30 and preceding years are from *Statistics of Public High Schools* and exclude graduates from high schools that failed to report to the Office of Education. Includes estimates for jurisdictions not reporting counts of graduates by sex.

[3] The averaged freshman graduation rate provides an estimate of the percentage of students who receive a regular diploma within 4 years of entering ninth grade. The rate uses aggregate student enrollment data to estimate the size of an incoming freshman class and aggregate counts of the number of diplomas awarded 4 years later. Averaged freshman graduation rates in this table are based on reported totals of enrollment by grade and high school graduates, rather than on details reported by race/ethnicity.

[4] Derived from Current Population Reports, Series P-25. For years 1869–70 through 1989–90, 17-year-old population is an estimate of the October 17-year-old population based on July data. Data for 1990–91 and later years are October resident population estimates prepared by the Census Bureau.

[5] Estimated.

[6] Includes imputations for nonreporting states.

[7] Projected by private schools responding to the Private School Universe Survey.

[8] Includes estimates for public schools in New York and Wisconsin. Without estimates for these two states, the averaged freshman graduation rate for the remaining 48 states and the District of Columbia is 75.0 percent.

[9] Includes estimate for Connecticut, which did not report graduates by sex.

[10] Projected by NCES.

NOTE: Includes graduates of regular day school programs. Excludes graduates of other programs, when separately reported, and recipients of high school equivalency certificates. Some data have been revised from previously published figures. Detail may not sum to totals because of rounding.

SOURCE: U.S. Department of Education, National Center for Education Statistics, *Annual Report of the Commissioner of Education*, 1870 through 1910; *Biennial Survey of Education in the United States*, 1919–20 through 1949–50; *Statistics of State School Systems*, 1951–52 through 1957–58; *Statistics of Public Elementary and Secondary School Systems*, 1958–59 through 1980–81; *Statistics of Nonpublic Elementary and Secondary Schools*, 1959 through 1980; Common Core of Data (CCD), "State Nonfiscal Survey of Public Elementary/Secondary Education," 1981–82 through 2009–10; "State Dropout and Completion Data File," 2005–06 through 2011–12; *Public School Graduates and Dropouts From the Common Core of Data*, 2007–08 and 2008–09; Private School Universe Survey (PSS), 1989 through 2011; and National High School Graduates Projection Model, 1972–73 through 2024–25. U.S. Department of Commerce, Census Bureau, Population Estimates, retrieved August 11, 2011, from http://www.census.gov/popest/national/asrh/2009-nat-res.html and Population Estimates, retrieved August 18, 2015, from http://www.census.gov/popest/data/national/asrh/2014/2014-nat-res.html. (This table was prepared August 2015.)

Table 10. Public high school graduates, by region, state, and jurisdiction: Selected years, 1980–81 through 2024–25

Region, state, and jurisdiction	Actual data							
	1980–81	1989–90	1999–2000	2005–06	2006–07	2007–08	2008–09	2009–10
1	2	3	4	5	6	7	8	9
United States	2,725,285	2,320,337 [1]	2,553,844	2,815,544 [1]	2,893,045	3,001,337	3,039,015 [1]	3,128,022
Region								
Northeast..................	593,727	446,045	453,814	521,015	536,697	552,289	552,973	556,400
Midwest....................	784,071	616,700	648,020	684,049	702,987	721,220	717,536	726,844
South........................	868,068	796,385	861,498	962,327	986,801	1,031,773	1,068,270	1,104,770
West.........................	479,419	461,207	590,512	648,153	666,560	696,055	700,236	740,008
State								
Alabama...................	44,894	40,485	37,819	37,918	38,912	41,346	42,082	43,166
Alaska	5,343	5,386	6,615	7,361	7,666	7,855	8,008	8,245
Arizona....................	28,416	32,103	38,304	54,091	55,954	61,667	62,374	61,145
Arkansas..................	29,577	26,475	27,335	28,790	27,166	28,725	28,057 [2]	28,276
California.................	242,172	236,291	309,866	343,515	356,641	374,561	372,310 [2]	404,987
Colorado	35,897	32,967	38,924	44,424	45,628	46,082	47,459	49,321
Connecticut..............	38,369	27,878	31,562	36,222	37,541	38,419	34,968	34,495
Delaware..................	7,349	5,550	6,108	7,275	7,205	7,388	7,839	8,133
District of Columbia[3]..	4,848	3,626	2,695	3,150 [4]	2,944	3,352	3,517	3,602
Florida.....................	88,755	88,934	106,708	134,686	142,284	149,046	153,461	156,130
Georgia....................	62,963	56,605	62,563	73,498	77,829	83,505	88,003	91,561
Hawaii	11,472	10,325	10,437	10,922	11,063	11,613	11,508	10,998
Idaho.......................	12,679	11,971	16,170	16,096	16,242	16,567	16,807	17,793
Illinois.....................	136,795	108,119	111,835	126,817	130,220	135,143	131,670	139,035
Indiana....................	73,381	60,012	57,012	57,920	59,887	61,901	63,663	64,551
Iowa	42,635	31,796	33,926	33,693	34,127	34,573	33,926	34,462
Kansas.....................	29,397	25,367	29,102	29,818	30,139	30,737	30,368	31,642
Kentucky	41,714	38,005	36,830	38,449	39,099	39,339	41,851	42,664
Louisiana	46,199	36,053	38,430	33,275	34,274	34,401	35,622	36,573
Maine......................	15,554	13,839	12,211	12,950	13,151	14,350 [5]	14,093 [5]	14,069
Maryland..................	54,050	41,566	47,849	55,536	57,564	59,171	58,304	59,078
Massachusetts...........	74,831	55,941 [6]	52,950	61,272	63,903	65,197	65,258	64,462
Michigan..................	124,372	93,807	97,679	102,582	111,838	115,183	112,742	110,682
Minnesota	64,166	49,087	57,372	58,898	59,497	60,409	59,729	59,667
Mississippi	28,083	25,182	24,232	23,848	24,186	24,795	24,505	25,478
Missouri	60,359	48,957	52,848	58,417	60,275	61,717	62,969	63,994
Montana	11,634	9,370	10,903	10,283	10,122	10,396	10,077	10,075
Nebraska..................	21,411	17,664	20,149	19,764	19,873	20,035	19,501	19,370
Nevada.....................	9,069	9,477	14,551	16,455	17,149	18,815	19,904 [2]	20,956
New Hampshire	11,552	10,766	11,829	13,988	14,452	14,982	14,757	15,034
New Jersey	93,168	69,824	74,420	90,049	93,013	94,994	95,085	96,225
New Mexico	17,915	14,884	18,031	17,822	16,131	18,264	17,931	18,595
New York..................	198,465	143,318	141,731	161,817	168,333	176,310	180,917	183,826
North Carolina	69,395	64,782	62,140	76,710	76,031	83,307	86,712	88,704
North Dakota.............	9,924	7,690	8,606	7,192	7,159	6,999	7,232	7,155
Ohio	143,503	114,513	111,668	117,356	117,658	120,758	122,203	123,437
Oklahoma	38,875	35,606	37,646	36,497	37,100	37,630	37,219	38,503
Oregon.....................	28,729	25,473	30,151	32,394	33,446	34,949	35,138	34,671
Pennsylvania.............	144,645	110,527	113,959	127,830 [4]	128,603	130,298	130,658	131,182
Rhode Island.............	10,719	7,825	8,477	10,108	10,384	10,347	10,028	9,908
South Carolina	38,347	32,483	31,617	34,970 [4]	35,108	35,303	39,114	40,438
South Dakota.............	10,385	7,650	9,278	8,589	8,346	8,582	8,123	8,162
Tennessee.................	50,648	46,094	41,568	50,880	54,502	57,486	60,368	62,408
Texas.......................	171,665	172,480	212,925	240,485	241,193	252,121	264,275	280,894
Utah	19,886	21,196	32,501	29,050	28,276	28,167	30,463	31,481
Vermont....................	6,424	6,127	6,675	6,779	7,317	7,392	7,209	7,199
Virginia....................	67,126	60,605	65,596	69,597	73,997	77,369	79,651	81,511
Washington	50,046	45,941	57,597	60,213	62,801	61,625	62,764	66,046
West Virginia.............	23,580	21,854	19,437	16,763	17,407	17,489	17,690	17,651
Wisconsin	67,743	52,038	58,545	63,003	63,968	65,183	65,410	64,687
Wyoming	6,161	5,823	6,462	5,527	5,441	5,494	5,493	5,695
Jurisdiction								
Bureau of Indian Education	—	—	—	—	—	—	—	—
DoD, overseas...........	—	—	2,642	—	—	—	—	—
DoD, domestic...........	—	—	560	—	—	—	—	—
Other jurisdictions								
American Samoa ...	—	703	698	879	954	—	—	—
Guam	—	1,033	1,406	—	—	—	—	—
Northern Marianas .	—	227	360	670	643	—	—	—
Puerto Rico	—	29,049	30,856	31,896	31,718	30,016	29,286	25,514
U.S. Virgin Islands..	—	1,260	1,060	—	820	820	940	958

See notes at end of table.

Table 10. Public high school graduates, by region, state, and jurisdiction: Selected years, 1980–81 through 2024–25—Continued

Region, state, and jurisdiction	Projected data															
	2010–11	2011–12	2012–13	2013–14	2014–15	2015–16	2016–17	2017–18	2018–19	2019–20	2020–21	2021–22	2022–23	2023–24	2024–25	Percent change, 2011–12 to 2024–25
1	10	11	12	13	14	15	16	17	18	19	20	21	22	23	24	25
United States	**3,143,879**	**3,147,790**	**3,170,700**	**3,154,960**	**3,136,920**	**3,151,390**	**3,168,410**	**3,212,490**	**3,211,480**	**3,185,810**	**3,206,080**	**3,231,310**	**3,246,200**	**3,290,220**	**3,325,870**	**5.7**
Region																
Northeast	556,620	554,770	554,060	544,390	535,500	535,210	532,570	534,290	530,990	524,630	530,120	532,010	527,360	534,460	534,070	-3.7
Midwest	718,540	716,080	713,900	705,900	695,640	696,020	700,840	708,400	707,040	698,430	700,690	710,250	703,910	706,610	709,720	-0.9
South	1,119,420	1,119,870	1,136,850	1,142,740	1,148,550	1,162,440	1,175,040	1,200,060	1,205,870	1,192,880	1,196,610	1,202,490	1,222,070	1,244,760	1,263,430	12.8
West	749,300	757,070	765,880	761,930	757,240	757,710	759,960	769,760	767,590	769,860	778,670	786,550	792,860	804,400	818,640	8.1
State																
Alabama	46,030	45,420	44,960	44,380	44,610	44,280	44,740	45,210	44,550	43,480	42,870	42,860	42,930	43,180	43,930	-3.3
Alaska	8,070	7,990	7,900	7,430	7,390	7,330	7,540	7,480	7,440	7,300	7,450	7,650	7,810	8,040	8,060	0.9
Arizona	64,480	63,210	65,420	65,430	64,080	62,040	63,040	63,240	64,400	65,090	67,030	68,240	69,940	70,660	72,220	14.2
Arkansas	28,210	28,420	28,730	29,340	29,910	29,750	29,910	29,960	30,070	29,910	29,580	29,750	29,580	29,300	29,680	4.4
California	410,470	418,670	421,270	419,180	414,790	413,440	410,860	416,960	411,330	413,160	415,780	419,050	421,050	425,530	432,530	3.3
Colorado	50,120	50,090	51,130	51,200	51,560	52,940	53,760	55,100	56,190	56,720	57,980	57,840	58,270	59,130	59,610	19.0
Connecticut	38,860	38,680	37,680	37,460	36,230	36,220	35,720	35,280	34,890	34,140	34,700	33,830	33,660	32,890	32,490	-16.0
Delaware	8,040	8,240	8,060	8,230	7,930	7,860	7,880	8,080	7,950	8,040	8,530	8,460	8,590	8,710	8,740	6.0
District of Columbia[3] ..	3,480	3,860	3,540	3,480	3,340	3,530	3,280	3,420	3,410	3,220	3,190	3,270	3,490	3,680	3,980	3.0
Florida	155,500	151,970	160,090	159,610	162,420	160,840	163,420	164,400	164,640	160,110	159,830	162,020	163,750	167,700	171,200	12.7
Georgia	92,340	90,580	93,090	95,320	95,420	97,490	98,500	100,670	101,060	99,290	98,990	99,360	100,710	102,580	103,690	14.5
Hawaii	10,720	11,360	10,950	11,000	10,870	10,810	10,870	11,410	10,830	11,390	11,460	11,550	11,770	11,860	12,040	5.9
Idaho	17,520	17,570	17,390	18,190	17,920	18,240	18,650	18,890	19,350	19,450	19,490	19,910	20,290	20,300	20,510	16.7
Illinois	134,960	139,580	139,130	138,970	134,300	134,050	136,030	139,410	137,800	138,530	140,520	141,780	140,140	136,670	136,740	-2.0
Indiana	66,140	65,670	66,570	67,550	66,000	66,810	66,810	67,610	69,100	66,010	63,490	65,840	63,740	64,370	65,220	-0.7
Iowa	33,850	33,230	32,590	32,660	32,630	32,670	32,900	33,400	33,300	33,160	33,610	33,760	34,260	35,140	35,530	6.9
Kansas	31,370	31,900	32,310	32,200	31,530	32,350	32,440	32,970	33,110	32,680	33,310	33,250	33,490	33,970	34,220	7.3
Kentucky	43,030	42,640	42,630	42,430	41,350	42,060	42,500	43,260	43,780	42,750	43,230	43,230	43,210	44,490	44,820	5.1
Louisiana	35,850	36,670	37,130	37,690	36,860	36,810	37,060	39,010	38,560	38,650	37,830	38,340	38,470	39,520	40,470	10.4
Maine	13,650	13,470	13,120	12,780	12,560	12,590	12,190	12,050	11,920	11,660	11,550	11,850	11,780	11,500	11,340	-15.8
Maryland	58,750	58,810	58,670	57,590	56,770	56,540	55,560	56,750	56,000	57,930	58,530	59,620	60,140	62,050	62,940	7.0
Massachusetts	64,730	65,160	65,000	64,470	64,430	65,070	64,520	64,530	64,550	63,920	64,030	64,050	63,020	63,640	63,230	-3.0
Michigan	105,750	105,450	103,880	101,580	101,090	99,050	99,550	99,310	98,120	95,950	94,920	95,710	92,860	92,940	92,710	-12.1
Minnesota	59,360	57,500	56,860	56,130	56,410	56,130	57,080	57,680	58,700	58,290	60,010	61,840	62,140	63,030	63,630	10.7
Mississippi	27,320	26,150	26,910	26,490	26,210	26,270	26,690	27,640	26,790	26,300	25,650	26,210	26,030	27,070	27,830	6.4
Missouri	63,000	61,310	61,200	61,190	60,640	61,180	60,790	61,010	60,480	59,590	59,750	60,410	60,570	61,280	61,340	#
Montana	9,730	9,760	9,320	9,490	9,370	9,340	9,440	9,250	9,500	9,520	9,610	9,820	9,820	10,410	10,700	9.7
Nebraska	20,330	20,460	21,240	21,190	21,030	20,930	21,190	21,800	22,050	22,450	22,750	23,420	23,150	23,560	23,720	15.9
Nevada	21,180	21,930	23,160	21,680	21,810	22,160	22,420	22,690	22,890	23,060	22,960	23,140	23,530	24,230	24,950	13.8
New Hampshire	14,500	14,430	14,150	13,730	13,540	13,340	12,990	12,920	12,620	12,610	12,330	12,340	12,040	12,050	11,840	-17.9
New Jersey	95,180	93,820	97,060	94,780	95,040	95,590	95,930	95,300	95,200	94,080	95,040	95,240	93,830	95,010	95,300	1.6
New Mexico	19,350	20,310	19,760	19,400	19,360	19,410	19,990	19,940	20,290	20,080	20,050	20,390	20,490	20,760	20,860	2.7
New York	182,760	181,050	182,970	180,480	178,720	177,710	176,780	179,000	176,920	175,960	178,550	179,330	179,070	184,170	185,060	2.2
North Carolina	89,900	93,980	94,420	95,450	96,940	98,410	99,840	102,030	103,160	101,460	101,980	94,650	102,930	104,790	105,400	12.1
North Dakota	7,160	6,940	6,950	7,020	6,940	7,250	7,230	7,090	7,400	7,610	7,900	8,440	8,600	9,550	10,000	44.1
Ohio	124,230	123,140	123,210	117,880	116,410	116,660	117,270	117,870	117,300	115,110	114,700	114,700	114,020	114,600	114,440	-7.1
Oklahoma	37,740	37,310	37,480	37,250	37,630	38,780	39,290	39,920	39,900	40,230	40,750	41,140	41,520	42,220	43,330	16.1
Oregon	34,720	34,260	35,040	34,940	34,590	35,110	35,080	35,000	35,050	34,660	34,880	35,310	35,400	36,260	36,850	7.6
Pennsylvania	130,290	131,740	127,590	124,360	118,900	118,990	119,700	120,310	119,450	116,930	118,630	119,890	118,660	120,320	120,020	-8.9
Rhode Island	9,730	9,560	9,850	9,840	9,680	9,440	8,610	8,900	9,480	9,430	9,430	9,540	9,280	9,000	8,770	-8.3
South Carolina	40,710	41,850	41,460	41,300	41,400	42,340	43,210	44,300	44,470	43,740	43,690	44,170	45,100	46,700	48,060	14.8
South Dakota	8,250	8,200	8,290	8,180	8,040	7,970	8,210	8,240	8,150	8,290	8,460	8,750	9,090	9,250	9,520	16.1
Tennessee	61,860	62,320	61,250	60,030	59,480	60,130	60,970	61,260	61,240	60,580	60,740	61,410	61,910	63,180	63,940	2.6
Texas	290,470	290,700	297,500	304,090	308,460	316,310	321,240	331,100	337,700	334,920	339,020	343,800	349,770	353,890	359,090	23.5
Utah	30,890	31,160	32,240	32,390	33,370	34,900	36,060	37,020	37,670	38,140	39,370	40,130	40,280	41,480	42,530	36.5
Vermont	6,930	6,860	6,650	6,510	6,400	6,270	6,140	6,000	5,980	5,890	5,850	5,940	6,020	5,890	6,020	-12.2
Virginia	82,900	83,340	83,170	82,730	82,490	83,530	83,690	85,450	85,390	84,890	85,300	87,050	86,940	88,870	89,380	7.2
Washington	66,450	65,210	66,850	66,060	66,490	66,170	66,380	66,870	66,740	65,330	66,340	67,240	67,660	69,040	70,860	8.7
West Virginia	17,310	17,600	17,790	17,340	17,330	17,520	17,270	17,620	17,230	17,390	16,910	17,160	17,020	16,820	16,980	-3.6
Wisconsin	64,140	62,710	61,670	61,350	60,610	60,980	61,350	62,010	61,540	60,760	61,270	62,370	61,850	62,250	62,650	-0.1
Wyoming	5,600	5,550	5,460	5,550	5,640	5,820	5,860	5,900	5,910	5,960	6,270	6,280	6,540	6,710	6,930	24.8
Jurisdiction																
Bureau of Indian Education	—	—	—	—	—	—	—	—	—	—	—	—	—	—	—	—
DoD, overseas	—	—	—	—	—	—	—	—	—	—	—	—	—	—	—	—
DoD, domestic	—	—	—	—	—	—	—	—	—	—	—	—	—	—	—	—
Other jurisdictions																
American Samoa ...	—	—	—	—	—	—	—	—	—	—	—	—	—	—	—	—
Guam	—	—	—	—	—	—	—	—	—	—	—	—	—	—	—	—
Northern Marianas .	—	—	—	—	—	—	—	—	—	—	—	—	—	—	—	—
Puerto Rico	—	—	—	—	—	—	—	—	—	—	—	—	—	—	—	—
U.S. Virgin Islands ..	—	—	—	—	—	—	—	—	—	—	—	—	—	—	—	—

—Not available.
#Rounds to zero.
[1]U.S. total includes estimates for nonreporting states.
[2]Estimated high school graduates from NCES 2011-312, *Public School Graduates and Dropouts from the Common Core of Data: School Year 2008–09.*
[3]Beginning in 1989–90, graduates from adult programs are excluded.
[4]Projected data from NCES 2009-062, *Projections of Education Statistics to 2018.*
[5]Includes 1,161 graduates in 2007–08 and 1,169 graduates in 2008–09 from private high schools that received a majority of their funding from public sources.
[6]Projected data from NCES 91-490, *Projections of Education Statistics to 2002.*

NOTE: Data include regular diploma recipients, but exclude students receiving a certificate of attendance and persons receiving high school equivalency certificates. DoD = Department of Defense. Some data have been revised from previously published figures. Detail may not sum to totals because of rounding.
SOURCE: U.S. Department of Education, National Center for Education Statistics, Common Core of Data (CCD), "State Nonfiscal Survey of Public Elementary/Secondary Education," 1981–82 through 2005–06; "State Dropout and Completion Data File," 2005–06 through 2009–10; *Public School Graduates and Dropouts from the Common Core of Data*, 2007–08 and 2008–09; and State High School Graduates Projection Model, 1980–81 through 2024–25. (This table was prepared August 2015.)

Table 11. Public high school graduates, by race/ethnicity: 1998–99 through 2024–25

Year	Number of high school graduates							Percentage distribution of graduates						
	Total	White	Black	Hispanic	Asian/ Pacific Islander	American Indian/ Alaska Native	Two or more races	Total	White	Black	Hispanic	Asian/ Pacific Islander	American Indian/ Alaska Native	Two or more races
1	2	3	4	5	6	7	8	9	10	11	12	13	14	15
1998–99	2,485,630	1,749,561	325,708	270,836	115,216	24,309	—	100.0	70.4	13.1	10.9	4.6	1.0	†
1999–2000	2,553,844	1,778,370	338,116	289,139	122,344	25,875	—	100.0	69.6	13.2	11.3	4.8	1.0	†
2000–01	2,569,200	1,775,036	339,578	301,740	126,465	26,381	—	100.0	69.1	13.2	11.7	4.9	1.0	†
2001–02	2,621,534	1,796,110	348,969	317,197	132,182	27,076	—	100.0	68.5	13.3	12.1	5.0	1.0	†
2002–03	2,719,947	1,856,454	359,920	340,182	135,588	27,803	—	100.0	68.3	13.2	12.5	5.0	1.0	†
2003–04	2,753,438	1,829,177	383,443	374,492	137,496	28,830	—	100.0	66.4	13.9	13.6	5.0	1.0	†
2004–05	2,799,250	1,855,198	385,987	383,714	143,729	30,622	—	100.0	66.3	13.8	13.7	5.1	1.1	†
2005–06	2,815,544	1,838,765	399,406	396,820	150,925	29,628	—	100.0	65.3	14.2	14.1	5.4	1.1	†
2006–07	2,893,045	1,868,056	418,113	421,036	154,837	31,003	—	100.0	64.6	14.5	14.6	5.4	1.1	†
2007–08	3,001,337	1,898,367	429,840	448,887	159,410	32,036	32,797 [1]	100.0	63.3	14.3	15.0	5.3	1.1	1.1 [1]
2008–09	3,039,015	1,883,382	451,384	481,698	163,575	32,213	26,763 [1]	100.0	62.0	14.9	15.9	5.4	1.1	0.9 [1]
2009–10	3,128,022	1,871,980	472,261	545,518	167,840	34,131	36,292 [1]	100.0	59.8	15.1	17.4	5.4	1.1	1.2 [1]
2010–11	3,143,879	1,835,156	471,410	583,907	168,880	32,778	51,748	100.0	58.4	15.0	18.6	5.4	1.0	1.6
2011–12	3,147,790	1,807,104	467,419	605,674	173,762	32,423	61,408	100.0	57.4	14.8	19.2	5.5	1.0	2.0
2012–13 [2]	3,170,700	1,794,490	460,680	636,100	180,300	31,060	68,070	100.0	56.6	14.5	20.1	5.7	1.0	2.1
2013–14 [2]	3,154,960	1,775,000	448,730	655,330	179,950	29,830	66,120	100.0	56.3	14.2	20.8	5.7	0.9	2.1
2014–15 [2]	3,136,920	1,747,580	439,490	672,100	180,030	28,780	68,940	100.0	55.7	14.0	21.4	5.7	0.9	2.2
2015–16 [2]	3,151,390	1,739,520	439,690	695,250	176,750	28,250	71,930	100.0	55.2	14.0	22.1	5.6	0.9	2.3
2016–17 [2]	3,168,410	1,733,160	443,830	712,300	175,940	29,380	73,800	100.0	54.7	14.0	22.5	5.6	0.9	2.3
2017–18 [2]	3,212,490	1,729,800	445,100	743,880	188,080	29,610	76,020	100.0	53.8	13.9	23.2	5.9	0.9	2.4
2018–19 [2]	3,211,480	1,706,400	437,760	775,350	185,290	28,900	77,770	100.0	53.1	13.6	24.1	5.8	0.9	2.4
2019–20 [2]	3,185,810	1,672,230	425,850	792,700	186,150	28,480	80,400	100.0	52.5	13.4	24.9	5.8	0.9	2.5
2020–21 [2]	3,206,080	1,666,820	413,890	823,390	191,440	27,680	82,870	100.0	52.0	12.9	25.7	6.0	0.9	2.6
2021–22 [2]	3,231,310	1,658,810	414,030	854,140	191,560	27,360	85,410	100.0	51.3	12.8	26.4	5.9	0.8	2.6
2022–23 [2]	3,246,200	1,633,360	415,730	895,040	187,680	26,660	87,730	100.0	50.3	12.8	27.6	5.8	0.8	2.7
2023–24 [2]	3,290,220	1,626,920	421,950	938,580	185,110	27,120	90,550	100.0	49.4	12.8	28.5	5.6	0.8	2.8
2024–25 [2]	3,325,870	1,623,940	432,000	961,270	187,850	27,420	93,390	100.0	48.8	13.0	28.9	5.6	0.8	2.8

—Not available.
†Not applicable.
[1]Data on students of Two or more races were not reported by all states; therefore, the data are not comparable to figures for 2010–11 and later years.
[2]Projected.
NOTE: Race categories exclude persons of Hispanic ethnicity. Prior to 2007–08, data on students of Two or more races were not collected separately. Some data have been revised from previously published figures. Detail may not sum to totals because of rounding.

SOURCE: U.S. Department of Education, National Center for Education Statistics, Common Core of Data (CCD), "State Nonfiscal Survey of Public Elementary/Secondary Education," 1999–2000 through 2005–06; "State Dropout and Completion Data File," 2005–06 through 2011–12; and National Public High School Graduates by Race/Ethnicity Projection Model, 1995–96 through 2024–25. (This table was prepared August 2015.)

Table 12. Current expenditures and current expenditures per pupil in public elementary and secondary schools: 1989–90 through 2024–25

School year	Current expenditures in unadjusted dollars[1]			Current expenditures in constant 2013–14 dollars[2]					
				Total current expenditures		Per pupil in fall enrollment		Per pupil in average daily attendance (ADA)	
	Total, in billions	Per pupil in fall enrollment	Per pupil in average daily attendance (ADA)	In billions	Annual percentage change	Per pupil enrolled	Annual percentage change	Per pupil in ADA	Annual percentage change
1	2	3	4	5	6	7	8	9	10
1989–90	$188.2	$4,643	$4,980	$343.0	3.8	$8,459	2.9	$9,073	2.3
1990–91	202.0	4,902	5,258	349.0	1.8	8,468	0.1	9,083	0.1
1991–92	211.2	5,023	5,421	353.6	1.3	8,409	-0.7	9,075	-0.1
1992–93	220.9	5,160	5,584	358.7	1.4	8,375	-0.4	9,064	-0.1
1993–94	231.5	5,327	5,767	366.4	2.1	8,429	0.6	9,126	0.7
1994–95	243.9	5,529	5,989	375.1	2.4	8,504	0.9	9,212	0.9
1995–96	255.1	5,689	6,147	382.0	1.8	8,519	0.2	9,205	-0.1
1996–97	270.2	5,923	6,393	393.3	3.0	8,624	1.2	9,307	1.1
1997–98	285.5	6,189	6,676	408.4	3.8	8,853	2.7	9,549	2.6
1998–99	302.9	6,508	7,013	425.9	4.3	9,151	3.4	9,861	3.3
1999–2000	323.9	6,912	7,394	442.6	3.9	9,446	3.2	10,104	2.5
2000–01	348.4	7,380	7,904	460.3	4.0	9,751	3.2	10,443	3.4
2001–02	368.4	7,727	8,259	478.3	3.9	10,033	2.9	10,723	2.7
2002–03	387.6	8,044	8,610	492.4	3.0	10,219	1.9	10,938	2.0
2003–04	403.4	8,310	8,900	501.5	1.8	10,332	1.1	11,064	1.2
2004–05	425.0	8,711	9,316	513.0	2.3	10,513	1.8	11,243	1.6
2005–06	449.1	9,145	9,778	522.2	1.8	10,632	1.1	11,368	1.1
2006–07	476.8	9,679	10,336	540.4	3.5	10,969	3.2	11,714	3.0
2007–08	506.9	10,298	10,982	553.9	2.5	11,254	2.6	12,001	2.5
2008–09	518.9	10,540	11,239	559.3	1.0	11,359	0.9	12,113	0.9
2009–10	524.7	10,636	11,427	568.9	0.1	11,531	-0.1	12,388	0.7
2010–11	527.3	10,663	11,433	560.4	-1.5	11,332	-1.7	12,151	-1.9
2011–12	527.1	10,667	11,363	544.2	-2.9	11,014	-2.8	11,732	-3.4
2012–13[3]	514.5	10,412	11,060	522.5	-4.0	10,574	0.7	11,232	1.1
2013–14[3]	529.9	10,610	11,352	529.9	1.4	10,610	0.9	11,352	0.9
2014–15[3]	542.4	10,851	11,610	539.2	1.8	10,787	2.0	11,541	2.0
2015–16[3]	559.5	11,169	11,950	548.3	1.7	10,946	1.8	11,711	1.8
2016–17[3]	584.8	11,643	12,457	560.0	2.1	11,150	2.0	11,929	2.0
2017–18[3]	615.3	12,164	13,015	575.2	2.7	11,370	2.0	12,166	2.0
2018–19[3]	644.0	12,660	13,546	587.3	2.1	11,545	1.5	12,353	1.5
2019–20[3]	674.9	13,185	14,108	600.7	2.3	11,737	1.3	12,558	1.3
2020–21[3]	706.4	13,705	14,663	613.7	2.2	11,906	1.0	12,739	1.0
2021–22[3]	736.8	14,193	15,186	626.0	2.0	12,059	1.0	12,902	1.0
2022–23[3]	768.0	14,696	15,723	638.2	2.0	12,212	1.1	13,066	1.1
2023–24[3]	800.2	15,213	16,277	650.5	1.9	12,366	0.7	13,231	0.7
2024–25[3]	824.9	15,589	16,679	659.4	1.4	12,460	#	13,332	#

—Not available.
#Rounds to zero.
[1] Unadjusted (or "current") dollars have not been adjusted to compensate for inflation.
[2] Constant dollars based on the Consumer Price Index, prepared by the Bureau of Labor Statistics, U.S. Department of Labor, adjusted to a school-year basis.
[3] Projected.

NOTE: Current expenditures include instruction, support services, food services, and enterprise operations. Some data have been revised from previously published figures.
SOURCE: U.S. Department of Education, National Center for Education Statistics, Common Core of Data (CCD), "National Public Education Financial Survey," 1989–90 through 2011–12; National Elementary and Secondary Enrollment Projection Model, 1972 through 2024; and Public Elementary and Secondary Education Current Expenditure Projection Model, 1973–74 through 2024–25. (This table was prepared August 2015.)

Table 13. Total fall enrollment in degree-granting postsecondary institutions, by attendance status, sex of student, and control of institution: Selected years, 1947 through 2024

Year	Total enrollment	Attendance status			Sex of student			Control of institution			
		Full-time	Part-time	Percent part-time	Male	Female	Percent female	Public	Private		
									Total	Nonprofit	For-profit
1	2	3	4	5	6	7	8	9	10	11	12
1947[1]	2,338,226	—	—	—	1,659,249	678,977	29.0	1,152,377	1,185,849	—	—
1948[1]	2,403,396	—	—	—	1,709,367	694,029	28.9	1,185,588	1,217,808	—	—
1949[1]	2,444,900	—	—	—	1,721,572	723,328	29.6	1,207,151	1,237,749	—	—
1950[1]	2,281,298	—	—	—	1,560,392	720,906	31.6	1,139,699	1,141,599	—	—
1951[1]	2,101,962	—	—	—	1,390,740	711,222	33.8	1,037,938	1,064,024	—	—
1952[1]	2,134,242	—	—	—	1,380,357	753,885	35.3	1,101,240	1,033,002	—	—
1953[1]	2,231,054	—	—	—	1,422,598	808,456	36.2	1,185,876	1,045,178	—	—
1954[1]	2,446,693	—	—	—	1,563,382	883,311	36.1	1,353,531	1,093,162	—	—
1955[1]	2,653,034	—	—	—	1,733,184	919,850	34.7	1,476,282	1,176,752	—	—
1956[1]	2,918,212	—	—	—	1,911,458	1,006,754	34.5	1,656,402	1,261,810	—	—
1957	3,323,783	—	—	—	2,170,765	1,153,018	34.7	1,972,673	1,351,110	—	—
1959	3,639,847	2,421,016	1,218,831 [2]	33.5	2,332,617	1,307,230	35.9	2,180,982	1,458,865	—	—
1961	4,145,065	2,785,133	1,359,932 [2]	32.8	2,585,821	1,559,244	37.6	2,561,447	1,583,618	—	—
1963	4,779,609	3,183,833	1,595,776 [2]	33.4	2,961,540	1,818,069	38.0	3,081,279	1,698,330	—	—
1964	5,280,020	3,573,238	1,706,782 [2]	32.3	3,248,713	2,031,307	38.5	3,467,708	1,812,312	—	—
1965	5,920,864	4,095,728	1,825,136 [2]	30.8	3,630,020	2,290,844	38.7	3,969,596	1,951,268	—	—
1966	6,389,872	4,438,606	1,951,266 [2]	30.5	3,856,216	2,533,656	39.7	4,348,917	2,040,955	—	—
1967	6,911,748	4,793,128	2,118,620 [2]	30.7	4,132,800	2,778,948	40.2	4,816,028	2,095,720	2,074,041	21,679
1968	7,513,091	5,210,155	2,302,936	30.7	4,477,649	3,035,442	40.4	5,430,652	2,082,439	2,061,211	21,228
1969	8,004,660	5,498,883	2,505,777	31.3	4,746,201	3,258,459	40.7	5,896,868	2,107,792	2,087,653	20,139
1970	8,580,887	5,816,290	2,764,597	32.2	5,043,642	3,537,245	41.2	6,428,134	2,152,753	2,134,420	18,333
1971	8,948,644	6,077,232	2,871,412	32.1	5,207,004	3,741,640	41.8	6,804,309	2,144,335	2,121,913	22,422
1972	9,214,860	6,072,389	3,142,471	34.1	5,238,757	3,976,103	43.1	7,070,635	2,144,225	2,123,245	20,980
1973	9,602,123	6,189,493	3,412,630	35.5	5,371,052	4,231,071	44.1	7,419,516	2,182,607	2,148,784	33,823
1974	10,223,729	6,370,273	3,853,456	37.7	5,622,429	4,601,300	45.0	7,988,500	2,235,229	2,200,963	34,266
1975	11,184,859	6,841,334	4,343,525	38.8	6,148,997	5,035,862	45.0	8,834,508	2,350,351	2,311,448	38,903
1976	11,012,137	6,717,058	4,295,079	39.0	5,810,828	5,201,309	47.2	8,653,477	2,358,660	2,314,298	44,362
1977	11,285,787	6,792,925	4,492,862	39.8	5,789,016	5,496,771	48.7	8,846,993	2,438,794	2,386,652	52,142
1978	11,260,092	6,667,657	4,592,435	40.8	5,640,998	5,619,094	49.9	8,785,893	2,474,199	2,408,331	65,868
1979	11,569,899	6,794,039	4,775,860	41.3	5,682,877	5,887,022	50.9	9,036,822	2,533,077	2,461,773	71,304
1980	12,096,895	7,097,958	4,998,937	41.3	5,874,374	6,222,521	51.4	9,457,394	2,639,501	2,527,787	111,714 [3]
1981	12,371,672	7,181,250	5,190,422	42.0	5,975,056	6,396,616	51.7	9,647,032	2,724,640	2,572,405	152,235 [3]
1982	12,425,780	7,220,618	5,205,162	41.9	6,031,384	6,394,396	51.5	9,696,087	2,729,693	2,552,739	176,954 [3]
1983	12,464,661	7,261,050	5,203,611	41.7	6,023,725	6,440,936	51.7	9,682,734	2,781,927	2,589,187	192,740
1984	12,241,940	7,098,388	5,143,552	42.0	5,863,574	6,378,366	52.1	9,477,370	2,764,570	2,574,419	190,151
1985	12,247,055	7,075,221	5,171,834	42.2	5,818,450	6,428,605	52.5	9,479,273	2,767,782	2,571,791	195,991
1986	12,503,511	7,119,550	5,383,961	43.1	5,884,515	6,618,996	52.9	9,713,893	2,789,618	2,572,479	217,139 [4]
1987	12,766,642	7,231,085	5,535,557	43.4	5,932,056	6,834,586	53.5	9,973,254	2,793,388	2,602,350	191,038 [4]
1988	13,055,337	7,436,768	5,618,569	43.0	6,001,896	7,053,441	54.0	10,161,388	2,893,949	2,673,567	220,382
1989	13,538,560	7,660,950	5,877,610	43.4	6,190,015	7,348,545	54.3	10,577,963	2,960,597	2,731,174	229,423
1990	13,818,637	7,820,985	5,997,652	43.4	6,283,909	7,534,728	54.5	10,844,717	2,973,920	2,760,227	213,693
1991	14,358,953	8,115,329	6,243,624	43.5	6,501,844	7,857,109	54.7	11,309,563	3,049,390	2,819,041	230,349
1992	14,487,359	8,162,118	6,325,241	43.7	6,523,989	7,963,370	55.0	11,384,567	3,102,792	2,872,523	230,269
1993	14,304,803	8,127,618	6,177,185	43.2	6,427,450	7,877,353	55.1	11,189,088	3,115,715	2,888,897	226,818
1994	14,278,790	8,137,776	6,141,014	43.0	6,371,898	7,906,892	55.4	11,133,680	3,145,110	2,910,107	235,003
1995	14,261,781	8,128,802	6,132,979	43.0	6,342,539	7,919,242	55.5	11,092,374	3,169,407	2,929,044	240,363
1996	14,367,520	8,302,953	6,064,567	42.2	6,352,825	8,014,695	55.8	11,120,499	3,247,021	2,942,556	304,465
1997	14,502,334	8,438,062	6,064,272	41.8	6,396,028	8,106,306	55.9	11,196,119	3,306,215	2,977,614	328,601
1998	14,506,967	8,563,338	5,943,629	41.0	6,369,265	8,137,702	56.1	11,137,769	3,369,198	3,004,925	364,273
1999	14,849,691	8,803,139	6,046,552	40.7	6,515,164	8,334,527	56.1	11,375,739	3,473,952	3,055,029	418,923
2000	15,312,289	9,009,600	6,302,689	41.2	6,721,769	8,590,520	56.1	11,752,786	3,559,503	3,109,419	450,084
2001	15,927,987	9,447,502	6,480,485	40.7	6,960,815	8,967,172	56.3	12,233,156	3,694,831	3,167,330	527,501
2002	16,611,711	9,946,359	6,665,352	40.1	7,202,116	9,409,595	56.6	12,751,993	3,859,718	3,265,476	594,242
2003	16,911,481	10,326,133	6,585,348	38.9	7,260,264	9,651,217	57.1	12,858,698	4,052,783	3,341,048	711,735
2004	17,272,044	10,610,177	6,661,867	38.6	7,387,262	9,884,782	57.2	12,980,112	4,291,932	3,411,685	880,247

See notes at end of table.

Year	Total enrollment	Attendance status			Sex of student			Control of institution			
		Full-time	Part-time	Percent part-time	Male	Female	Percent female	Public	Private		
									Total	Nonprofit	For-profit
1	2	3	4	5	6	7	8	9	10	11	12
2005	17,487,475	10,797,011	6,690,464	38.3	7,455,925	10,031,550	57.4	13,021,834	4,465,641	3,454,692	1,010,949
2006	17,758,870	10,957,305	6,801,565	38.3	7,574,815	10,184,055	57.3	13,180,133	4,578,737	3,512,866	1,065,871
2007	18,248,128	11,269,892	6,978,236	38.2	7,815,914	10,432,214	57.2	13,490,780	4,757,348	3,571,150	1,186,198
2008	19,102,814	11,747,743	7,355,071	38.5	8,188,895	10,913,919	57.1	13,972,153	5,130,661	3,661,519	1,469,142
2009	20,313,594	12,605,355	7,708,239	37.9	8,732,953	11,580,641	57.0	14,810,768	5,502,826	3,767,672	1,735,154
2010	21,019,438	13,087,182	7,932,256	37.7	9,045,759	11,973,679	57.0	15,142,171	5,877,267	3,854,482	2,022,785
2011	21,010,590	13,002,531	8,008,059	38.1	9,034,256	11,976,334	57.0	15,116,303	5,894,287	3,926,819	1,967,468
2012	20,642,819	12,737,013	7,905,806	38.3	8,919,087	11,723,732	56.8	14,880,343	5,762,476	3,953,578	1,808,898
2013	20,375,789	12,597,112	7,778,677	38.2	8,860,786	11,515,003	56.5	14,745,558	5,630,231	3,974,004	1,656,227
2014[5]	20,255,000	12,664,000	7,590,000	38.2	8,726,000	11,528,000	57.0	14,660,000	5,595,000	—	—
2015[5]	20,234,000	12,615,000	7,619,000	38.3	8,717,000	11,516,000	57.3	14,646,000	5,588,000	—	—
2016[5]	20,486,000	12,783,000	7,703,000	38.5	8,783,000	11,702,000	57.6	14,820,000	5,666,000	—	—
2017[5]	20,925,000	13,064,000	7,860,000	38.6	8,941,000	11,984,000	57.9	15,129,000	5,796,000	—	—
2018[5]	21,330,000	13,305,000	8,025,000	38.7	9,105,000	12,225,000	58.1	15,421,000	5,909,000	—	—
2019[5]	21,630,000	13,467,000	8,162,000	38.8	9,217,000	12,412,000	58.2	15,639,000	5,991,000	—	—
2020[5]	21,859,000	13,595,000	8,264,000	38.9	9,297,000	12,561,000	58.4	15,802,000	6,057,000	—	—
2021[5]	22,168,000	13,774,000	8,394,000	39.0	9,423,000	12,745,000	58.5	16,022,000	6,146,000	—	—
2022[5]	22,511,000	13,972,000	8,538,000	39.0	9,567,000	12,943,000	58.7	16,267,000	6,243,000	—	—
2023[5]	22,881,000	14,202,000	8,679,000	39.1	9,719,000	13,162,000	58.8	16,531,000	6,350,000	—	—
2024[5]	23,135,000	14,352,000	8,783,000	39.1	9,830,000	13,304,000	58.8	16,716,000	6,419,000	—	—

—Not available.

[1] Degree-credit enrollment only.

[2] Includes part-time resident students and all extension students (students attending courses at sites separate from the primary reporting campus). In later years, part-time student enrollment was collected as a distinct category.

[3] Large increases are due to the addition of schools accredited by the Accrediting Commission of Career Schools and Colleges of Technology.

[4] Because of imputation techniques, data are not consistent with figures for other years.

[5] Projected.

NOTE: Data through 1995 are for institutions of higher education, while later data are for degree-granting institutions. Degree-granting institutions grant associate's or higher degrees and partici-pate in Title IV federal financial aid programs. The degree-granting classification is very similar to the earlier higher education classification, but it includes more 2-year colleges and excludes a few higher education institutions that did not grant degrees. Some data have been revised from previously published figures.

SOURCE: U.S. Department of Education, National Center for Education Statistics, *Biennial Survey of Education in the United States*; *Opening Fall Enrollment in Higher Education*, 1963 through 1965; Higher Education General Information Survey (HEGIS), "Fall Enrollment in Colleges and Universities" surveys, 1966 through 1985; Integrated Postsecondary Education Data System (IPEDS), "Fall Enrollment Survey" (IPEDS-EF:86–99); IPEDS Spring 2001 through Spring 2014, Enrollment component; and Enrollment in Degree-Granting Institutions Projection Model, 1980 through 2024. (This table was prepared March 2015.)

Table 14. Total fall enrollment in degree-granting postsecondary institutions, by level and control of institution, attendance status, and sex of student: Selected years, 1970 through 2024

Level and control of institution, attendance status, and sex of student	Actual													
	1970	1975	1980[1]	1985	1990	1995	2000	2005	2008	2009	2010	2011	2012	2013
1	2	3	4	5	6	7	8	9	10	11	12	13	14	15
Total	8,580,887	11,184,859	12,096,895	12,247,055	13,818,637	14,261,781	15,312,289	17,487,475	19,102,814	20,313,594	21,019,438	21,010,590	20,642,819	20,375,789
Full-time	5,816,290	6,841,334	7,097,958	7,075,221	7,820,985	8,128,802	9,009,600	10,797,011	11,747,743	12,605,355	13,087,182	13,002,531	12,737,013	12,597,112
Males	3,504,095	3,926,753	3,689,244	3,607,720	3,807,752	3,807,392	4,111,093	4,803,388	5,234,357	5,632,097	5,838,383	5,792,818	5,709,792	5,682,166
Females	2,312,195	2,914,581	3,408,714	3,467,501	4,013,233	4,321,410	4,898,507	5,993,623	6,513,386	6,973,258	7,248,799	7,209,713	7,027,221	6,914,946
Part-time	2,764,597	4,343,525	4,998,937	5,171,834	5,997,652	6,132,979	6,302,689	6,690,464	7,355,071	7,708,239	7,932,256	8,008,059	7,905,806	7,778,677
Males	1,539,547	2,222,244	2,185,130	2,210,730	2,476,157	2,535,147	2,610,676	2,652,537	2,954,538	3,100,856	3,207,376	3,241,438	3,209,295	3,178,620
Females	1,225,050	2,121,281	2,813,807	2,961,104	3,521,495	3,597,832	3,692,013	4,037,927	4,400,533	4,607,383	4,724,880	4,766,621	4,696,511	4,600,057
4-year	6,261,502	7,214,740	7,570,608	7,715,978	8,578,554	8,769,252	9,363,858	10,999,420	12,131,436	12,791,013	13,335,841	13,499,440	13,478,846	13,407,050
Full-time	4,587,379	5,080,256	5,344,163	5,384,614	5,937,023	6,151,755	6,792,551	8,150,209	8,915,546	9,361,404	9,721,803	9,832,324	9,794,436	9,764,196
Males	2,732,796	2,891,192	2,809,528	2,781,412	2,926,360	2,929,177	3,115,252	3,649,622	3,984,494	4,185,726	4,355,153	4,401,635	4,403,960	4,403,914
Females	1,854,583	2,189,064	2,534,635	2,603,202	3,010,663	3,222,578	3,677,299	4,500,587	4,931,052	5,175,678	5,366,650	5,430,689	5,390,476	5,360,282
Part-time	1,674,123	2,134,484	2,226,445	2,331,364	2,641,531	2,617,497	2,571,307	2,849,211	3,215,890	3,429,609	3,614,038	3,667,116	3,684,410	3,642,854
Males	936,189	1,092,461	1,017,813	1,034,804	1,124,780	1,084,753	1,047,917	1,125,935	1,268,517	1,349,890	1,424,721	1,456,818	1,470,423	1,458,956
Females	737,934	1,042,023	1,208,632	1,296,560	1,516,751	1,532,744	1,523,390	1,723,276	1,947,373	2,079,719	2,189,317	2,210,298	2,213,987	2,183,898
Public 4-year	4,232,722	4,998,142	5,128,612	5,209,540	5,848,242	5,814,545	6,055,398	6,837,605	7,331,809	7,709,198	7,924,108	8,048,145	8,092,683	8,120,417
Full-time	3,086,491	3,469,821	3,592,193	3,623,341	4,033,654	4,084,711	4,371,218	5,021,745	5,378,123	5,649,722	5,811,214	5,890,689	5,910,198	5,934,852
Males	1,813,584	1,947,823	1,873,397	1,863,689	1,982,369	1,951,140	2,008,618	2,295,456	2,488,168	2,626,174	2,707,307	2,743,773	2,756,941	2,772,506
Females	1,272,907	1,521,998	1,718,796	1,759,652	2,051,285	2,133,571	2,362,600	2,726,289	2,889,955	3,023,548	3,103,907	3,146,916	3,153,257	3,162,346
Part-time	1,146,231	1,528,321	1,536,419	1,586,199	1,814,588	1,729,834	1,684,180	1,815,860	1,953,686	2,059,476	2,112,894	2,157,456	2,182,485	2,185,565
Males	609,422	760,469	685,051	693,115	764,248	720,402	683,100	724,375	788,594	833,155	860,968	885,045	901,197	911,040
Females	536,809	767,852	851,368	893,084	1,050,340	1,009,432	1,001,080	1,091,485	1,165,092	1,226,321	1,251,926	1,272,411	1,281,288	1,274,525
Private 4-year	2,028,780	2,216,598	2,441,996	2,506,438	2,730,312	2,954,707	3,308,460	4,161,815	4,799,627	5,081,815	5,411,733	5,451,295	5,386,163	5,286,633
Full-time	1,500,888	1,610,435	1,751,970	1,761,273	1,903,369	2,067,044	2,421,333	3,128,464	3,537,423	3,711,682	3,910,589	3,941,635	3,884,238	3,829,344
Males	919,212	943,369	936,131	917,723	943,991	978,037	1,106,634	1,354,166	1,496,326	1,559,552	1,647,846	1,657,862	1,647,019	1,631,408
Females	581,676	667,066	815,839	843,550	959,378	1,089,007	1,314,699	1,774,298	2,041,097	2,152,130	2,262,743	2,283,773	2,237,219	2,197,936
Part-time	527,892	606,163	690,026	745,165	826,943	887,663	887,127	1,033,351	1,262,204	1,370,133	1,501,144	1,509,660	1,501,925	1,457,289
Males	326,767	331,992	332,762	341,689	360,532	364,351	364,817	401,560	479,923	516,735	563,753	571,773	569,226	547,916
Females	201,125	274,171	357,264	403,476	466,411	523,312	522,310	631,791	782,281	853,398	937,391	937,887	932,699	909,373
Nonprofit 4-year	2,021,121	2,198,451	2,413,693	2,463,000	2,671,069	2,853,890	3,050,575	3,411,170	3,626,168	3,732,900	3,821,799	3,886,964	3,915,972	3,941,806
Full-time	1,494,625	1,596,074	1,733,014	1,727,707	1,859,124	1,989,457	2,226,028	2,534,793	2,698,819	2,787,321	2,864,640	2,905,674	2,928,938	2,961,998
Males	914,020	930,842	921,253	894,080	915,100	931,956	996,113	1,109,075	1,184,895	1,223,333	1,259,638	1,275,590	1,290,080	1,303,567
Females	580,605	665,232	811,761	833,627	944,024	1,057,501	1,229,915	1,425,718	1,513,924	1,563,988	1,605,002	1,630,084	1,638,858	1,658,431
Part-time	526,496	602,377	680,679	735,293	811,945	864,433	824,547	876,377	927,349	945,579	957,159	981,290	987,034	979,808
Males	325,693	329,662	327,986	336,168	352,106	351,874	332,814	339,572	357,974	363,789	366,735	375,713	377,740	377,480
Females	200,803	272,715	352,693	399,125	459,839	512,559	491,733	536,805	569,375	581,790	590,424	605,577	609,294	602,328
For-profit 4-year	7,659	18,147	28,303	43,438	59,243	100,817	257,885	750,645	1,173,459	1,348,915	1,589,934	1,564,331	1,470,191	1,344,827
2-year	2,319,385	3,970,119	4,526,287	4,531,077	5,240,083	5,492,529	5,948,431	6,488,055	6,971,378	7,522,581	7,683,597	7,511,150	7,163,973	6,968,739
Full-time	1,228,911	1,761,078	1,753,795	1,690,607	1,883,962	1,977,047	2,217,049	2,646,802	2,832,197	3,243,951	3,365,379	3,170,207	2,942,577	2,832,916
Males	771,299	1,035,561	879,716	826,308	881,392	878,215	995,841	1,153,766	1,249,863	1,446,371	1,483,230	1,391,183	1,305,832	1,278,252
Females	457,612	725,517	874,079	864,299	1,002,570	1,098,832	1,221,208	1,493,036	1,582,334	1,797,580	1,882,149	1,779,024	1,636,745	1,554,664
Part-time	1,090,474	2,209,041	2,772,492	2,840,470	3,356,121	3,515,482	3,731,382	3,841,253	4,139,181	4,278,630	4,318,218	4,340,943	4,221,396	4,135,823
Males	603,358	1,129,783	1,167,317	1,175,926	1,351,377	1,450,394	1,562,759	1,526,602	1,686,021	1,750,966	1,782,655	1,784,620	1,738,872	1,719,664
Females	487,116	1,079,258	1,605,175	1,664,544	2,004,744	2,065,088	2,168,623	2,314,651	2,453,160	2,527,664	2,535,563	2,556,323	2,482,524	2,416,159
Public 2-year	2,195,412	3,836,366	4,328,782	4,269,733	4,996,475	5,277,829	5,697,388	6,184,229	6,640,344	7,101,569	7,218,063	7,068,158	6,787,660	6,625,141
Full-time	1,129,165	1,662,621	1,595,493	1,496,905	1,716,843	1,840,590	2,000,008	2,387,016	2,548,488	2,875,291	2,950,024	2,781,419	2,615,620	2,529,957
Males	720,440	988,701	811,871	742,673	810,664	818,605	891,282	1,055,029	1,152,037	1,315,200	1,340,820	1,260,759	1,197,173	1,176,699
Females	408,725	673,920	783,622	754,232	906,179	1,021,985	1,108,726	1,331,987	1,396,451	1,560,091	1,609,204	1,520,660	1,418,447	1,353,258
Part-time	1,066,247	2,173,745	2,733,289	2,772,828	3,279,632	3,437,239	3,697,380	3,797,213	4,091,856	4,226,278	4,268,039	4,286,739	4,172,040	4,095,184
Males	589,439	1,107,680	1,152,268	1,138,011	1,317,730	1,417,488	1,549,407	1,514,363	1,671,716	1,735,300	1,769,737	1,770,197	1,725,988	1,708,594
Females	476,808	1,066,065	1,581,021	1,634,817	1,961,902	2,019,751	2,147,973	2,282,850	2,420,140	2,490,978	2,498,302	2,516,542	2,446,052	2,386,590
Private 2-year	123,973	133,753	197,505	261,344	243,608	214,700	251,043	303,826	331,034	421,012	465,534	442,992	376,313	343,598
Full-time	99,746	98,457	158,302	193,702	167,119	136,457	217,041	259,786	283,709	368,660	415,355	388,788	326,957	302,959
Males	50,859	46,860	67,845	83,635	70,728	59,610	104,559	98,737	97,826	131,171	142,410	130,424	108,659	101,553
Females	48,887	51,597	90,457	110,067	96,391	76,847	112,482	161,049	185,883	237,489	272,945	258,364	218,298	201,406
Part-time	24,227	35,296	39,203	67,642	76,489	78,243	34,002	44,040	47,325	52,352	50,179	54,204	49,356	40,639
Males	13,919	22,103	15,049	37,915	33,647	32,906	13,352	12,239	14,305	15,666	12,918	14,423	12,884	11,070
Females	10,308	13,193	24,154	29,727	42,842	45,337	20,650	31,801	33,020	36,686	37,261	39,781	36,472	29,569
Nonprofit 2-year	113,299	112,997	114,094	108,791	89,158	75,154	58,844	43,522	35,351	34,772	32,683	39,855	37,606	32,198
Full-time	91,514	82,158	83,009	76,547	62,003	54,033	46,670	28,939	23,270	23,488	23,127	30,584	29,320	24,055
Males	46,030	40,548	34,968	30,878	25,946	23,265	21,950	12,086	9,244	9,578	9,944	11,298	10,459	9,470
Females	45,484	41,610	48,041	45,669	36,057	30,768	24,720	16,853	14,026	13,910	13,183	19,286	18,861	14,585
Part-time	21,785	30,839	31,085	32,244	27,155	21,121	12,174	14,583	12,081	11,284	9,556	9,271	8,286	8,143
Males	12,097	18,929	11,445	10,786	7,970	6,080	4,499	3,566	2,867	2,721	2,585	2,540	2,465	2,386
Females	9,688	11,910	19,640	21,458	19,185	15,041	7,675	11,017	9,214	8,563	6,971	6,731	5,821	5,757
For-profit 2-year	10,674	20,756	83,411	152,553	154,450	139,546	192,199	260,304	295,683	386,240	432,851	403,137	338,707	311,400

See notes at end of table.

Table 14. Total fall enrollment in degree-granting postsecondary institutions, by level and control of institution, attendance status, and sex of student: Selected years, 1970 through 2024—Continued

Level and control of institution, attendance status, and sex of student	Projected										
	2014	2015	2016	2017	2018	2019	2020	2021	2022	2023	2024
1	16	17	18	19	20	21	22	23	24	25	26
Total	20,255,000	20,234,000	20,486,000	20,925,000	21,330,000	21,630,000	21,859,000	22,168,000	22,511,000	22,881,000	23,135,000
Full-time	12,664,000	12,615,000	12,783,000	13,064,000	13,305,000	13,467,000	13,595,000	13,774,000	13,972,000	14,202,000	14,352,000
Males	5,654,000	5,671,000	5,721,000	5,811,000	5,903,000	5,972,000	6,021,000	6,089,000	6,167,000	6,254,000	6,316,000
Females	7,010,000	6,943,000	7,062,000	7,253,000	7,402,000	7,495,000	7,574,000	7,685,000	7,805,000	7,948,000	8,035,000
Part-time	7,590,000	7,619,000	7,703,000	7,861,000	8,025,000	8,163,000	8,264,000	8,394,000	8,539,000	8,679,000	8,783,000
Males	3,072,000	3,046,000	3,063,000	3,130,000	3,202,000	3,245,000	3,277,000	3,333,000	3,400,000	3,465,000	3,514,000
Females	4,519,000	4,573,000	4,640,000	4,731,000	4,823,000	4,918,000	4,987,000	5,061,000	5,139,000	5,214,000	5,269,000
4-year	**13,246,000**	**13,222,000**	**13,395,000**	**13,690,000**	**13,952,000**	**14,142,000**	**14,297,000**	**14,505,000**	**14,728,000**	**14,975,000**	**15,140,000**
Full-time	9,739,000	9,699,000	9,826,000	10,039,000	10,219,000	10,341,000	10,443,000	10,581,000	10,729,000	10,903,000	11,016,000
Males	4,358,000	4,371,000	4,409,000	4,478,000	4,546,000	4,599,000	4,638,000	4,692,000	4,751,000	4,816,000	4,863,000
Females	5,381,000	5,328,000	5,417,000	5,561,000	5,673,000	5,742,000	5,804,000	5,889,000	5,979,000	6,087,000	6,153,000
Part-time	3,506,000	3,523,000	3,569,000	3,651,000	3,733,000	3,801,000	3,855,000	3,924,000	3,999,000	4,072,000	4,123,000
Males	1,412,000	1,403,000	1,415,000	1,450,000	1,487,000	1,510,000	1,527,000	1,557,000	1,593,000	1,626,000	1,651,000
Females	2,094,000	2,120,000	2,154,000	2,201,000	2,246,000	2,292,000	2,328,000	2,366,000	2,407,000	2,445,000	2,472,000
Public 4-year	8,008,000	7,991,000	8,091,000	8,265,000	8,421,000	8,535,000	8,627,000	8,750,000	8,883,000	9,030,000	9,130,000
Full-time	5,911,000	5,884,000	5,958,000	6,083,000	6,191,000	6,265,000	6,325,000	6,408,000	6,496,000	6,600,000	6,669,000
Males	2,734,000	2,741,000	2,763,000	2,805,000	2,847,000	2,879,000	2,904,000	2,937,000	2,973,000	3,013,000	3,043,000
Females	3,177,000	3,144,000	3,195,000	3,279,000	3,344,000	3,385,000	3,422,000	3,472,000	3,524,000	3,587,000	3,626,000
Part-time	2,097,000	2,107,000	2,133,000	2,181,000	2,230,000	2,270,000	2,302,000	2,342,000	2,387,000	2,430,000	2,461,000
Males	877,000	872,000	878,000	900,000	922,000	936,000	947,000	965,000	987,000	1,007,000	1,023,000
Females	1,220,000	1,235,000	1,255,000	1,281,000	1,307,000	1,334,000	1,355,000	1,377,000	1,400,000	1,423,000	1,438,000
Private 4-year	5,237,000	5,231,000	5,304,000	5,425,000	5,531,000	5,608,000	5,671,000	5,754,000	5,845,000	5,945,000	6,010,000
Full-time	3,828,000	3,814,000	3,868,000	3,956,000	4,028,000	4,077,000	4,117,000	4,173,000	4,233,000	4,303,000	4,347,000
Males	1,624,000	1,630,000	1,646,000	1,673,000	1,699,000	1,719,000	1,735,000	1,755,000	1,778,000	1,803,000	1,820,000
Females	2,205,000	2,184,000	2,222,000	2,282,000	2,329,000	2,357,000	2,383,000	2,418,000	2,455,000	2,500,000	2,527,000
Part-time	1,409,000	1,417,000	1,436,000	1,470,000	1,503,000	1,531,000	1,553,000	1,581,000	1,612,000	1,642,000	1,663,000
Males	535,000	532,000	537,000	550,000	564,000	573,000	580,000	592,000	606,000	619,000	628,000
Females	874,000	885,000	900,000	919,000	939,000	958,000	973,000	989,000	1,006,000	1,023,000	1,034,000
Nonprofit 4-year	—	—	—	—	—	—	—	—	—	—	—
Full-time	—	—	—	—	—	—	—	—	—	—	—
Males	—	—	—	—	—	—	—	—	—	—	—
Females	—	—	—	—	—	—	—	—	—	—	—
Part-time	—	—	—	—	—	—	—	—	—	—	—
Males	—	—	—	—	—	—	—	—	—	—	—
Females	—	—	—	—	—	—	—	—	—	—	—
For-profit 4-year	—	—	—	—	—	—	—	—	—	—	—
2-year	**7,009,000**	**7,011,000**	**7,090,000**	**7,235,000**	**7,378,000**	**7,487,000**	**7,562,000**	**7,664,000**	**7,782,000**	**7,907,000**	**7,996,000**
Full-time	2,925,000	2,916,000	2,957,000	3,026,000	3,085,000	3,126,000	3,153,000	3,193,000	3,243,000	3,299,000	3,335,000
Males	1,296,000	1,300,000	1,311,000	1,333,000	1,356,000	1,374,000	1,383,000	1,398,000	1,416,000	1,438,000	1,453,000
Females	1,629,000	1,616,000	1,645,000	1,692,000	1,729,000	1,752,000	1,770,000	1,796,000	1,826,000	1,862,000	1,882,000
Part-time	4,084,000	4,096,000	4,134,000	4,210,000	4,292,000	4,362,000	4,409,000	4,470,000	4,540,000	4,607,000	4,660,000
Males	1,660,000	1,643,000	1,648,000	1,680,000	1,716,000	1,736,000	1,749,000	1,776,000	1,808,000	1,839,000	1,863,000
Females	2,425,000	2,453,000	2,485,000	2,530,000	2,577,000	2,626,000	2,660,000	2,694,000	2,732,000	2,769,000	2,797,000
Public 2-year	6,651,000	6,655,000	6,729,000	6,865,000	7,000,000	7,104,000	7,175,000	7,272,000	7,384,000	7,502,000	7,586,000
Full-time	2,611,000	2,603,000	2,639,000	2,700,000	2,754,000	2,790,000	2,813,000	2,850,000	2,894,000	2,944,000	2,976,000
Males	1,193,000	1,197,000	1,207,000	1,227,000	1,249,000	1,264,000	1,273,000	1,287,000	1,304,000	1,323,000	1,338,000
Females	1,418,000	1,406,000	1,432,000	1,473,000	1,505,000	1,525,000	1,540,000	1,563,000	1,590,000	1,620,000	1,638,000
Part-time	4,040,000	4,052,000	4,089,000	4,165,000	4,246,000	4,315,000	4,362,000	4,422,000	4,491,000	4,558,000	4,610,000
Males	1,648,000	1,631,000	1,637,000	1,668,000	1,704,000	1,724,000	1,737,000	1,764,000	1,795,000	1,826,000	1,850,000
Females	2,392,000	2,420,000	2,452,000	2,496,000	2,543,000	2,591,000	2,624,000	2,658,000	2,695,000	2,732,000	2,760,000
Private 2-year	358,000	357,000	362,000	371,000	378,000	383,000	387,000	392,000	398,000	405,000	410,000
Full-time	314,000	313,000	317,000	325,000	332,000	336,000	339,000	344,000	349,000	355,000	359,000
Males	103,000	103,000	104,000	106,000	108,000	109,000	110,000	111,000	113,000	114,000	115,000
Females	211,000	209,000	213,000	219,000	224,000	227,000	229,000	233,000	237,000	241,000	244,000
Part-time	44,000	44,000	45,000	45,000	46,000	47,000	48,000	48,000	49,000	50,000	50,000
Males	11,000	11,000	11,000	12,000	12,000	12,000	12,000	12,000	12,000	13,000	13,000
Females	32,000	33,000	33,000	34,000	34,000	35,000	36,000	36,000	37,000	37,000	37,000
Nonprofit 2-year	—	—	—	—	—	—	—	—	—	—	—
Full-time	—	—	—	—	—	—	—	—	—	—	—
Males	—	—	—	—	—	—	—	—	—	—	—
Females	—	—	—	—	—	—	—	—	—	—	—
Part-time	—	—	—	—	—	—	—	—	—	—	—
Males	—	—	—	—	—	—	—	—	—	—	—
Females	—	—	—	—	—	—	—	—	—	—	—
For-profit 2-year	—	—	—	—	—	—	—	—	—	—	—

—Not available.

[1]Large increase in private 2-year institutions in 1980 is due to the addition of schools accredited by the Accrediting Commission of Career Schools and Colleges of Technology. NOTE: Data through 1995 are for institutions of higher education, while later data are for degree-granting institutions. Degree-granting institutions grant associate's or higher degrees and participate in Title IV federal financial aid programs. The degree-granting classification is very similar to the earlier higher education classification, but it includes more 2-year colleges and excludes a few higher education institutions that did not grant degrees. Some data have been revised from previously published figures.

SOURCE: U.S. Department of Education, National Center for Education Statistics, Higher Education General Information Survey (HEGIS), "Fall Enrollment in Colleges and Universities" surveys, 1970 through 1985; Integrated Postsecondary Education Data System (IPEDS), "Fall Enrollment Survey" (IPEDS-EF:90–99); IPEDS Spring 2001 through Spring 2014, Enrollment component; and Enrollment in Degree-Granting Institutions Projection Model, 1980 through 2024. (This table was prepared March 2015.)

Table 15. Total fall enrollment in degree-granting postsecondary institutions, by attendance status, sex, and age: Selected years, 1970 through 2024

[In thousands]

Attendance status, sex, and age	1970	1980	1990	2000	2003	2004	2005	2006	2007	2008	2009	2010	2011	2012	2013	Projected 2014	2015	2019	2024
1	2	3	4	5	6	7	8	9	10	11	12	13	14	15	16	17	18	19	20
All students	8,581	12,097	13,819	15,312	16,911	17,272	17,487	17,759	18,248	19,103	20,314	21,019	21,011	20,643	20,376	20,255	20,234	21,630	23,135
14 to 17 years old	263	257	153	131	169	166	187	184	200	195	215	202	221	242	270	254	259	278	311
18 and 19 years old	2,579	2,852	2,777	3,258	3,355	3,367	3,444	3,561	3,690	3,813	4,009	4,057	3,956	3,782	3,710	3,879	3,850	4,132	4,313
20 and 21 years old	1,885	2,395	2,593	3,005	3,391	3,516	3,563	3,573	3,570	3,649	3,916	4,103	4,269	4,235	4,248	4,472	4,414	4,526	4,747
22 to 24 years old	1,469	1,947	2,202	2,600	3,086	3,166	3,114	3,185	3,280	3,443	3,571	3,759	3,793	3,950	3,949	4,075	4,035	4,121	4,429
25 to 29 years old	1,091	1,843	2,083	2,044	2,311	2,418	2,469	2,506	2,651	2,840	3,082	3,254	3,272	3,154	3,031	2,995	3,071	3,467	3,525
30 to 34 years old	527	1,227	1,384	1,333	1,418	1,440	1,438	1,472	1,519	1,609	1,735	1,805	1,788	1,683	1,629	1,494	1,508	1,685	1,931
35 years old and over	767	1,577	2,627	2,942	3,181	3,199	3,272	3,277	3,339	3,554	3,785	3,840	3,712	3,595	3,538	3,086	3,097	3,421	3,879
Males	5,044	5,874	6,284	6,722	7,260	7,387	7,456	7,575	7,816	8,189	8,733	9,046	9,034	8,919	8,861	8,726	8,717	9,217	9,831
14 to 17 years old	125	106	66	58	67	62	68	69	88	93	103	94	104	119	130	118	119	124	136
18 and 19 years old	1,355	1,368	1,298	1,464	1,474	1,475	1,523	1,604	1,669	1,704	1,795	1,820	1,782	1,707	1,682	1,696	1,688	1,792	1,860
20 and 21 years old	1,064	1,219	1,259	1,411	1,541	1,608	1,658	1,628	1,634	1,695	1,866	1,948	1,985	1,960	1,956	2,025	1,997	2,022	2,108
22 to 24 years old	1,004	1,075	1,129	1,222	1,411	1,437	1,410	1,445	1,480	1,555	1,599	1,723	1,769	1,864	1,879	1,931	1,917	1,918	2,029
25 to 29 years old	796	983	1,024	908	1,007	1,039	1,057	1,040	1,148	1,222	1,378	1,410	1,404	1,353	1,327	1,282	1,316	1,489	1,524
30 to 34 years old	333	564	605	581	602	619	591	628	638	691	707	731	700	661	638	587	593	667	777
35 years old and over	366	559	902	1,077	1,158	1,147	1,149	1,160	1,159	1,228	1,285	1,320	1,290	1,255	1,249	1,087	1,088	1,205	1,397
Females	3,537	6,223	7,535	8,591	9,651	9,885	10,032	10,184	10,432	10,914	11,581	11,974	11,976	11,724	11,515	11,529	11,516	12,412	13,305
14 to 17 years old	137	151	87	73	102	104	119	115	112	102	113	108	116	123	140	137	140	154	175
18 and 19 years old	1,224	1,484	1,479	1,794	1,880	1,892	1,920	1,956	2,021	2,109	2,214	2,237	2,173	2,075	2,028	2,182	2,162	2,340	2,453
20 and 21 years old	821	1,177	1,334	1,593	1,851	1,908	1,905	1,945	1,936	1,954	2,050	2,155	2,284	2,276	2,293	2,447	2,417	2,504	2,639
22 to 24 years old	464	871	1,073	1,378	1,675	1,729	1,704	1,740	1,800	1,888	1,972	2,036	2,024	2,087	2,070	2,144	2,118	2,203	2,400
25 to 29 years old	296	859	1,059	1,136	1,304	1,379	1,413	1,466	1,502	1,618	1,704	1,844	1,868	1,801	1,704	1,713	1,755	1,978	2,002
30 to 34 years old	194	663	779	752	816	821	847	844	881	918	1,028	1,074	1,088	1,022	991	907	916	1,018	1,154
35 years old and over	401	1,018	1,725	1,865	2,023	2,052	2,123	2,117	2,180	2,326	2,500	2,520	2,422	2,340	2,289	1,999	2,009	2,215	2,482
Full-time	5,816	7,098	7,821	9,010	10,326	10,610	10,797	10,957	11,270	11,748	12,605	13,087	13,003	12,737	12,597	12,664	12,615	13,467	14,352
14 to 17 years old	246	231	134	121	146	138	152	148	169	168	179	170	185	207	226	214	218	235	263
18 and 19 years old	2,374	2,544	2,471	2,823	2,934	2,960	3,026	3,120	3,244	3,359	3,481	3,496	3,351	3,227	3,151	3,171	3,147	3,393	3,553
20 and 21 years old	1,649	2,007	2,137	2,452	2,841	2,926	2,976	2,972	2,985	3,043	3,241	3,364	3,427	3,386	3,362	3,443	3,391	3,496	3,680
22 to 24 years old	904	1,181	1,405	1,714	2,083	2,143	2,122	2,127	2,205	2,347	2,511	2,585	2,580	2,603	2,630	2,688	2,651	2,729	2,946
25 to 29 years old	426	641	791	886	1,086	1,132	1,174	1,225	1,299	1,369	1,506	1,605	1,600	1,555	1,515	1,487	1,531	1,745	1,784
30 to 34 years old	113	272	383	418	489	517	547	571	556	571	657	745	763	711	701	688	697	784	900
35 years old and over	104	221	500	596	747	795	800	794	812	890	1,030	1,122	1,096	1,047	1,012	974	979	1,085	1,225
Males	3,504	3,689	3,808	4,111	4,638	4,739	4,803	4,879	5,029	5,234	5,632	5,838	5,793	5,710	5,682	5,654	5,671	5,972	6,316
14 to 17 years old	121	95	55	51	58	49	53	52	74	73	77	71	85	102	110	98	100	104	114
18 and 19 years old	1,261	1,219	1,171	1,252	1,291	1,297	1,339	1,404	1,465	1,516	1,570	1,574	1,510	1,462	1,435	1,412	1,411	1,502	1,560
20 and 21 years old	955	1,046	1,035	1,156	1,305	1,360	1,398	1,372	1,366	1,407	1,536	1,586	1,586	1,537	1,520	1,536	1,518	1,542	1,608
22 to 24 years old	686	717	768	834	995	1,001	982	992	1,043	1,105	1,169	1,215	1,217	1,254	1,267	1,294	1,289	1,294	1,371
25 to 29 years old	346	391	433	410	503	498	506	533	578	597	661	715	727	728	733	720	747	849	871
30 to 34 years old	77	142	171	186	209	231	225	235	231	249	279	301	299	278	274	268	275	310	363
35 years old and over	58	80	174	222	277	302	300	291	273	287	341	376	369	349	344	326	332	370	430
Females	2,312	3,409	4,013	4,899	5,688	5,871	5,994	6,078	6,240	6,513	6,973	7,249	7,210	7,027	6,915	7,010	6,943	7,495	8,035
14 to 17 years old	125	136	78	70	88	89	98	95	95	95	102	99	100	105	117	116	119	131	149
18 and 19 years old	1,113	1,325	1,300	1,571	1,643	1,662	1,687	1,716	1,779	1,843	1,911	1,922	1,842	1,765	1,716	1,759	1,736	1,891	1,993
20 and 21 years old	693	961	1,101	1,296	1,536	1,566	1,578	1,601	1,619	1,636	1,705	1,778	1,840	1,849	1,842	1,907	1,873	1,954	2,071
22 to 24 years old	218	464	638	880	1,088	1,142	1,140	1,135	1,163	1,242	1,343	1,370	1,364	1,349	1,363	1,394	1,363	1,434	1,575
25 to 29 years old	80	250	358	476	583	634	668	692	721	772	845	891	873	827	782	767	784	896	914
30 to 34 years old	37	130	212	232	280	286	322	336	324	322	378	444	464	433	427	420	422	473	537
35 years old and over	46	141	326	374	471	493	500	503	539	603	690	746	727	698	667	648	647	715	795
Part-time	2,765	4,999	5,998	6,303	6,585	6,662	6,690	6,802	6,978	7,355	7,708	7,932	8,008	7,906	7,779	7,590	7,619	8,163	8,783
14 to 17 years old	16	26	19	10	23	28	36	36	31	27	36	32	36	35	44	40	40	43	48
18 and 19 years old	205	308	306	435	421	407	417	440	446	453	528	561	604	555	559	708	702	739	759
20 and 21 years old	236	388	456	553	551	590	586	601	585	606	675	738	842	849	886	1,029	1,023	1,030	1,067
22 to 24 years old	564	765	796	886	1,003	1,023	992	1,058	1,074	1,096	1,059	1,174	1,212	1,347	1,319	1,387	1,383	1,393	1,483
25 to 29 years old	665	1,202	1,291	1,158	1,224	1,286	1,296	1,282	1,352	1,471	1,576	1,648	1,672	1,599	1,516	1,508	1,540	1,722	1,741
30 to 34 years old	414	954	1,001	915	929	923	891	901	963	1,037	1,079	1,060	1,025	972	928	806	812	901	1,031
35 years old and over	663	1,356	2,127	2,345	2,434	2,404	2,472	2,483	2,527	2,664	2,754	2,718	2,616	2,548	2,527	2,113	2,119	2,335	2,654
Males	1,540	2,185	2,476	2,611	2,622	2,648	2,653	2,696	2,786	2,955	3,101	3,207	3,241	3,209	3,179	3,072	3,046	3,245	3,514
14 to 17 years old	4	12	11	7	9	13	15	17	14	20	25	23	20	17	21	19	19	20	22
18 and 19 years old	94	149	127	212	183	178	184	200	204	188	226	245	273	246	247	284	276	290	300
20 and 21 years old	108	172	224	255	236	248	260	257	269	289	330	362	398	423	436	489	479	481	499
22 to 24 years old	318	359	361	388	416	436	428	452	438	450	430	508	552	609	613	637	628	623	659
25 to 29 years old	450	592	591	498	504	540	551	507	570	625	718	695	677	625	594	562	569	640	653
30 to 34 years old	257	422	435	395	392	388	365	393	406	442	428	430	401	383	364	319	318	356	414
35 years old and over	309	479	728	855	882	845	850	869	886	941	944	944	921	906	905	762	757	835	967
Females	1,225	2,814	3,521	3,692	3,963	4,014	4,038	4,106	4,192	4,401	4,607	4,725	4,767	4,697	4,600	4,519	4,573	4,918	5,269
14 to 17 years old	12	14	9	3	14	15	21	20	17	7	11	9	16	18	23	21	21	23	26
18 and 19 years old	112	159	179	223	238	230	233	240	242	265	303	316	332	310	312	424	426	449	460
20 and 21 years old	128	216	233	298	315	342	327	344	317	318	345	377	444	427	450	540	544	549	568
22 to 24 years old	246	407	435	497	587	588	564	605	637	646	629	666	660	738	706	750	755	769	824
25 to 29 years old	216	609	700	660	721	746	745	774	781	846	859	953	995	974	922	946	971	1,083	1,088
30 to 34 years old	158	532	567	520	537	535	526	508	557	595	651	630	624	589	564	487	493	545	617
35 years old and over	354	876	1,399	1,491	1,552	1,560	1,623	1,614	1,640	1,723	1,810	1,774	1,695	1,642	1,622	1,351	1,362	1,500	1,687

NOTE: Distributions by age are estimates based on samples of the civilian noninstitutional population from the U.S. Census Bureau's Current Population Survey. Data through 1995 are for institutions of higher education, while later data are for degree-granting institutions. Degree-granting institutions grant associate's or higher degrees and participate in Title IV federal financial aid programs. The degree-granting classification is very similar to the earlier higher education classification, but it includes more 2-year colleges and excludes a few higher education institutions that did not grant degrees. Some data have been revised from previously published figures. Detail may not sum to totals because of rounding.

SOURCE: U.S. Department of Education, National Center for Education Statistics, Higher Education General Information Survey (HEGIS), "Fall Enrollment in Colleges and Universities" surveys, 1970 and 1980; Integrated Postsecondary Education Data System (IPEDS), "Fall Enrollment Survey" (IPEDS-EF:90–99); IPEDS Spring 2001 through Spring 2014, Enrollment component; and Enrollment in Degree-Granting Institutions Projection Model, 1980 through 2024. U.S. Department of Commerce, Census Bureau, Current Population Survey (CPS), October, selected years, 1970 through 2013. (This table was prepared May 2015.)

This page intentionally left blank.

Table 16. Total undergraduate fall enrollment in degree-granting postsecondary institutions, by attendance status, sex of student, and control and level of institution: Selected years, 1970 through 2024

						Males		Females			Private		
Level and year	Total	Full-time	Part-time	Males	Females	Full-time	Part-time	Full-time	Part-time	Public	Total	Nonprofit	For-profit
1	2	3	4	5	6	7	8	9	10	11	12	13	14
Total, all levels													
1970	7,368,644	5,280,064	2,088,580	4,249,702	3,118,942	3,096,371	1,153,331	2,183,693	935,249	5,620,255	1,748,389	1,730,133	18,256
1975	9,679,455	6,168,396	3,511,059	5,257,005	4,422,450	3,459,328	1,797,677	2,709,068	1,713,382	7,826,032	1,853,423	1,814,844	38,579
1980	10,475,055	6,361,744	4,113,311	5,000,177	5,474,878	3,226,857	1,773,320	3,134,887	2,339,991	8,441,955	2,033,100	1,926,703	106,397
1981	10,754,522	6,449,068	4,305,454	5,108,271	5,646,251	3,260,473	1,847,798	3,188,595	2,457,656	8,648,363	2,106,159	1,958,848	147,311
1982	10,825,062	6,483,805	4,341,257	5,170,494	5,654,568	3,299,436	1,871,058	3,184,369	2,470,199	8,713,073	2,111,989	1,939,389	172,600
1983	10,845,995	6,514,034	4,331,961	5,158,300	5,687,695	3,304,247	1,854,053	3,209,787	2,477,908	8,697,118	2,148,877	1,961,076	187,801
1984	10,618,071	6,347,653	4,270,418	5,006,813	5,611,258	3,194,930	1,811,883	3,152,723	2,458,535	8,493,491	2,124,580	1,940,310	184,270
1985	10,596,674	6,319,592	4,277,082	4,962,080	5,634,594	3,156,446	1,805,634	3,163,146	2,471,448	8,477,125	2,119,549	1,928,996	190,553
1986	10,797,975	6,352,073	4,445,902	5,017,505	5,780,470	3,146,330	1,871,175	3,205,743	2,574,727	8,660,716	2,137,259	1,928,294	208,965
1987	11,046,235	6,462,549	4,583,686	5,068,457	5,977,778	3,163,676	1,904,781	3,298,873	2,678,905	8,918,589	2,127,646	1,939,942	187,704
1988	11,316,548	6,642,428	4,674,120	5,137,644	6,178,904	3,206,442	1,931,202	3,435,986	2,742,918	9,103,146	2,213,402	—	—
1989	11,742,531	6,840,696	4,901,835	5,310,990	6,431,541	3,278,647	2,032,343	3,562,049	2,869,492	9,487,742	2,254,789	—	—
1990	11,959,106	6,976,030	4,983,076	5,379,759	6,579,347	3,336,535	2,043,224	3,639,495	2,939,852	9,709,596	2,249,510	2,043,407	206,103
1991	12,439,287	7,221,412	5,217,875	5,571,003	6,868,284	3,435,526	2,135,477	3,785,886	3,082,398	10,147,957	2,291,330	2,072,354	218,976
1992	12,537,700	7,244,442	5,293,258	5,582,936	6,954,764	3,424,739	2,158,197	3,819,703	3,135,061	10,216,297	2,321,403	2,101,721	219,682
1993	12,323,959	7,179,482	5,144,477	5,483,682	6,840,277	3,381,997	2,101,685	3,797,485	3,042,792	10,011,787	2,312,172	2,099,197	212,975
1994	12,262,608	7,168,706	5,093,902	5,422,113	6,840,495	3,341,591	2,080,522	3,827,115	3,013,380	9,945,128	2,317,480	2,100,465	217,015
1995	12,231,719	7,145,268	5,086,451	5,401,130	6,830,589	3,296,610	2,104,520	3,848,658	2,981,931	9,903,626	2,328,093	2,104,693	223,400
1996	12,326,948	7,298,839	5,028,109	5,420,672	6,906,276	3,339,108	2,081,564	3,959,731	2,946,545	9,935,283	2,391,665	2,112,318	279,347
1997	12,450,587	7,418,598	5,031,989	5,468,532	6,982,055	3,379,597	2,088,935	4,039,001	2,943,054	10,007,479	2,443,108	2,139,824	303,284
1998	12,436,937	7,538,711	4,898,226	5,446,133	6,990,804	3,428,161	2,017,972	4,110,550	2,880,254	9,950,212	2,486,725	2,152,655	334,070
1999	12,739,445	7,753,548	4,985,897	5,584,234	7,155,211	3,524,586	2,059,648	4,228,962	2,926,249	10,174,228	2,565,217	2,185,290	379,927
2000	13,155,393	7,922,926	5,232,467	5,778,268	7,377,125	3,588,246	2,190,022	4,334,680	3,042,445	10,539,322	2,616,071	2,213,180	402,891
2001	13,715,610	8,327,640	5,387,970	6,004,431	7,711,179	3,768,630	2,235,801	4,559,010	3,152,169	10,985,871	2,729,739	2,257,718	472,021
2002	14,257,077	8,734,252	5,522,825	6,192,390	8,064,687	3,934,168	2,258,222	4,800,084	3,264,603	11,432,855	2,824,222	2,306,091	518,131
2003	14,480,364	9,045,253	5,435,111	6,227,372	8,252,992	4,048,682	2,178,690	4,996,571	3,256,421	11,523,103	2,957,261	2,346,673	610,588
2004	14,780,630	9,284,336	5,496,294	6,340,048	8,440,582	4,140,628	2,199,420	5,143,708	3,296,874	11,650,580	3,130,050	2,389,366	740,684
2005	14,963,964	9,446,430	5,517,534	6,408,871	8,555,093	4,200,863	2,208,008	5,245,567	3,309,526	11,697,730	3,266,234	2,418,368	847,866
2006	15,184,302	9,571,079	5,613,223	6,513,756	8,670,546	4,264,606	2,249,150	5,306,473	3,364,073	11,847,426	3,336,876	2,448,240	888,636
2007	15,603,771	9,840,978	5,762,793	6,727,600	8,876,171	4,396,868	2,330,732	5,444,110	3,432,061	12,137,583	3,466,188	2,470,327	995,861
2008	16,365,738	10,254,930	6,110,808	7,066,623	9,299,115	4,577,431	2,489,192	5,677,499	3,621,616	12,591,217	3,774,521	2,536,532	1,237,989
2009	17,464,179	11,038,275	6,425,904	7,563,176	9,901,003	4,942,120	2,621,056	6,096,155	3,804,848	13,386,375	4,077,804	2,595,171	1,482,633
2010	18,082,427	11,457,040	6,625,387	7,836,282	10,246,145	5,118,975	2,717,307	6,338,065	3,908,080	13,703,000	4,379,427	2,652,993	1,726,434
2011	18,077,303	11,365,175	6,712,128	7,822,992	10,254,311	5,070,553	2,752,439	6,294,622	3,959,689	13,694,899	4,382,404	2,718,923	1,663,481
2012	17,732,431	11,097,779	6,634,652	7,713,901	10,018,530	4,984,696	2,729,205	6,113,083	3,905,447	13,473,743	4,258,688	2,745,075	1,513,613
2013	17,474,835	10,938,494	6,536,341	7,659,626	9,815,209	4,949,572	2,710,054	5,988,922	3,826,287	13,347,002	4,127,833	2,757,447	1,370,386
2014[1]	17,322,000	10,966,000	6,356,000	7,466,000	9,855,000	4,874,000	2,592,000	6,092,000	3,763,000	13,245,000	4,077,000	—	—
2015[1]	17,280,000	10,904,000	6,376,000	7,446,000	9,834,000	4,878,000	2,568,000	6,026,000	3,808,000	13,221,000	4,059,000	—	—
2016[1]	17,472,000	11,033,000	6,439,000	7,490,000	9,982,000	4,911,000	2,579,000	6,122,000	3,859,000	13,366,000	4,106,000	—	—
2017[1]	17,823,000	11,261,000	6,562,000	7,612,000	10,210,000	4,981,000	2,631,000	6,280,000	3,931,000	13,633,000	4,189,000	—	—
2018[1]	18,156,000	11,463,000	6,693,000	7,745,000	10,412,000	5,055,000	2,689,000	6,407,000	4,004,000	13,890,000	4,266,000	—	—
2019[1]	18,404,000	11,601,000	6,804,000	7,836,000	10,569,000	5,113,000	2,723,000	6,488,000	4,081,000	14,083,000	4,321,000	—	—
2020[1]	18,591,000	11,708,000	6,883,000	7,898,000	10,692,000	5,152,000	2,747,000	6,556,000	4,136,000	14,225,000	4,365,000	—	—
2021[1]	18,843,000	11,857,000	6,986,000	7,998,000	10,845,000	5,207,000	2,791,000	6,650,000	4,194,000	14,418,000	4,425,000	—	—
2022[1]	19,119,000	12,019,000	7,100,000	8,113,000	11,006,000	5,269,000	2,844,000	6,750,000	4,256,000	14,631,000	4,488,000	—	—
2023[1]	19,423,000	12,211,000	7,211,000	8,236,000	11,187,000	5,340,000	2,895,000	6,871,000	4,316,000	14,863,000	4,560,000	—	—
2024[1]	19,640,000	12,345,000	7,295,000	8,330,000	11,310,000	5,395,000	2,935,000	6,949,000	4,361,000	15,029,000	4,611,000	—	—
2-year institutions[2]													
1970	2,318,956	1,228,909	1,090,047	1,374,426	944,530	771,298	603,128	457,611	486,919	2,194,983	123,973	113,299	10,674
1975	3,965,726	1,761,009	2,204,717	2,163,604	1,802,122	1,035,531	1,128,073	725,478	1,076,644	3,831,973	133,753	112,997	20,756
1980	4,525,097	1,753,637	2,771,460	2,046,642	2,478,455	879,619	1,167,023	874,018	1,604,437	4,327,592	197,505	114,094	83,411
1981	4,715,403	1,795,858	2,919,545	2,124,136	2,591,267	897,657	1,226,479	898,201	1,693,066	4,479,900	235,503	119,166	116,337
1982	4,770,712	1,839,704	2,931,008	2,169,802	2,600,910	930,606	1,239,196	909,098	1,691,812	4,518,659	252,053	114,976	137,077
1983	4,723,466	1,826,801	2,896,665	2,131,109	2,592,357	914,704	1,216,405	912,097	1,680,260	4,459,330	264,136	116,293	147,843
1984	4,530,337	1,703,786	2,826,551	2,016,463	2,513,874	841,347	1,175,116	862,439	1,651,435	4,278,661	251,676	108,247	143,429
1985	4,531,077	1,690,607	2,840,470	2,002,234	2,528,843	826,308	1,175,926	864,299	1,664,544	4,269,733	261,344	108,791	152,553
1986	4,679,548	1,696,261	2,983,287	2,060,932	2,618,616	824,551	1,236,381	871,710	1,746,906	4,413,691	265,857	101,498	164,359
1987	4,776,222	1,708,669	3,067,553	2,072,823	2,703,399	820,167	1,252,656	888,502	1,814,897	4,541,054	235,168	90,102	145,066
1988	4,875,155	1,743,592	3,131,563	2,089,689	2,785,466	818,593	1,271,096	924,999	1,860,467	4,615,487	259,668	—	—
1989	5,150,889	1,855,701	3,295,188	2,216,800	2,934,089	869,688	1,347,112	986,013	1,948,076	4,883,660	267,229	—	—
1990	5,240,083	1,883,962	3,356,121	2,232,769	3,007,314	881,392	1,351,377	1,002,570	2,004,744	4,996,475	243,608	89,158	154,450
1991	5,651,900	2,074,530	3,577,370	2,401,910	3,249,990	961,397	1,440,513	1,113,133	2,136,857	5,404,815	247,085	89,289	157,796
1992	5,722,349	2,080,005	3,642,344	2,413,266	3,309,083	951,816	1,461,450	1,128,189	2,180,894	5,484,514	237,835	83,288	154,547
1993	5,565,561	2,043,319	3,522,242	2,345,396	3,220,165	928,216	1,417,180	1,115,103	2,105,062	5,337,022	228,539	86,357	142,182
1994	5,529,609	2,031,713	3,497,896	2,323,161	3,206,448	911,589	1,411,572	1,120,124	2,086,324	5,308,366	221,243	85,607	135,636
1995	5,492,098	1,977,046	3,515,052	2,328,500	3,163,598	878,215	1,450,285	1,098,831	2,064,767	5,277,398	214,700	75,154	139,546
1996	5,562,780	2,072,215	3,490,565	2,358,792	3,203,988	916,452	1,442,340	1,155,763	2,048,225	5,314,038	248,742	75,253	173,489
1997	5,605,569	2,095,171	3,510,398	2,389,711	3,215,858	931,394	1,458,317	1,163,777	2,052,081	5,360,686	244,883	71,794	173,089
1998	5,489,314	2,085,906	3,403,408	2,333,334	3,155,980	936,421	1,396,913	1,149,485	2,006,495	5,245,963	243,351	65,870	177,481
1999	5,653,256	2,167,242	3,486,014	2,413,322	3,239,934	979,203	1,434,119	1,188,039	2,051,895	5,397,786	255,470	63,301	192,169
2000	5,948,104	2,217,044	3,731,060	2,558,520	3,389,584	995,839	1,562,681	1,221,205	2,168,379	5,697,061	251,043	58,844	192,199
2001	6,250,529	2,374,490	3,876,039	2,675,193	3,575,336	1,066,281	1,608,912	1,308,209	2,267,127	5,996,651	253,878	47,549	206,329
2002	6,529,198	2,556,032	3,973,166	2,753,405	3,775,793	1,135,669	1,617,736	1,420,363	2,355,430	6,270,199	258,999	47,087	211,912
2003	6,493,862	2,650,337	3,843,525	2,689,928	3,803,934	1,162,555	1,527,373	1,487,782	2,316,152	6,208,885	284,977	43,868	241,109
2004	6,545,570	2,683,489	3,862,081	2,697,507	3,848,063	1,166,554	1,530,953	1,516,935	2,331,128	6,243,344	302,226	42,250	259,976

See notes at end of table.

Table 16. Total undergraduate fall enrollment in degree-granting postsecondary institutions, by attendance status, sex of student, and control and level of institution: Selected years, 1970 through 2024—Continued

Level and year	Total	Full-time	Part-time	Males	Females	Males		Females		Public	Private		
						Full-time	Part-time	Full-time	Part-time		Total	Nonprofit	For-profit
1	2	3	4	5	6	7	8	9	10	11	12	13	14
2005	6,487,826	2,646,763	3,841,063	2,680,299	3,807,527	1,153,759	1,526,540	1,493,004	2,314,523	6,184,000	303,826	43,522	260,304
2006	6,518,291	2,643,222	3,875,069	2,704,654	3,813,637	1,159,800	1,544,854	1,483,422	2,330,215	6,224,871	293,420	39,156	254,264
2007	6,617,621	2,692,491	3,925,130	2,770,457	3,847,164	1,190,067	1,580,390	1,502,424	2,344,740	6,323,810	293,811	33,486	260,325
2008	6,971,105	2,832,110	4,138,995	2,935,793	4,035,312	1,249,832	1,685,961	1,582,278	2,453,034	6,640,071	331,034	35,351	295,683
2009	7,522,581	3,243,952	4,278,629	3,197,338	4,325,243	1,446,372	1,750,966	1,797,580	2,527,663	7,101,569	421,012	34,772	386,240
2010	7,683,597	3,365,379	4,318,218	3,265,885	4,417,712	1,483,230	1,782,655	1,882,149	2,535,563	7,218,063	465,534	32,683	432,851
2011	7,511,150	3,170,207	4,340,943	3,175,803	4,335,347	1,391,183	1,784,620	1,779,024	2,556,323	7,068,158	442,992	39,855	403,137
2012	7,163,973	2,942,577	4,221,396	3,044,704	4,119,269	1,305,832	1,738,872	1,636,745	2,482,524	6,787,660	376,313	37,606	338,707
2013	6,968,739	2,832,916	4,135,823	2,997,916	3,970,823	1,278,252	1,719,664	1,554,664	2,416,159	6,625,141	343,598	32,198	311,400
2014[1]	7,009,000	2,925,000	4,084,000	2,956,000	4,053,000	1,296,000	1,660,000	1,629,000	2,425,000	6,651,000	358,000	—	—
2015[1]	7,011,000	2,916,000	4,096,000	2,943,000	4,069,000	1,300,000	1,643,000	1,616,000	2,453,000	6,655,000	357,000	—	—
2016[1]	7,090,000	2,957,000	4,134,000	2,960,000	4,131,000	1,311,000	1,648,000	1,645,000	2,485,000	6,729,000	362,000	—	—
2017[1]	7,235,000	3,026,000	4,210,000	3,013,000	4,222,000	1,333,000	1,680,000	1,692,000	2,530,000	6,865,000	371,000	—	—
2018[1]	7,378,000	3,085,000	4,292,000	3,072,000	4,306,000	1,356,000	1,716,000	1,729,000	2,577,000	7,000,000	378,000	—	—
2019[1]	7,487,000	3,126,000	4,362,000	3,109,000	4,378,000	1,374,000	1,736,000	1,752,000	2,626,000	7,104,000	383,000	—	—
2020[1]	7,562,000	3,153,000	4,409,000	3,132,000	4,429,000	1,383,000	1,749,000	1,770,000	2,660,000	7,175,000	387,000	—	—
2021[1]	7,664,000	3,193,000	4,470,000	3,174,000	4,490,000	1,398,000	1,776,000	1,796,000	2,694,000	7,272,000	392,000	—	—
2022[1]	7,782,000	3,243,000	4,540,000	3,224,000	4,558,000	1,416,000	1,808,000	1,826,000	2,732,000	7,384,000	398,000	—	—
2023[1]	7,907,000	3,299,000	4,607,000	3,276,000	4,630,000	1,438,000	1,839,000	1,862,000	2,769,000	7,502,000	405,000	—	—
2024[1]	7,996,000	3,335,000	4,660,000	3,316,000	4,679,000	1,453,000	1,863,000	1,882,000	2,797,000	7,586,000	410,000	—	—
4-year institutions													
1970	5,049,688	4,051,155	998,533	2,875,276	2,174,412	2,325,073	550,203	1,726,082	448,330	3,425,272	1,624,416	1,616,834	7,582
1975	5,713,729	4,407,387	1,306,342	3,093,401	2,620,328	2,423,797	669,604	1,983,590	636,738	3,994,059	1,719,670	1,701,847	17,823
1980	5,949,958	4,608,107	1,341,851	2,953,535	2,996,423	2,347,238	606,297	2,260,869	735,554	4,114,363	1,835,595	1,812,609	22,986
1981	6,039,119	4,653,210	1,385,909	2,984,135	3,054,984	2,362,816	621,319	2,290,394	764,590	4,168,463	1,870,656	1,839,682	30,974
1982	6,054,350	4,644,101	1,410,249	3,000,692	3,053,658	2,368,830	631,862	2,275,271	778,387	4,194,414	1,859,936	1,824,413	35,523
1983	6,122,529	4,687,233	1,435,296	3,027,191	3,095,338	2,389,543	637,648	2,297,690	797,648	4,237,788	1,884,741	1,844,783	39,958
1984	6,087,734	4,643,867	1,443,867	2,990,350	3,097,384	2,353,583	636,767	2,290,284	807,100	4,214,830	1,872,904	1,832,063	40,841
1985	6,065,597	4,628,985	1,436,612	2,959,846	3,105,751	2,330,138	629,708	2,298,847	806,904	4,207,392	1,858,205	1,820,205	38,000
1986	6,118,427	4,655,812	1,462,615	2,956,573	3,161,854	2,321,779	634,794	2,334,033	827,821	4,247,025	1,871,402	1,826,796	44,606
1987	6,270,013	4,753,880	1,516,133	2,995,634	3,274,379	2,343,509	652,125	2,410,371	864,008	4,377,535	1,892,478	1,849,840	42,638
1988	6,441,393	4,898,836	1,542,557	3,047,955	3,393,438	2,387,849	660,106	2,510,987	882,451	4,487,659	1,953,734	—	—
1989	6,591,642	4,984,995	1,606,647	3,094,190	3,497,452	2,408,959	685,231	2,576,036	921,416	4,604,082	1,987,560	—	—
1990	6,719,023	5,092,068	1,626,955	3,146,990	3,572,033	2,455,143	691,847	2,636,925	935,108	4,713,121	2,005,902	1,954,249	51,653
1991	6,787,387	5,146,882	1,640,505	3,169,093	3,618,294	2,474,129	694,964	2,672,753	945,541	4,743,142	2,044,245	1,983,065	61,180
1992	6,815,351	5,164,437	1,650,914	3,169,670	3,645,681	2,472,923	696,747	2,691,514	954,167	4,731,783	2,083,568	2,018,433	65,135
1993	6,758,398	5,136,163	1,622,235	3,138,286	3,620,112	2,453,781	684,505	2,682,382	937,730	4,674,765	2,083,633	2,012,840	70,793
1994	6,732,999	5,136,993	1,596,006	3,098,952	3,634,047	2,430,002	668,950	2,706,991	927,056	4,636,762	2,096,237	2,014,858	81,379
1995	6,739,621	5,168,222	1,571,399	3,072,630	3,666,991	2,418,395	654,235	2,749,827	917,164	4,626,228	2,113,393	2,029,539	83,854
1996	6,764,168	5,226,624	1,537,544	3,061,880	3,702,288	2,422,656	639,224	2,803,968	898,320	4,621,245	2,142,923	2,037,065	105,858
1997	6,845,018	5,323,427	1,521,591	3,078,821	3,766,197	2,448,203	630,618	2,875,224	890,973	4,646,793	2,198,225	2,068,030	130,195
1998	6,947,623	5,452,805	1,494,818	3,112,799	3,834,824	2,491,740	621,059	2,961,065	873,759	4,704,249	2,243,374	2,086,785	156,589
1999	7,086,189	5,586,306	1,499,883	3,170,912	3,915,277	2,545,383	625,529	3,040,923	874,354	4,776,442	2,309,747	2,121,989	187,758
2000	7,207,289	5,705,882	1,501,407	3,219,748	3,987,541	2,592,407	627,341	3,113,475	874,066	4,842,261	2,365,028	2,154,336	210,692
2001	7,465,081	5,953,150	1,511,931	3,329,238	4,135,843	2,702,349	626,889	3,250,801	885,042	4,989,220	2,475,861	2,210,169	265,692
2002	7,727,879	6,178,220	1,549,659	3,438,985	4,288,894	2,798,499	640,486	3,379,721	909,173	5,162,656	2,565,223	2,259,004	306,219
2003	7,986,502	6,394,916	1,591,586	3,537,444	4,449,058	2,886,127	651,317	3,508,789	940,269	5,314,218	2,672,284	2,302,805	369,479
2004	8,235,060	6,600,847	1,634,213	3,642,541	4,592,519	2,974,074	668,467	3,626,773	965,746	5,407,236	2,827,824	2,347,116	480,708
2005	8,476,138	6,799,667	1,676,471	3,728,572	4,747,566	3,047,104	681,468	3,752,563	995,003	5,513,730	2,962,408	2,374,846	587,562
2006	8,666,011	6,927,857	1,738,154	3,809,102	4,856,909	3,104,806	704,296	3,823,051	1,033,858	5,622,555	3,043,456	2,409,084	634,372
2007	8,986,150	7,148,487	1,837,663	3,957,143	5,029,007	3,206,801	750,342	3,941,686	1,087,321	5,813,773	3,172,377	2,436,841	735,536
2008	9,394,633	7,422,820	1,971,813	4,130,830	5,263,803	3,327,599	803,231	4,095,221	1,168,582	5,951,146	3,443,487	2,501,181	942,306
2009	9,941,598	7,794,323	2,147,275	4,365,838	5,575,760	3,495,748	870,090	4,298,575	1,277,185	6,284,806	3,656,792	2,560,399	1,096,393
2010	10,398,830	8,091,661	2,307,169	4,570,397	5,828,433	3,635,745	934,652	4,455,916	1,372,517	6,484,937	3,913,893	2,620,310	1,293,583
2011	10,566,153	8,194,968	2,371,185	4,647,189	5,918,964	3,679,370	967,819	4,515,598	1,403,366	6,626,741	3,939,412	2,679,068	1,260,344
2012	10,568,458	8,155,202	2,413,256	4,669,197	5,899,261	3,678,864	990,333	4,476,338	1,422,923	6,686,083	3,882,375	2,707,469	1,174,906
2013	10,506,096	8,105,578	2,400,518	4,661,710	5,844,386	3,671,320	990,390	4,434,258	1,410,128	6,721,861	3,784,235	2,725,249	1,058,986
2014[1]	10,312,000	8,041,000	2,271,000	4,510,000	5,802,000	3,578,000	933,000	4,463,000	1,339,000	6,594,000	3,719,000	—	—
2015[1]	10,269,000	7,989,000	2,280,000	4,503,000	5,765,000	3,578,000	925,000	4,411,000	1,355,000	6,566,000	3,702,000	—	—
2016[1]	10,381,000	8,077,000	2,305,000	4,531,000	5,851,000	3,600,000	931,000	4,477,000	1,374,000	6,638,000	3,744,000	—	—
2017[1]	10,587,000	8,235,000	2,352,000	4,599,000	5,988,000	3,647,000	952,000	4,588,000	1,401,000	6,768,000	3,819,000	—	—
2018[1]	10,778,000	8,377,000	2,401,000	4,673,000	6,105,000	3,699,000	974,000	4,678,000	1,427,000	6,890,000	3,888,000	—	—
2019[1]	10,917,000	8,475,000	2,442,000	4,726,000	6,191,000	3,739,000	987,000	4,736,000	1,455,000	6,979,000	3,938,000	—	—
2020[1]	11,029,000	8,555,000	2,474,000	4,766,000	6,263,000	3,769,000	997,000	4,786,000	1,477,000	7,050,000	3,979,000	—	—
2021[1]	11,179,000	8,664,000	2,515,000	4,824,000	6,355,000	3,809,000	1,015,000	4,855,000	1,500,000	7,146,000	4,033,000	—	—
2022[1]	11,337,000	8,776,000	2,561,000	4,889,000	6,448,000	3,853,000	1,036,000	4,924,000	1,524,000	7,247,000	4,090,000	—	—
2023[1]	11,516,000	8,912,000	2,604,000	4,959,000	6,557,000	3,903,000	1,057,000	5,009,000	1,547,000	7,361,000	4,155,000	—	—
2024[1]	11,645,000	9,009,000	2,635,000	5,014,000	6,631,000	3,942,000	1,072,000	5,067,000	1,564,000	7,443,000	4,201,000	—	—

—Not available.
[1]Projected.
[2]Beginning in 1980, 2-year institutions include schools accredited by the Accrediting Commission of Career Schools and Colleges of Technology.
NOTE: Data include unclassified undergraduate students. Data through 1995 are for institutions of higher education, while later data are for degree-granting institutions. Degree-granting institutions grant associate's or higher degrees and participate in Title IV federal financial aid programs. The degree-granting classification is very similar to the earlier higher education classification, but it includes more 2-year colleges and excludes a few higher education institutions that did not grant degrees. Some data have been revised from previously published figures.
SOURCE: U.S. Department of Education, National Center for Education Statistics, Higher Education General Information Survey (HEGIS), "Fall Enrollment in Colleges and Universities" surveys, 1970 through 1985; Integrated Postsecondary Education Data System (IPEDS), "Fall Enrollment Survey" (IPEDS-EF:86–99); IPEDS Spring 2001 through Spring 2014, Enrollment component; and Enrollment in Degree-Granting Institutions Projection Model, 1980 through 2024. (This table was prepared March 2015.)

Year	Total	Full-time	Part-time	Males	Females	Males Full-time	Males Part-time	Females Full-time	Females Part-time	Public	Private Total	Private Nonprofit	Private For-profit
1	2	3	4	5	6	7	8	9	10	11	12	13	14
1967	896,065	448,238	447,827	630,701	265,364	354,628	276,073	93,610	171,754	522,623	373,442	373,336	106
1968	1,037,377	469,747	567,630	696,649	340,728	358,686	337,963	111,061	229,667	648,657	388,720	388,681	39
1969	1,120,175	506,833	613,342	738,673	381,502	383,630	355,043	123,203	258,299	738,551	381,624	381,558	66
1970	1,212,243	536,226	676,017	793,940	418,303	407,724	386,216	128,502	289,801	807,879	404,364	404,287	77
1971	1,204,390	564,236	640,154	789,131	415,259	428,167	360,964	136,069	279,190	796,516	407,874	407,804	70
1972	1,272,421	583,299	689,122	810,164	462,257	436,533	373,631	146,766	315,491	848,031	424,390	424,278	112
1973	1,342,452	610,935	731,517	833,453	508,999	444,219	389,234	166,716	342,283	897,104	445,348	445,205	143
1974	1,425,001	643,927	781,074	856,847	568,154	454,706	402,141	189,221	378,933	956,770	468,231	467,950	281
1975	1,505,404	672,938	832,466	891,992	613,412	467,425	424,567	205,513	407,899	1,008,476	496,928	496,604	324
1976	1,577,546	683,825	893,721	904,551	672,995	459,286	445,265	224,539	448,456	1,033,115	544,431	541,064	3,367
1977	1,569,084	698,902	870,182	891,819	677,265	462,038	429,781	236,864	440,401	1,004,013	565,071	561,384	3,687
1978	1,575,693	704,831	870,862	879,931	695,762	458,865	421,066	245,966	449,796	998,608	577,085	573,563	3,522
1979	1,571,922	714,624	857,298	862,754	709,168	456,197	406,557	258,427	450,741	989,991	581,931	578,425	3,506
1980	1,621,840	736,214	885,626	874,197	747,643	462,387	411,810	273,827	473,816	1,015,439	606,401	601,084	5,317
1981	1,617,150	732,182	884,968	866,785	750,365	452,364	414,421	279,818	470,547	998,669	618,481	613,557	4,924
1982	1,600,718	736,813	863,905	860,890	739,828	453,519	407,371	283,294	456,534	983,014	617,704	613,350	4,354
1983	1,618,666	747,016	871,650	865,425	753,241	455,540	409,885	291,476	461,765	985,616	633,050	628,111	4,939
1984	1,623,869	750,735	873,134	856,761	767,108	452,579	404,182	298,156	468,952	983,879	639,990	634,109	5,881
1985	1,650,381	755,629	894,752	856,370	794,011	451,274	405,096	304,355	489,656	1,002,148	648,233	642,795	5,438
1986	1,705,536	767,477	938,059	867,010	838,526	452,717	414,293	314,760	523,766	1,053,177	652,359	644,185	8,174
1987	1,720,407	768,536	951,871	863,599	856,808	447,212	416,387	321,324	535,484	1,054,665	665,742	662,408	3,334
1988	1,738,789	794,340	944,449	864,252	874,537	455,337	408,915	339,003	535,534	1,058,242	680,547	—	—
1989	1,796,029	820,254	975,775	879,025	917,004	461,596	417,429	358,658	558,346	1,090,221	705,808	—	—
1990	1,859,531	844,955	1,014,576	904,150	955,381	471,217	432,933	373,738	581,643	1,135,121	724,410	716,820	7,590
1991	1,919,666	893,917	1,025,749	930,841	988,825	493,849	436,992	400,068	588,757	1,161,606	758,060	746,687	11,373
1992	1,949,659	917,676	1,031,983	941,053	1,008,606	502,166	438,887	415,510	593,096	1,168,270	781,389	770,802	10,587
1993	1,980,844	948,136	1,032,708	943,768	1,037,076	508,574	435,194	439,562	597,514	1,177,301	803,543	789,700	13,843
1994	2,016,182	969,070	1,047,112	949,785	1,066,397	513,592	436,193	455,478	610,919	1,188,552	827,630	809,642	17,988
1995	2,030,062	983,534	1,046,528	941,409	1,088,653	510,782	430,627	472,752	615,901	1,188,748	841,314	824,351	16,963
1996	2,040,572	1,004,114	1,036,458	932,153	1,108,419	512,100	420,053	492,014	616,405	1,185,216	855,356	830,238	25,118
1997	2,051,747	1,019,464	1,032,283	927,496	1,124,251	510,845	416,651	508,619	615,632	1,188,640	863,107	837,790	25,317
1998	2,070,030	1,024,627	1,045,403	923,132	1,146,898	505,492	417,640	519,135	627,763	1,187,557	882,473	852,270	30,203
1999	2,110,246	1,049,591	1,060,655	930,930	1,179,316	508,930	422,000	540,661	638,655	1,201,511	908,735	869,739	38,996
2000	2,156,896	1,086,674	1,070,222	943,501	1,213,395	522,847	420,654	563,827	649,568	1,213,464	943,432	896,239	47,193
2001	2,212,377	1,119,862	1,092,515	956,384	1,255,993	531,260	425,124	588,602	667,391	1,247,285	965,092	909,612	55,480
2002	2,354,634	1,212,107	1,142,527	1,009,726	1,344,908	566,930	442,796	645,177	699,731	1,319,138	1,035,496	959,385	76,111
2003	2,431,117	1,280,880	1,150,237	1,032,892	1,398,225	589,190	443,702	691,690	706,535	1,335,595	1,095,522	994,375	101,147
2004	2,491,414	1,325,841	1,165,573	1,047,214	1,444,200	598,727	448,487	727,114	717,086	1,329,532	1,161,882	1,022,319	139,563
2005	2,523,511	1,350,581	1,172,930	1,047,054	1,476,457	602,525	444,529	748,056	728,401	1,324,104	1,199,407	1,036,324	163,083
2006	2,574,568	1,386,226	1,188,342	1,061,059	1,513,509	614,709	446,350	771,517	741,992	1,332,707	1,241,861	1,064,626	177,235
2007	2,644,357	1,428,914	1,215,443	1,088,314	1,556,043	632,576	455,738	796,338	759,705	1,353,197	1,291,160	1,100,823	190,337
2008	2,737,076	1,492,813	1,244,263	1,122,272	1,614,804	656,926	465,346	835,887	778,917	1,380,936	1,356,140	1,124,987	231,153
2009	2,849,415	1,567,080	1,282,335	1,169,777	1,679,638	689,977	479,800	877,103	802,535	1,424,393	1,425,022	1,172,501	252,521
2010	2,937,011	1,630,142	1,306,869	1,209,477	1,727,534	719,408	490,069	910,734	816,800	1,439,171	1,497,840	1,201,489	296,351
2011	2,933,287	1,637,356	1,295,931	1,211,264	1,722,023	722,265	488,999	915,091	806,932	1,421,404	1,511,883	1,207,896	303,987
2012	2,910,388	1,639,234	1,271,154	1,205,186	1,705,202	725,096	480,090	914,138	791,064	1,406,600	1,503,788	1,208,503	295,285
2013	2,900,954	1,658,618	1,242,336	1,201,160	1,699,794	732,594	468,566	926,024	773,770	1,398,556	1,502,398	1,216,557	285,841
2014[1]	2,933,000	1,698,000	1,234,000	1,260,000	1,673,000	780,000	479,000	918,000	755,000	1,415,000	1,518,000	—	—
2015[1]	2,953,000	1,710,000	1,243,000	1,271,000	1,682,000	793,000	478,000	917,000	765,000	1,425,000	1,529,000	—	—
2016[1]	3,013,000	1,749,000	1,264,000	1,293,000	1,720,000	809,000	484,000	940,000	780,000	1,454,000	1,560,000	—	—
2017[1]	3,102,000	1,804,000	1,298,000	1,329,000	1,773,000	830,000	498,000	973,000	800,000	1,496,000	1,606,000	—	—
2018[1]	3,173,000	1,842,000	1,331,000	1,360,000	1,813,000	847,000	513,000	995,000	818,000	1,531,000	1,643,000	—	—
2019[1]	3,225,000	1,866,000	1,359,000	1,382,000	1,843,000	859,000	522,000	1,007,000	836,000	1,556,000	1,670,000	—	—
2020[1]	3,268,000	1,888,000	1,381,000	1,399,000	1,869,000	869,000	530,000	1,018,000	851,000	1,577,000	1,692,000	—	—
2021[1]	3,325,000	1,917,000	1,408,000	1,424,000	1,901,000	882,000	542,000	1,035,000	866,000	1,604,000	1,721,000	—	—
2022[1]	3,391,000	1,953,000	1,438,000	1,454,000	1,937,000	898,000	556,000	1,055,000	882,000	1,636,000	1,755,000	—	—
2023[1]	3,458,000	1,991,000	1,467,000	1,483,000	1,975,000	913,000	569,000	1,078,000	898,000	1,669,000	1,790,000	—	—
2024[1]	3,495,000	2,007,000	1,488,000	1,500,000	1,994,000	921,000	579,000	1,086,000	908,000	1,686,000	1,809,000	—	—

—Not available.

[1]Projected.

NOTE: Data include unclassified graduate students. Data through 1995 are for institutions of higher education, while later data are for degree-granting institutions. Degree-granting institutions grant associate's or higher degrees and participate in Title IV federal financial aid programs. The degree-granting classification is very similar to the earlier higher education classification, but it includes more 2-year colleges and excludes a few higher education institutions that did not grant degrees. Some data have been revised from previously published figures.

SOURCE: U.S. Department of Education, National Center for Education Statistics, Higher Education General Information Survey (HEGIS), "Fall Enrollment in Colleges and Universities" surveys, 1967 through 1985; Integrated Postsecondary Education Data System (IPEDS), "Fall Enrollment Survey" (IPEDS-EF:86–99); IPEDS Spring 2001 through Spring 2014, Enrollment component; and Enrollment in Degree-Granting Institutions Projection Model, 1980 through 2024. (This table was prepared March 2015.)

Table 18. Total fall enrollment of first-time degree/certificate-seeking students in degree-granting postsecondary institutions, by attendance status, sex of student, and level and control of institution: 1955 through 2024

Year	Total	Full-time	Part-time	Males Total	Males Full-time	Males Part-time	Females Total	Females Full-time	Females Part-time	4-year Public	4-year Private	2-year Public	2-year Private
1	2	3	4	5	6	7	8	9	10	11	12	13	14
1955[1]	670,013	—	—	415,604	—	—	254,409	—	—	283,084[2]	246,960[2]	117,288[2]	22,681[2]
1956[1]	717,504	—	—	442,903	—	—	274,601	—	—	292,743[2]	261,951[2]	137,406[2]	25,404[2]
1957[1]	723,879	—	—	441,969	—	—	281,910	—	—	293,544[2]	262,695[2]	140,522[2]	27,118[2]
1958[1]	775,308	—	—	465,422	—	—	309,886	—	—	328,242[2]	272,117[2]	146,379[2]	28,570[2]
1959[1]	821,520	—	—	487,890	—	—	333,630	—	—	348,150[2]	291,691[2]	153,393[2]	28,286[2]
1960[1]	923,069	—	—	539,512	—	—	383,557	—	—	395,884[2]	313,209[2]	181,860[2]	32,116[2]
1961[1]	1,018,361	—	—	591,913	—	—	426,448	—	—	438,135[2]	336,449[2]	210,101[2]	33,676[2]
1962[1]	1,030,554	—	—	598,099	—	—	432,455	—	—	445,191[2]	324,923[2]	224,537[2]	35,903[2]
1963[1]	1,046,424	—	—	604,282	—	—	442,142	—	—	—	—	—	—
1964[1]	1,224,840	—	—	701,524	—	—	523,316	—	—	539,251[2]	363,348[2]	275,413[2]	46,828[2]
1965[1]	1,441,822	—	—	829,215	—	—	612,607	—	—	642,233[2]	398,792[2]	347,788[2]	53,009[2]
1966	1,554,337	—	—	889,516	—	—	664,821	—	—	626,472[2]	382,889[2]	478,459[2]	66,517[2]
1967[1]	1,640,936	1,335,512	305,424	931,127	761,299	169,828	709,809	574,213	135,596	644,525	368,300	561,488	66,623
1968	1,892,849	1,470,653	422,196	1,082,367	847,005	235,362	810,482	623,648	186,834	724,377	378,052	718,562	71,858
1969	1,967,104	1,525,290	441,814	1,118,269	876,280	241,989	848,835	649,010	199,825	699,167	391,508	814,132	62,297
1970	2,063,397	1,587,072	476,325	1,151,960	896,281	255,679	911,437	690,791	220,646	717,449	395,886	890,703	59,359
1971	2,119,018	1,606,036	512,982	1,170,518	895,715	274,803	948,500	710,321	238,179	704,052	384,695	971,295	58,976
1972	2,152,778	1,574,197	578,581	1,157,501	858,254	299,247	995,277	715,943	279,334	680,337	380,982	1,036,616	54,843
1973	2,226,041	1,607,269	618,772	1,182,173	867,314	314,859	1,043,868	739,955	303,913	698,777	378,994	1,089,182	59,088
1974	2,365,761	1,673,333	692,428	1,243,790	896,077	347,713	1,121,971	777,256	344,715	745,637	386,391	1,175,759	57,974
1975	2,515,155	1,763,296	751,859	1,327,935	942,198	385,737	1,187,220	821,098	366,122	771,725	395,440	1,283,523	64,467
1976	2,347,014	1,662,333	684,681	1,170,326	854,597	315,729	1,176,688	807,736	368,952	717,373	413,961	1,152,944	62,736
1977	2,394,426	1,680,916	713,510	1,155,856	839,848	316,008	1,238,570	841,068	397,502	737,497	404,631	1,185,648	66,650
1978	2,389,627	1,650,848	738,779	1,141,777	817,294	324,483	1,247,850	833,554	414,296	736,703	406,669	1,173,544	72,711
1979	2,502,896	1,706,732	796,164	1,179,846	840,315	339,531	1,323,050	866,417	456,633	760,119	415,126	1,253,854	73,797
1980	2,587,644	1,749,928	837,716	1,218,961	862,458	356,503	1,368,683	887,470	481,213	765,395	417,937	1,313,591	90,721[3]
1981	2,595,421	1,737,714	857,707	1,217,680	851,833	365,847	1,377,741	885,881	491,860	754,007	419,257	1,318,436	103,721[3]
1982	2,505,466	1,688,620	816,846	1,199,237	837,223	362,014	1,306,229	851,397	454,832	730,775	404,252	1,254,193	116,246[3]
1983	2,443,703	1,678,071	765,632	1,159,049	824,609	334,440	1,284,654	853,462	431,192	728,244	403,882	1,189,869	121,708
1984	2,356,898	1,613,185	743,713	1,112,303	786,099	326,204	1,244,595	827,086	417,509	713,790	402,959	1,130,311	109,838
1985	2,292,222	1,602,038	690,184	1,075,736	774,858	300,878	1,216,486	827,180	389,306	717,199	398,556	1,060,275	116,192
1986	2,219,208	1,589,451	629,757	1,046,527	768,856	277,671	1,172,681	820,595	352,086	719,974	391,673	990,973	116,588
1987	2,246,359	1,626,719	619,640	1,046,615	779,226	267,389	1,199,744	847,493	352,251	757,833	405,113	979,820	103,593
1988	2,378,803	1,698,927	679,876	1,100,026	807,319	292,707	1,278,777	891,608	387,169	783,358	425,907	1,048,914	120,624
1989	2,341,035	1,656,594	684,441	1,094,750	791,295	303,455	1,246,285	865,299	380,986	762,217	413,836	1,048,529	116,453
1990	2,256,624	1,617,118	639,506	1,045,191	771,372	273,819	1,211,433	845,746	365,687	727,264	400,120	1,041,097	88,143
1991	2,277,920	1,652,983	624,937	1,068,433	798,043	270,390	1,209,487	854,940	354,547	717,697	392,904	1,070,048	97,271
1992	2,184,113	1,603,737	580,376	1,013,058	760,290	252,768	1,171,055	843,447	327,608	697,393	408,306	993,074	85,340
1993	2,160,710	1,608,274	552,436	1,007,647	762,240	245,407	1,153,063	846,034	307,029	702,273	410,688	973,545	74,204
1994	2,133,205	1,603,106	530,099	984,558	751,081	233,477	1,148,647	852,025	296,622	709,042	405,917	952,468	65,778
1995	2,168,831	1,646,812	522,019	1,001,052	767,185	233,867	1,167,779	879,627	288,152	731,836	419,025	954,595	63,375
1996	2,274,319	1,739,852	534,467	1,046,662	805,982	240,680	1,227,657	933,870	293,787	741,164	427,442	989,536	116,177
1997	2,219,255	1,733,512	485,743	1,026,058	806,054	220,004	1,193,197	927,458	265,739	755,362	442,397	923,954	97,542
1998	2,212,593	1,775,412	437,181	1,022,656	825,577	197,079	1,189,937	949,835	240,102	792,772	460,948	858,417	100,456
1999	2,357,590	1,849,741	507,849	1,094,539	865,545	228,994	1,263,051	984,196	278,855	819,503	474,223	955,499	108,365
2000	2,427,551	1,918,093	509,458	1,123,948	894,432	229,516	1,303,603	1,023,661	279,942	842,228	498,532	952,175	134,616
2001	2,497,078	1,989,179	507,899	1,152,837	926,393	226,444	1,344,241	1,062,786	281,455	866,619	508,030	988,726	133,703
2002	2,570,611	2,053,065	517,546	1,170,609	945,938	224,671	1,400,002	1,107,127	292,875	886,297	517,621	1,037,267	129,426
2003	2,591,754	2,102,394	489,360	1,175,856	965,075	210,781	1,415,898	1,137,319	278,579	918,602	537,726	1,004,428	130,998
2004	2,630,243	2,147,546	482,697	1,190,268	981,591	208,677	1,439,975	1,165,955	274,020	925,249	562,485	1,009,082	133,427
2005	2,657,338	2,189,884	467,454	1,200,055	995,610	204,445	1,457,283	1,194,274	263,009	953,903	606,712	977,224	119,499
2006	2,707,213	2,219,853	487,360	1,228,665	1,015,585	213,080	1,478,548	1,204,268	274,280	990,262	598,412	1,013,080	105,459
2007	2,776,168	2,293,855	482,313	1,267,030	1,052,600	214,430	1,509,138	1,241,255	267,883	1,023,543	633,296	1,016,262	103,067
2008	3,024,723	2,427,740	596,983	1,389,302	1,115,500	273,802	1,635,421	1,312,240	323,181	1,053,838	673,581	1,186,576	110,728
2009	3,156,882	2,534,440	622,442	1,464,424	1,177,119	287,305	1,692,458	1,357,321	335,137	1,090,980	658,808	1,275,974	131,120
2010	3,156,727	2,533,636	623,091	1,461,016	1,171,090	289,926	1,695,711	1,362,546	333,165	1,110,601	674,573	1,238,491	133,062
2011	3,091,496	2,479,155	612,341	1,424,140	1,140,843	283,297	1,667,356	1,338,312	329,044	1,131,091	656,864	1,195,083	108,458
2012	2,990,280	2,406,038	584,242	1,385,096	1,114,025	271,071	1,605,184	1,292,013	313,171	1,127,832	642,686	1,133,486	86,276
2013	2,986,596	2,415,925	570,671	1,384,314	1,117,375	266,939	1,602,282	1,298,550	303,732	1,143,870	633,041	1,128,054	81,631
2014[4]	2,958,000	—	—	1,349,000	—	—	1,609,000	—	—	—	—	—	—
2015[4]	2,950,000	—	—	1,345,000	—	—	1,605,000	—	—	—	—	—	—
2016[4]	2,983,000	—	—	1,353,000	—	—	1,629,000	—	—	—	—	—	—
2017[4]	3,042,000	—	—	1,375,000	—	—	1,667,000	—	—	—	—	—	—
2018[4]	3,099,000	—	—	1,399,000	—	—	1,700,000	—	—	—	—	—	—
2019[4]	3,141,000	—	—	1,415,000	—	—	1,725,000	—	—	—	—	—	—
2020[4]	3,172,000	—	—	1,427,000	—	—	1,745,000	—	—	—	—	—	—
2021[4]	3,215,000	—	—	1,445,000	—	—	1,770,000	—	—	—	—	—	—
2022[4]	3,262,000	—	—	1,466,000	—	—	1,797,000	—	—	—	—	—	—
2023[4]	3,314,000	—	—	1,488,000	—	—	1,826,000	—	—	—	—	—	—
2024[4]	3,351,000	—	—	1,505,000	—	—	1,846,000	—	—	—	—	—	—

—Not available.

[1] Excludes first-time degree/certificate-seeking students in occupational programs not creditable towards a bachelor's degree.

[2] Data for 2-year branches of 4-year college systems are aggregated with the 4-year institutions.

[3] Large increases are due to the addition of schools accredited by the Accrediting Commission of Career Schools and Colleges of Technology.

[4] Projected.

NOTE: Data through 1995 are for institutions of higher education, while later data are for degree-granting institutions. Degree-granting institutions grant associate's or higher degrees and participate in Title IV federal financial aid programs. The degree-granting classification is very similar to the earlier higher education classification, but it includes more 2-year colleges and excludes a few higher education institutions that did not grant degrees. Alaska and Hawaii are included in all years. Some data have been revised from previously published figures.

SOURCE: U.S. Department of Education, National Center for Education Statistics, *Biennial Survey of Education in the United States; Opening Fall Enrollment in Higher Education*, 1963 through 1965; Higher Education General Information Survey (HEGIS), "Fall Enrollment in Colleges and Universities" surveys, 1966 through 1985; Integrated Postsecondary Education Data System (IPEDS), "Fall Enrollment Survey" (IPEDS-EF:86–99); IPEDS Spring 2001 through Spring 2014, Enrollment component; and First-Time Freshmen Projection Model, 1980 through 2024. (This table was prepared March 2015.)

Table 19. Fall enrollment of U.S. residents in degree-granting postsecondary institutions, by race/race/ethnicity: Selected years, 1976 through 2024

Year	Enrollment (in thousands)									Percentage distribution								
					Asian/Pacific Islander			American Indian/ Alaska Native	Two or more races					Asian/Pacific Islander			American Indian/ Alaska Native	Two or more races
	Total	White	Black	Hispanic	Total	Asian	Pacific Islander			Total	White	Black	Hispanic	Total	Asian	Pacific Islander		
1	2	3	4	5	6	7	8	9	10	11	12	13	14	15	16	17	18	19
1976	10,767	9,076	1,033	384	198	—	—	76	—	100.0	84.3	9.6	3.6	1.8	—	—	0.7	—
1980	11,782	9,833	1,107	472	286	—	—	84	—	100.0	83.5	9.4	4.0	2.4	—	—	0.7	—
1990	13,427	10,722	1,247	782	572	—	—	103	—	100.0	79.9	9.3	5.8	4.3	—	—	0.8	—
1994	13,823	10,427	1,449	1,046	774	—	—	127	—	100.0	75.4	10.5	7.6	5.6	—	—	0.9	—
1995	13,807	10,311	1,474	1,094	797	—	—	131	—	100.0	74.7	10.7	7.9	5.8	—	—	1.0	—
1996	13,901	10,264	1,506	1,166	828	—	—	138	—	100.0	73.8	10.8	8.4	6.0	—	—	1.0	—
1997	14,037	10,266	1,551	1,218	859	—	—	142	—	100.0	73.1	11.0	8.7	6.1	—	—	1.0	—
1998	14,063	10,179	1,583	1,257	900	—	—	144	—	100.0	72.4	11.3	8.9	6.4	—	—	1.0	—
1999	14,361	10,329	1,649	1,324	914	—	—	146	—	100.0	71.9	11.5	9.2	6.4	—	—	1.0	—
2000	14,784	10,462	1,730	1,462	978	—	—	151	—	100.0	70.8	11.7	9.9	6.6	—	—	1.0	—
2001	15,363	10,775	1,850	1,561	1,019	—	—	158	—	100.0	70.1	12.0	10.2	6.6	—	—	1.0	—
2002	16,021	11,140	1,979	1,662	1,074	—	—	166	—	100.0	69.5	12.4	10.4	6.7	—	—	1.0	—
2003	16,314	11,281	2,068	1,716	1,076	—	—	173	—	100.0	69.1	12.7	10.5	6.6	—	—	1.1	—
2004	16,682	11,423	2,165	1,810	1,109	—	—	176	—	100.0	68.5	13.0	10.8	6.6	—	—	1.1	—
2005	16,903	11,495	2,215	1,882	1,134	—	—	176	—	100.0	68.0	13.1	11.1	6.7	—	—	1.0	—
2006	17,163	11,572	2,280	1,964	1,165	—	—	181	—	100.0	67.4	13.3	11.4	6.8	—	—	1.1	—
2007	17,624	11,756	2,383	2,076	1,218	—	—	190	—	100.0	66.7	13.5	11.8	6.9	—	—	1.1	—
2008	18,442	12,089	2,584	2,273	1,303	—	—	193	—	100.0	65.5	14.0	12.3	7.1	—	—	1.0	—
2009	19,631	12,669	2,884	2,537	1,335	—	—	206	—	100.0	64.5	14.7	12.9	6.8	—	—	1.0	—
2010	20,312	12,721	3,039	2,749	1,282	1,218	64	196	325	100.0	62.6	15.0	13.5	6.3	6.0	0.3	1.0	1.6
2011	20,270	12,402	3,079	2,893	1,277	1,211	66	186	433	100.0	61.2	15.2	14.3	6.3	6.0	0.3	0.9	2.1
2012	19,860	11,981	2,962	2,979	1,259	1,196	64	173	505	100.0	60.3	14.9	15.0	6.3	6.0	0.3	0.9	2.5
2013	19,535	11,591	2,872	3,091	1,260	1,199	61	163	559	100.0	59.3	14.7	15.8	6.4	6.1	0.3	0.8	2.9
2014[1]	19,426	11,582	2,966	2,951	1,214	—	—	156	556	100.0	59.6	15.3	15.2	6.3	—	—	0.8	2.9
2015[1]	19,399	11,460	3,016	3,013	1,200	—	—	154	555	100.0	59.1	15.5	15.5	6.2	—	—	0.8	2.9
2016[1]	19,632	11,509	3,100	3,099	1,208	—	—	154	562	100.0	58.6	15.8	15.8	6.2	—	—	0.8	2.9
2017[1]	20,045	11,674	3,204	3,208	1,230	—	—	155	574	100.0	58.2	16.0	16.0	6.1	—	—	0.8	2.9
2018[1]	20,421	11,835	3,286	3,306	1,252	—	—	157	585	100.0	58.0	16.1	16.2	6.1	—	—	0.8	2.9
2019[1]	20,696	11,935	3,349	3,390	1,272	—	—	158	593	100.0	57.7	16.2	16.4	6.1	—	—	0.8	2.9
2020[1]	20,902	11,982	3,407	3,468	1,287	—	—	159	598	100.0	57.3	16.3	16.6	6.2	—	—	0.8	2.9
2021[1]	21,184	12,074	3,477	3,556	1,311	—	—	160	607	100.0	57.0	16.4	16.8	6.2	—	—	0.8	2.9
2022[1]	21,496	12,184	3,546	3,651	1,339	—	—	161	615	100.0	56.7	16.5	17.0	6.2	—	—	0.7	2.9
2023[1]	21,836	12,298	3,626	3,758	1,366	—	—	162	625	100.0	56.3	16.6	17.2	6.3	—	—	0.7	2.9
2024[1]	22,064	12,346	3,683	3,851	1,389	—	—	162	632	100.0	56.0	16.7	17.5	6.3	—	—	0.7	2.9

—Not available.

[1]Projected.

NOTE: Race categories exclude persons of Hispanic ethnicity. Prior to 2010, institutions were not required to report separate data on Asians, Pacific Islanders, and students of Two or more races. Detail may not sum to totals because of rounding. Some data have been revised from previously published figures.

SOURCE: U.S. Department of Education, National Center for Education Statistics, Higher Education General Information Survey (HEGIS), "Fall Enrollment in Colleges and Universities" surveys, 1976 and 1980; Integrated Postsecondary Education Data System (IPEDS), "Fall Enrollment Survey" (IPEDS-EF:90–99); IPEDS Spring 2001 through Spring 2014, Enrollment component; and Enrollment in Degree-Granting Institutions by Race/Ethnicity Projection Model, 1980 through 2024. (This table was prepared March 2015.)

Table 20. Full-time-equivalent fall enrollment in degree-granting postsecondary institutions, by control and level of institution: 1967 through 2024

Year	All institutions Total	4-year	2-year	Public institutions Total	4-year	2-year	Private institutions Total	4-year Total	Nonprofit	For-profit	2-year Total	Nonprofit	For-profit
1	2	3	4	5	6	7	8	9	10	11	12	13	14
1967	5,499,360	4,448,302	1,051,058	3,777,701	2,850,432	927,269	1,721,659	1,597,870	—	—	123,789	—	—
1968	5,977,768	4,729,522	1,248,246	4,248,639	3,128,057	1,120,582	1,729,129	1,601,465	—	—	127,664	—	—
1969	6,333,357	4,899,034	1,434,323	4,577,353	3,259,323	1,318,030	1,756,004	1,639,711	—	—	116,293	—	—
1970	6,737,819	5,145,422	1,592,397	4,953,144	3,468,569	1,484,575	1,784,675	1,676,853	—	—	107,822	—	—
1971	7,148,558	5,357,647	1,790,911	5,344,402	3,660,626	1,683,776	1,804,156	1,697,021	—	—	107,135	—	—
1972	7,253,757	5,406,833	1,846,924	5,452,854	3,706,238	1,746,616	1,800,903	1,700,595	—	—	100,308	—	—
1973	7,453,463	5,439,230	2,014,233	5,629,563	3,721,037	1,908,526	1,823,900	1,718,193	—	—	105,707	—	—
1974	7,805,452	5,606,247	2,199,205	5,944,799	3,847,543	2,097,256	1,860,653	1,758,704	—	—	101,949	—	—
1975	8,479,698	5,900,408	2,579,290	6,522,319	4,056,502	2,465,817	1,957,379	1,843,906	—	—	113,473	—	—
1976	8,312,502	5,848,001	2,464,501	6,349,903	3,998,450	2,351,453	1,962,599	1,849,551	—	—	113,048	—	—
1977	8,415,339	5,935,076	2,480,263	6,396,476	4,039,071	2,357,405	2,018,863	1,896,005	—	—	122,858	—	—
1978	8,348,482	5,932,357	2,416,125	6,279,199	3,996,126	2,283,073	2,069,283	1,936,231	—	—	133,052	—	—
1979	8,487,317	6,016,072	2,471,245	6,392,617	4,059,304	2,333,313	2,094,700	1,956,768	—	—	137,932	—	—
1980	8,819,013	6,161,372	2,657,641	6,642,294	4,158,267	2,484,027	2,176,719	2,003,105	—	—	173,614 [1]	—	—
1981	9,014,521	6,249,847	2,764,674	6,781,300	4,208,506	2,572,794	2,233,221	2,041,341	—	—	191,880 [1]	—	—
1982	9,091,648	6,248,923	2,842,725	6,850,589	4,220,648	2,629,941	2,241,059	2,028,275	—	—	212,784 [1]	—	—
1983	9,166,398	6,325,222	2,841,176	6,881,479	4,265,807	2,615,672	2,284,919	2,059,415	—	—	225,504	—	—
1984	8,951,695	6,292,711	2,658,984	6,684,664	4,237,895	2,446,769	2,267,031	2,054,816	—	—	212,215	—	—
1985	8,943,433	6,294,339	2,649,094	6,667,781	4,239,622	2,428,159	2,275,652	2,054,717	—	—	220,935	—	—
1986	9,064,165	6,360,325	2,703,842	6,778,045	4,295,494	2,482,551	2,286,122	2,064,831	—	—	221,291 [2]	—	—
1987	9,229,736	6,486,504	2,743,230	6,937,690	4,395,728	2,541,961	2,292,045	2,090,776	—	—	201,269 [2]	—	—
1988	9,464,271	6,664,146	2,800,125	7,096,905	4,505,774	2,591,131	2,367,366	2,158,372	—	—	208,994	—	—
1989	9,780,881	6,813,602	2,967,279	7,371,590	4,619,828	2,751,762	2,409,291	2,193,774	—	—	215,517	—	—
1990	9,983,436	6,968,008	3,015,428	7,557,982	4,740,049	2,817,933	2,425,454	2,227,959	2,177,668	50,291	197,495	72,785	124,710
1991	10,360,606	7,081,454	3,279,152	7,862,845	4,795,704	3,067,141	2,497,761	2,285,750	2,223,463	62,287	212,011	72,545	139,466
1992	10,436,776	7,129,379	3,307,397	7,911,701	4,797,884	3,113,817	2,525,075	2,331,495	2,267,373	64,122	193,580	66,647	126,933
1993	10,351,415	7,120,921	3,230,494	7,812,394	4,765,983	3,046,411	2,539,021	2,354,938	2,282,643	72,295	184,083	70,469	113,614
1994	10,348,072	7,137,341	3,210,731	7,784,396	4,749,524	3,034,872	2,563,676	2,387,817	2,301,063	86,754	175,859	69,578	106,281
1995	10,334,956	7,172,844	3,162,112	7,751,815	4,757,223	2,994,592	2,583,141	2,415,621	2,328,730	86,891	167,520	62,416	105,104
1996	10,481,886	7,234,541	3,247,345	7,794,895	4,767,117	3,027,778	2,686,991	2,467,424	2,353,561	113,863	219,567	63,954	155,613
1997	10,615,028	7,338,794	3,276,234	7,869,764	4,813,849	3,055,915	2,745,264	2,524,945	2,389,627	135,318	220,319	61,761	158,558
1998	10,698,775	7,467,828	3,230,947	7,880,135	4,868,857	3,011,278	2,818,640	2,598,971	2,436,188	162,783	219,669	56,834	162,835
1999	10,974,519	7,634,247	3,340,272	8,059,240	4,949,851	3,109,389	2,915,279	2,684,396	2,488,140	196,256	230,883	53,956	176,927
2000	11,267,025	7,795,139	3,471,886	8,266,932	5,025,588	3,241,344	3,000,093	2,769,551	2,549,676	219,875	230,542	51,503	179,039
2001	11,765,945	8,087,980	3,677,965	8,639,154	5,194,035	3,445,119	3,126,791	2,893,945	2,612,833	281,112	232,846	41,037	191,809
2002	12,331,319	8,439,064	3,892,255	9,061,411	5,406,283	3,655,128	3,269,908	3,032,781	2,699,702	333,079	237,127	40,110	197,017
2003	12,687,597	8,744,188	3,943,409	9,240,724	5,557,680	3,683,044	3,446,873	3,186,508	2,776,850	409,658	260,365	36,815	223,550
2004	13,000,994	9,018,024	3,982,970	9,348,081	5,640,650	3,707,431	3,652,913	3,377,374	2,837,251	540,123	275,539	34,202	241,337
2005	13,200,790	9,261,634	3,939,156	9,390,216	5,728,327	3,661,889	3,810,574	3,533,307	2,878,354	654,953	277,267	34,729	242,538
2006	13,403,097	9,456,166	3,946,931	9,503,558	5,824,768	3,678,790	3,899,539	3,631,398	2,936,172	695,226	268,141	31,203	236,938
2007	13,782,702	9,769,560	4,013,142	9,739,709	5,994,230	3,745,479	4,042,993	3,775,330	2,993,729	781,601	267,663	26,134	241,529
2008	14,394,238	10,169,454	4,224,784	10,061,812	6,139,525	3,922,287	4,332,426	4,029,929	3,060,308	969,621	302,497	28,065	274,432
2009	15,379,473	10,695,816	4,683,657	10,746,637	6,452,414	4,294,223	4,632,836	4,243,402	3,153,294	1,090,108	389,434	27,964	361,470
2010	15,947,474	11,129,239	4,818,235	11,018,756	6,635,799	4,382,957	4,928,718	4,493,440	3,235,149	1,258,291	435,278	26,920	408,358
2011	15,892,792	11,261,845	4,630,947	10,954,754	6,734,116	4,220,638	4,938,038	4,527,729	3,285,711	1,242,018	410,309	34,267	376,042
2012	15,594,638	11,231,758	4,362,880	10,780,749	6,764,423	4,016,326	4,813,889	4,467,335	3,311,250	1,156,085	346,554	32,609	313,945
2013	15,409,944	11,185,987	4,223,957	10,695,774	6,790,901	3,904,873	4,714,170	4,395,086	3,341,575	1,053,511	319,084	27,290	291,794
2014 [3]	15,407,000	11,108,000	4,299,000	10,699,000	6,732,000	3,967,000	4,707,000	4,376,000	—	—	331,000	—	—
2015 [3]	15,367,000	11,074,000	4,293,000	10,672,000	6,709,000	3,963,000	4,695,000	4,365,000	—	—	330,000	—	—
2016 [3]	15,566,000	11,219,000	4,347,000	10,805,000	6,793,000	4,012,000	4,761,000	4,426,000	—	—	335,000	—	—
2017 [3]	15,905,000	11,464,000	4,441,000	11,035,000	6,937,000	4,098,000	4,870,000	4,527,000	—	—	343,000	—	—
2018 [3]	16,205,000	11,676,000	4,529,000	11,243,000	7,064,000	4,179,000	4,962,000	4,612,000	—	—	350,000	—	—
2019 [3]	16,417,000	11,825,000	4,593,000	11,391,000	7,153,000	4,238,000	5,027,000	4,672,000	—	—	355,000	—	—
2020 [3]	16,582,000	11,947,000	4,635,000	11,503,000	7,226,000	4,277,000	5,079,000	4,721,000	—	—	358,000	—	—
2021 [3]	16,809,000	12,112,000	4,697,000	11,658,000	7,324,000	4,334,000	5,150,000	4,788,000	—	—	363,000	—	—
2022 [3]	17,059,000	12,290,000	4,769,000	11,831,000	7,430,000	4,401,000	5,228,000	4,860,000	—	—	369,000	—	—
2023 [3]	17,341,000	12,492,000	4,849,000	12,024,000	7,551,000	4,474,000	5,316,000	4,941,000	—	—	375,000	—	—
2024 [3]	17,528,000	12,625,000	4,903,000	12,155,000	7,632,000	4,524,000	5,373,000	4,993,000	—	—	379,000	—	—

—Not available.

[1] Large increases are due to the addition of schools accredited by the Accrediting Commission of Career Schools and Colleges of Technology.

[2] Because of imputation techniques, data are not consistent with figures for other years.

[3] Projected.

NOTE: Full-time-equivalent enrollment is the full-time enrollment, plus the full-time equivalent of the part-time students. Data through 1995 are for institutions of higher education, while later data are for degree-granting institutions. Degree-granting institutions grant associate's or higher degrees and participate in Title IV federal financial aid programs. The degree-granting classification is very similar to the earlier higher education classification, but it includes more 2-year colleges and excludes a few higher education institutions that did not grant degrees. Some data have been revised from previously published figures.

SOURCE: U.S. Department of Education, National Center for Education Statistics, Higher Education General Information Survey (HEGIS), "Fall Enrollment in Colleges and Universities" surveys, 1967 through 1985; Integrated Postsecondary Education Data System (IPEDS), "Fall Enrollment Survey" (IPEDS-EF:86-99); IPEDS Spring 2001 through Spring 2014, Enrollment component; and Enrollment in Degree-Granting Institutions Projection Model, 1980 through 2024. (This table was prepared March 2015.)

Table 21. Degrees conferred by degree-granting postsecondary institutions, by level of degree and sex of student: Selected years, 1869–70 through 2024–25

Year	Associate's degrees				Bachelor's degrees				Master's degrees				Doctor's degrees[1]			
	Total	Males	Females	Percent female	Total	Males	Females	Percent female	Total	Males	Females	Percent female	Total	Males	Females	Percent female
1	2	3	4	5	6	7	8	9	10	11	12	13	14	15	16	17
1869–70	—	—	—	—	9,371 [2]	7,993 [2]	1,378 [2]	14.7	0	0	0	—	1	1	0	0.0
1879–80	—	—	—	—	12,896 [2]	10,411 [2]	2,485 [2]	19.3	879	868	11	1.3	54	51	3	5.6
1889–90	—	—	—	—	15,539 [2]	12,857 [2]	2,682 [2]	17.3	1,015	821	194	19.1	149	147	2	1.3
1899–1900	—	—	—	—	27,410 [2]	22,173 [2]	5,237 [2]	19.1	1,583	1,280	303	19.1	382	359	23	6.0
1909–10	—	—	—	—	37,199 [2]	28,762 [2]	8,437 [2]	22.7	2,113	1,555	558	26.4	443	399	44	9.9
1919–20	—	—	—	—	48,622 [2]	31,980 [2]	16,642 [2]	34.2	4,279	2,985	1,294	30.2	615	522	93	15.1
1929–30	—	—	—	—	122,484 [2]	73,615 [2]	48,869 [2]	39.9	14,969	8,925	6,044	40.4	2,299	1,946	353	15.4
1939–40	—	—	—	—	186,500 [2]	109,546 [2]	76,954 [2]	41.3	26,731	16,508	10,223	38.2	3,290	2,861	429	13.0
1949–50	—	—	—	—	432,058 [2]	328,841 [2]	103,217 [2]	23.9	58,183	41,220	16,963	29.2	6,420	5,804	616	9.6
1959–60	—	—	—	—	392,440 [2]	254,063 [2]	138,377 [2]	35.3	74,435	50,898	23,537	31.6	9,829	8,801	1,028	10.5
1969–70	206,023	117,432	88,591	43.0	792,316	451,097	341,219	43.1	213,589	130,799	82,790	38.8	59,486	53,792	5,694	9.6
1970–71	252,311	144,144	108,167	42.9	839,730	475,594	364,136	43.4	235,564	143,083	92,481	39.3	64,998	58,137	6,861	10.6
1971–72	292,014	166,227	125,787	43.1	887,273	500,590	386,683	43.6	257,201	155,010	102,191	39.7	71,206	63,353	7,853	11.0
1972–73	316,174	175,413	140,761	44.5	922,362	518,191	404,171	43.8	268,654	159,569	109,085	40.6	79,512	69,959	9,553	12.0
1973–74	343,924	188,591	155,333	45.2	945,776	527,313	418,463	44.2	282,074	162,606	119,468	42.4	82,591	71,131	11,460	13.9
1974–75	360,171	191,017	169,154	47.0	922,933	504,841	418,092	45.3	297,545	166,318	131,227	44.1	84,904	71,025	13,879	16.3
1975–76	391,454	209,996	181,458	46.4	925,746	504,925	420,821	45.5	317,477	172,519	144,958	45.7	91,007	73,888	17,119	18.8
1976–77	406,377	210,842	195,535	48.1	919,549	495,545	424,004	46.1	323,025	173,090	149,935	46.4	91,730	72,209	19,521	21.3
1977–78	412,246	204,718	207,528	50.3	921,204	487,347	433,857	47.1	317,987	166,857	151,130	47.5	92,345	70,283	22,062	23.9
1978–79	402,702	192,091	210,611	52.3	921,390	477,344	444,046	48.2	307,686	159,111	148,575	48.3	94,971	70,452	24,519	25.8
1979–80	400,910	183,737	217,173	54.2	929,417	473,611	455,806	49.0	305,196	156,882	148,314	48.6	95,631	69,526	26,105	27.3
1980–81	416,377	188,638	227,739	54.7	935,140	469,883	465,257	49.8	302,637	152,979	149,658	49.5	98,016	69,567	28,449	29.0
1981–82	434,526	196,944	237,582	54.7	952,998	473,364	479,634	50.3	302,447	151,349	151,098	50.0	97,838	68,630	29,208	29.9
1982–83	449,620	203,991	245,629	54.6	969,510	479,140	490,370	50.6	296,415	150,092	146,323	49.4	99,335	67,757	31,578	31.8
1983–84	452,240	202,704	249,536	55.2	974,309	482,319	491,990	50.5	291,141	149,268	141,873	48.7	100,799	67,769	33,030	32.8
1984–85	454,712	202,932	251,780	55.4	979,477	482,528	496,949	50.7	293,472	149,276	144,196	49.1	100,785	66,269	34,516	34.2
1985–86	446,047	196,166	249,881	56.0	987,823	485,923	501,900	50.8	295,850	149,373	146,477	49.5	100,280	65,215	35,065	35.0
1986–87	436,304	190,839	245,465	56.3	991,264	480,782	510,482	51.5	296,530	147,063	149,467	50.4	98,477	62,790	35,687	36.2
1987–88	435,085	190,047	245,038	56.3	994,829	477,203	517,626	52.0	305,783	150,243	155,540	50.9	99,139	63,019	36,120	36.4
1988–89	436,764	186,316	250,448	57.3	1,018,755	483,346	535,409	52.6	316,626	153,993	162,633	51.4	100,571	63,055	37,516	37.3
1989–90	455,102	191,195	263,907	58.0	1,051,344	491,696	559,648	53.2	330,152	158,052	172,100	52.1	103,508	63,963	39,545	38.2
1990–91	481,720	198,634	283,086	58.8	1,094,538	504,045	590,493	53.9	342,863	160,842	182,021	53.1	105,547	64,242	41,305	39.1
1991–92	504,231	207,481	296,750	58.9	1,136,553	520,811	615,742	54.2	358,089	165,867	192,222	53.7	109,554	66,603	42,951	39.2
1992–93	514,756	211,964	302,792	58.8	1,165,178	532,881	632,297	54.3	375,032	173,354	201,678	53.8	112,072	67,130	44,942	40.1
1993–94	530,632	215,261	315,371	59.4	1,169,275	532,422	636,853	54.5	393,037	180,571	212,466	54.1	112,636	66,773	45,863	40.7
1994–95	539,691	218,352	321,339	59.5	1,160,134	526,131	634,003	54.6	403,609	183,043	220,566	54.6	114,266	67,324	46,942	41.1
1995–96	555,216	219,514	335,702	60.5	1,164,792	522,454	642,338	55.1	412,180	183,481	228,699	55.5	115,507	67,189	48,318	41.8
1996–97	571,226	223,948	347,278	60.8	1,172,879	520,515	652,364	55.6	425,260	185,270	239,990	56.4	118,747	68,387	50,360	42.4
1997–98	558,555	217,613	340,942	61.0	1,184,406	519,956	664,450	56.1	436,037	188,718	247,319	56.7	118,735	67,232	51,503	43.4
1998–99	564,984	220,508	344,476	61.0	1,202,239	519,961	682,278	56.8	446,038	190,230	255,808	57.4	116,700	65,340	51,360	44.0
1999–2000	564,933	224,721	340,212	60.2	1,237,875	530,367	707,508	57.2	463,185	196,129	267,056	57.7	118,736	64,930	53,806	45.3
2000–01	578,865	231,645	347,220	60.0	1,244,171	531,840	712,331	57.3	473,502	197,770	275,732	58.2	119,585	64,171	55,414	46.3
2001–02	595,133	238,109	357,024	60.0	1,291,900	549,816	742,084	57.4	487,313	202,604	284,709	58.4	119,663	62,731	56,932	47.6
2002–03	634,016	253,451	380,565	60.0	1,348,811	573,258	775,553	57.5	518,699	215,172	303,527	58.5	121,579	62,730	58,849	48.4
2003–04	665,301	260,033	405,268	60.9	1,399,542	595,425	804,117	57.5	564,272	233,056	331,216	58.7	126,087	63,981	62,106	49.3
2004–05	696,660	267,536	429,124	61.6	1,439,264	613,000	826,264	57.4	580,151	237,155	342,996	59.1	134,387	67,257	67,130	50.0
2005–06	713,066	270,095	442,971	62.1	1,485,242	630,600	854,642	57.5	599,731	241,656	358,075	59.7	138,056	68,912	69,144	50.1
2006–07	728,114	275,187	452,927	62.2	1,524,092	649,570	874,522	57.4	610,597	242,189	368,408	60.3	144,690	71,308	73,382	50.7
2007–08	750,164	282,521	467,643	62.3	1,563,069	667,928	895,141	57.3	630,666	250,169	380,497	60.3	149,378	73,453	75,925	50.8
2008–09	787,243	298,066	489,177	62.1	1,601,399	685,422	915,977	57.2	662,082	263,515	398,567	60.2	154,564	75,674	78,890	51.0
2009–10	848,856	322,747	526,109	62.0	1,649,919	706,660	943,259	57.2	693,313	275,317	417,996	60.3	158,590	76,610	81,980	51.7
2010–11	943,506	361,408	582,098	61.7	1,716,053	734,159	981,894	57.2	730,922	291,680	439,242	60.1	163,827	79,672	84,155	51.4
2011–12	1,021,718	393,479	628,239	61.5	1,792,163	765,772	1,026,391	57.3	755,967	302,484	453,483	60.0	170,217	82,670	87,547	51.4
2012–13	1,006,961	388,846	618,115	61.4	1,840,164	787,231	1,052,933	57.2	751,751	301,575	450,176	59.9	175,038	85,104	89,934	51.4
2013–14[3]	964,000	379,000	585,000	60.7	1,859,000	794,000	1,065,000	57.3	760,000	305,000	455,000	59.9	178,000	86,000	91,000	51.1
2014–15[3]	949,000	375,000	574,000	60.5	1,852,000	789,000	1,063,000	57.4	778,000	318,000	459,000	59.0	178,000	86,000	91,000	51.1
2015–16[3]	952,000	375,000	577,000	60.6	1,847,000	788,000	1,059,000	57.3	802,000	335,000	467,000	58.2	179,000	87,000	92,000	51.4
2016–17[3]	973,000	380,000	593,000	60.9	1,845,000	775,000	1,069,000	57.9	824,000	344,000	480,000	58.3	182,000	89,000	93,000	51.1
2017–18[3]	991,000	385,000	606,000	61.2	1,847,000	779,000	1,069,000	57.9	851,000	354,000	496,000	58.3	187,000	93,000	94,000	50.3
2018–19[3]	1,016,000	391,000	625,000	61.5	1,871,000	785,000	1,086,000	58.0	877,000	365,000	511,000	58.3	190,000	94,000	96,000	50.5
2019–20[3]	1,041,000	398,000	644,000	61.9	1,903,000	795,000	1,108,000	58.2	899,000	374,000	525,000	58.4	194,000	96,000	98,000	50.5
2020–21[3]	1,062,000	403,000	659,000	62.1	1,933,000	805,000	1,128,000	58.4	920,000	382,000	539,000	58.6	198,000	98,000	100,000	50.5
2021–22[3]	1,082,000	409,000	673,000	62.2	1,956,000	814,000	1,142,000	58.4	943,000	389,000	554,000	58.7	201,000	99,000	102,000	50.7
2022–23[3]	1,103,000	415,000	688,000	62.4	1,977,000	821,000	1,156,000	58.5	969,000	398,000	571,000	58.9	203,000	100,000	103,000	50.7
2023–24[3]	1,126,000	421,000	706,000	62.7	2,004,000	830,000	1,173,000	58.5	996,000	408,000	588,000	59.0	206,000	101,000	105,000	51.0
2024–25[3]	1,150,000	427,000	723,000	62.9	2,029,000	840,000	1,190,000	58.6	1,019,000	416,000	603,000	59.2	209,000	102,000	107,000	51.2

—Not available.

[1]Includes Ph.D., Ed.D., and comparable degrees at the doctoral level. Includes most degrees formerly classified as first-professional, such as M.D., D.D.S., and law degrees.

[2]Includes some degrees classified as master's or doctor's degrees in later years.

[3]Projected.

NOTE: Data through 1994–95 are for institutions of higher education, while later data are for degree-granting institutions. Degree-granting institutions grant associate's or higher degrees and participate in Title IV federal financial aid programs. Some data have been revised from previously published figures. Detail may not sum to totals because of rounding.

SOURCE: U.S. Department of Education, National Center for Education Statistics, *Earned Degrees Conferred*, 1869–70 through 1964–65; Higher Education General Information Survey (HEGIS), "Degrees and Other Formal Awards Conferred" surveys, 1965–66 through 1985–86; Integrated Postsecondary Education Data System (IPEDS), "Completions Survey" (IPEDS-C:87–99); IPEDS Fall 2000 through Fall 2013, Completions component; and Degrees Conferred Projection Model, 1980–81 through 2024–25. (This table was prepared April 2015.

Technical Appendixes

This page intentionally left blank.

Appendix A
Introduction to Projection Methodology

A.0. INTRODUCTION TO PROJECTION METHODOLOGY

Content of appendix A

Since its inception in 1964, the *Projections of Education Statistics* series has been providing projections of key education statistics to policy makers, educators, researchers, the press, and the general public. This edition of *Projections of Education Statistics* is the forty-third in the series.

Appendix A contains this introduction, which provides a general overview of the projection methodology, as well as six additional sections that discuss the specific methodology for the different statistics projected:

- » A.0. Introduction to Projection Methodology;
- » A.1. Elementary and Secondary Enrollment;
- » A.2. High School Graduates;
- » A.3. Elementary and Secondary Teachers;
- » A.4. Expenditures for Public Elementary and Secondary Education;
- » A.5. Enrollment in Degree-granting Postsecondary Institutions; and
- » A.6. Postsecondary Degrees Conferred.

This introduction

- » outlines the two major techniques used to make the projections;
- » summarizes key demographic and economic assumptions underlying the projections;
- » examines the accuracy of the projections; and
- » introduces the subsequent sections of appendix A.

Projection techniques

Two main projection techniques were used to develop the projections presented in this publication:

- » Exponential smoothing was the technique used in the projections of elementary and secondary enrollments and high school graduates. This technique also played a role in the projections of teachers at the elementary and secondary level, as well as enrollments and degrees conferred at the postsecondary level.
- » Multiple linear regression was the primary technique used in the projections of teachers and expenditures at the elementary and secondary level, as well as enrollments and degrees conferred at the postsecondary level.

Exponential smoothing

Two different types of exponential smoothing, single exponential smoothing and double exponential smoothing, were used in producing the projections presented in this publication.

Single exponential smoothing was used when the historical data had a basically horizontal pattern. Single exponential smoothing produces a single forecast for all years in the forecast period. In developing projections of elementary and secondary enrollments, for example, the rate at which students progress from one particular grade to the next (e.g., from grade 2 to grade 3) was projected using single exponential smoothing. Thus, this percentage was assumed to be constant over the forecast period.

In general, exponential smoothing places more weight on recent observations than on earlier ones. The weights for observations decrease exponentially as one moves further into the past. As a result, the older data have less influence on the projections. The rate at which the weights of older observations decrease is determined by the smoothing constant.

When using single exponential smoothing for a time series, P_t, a smoothed series, $\hat{P}$, is computed recursively by evaluating

$$\hat{P}_t = \propto P_t + (1 - \propto) \hat{P}_{t-1}$$

where $0 < \propto \leq 1$ is the smoothing constant.

By repeated substitution, we can rewrite the equation as

$$\hat{P}_t = \propto \sum_{s=0}^{t-1} (1 - \propto)^s P_{t-s}$$

where time, s, goes from the first period in the time series, 0, to time period $t\text{-}1$.

The forecasts are constant for all years in the forecast period. The constant equals

$$\hat{P}_{T+k} = \hat{P}_T$$

where T is the last year of actual data and k is the kth year in the forecast period where $k > 0$.

These equations illustrate that the projection is a weighted average based on exponentially decreasing weights. For higher smoothing constants, weights for earlier observations decrease more rapidly than for lower smoothing constants.

For each of the approximately 1,200 single exponential smoothing equations in this edition of *Projections of Education Statistics*, a smoothing constant was individually chosen to minimize the sum of squared forecast errors for that equation. The smoothing constants used to produce the projections in this report ranged from 0.001 to 0.999.

Double exponential smoothing is an extension of single exponential smoothing that allows the forecasting of data with trends. It produces different forecasts for different years in the forecast period. Double exponential smoothing with two smoothing constants was used to forecast the number of doctor's degrees awarded to males and females.

The smoothing forecast using double exponential smoothing is found using the three equations:

$$\hat{P}_{t+k} = a_t + b_t k$$

$$a_t = \propto P_t + (1 - \propto)(a_{t-1} + b_{t-1})$$

$$b_t = \beta (a_t - a_{t-1}) + (1 - \beta) b_{t-1}$$

where a_t denotes an estimate of the level of the series at time t, b_t denotes an estimate of the level of the series at time t, and $0 < \propto, \beta < 1$ are the smoothing constants.

Forecasts from double smoothing are computed as

$$\hat{P}_{T+k} = a_T + b_T k$$

where T is the last year of actual data and k is the kth year in the forecast period where $k > 0$. The last expression shows that forecasts from double smoothing lie on a linear trend with intercept a_T and slope b_T. Single exponential smoothing can be viewed as a special case of double exponential smoothing where the impact that time has on the forecasts has been eliminated (i.e., requiring the slope term b_t to equal 0.0).

The smoothing constants for each of the two double exponential smoothing equations used for this report were selected using a search algorithm that finds the pair of smoothing constants that together minimize the sum of forecast errors for their equation.

Beginning with the *Projections of Education Statistics to 2020*, each smoothing constant was chosen separately. In earlier editions all the smoothing constants had been set to 0.4. Also beginning with that edition, two smoothing constants, rather than one, were used for double exponential smoothing.

Multiple linear regression

Multiple linear regression was used in cases where a strong relationship exists between the variable being projected (the dependent variable) and independent variables. This technique can be used only when accurate data and reliable projections of the independent variables are available. Key independent variables for this publication include demographic and economic factors. For example, current expenditures for public elementary and secondary education are related to economic factors such as disposable income and education revenues from state sources. The sources of the demographic and economic projections used for this publication are discussed below, under "Assumptions."

The equations in this appendix should be viewed as forecasting rather than structural equations. That is, the equations are intended only to project values for the dependent variables, not to reflect all elements of underlying social, political, and economic structures. Lack of available data precluded the building of large-scale structural models. The particular equations shown were selected on the basis of their statistical properties, such as coefficients of determination (R^2s), the *t*-statistics of the coefficients, the Durbin-Watson statistic, the Breusch-Godfrey Serial Correlation LM test statistic, and residual plots.

The functional form primarily used is the multiplicative model. When used with two independent variables, this model takes the form:

$$Y = a \cdot X_1^{b_1} \cdot X_2^{b_2}$$

This equation can easily be transformed into the linear form by taking the natural log (ln) of both sides of the equation:

$$ln(Y) = ln(a) + b_1 lnX_1 + b_2 lnX_2$$

One property of this model is that the coefficient of an independent variable shows how responsive in percentage terms the dependent variable is to a one percent change in that independent variable (also called the elasticity). For example, a 1 percent change in X_1 in the above equation would lead to a b_1 percent change in Y.

Assumptions

All projections are based on underlying assumptions, and these assumptions determine projection results to a large extent. It is important that users of projections understand the assumptions to determine the acceptability of projected time series for their purposes. All the projections in this publication are to some extent dependent on demographic and/or economic assumptions.

Demographic assumptions

Many of the projections in this publication are demographically based on the U.S. Census Bureau's 2012 National Population Projections (December 2012) and the Interim State Population Projections (April 2005).

The two sets of Census Bureau population projections are produced using cohort-component models. In order for the national-level population projections by age, sex, and race/ethnicity to be consistent with the most recent historical estimates released by the Census Bureau, the projections were ratio-adjusted by applying the ratio of the last historical estimate to the corresponding projections year to the projections for each age, sex, and race/ethnicity combination. This allows for a consistent set of historical estimates and projections. For more information on the methodology used for Census Bureau population projections, see appendix C, Data Sources.

The enrollment projections in this publication depend on Census Bureau population projections for the various age groups that attend school. The future fertility rate assumption (along with corresponding projections of female populations) determines projections of the number of births, a key factor for population projections. The fertility rate assumption plays a major role in determining population projections for the age groups enrolled in nursery school, kindergarten, and elementary grades. The effects of the fertility rate assumption are more pronounced toward the end of the forecast period, while immigration assumptions affect all years. For enrollments in secondary grades and college, the fertility rate assumption is of no consequence, since all the population cohorts for these enrollment ranges have already been born.

Economic assumptions

Various economic variables are used in the forecasting models for numbers of elementary and secondary teachers, public elementary and secondary school expenditures, and postsecondary enrollment.

Projections of the economic variables were from the trend scenario of the "U.S. Quarterly Model 1st Quarter 2015 Short-Term Baseline Projections" developed by the economic consulting firm IHS Global Inc. This set of projections was IHS Global Inc.'s most recent set at the time the education projections in this report were produced. The trend scenario depicts a mean of possible paths that the economy could take over the forecast period, barring major shocks. The economy, in this scenario, evolves smoothly, without major fluctuations.

More information about specific assumptions

For details about the primary assumptions used in this edition of *Projections of Education Statistics*, see table A-1 on page 73.

Accuracy of the projections

Projections of time series usually differ from the final reported data due to errors from many sources. This is because of the inherent nature of the statistical universe from which the basic data are obtained and the properties of projection methodologies, which depend on the validity of many assumptions.

The mean absolute percentage error (MAPE) is one way to express the forecast accuracy of past projections. This measure expresses the average absolute value of errors over past projections in percentage terms. For example, an analysis of projection errors over the past 31 editions of *Projections of Education Statistics* indicates that the MAPEs for public school enrollment in grades prekindergarten–12 for lead times of 1, 2, 5, and 10 years were 0.3, 0.5, 1.3, and 2.4 percent, respectively. For the 1-year-out projection, this means that one would expect the projection to be within 0.3 percent of the actual value, on average.

For a list of MAPEs for selected national statistics in this publication, see table A-2 on page 74. Sections A.1 through A.6 each contains at least one text table (tables A through J) that presents the MAPEs for the key national statistics of that section. Each text table appears directly after the discussion of accuracy of that section's national projections. For a list of MAPEs by state and region for public elementary and secondary enrollment, see tables A-7 through A-9 on pages 83–85 and for a list of MAPEs by state and region for the number of high school graduates in public schools, see table A-10 on page 91.

Tables A-3 and A-4 present an example of how the MAPEs were constructed using actual values for total enrollment in degree-granting postsecondary institutions projections for schools years 2010–11 through 2013–14 and enrollment projections from the last four editions of *Projections of Education Statistics*. The top two panels of table A-3 shows the actual values for school years 2010–11 through 2013–14 and enrollment projections for each year from *Projections of Education Statistics to 2020* with the number of projections generally decreasing by one for each subsequent edition. The bottom panel of table A-3 shows the percentage differences between the actual values and the projected values. For example, the projected value for 2010–11 presented in *Projections of Education Statistics to 2020* was 2.1 lower than the actual value for that year.

The top panel of table A-4 shows the absolute value of the percent differences from table A-3 arranged by lead time rather than year. For example, in the *Projections of Education Statistics to 2020*, the last year of actual data reported was 2010–11 and thus the lead time for the projection of 2010–11 data was 1 year. Thus, the 2.1 appearing in the 2010–11 column of Table A-3 for *Projections of Education Statistics to 2020* appears in the column for lead times of 1 year in Table A-4, indicating that projection of the one-year-out forecast from *Projections of Education Statistics to 2020* differed by 2.1 percent in absolute terms from its actual value. The MAPEs for each lead time shown in the bottom panel of table A-4 were calculated by computing the average of the absolute values of the percentage differences for that lead time. For example, actual values are available to calculate the absolute values of the percentage differences for a lead time of 2 years for the first three editions of the *Projections of Education Statistics* listed in table A-4. These absolute values are 1.5, 4.4, and 4.1. The MAPE for a lead time of 2 years was then calculated by taking the average of these numbers, or 3.3. This matches the MAPE that appears in the bottom panel for a lead time of 2 years. (Calculations for table A-3 are based on unrounded numbers.) These MAPEs are different from the MAPEs for public elementary and secondary enrollment projections elsewhere in this report because the MAPEs in the example were calculated using only the last 4 editions of *Projections of Education Statistics*.

The number of years used in the analyses of the projection errors differ both because projections of additional education statistics have been added to the report over time and because, in some cases, there have been substantial changes in the methodology used to produce the projections such that the MAPEs for the earlier projections are no longer relevant. MAPEs are presented for a statistic only after it has been produced using substantially the same methodology in five previous editions of *Projections of Education Statistics* and there are at least three additional years of historical data for use in calculating the MAPEs.

Table A-1. Summary of forecast assumptions to 2024

Variable	Assumption
1	2
Demographic assumptions	
Population..	Projections are consistent with the Census Bureau estimates[1]
18- to 24-year-old population..	Census Bureau projection: average annual growth rate of -0.4%
25- to 29-year-old population..	Census Bureau projection: average annual growth rate of 0.4%
30- to 34-year-old population..	Census Bureau projection: average annual growth rate of 1.2%
35- to 44-year-old population..	Census Bureau projection: average annual growth rate of 0.9%
Economic assumptions	
Disposable income per capita in constant dollars..	Annual percent changes range between 1.0% and 2.6% with an annual growth rate of 2.0%
Education revenue receipts from state sources per capita in constant dollars...............	Annual percent changes range between 0.7% and 2.9% with an annual growth rate of 1.9%
Inflation rate	Inflation rate ranges between 1.4% and 2.5%
Unemployment rate (men)	
Ages 18 and 19	Remains between 17.4% and 18.0%
Ages 20 to 24	Remains between 10.0% and 10.4%
Age 25 and over	Remains between 4.3% and 4.4%
Unemployment rate (women)	
Ages 18 and 19	Remains between 13.4% and 14.1%
Ages 20 to 24	Remains between 8.1% and 8.5%
Age 25 and over	Remains between 4.2% and 4.4%

[1]As the Census Bureau projections were not updated to reflect the most recent 2013 Census Bureau population estimates, the Census Bureau age-specific population projections for each year were adjusted by multiplying the ratio of the total Census Bureau estimate for 2013 to the total Census Bureau projection for 2013.

SOURCE: U.S. Department of Commerce, Census Bureau, Population Estimates, retrieved January 5, 2015 from http://www.census.gov/popest/data/index.html; and Population Projections, retrieved January 5, 2015, from http://www.census.gov/population/projections/data/national/2012.html; and IHS Global Inc., "U.S. Quarterly Macroeconomic Model, 1st Quarter 2015 Short-Term Baseline Projections." (This table was prepared March 2015.)

Table A-2. Mean absolute percentage errors (MAPEs), by lead time for selected statistics in all elementary and secondary schools and degree-granting postsecondary institutions: *Projections of Education Statistics to 1984–85* through *Projections of Education Statistics to 2023*

Statistic	Lead time (years)									
	1	2	3	4	5	6	7	8	9	10
1	2	3	4	5	6	7	8	9	10	11
Public elementary and secondary schools										
Prekindergarten–12 enrollment[1]	0.3	0.5	0.8	1.0	1.3	1.5	1.7	1.9	2.1	2.4
Prekindergarten–8 enrollment[1]	0.3	0.6	1.0	1.2	1.5	1.8	2.1	2.3	2.6	3.0
9–12 enrollment[1]	0.4	0.6	0.9	1.1	1.2	1.4	1.7	2.0	2.3	2.5
White[1]	0.5	1.7	3.6	4.3	4.0	—	—	—	—	—
Black or African American[2]	0.7	2.1	4.0	4.2	2.7	—	—	—	—	—
Hispanic or Latino[2]	1.1	2.2	2.8	3.3	0.5	—	—	—	—	—
Asian/Hawaiian or other Pacific Islander[2]	0.8	3.1	6.2	7.3	7.0	—	—	—	—	—
American Indian/Alaska Native[2]	1.6	4.9	7.6	12.0	13.8	—	—	—	—	—
Elementary and secondary teachers[3]	0.8	1.6	1.8	2.4	3.0	3.7	4.6	5.1	5.0	5.4
High school graduates[4]	1.0	1.1	1.8	2.3	2.2	2.6	3.2	4.1	4.7	5.0
White[1]	1.2	0.5	1.0	1.6	2.9	—	—	—	—	—
Black or African American[2]	2.7	3.1	5.6	5.5	7.6	—	—	—	—	—
Hispanic or Latino[2]	4.1	4.7	10.4	15.3	14.4	—	—	—	—	—
Asian/Hawaiian or other Pacific Islander[2]	1.7	2.6	1.7	2.2	0.7	—	—	—	—	—
American Indian/Alaska Native[2]	2.3	1.7	4.9	8.9	10.6	—	—	—	—	—
Total current expenditures[5]	1.6	2.4	2.2	2.1	2.5	3.9	4.9	5.0	4.7	4.5
Current expenditures per pupil in fall enrollment[5]	1.6	2.3	2.2	2.1	2.6	3.8	4.9	5.3	5.7	5.7
Private elementary and secondary schools[6]										
Prekindergarten–12 enrollment	2.2	5.5	3.7	8.4	8.3	11.7	12.1	15.1	16.2	15.2
Prekindergarten–8 enrollment	2.6	5.8	4.3	9.5	10.0	14.0	15.0	17.4	19.3	17.9
9–12 enrollment	2.7	4.2	2.5	4.5	3.0	4.6	4.0	7.8	6.2	6.6
High school graduates	0.9	1.2	1.6	2.8	4.1	5.2	3.3	5.6	4.6	4.9
Degree-granting postsecondary institutions										
Total enrollment[7]	1.6	2.6	3.8	4.7	5.4	6.3	7.4	8.5	10.7	12.4
Males[7]	1.6	3.0	4.1	5.2	6.3	7.3	8.5	9.7	11.5	13.0
Females[7]	1.7	2.7	4.0	4.5	4.8	5.5	6.7	7.7	10.1	11.9
4-year institutions[7]	1.5	2.9	4.1	5.4	6.5	7.6	9.0	10.3	12.6	14.5
2-year institutions[7]	2.5	3.5	5.0	5.0	4.9	4.6	5.1	6.0	8.1	9.0
White[8]	2.3	4.0	4.7	4.7	4.8	3.4	3.0	3.2	4.3	—
Black or African American[8]	3.3	8.1	11.0	12.8	13.2	14.0	13.0	10.2	8.2	—
Hispanic or Latino[8]	3.7	6.9	10.4	14.9	18.6	20.5	21.2	21.2	22.3	—
Asian/Hawaiian or other Pacific Islander[8]	3.2	6.1	7.4	8.1	6.7	5.2	4.7	6.9	6.6	—
American Indian/Alaska Native[8]	6.1	8.2	10.2	11.6	13.9	21.3	24.4	30.7	35.8	—
Total first-time freshman enrollment[9]	3.6	6.3	6.6	5.1	1.9	0.3	—	—	—	—
Males[9]	3.7	6.3	6.6	4.9	2.3	2.6	—	—	—	—
Females[9]	3.6	6.2	6.6	5.3	2.5	2.8	—	—	—	—
Associate's degrees[8]	2.7	6.1	10.2	14.9	18.3	18.3	—	—	—	—
Bachelor's degrees[8]	0.7	0.4	0.9	3.1	5.0	6.6	—	—	—	—

— Not available.

[1] MAPEs for public prekindergarten–12 enrollments were calculated using the last 31 editions of *Projections of Education Statistics*, from *Projections of Education Statistics to 1984–1985* through *Projections of Education Statistics to 2023*.

[2] Data for public prekindergarten–12 enrollments and high school graduates by race/ethnicity were calculated using the last 5 editions of *Projections of Education Statistics*, from *Projections of Education Statistics to 2019* through *Projections of Education Statistics to 2023*.

[3] Data for teachers expressed in full-time equivalents. MAPEs for teachers were calculated from the past 24 editions of *Projections of Education Statistics*, from *Projections of Education Statistics to 1997–98* through *Projections of Education Statistics to 2023*, excluding *Projections of Education Statistics to 2012* which did not include projections of teachers.

[4] MAPEs for public high school graduates were calculated from the past 24 editions of *Projections of Education Statistics*, from *Projections of Education Statistics to 2000* through *Projections of Education Statistics to 2023*.

[5] In constant dollars based on the Consumer Price Index for all urban consumers, Bureau of Labor Statistics, U.S. Department of Labor. MAPEs for current expenditures were calculated using projections from the past 24 editions of *Projections of Education Statistics*, from *Projections of Education Statistics to 1997–98* through *Projections of Education Statistics to 2023*, excluding *Projections of Education Statistics to 2012* which did not include projections of current expenditures.

[6] MAPEs for private prekindergarten–12 enrollments and high school graduates were calculated from the past 13 editions of *Projections of Education Statistics*, from *Projections of Education Statistics 2011* through *Projections of Education Statistics to 2023*.

[7] MAPEs for total degree-granting postsecondary institution enrollment and degree-granting postsecondary institution enrollment by sex and level of institution were calculated using the last 17 editions of *Projections of Education Statistics*, from *Projections of Education Statistics to 2007* through *Projections of Education Statistics to 2023*.

[8] MAPEs for degree-granting postsecondary institution enrollment by race/ethnicity and associate's degrees, and bachelor's degrees were calculated using the last 9 editions of *Projections of Education Statistics*, from *Projections of Education Statistics to 2015* through *Projections of Education Statistics to 2023*.

[9] MAPEs for degree-granting postsecondary institution first-time freshmen enrollment by race/ethnicity were calculated using the last 6 editions of *Projections of Education Statistics*, from *Projections of Education Statistics to 2018* through *Projections of Education Statistics to 2023*.

NOTE: Mean absolute percentage error is the average value over past projections of the absolute values of errors expressed in percentage terms. No MAPEs are presented for certain degrees conferred as the current models used for producing these projections have only been used for three other editions of *Projections of Education Statistics*. Calculations were made using unrounded numbers. Some data have been revised from previously published figures.

SOURCE: U.S. Department of Education, National Center for Education Statistics, *Projections of Education Statistics*, various issues. (This table was prepared April 2015.)

Table A-3. Example of constructing mean absolute percentage errors (MAPEs) on fall enrollment in degree-granting institutions, part 1

Source	Year of data			
	2010–11	2011–12	2012–13	2013–14
1	2	3	4	5
	Enrollment in thousands			
Actual..	21,016	20,994	20,643	20,376
	Projected enrollment in thousands			
Projections of Education Statistics to 2020	20,582	20,688	20,727	20,948
Projections of Education Statistics to 2021	†	21,294	21,556	21,792
Projections of Education Statistics to 2022	†	†	20,968	21,216
Projections of Education Statistics to 2023	†	†	†	20,597
	Percentage difference between actual and projected values			
Projections of Education Statistics to 2020	-2.1	-1.5	0.4	2.8
Projections of Education Statistics to 2021	†	1.4	4.4	7.0
Projections of Education Statistics to 2022	†	†	1.6	4.1
Projections of Education Statistics to 2023	†	†	†	1.1

† Not applicable.
SOURCE: U.S. Department of Education, National Center for Education Statistics, Integrated Postsecondary Education Data System (IPEDS), IPEDS Spring 2010 through Spring 2014, Enrollment component; and *Projections of Education Statistics*, various editions. (This exhibit was prepared February 2015.)

Table A-4. Example of constructing mean absolute percentage errors (MAPEs) on fall enrollment in degree-granting institutions, part 2

Source	Lead time (years)			
	1	2	3	4
1	2	3	4	5
	Absolute value of percentage difference between actual and projected values			
Projections of Education Statistics to 2020	2.1	1.5	0.4	2.8
Projections of Education Statistics to 2021	1.4	4.4	7.0	†
Projections of Education Statistics to 2022	1.6	4.1	†	†
Projections of Education Statistics to 2023	1.1	†	†	†
	Mean absolute percentage error			
Example..	1.5	3.3	3.7	2.8

† Not applicable.
NOTE: The mean absolute percentage errors presented in this table are for illustrative purpose only.

SOURCE: U.S. Department of Education, National Center for Education Statistics, Integrated Postsecondary Education Data System (IPEDS), IPEDS Spring 2010 through Spring 2014, Enrollment component; and *Projections of Education Statistics*, various editions. (This exhibit was prepared February 2015.)

A.1. ELEMENTARY AND SECONDARY ENROLLMENT

Projections in this edition

This edition of *Projections of Education Statistics* presents projected trends in elementary and secondary enrollment from 2013 to 2024. These projections were made using three models:

» The *National Elementary and Secondary Enrollment Projection Model* was used to project total, public, and private school enrollments for the nation by grade level and for ungraded elementary and ungraded secondary programs.

» The *State Public Elementary and Secondary Enrollment Projection Model* was used to project total public school enrollments by grade level for individual states and regions.

» The *National Public Elementary and Secondary Enrollment by Race/Ethnicity Projection Model* was used to project public school enrollments for the nation by race/ethnicity and grade level.

All three elementary and secondary enrollment models used the following same methods.

Overview of approach

Two methods were used in all the elementary and secondary enrollment models:

» The *grade progression rate method* was used to project enrollments in grades 2 through 12. In this method, a rate of progression from each grade (1 through 11) to the next grade (2 through 12) was projected using single exponential smoothing. (For example, the rate of progression from grade 2 to grade 3 is the current year's grade 3 enrollment expressed as a percentage of the previous year's grade 2 enrollment.) To calculate enrollment for each year in the forecast period, the progression rate for each grade was applied to the previous year's enrollment in the previous grade.

» The *enrollment rate method* was used to project prekindergarten, kindergarten, and first-grade enrollments as well as elementary special and ungraded and secondary special and ungraded enrollments. For each of these enrollment categories, the enrollment rate for the last year of actual data was used as the projected enrollment rate. To calculate enrollment for each year in the forecast period, the enrollment rate for each category was applied to the projected population in the appropriate age group.

Assumptions underlying these methods

The grade progression and enrollment rate methods assume that past trends in factors affecting public and private elementary and secondary school enrollments will continue over the forecast period. This assumption implies that all factors influencing enrollments will display future patterns consistent with past patterns. This method implicitly includes the net effect of such factors as migration, dropouts, deaths, nonpromotion, and transfers between public and private schools.

Procedures and equations used in all three elementary and secondary enrollment projection models

The notation and equations that follow describe the basic procedures used to project elementary and secondary enrollments in each of the three elementary and secondary enrollment projection models.

Let:

i = Subscript denoting age

j = Subscript denoting grade

t = Subscript denoting time

T = Subscript of the first year in the forecast period

N_t = Enrollment at the prekindergarten (nursery) level

K_t = Enrollment at the kindergarten level

$G_{j,t}$ = Enrollment in grade j

E_t = Enrollment in elementary special and ungraded programs

S_t = Enrollment in secondary special and ungraded programs

$P_{i,t}$ = Population age i

$R_{j,t}$ = Progression rate for grade j

RN_t = Enrollment rate for prekindergarten (nursery school)

RK_t = Enrollment rate for kindergarten

$RG_{1,t}$ = Enrollment rate for grade 1

RE_t = Enrollment rate for elementary special and ungraded programs

RS_t = Enrollment rate for secondary special and ungraded programs.

Step 1. *Calculate historical grade progression rates for each of grades 2 through 12.* The first step in projecting the enrollments for grades 2 through 12 using the grade progression method was to calculate, for each grade, a progression rate for each year of actual data used to produce the projections except for the first year. The progression rate for grade j in year t equals

$$R_{j,t} = G_{j,t}/G_{j-1,t-1}$$

Step 2. *Produce a projected progression rate for each of grades 2 through 12.* Projections for each grade's progression rate were then produced for the forecast period using single exponential smoothing. A separate smoothing constant, chosen to minimize the sum of squared forecast errors, was used to calculate the projected progression rate for each grade. Single exponential smoothing produces a single forecast for all years in the forecast period. Therefore, for each grade j, the projected progression rate, $\hat{R}_j$, is the same for each year in the forecast period.

Step 3. *Calculate enrollment projections for each of grades 2 through 12.* For the first year in the forecast period, T, enrollment projections, $G_{j,t}$, for grades 2 through 12, were produced using the projected progression rates and the enrollments of grades 1 through 11 from the last year of actual data, $T-1$. Specifically,

$$\hat{G}_{j,T} = \hat{R}_j \cdot G_{j-1,T-1}$$

This same procedure was then used to produce the projections for the following year, $T+1$, except that enrollment projections for year T were used rather than actual numbers:

$$\hat{G}_{j,T+1} = \hat{R}_j \cdot \hat{G}_{j,T}$$

The enrollment projections for grades 2 through 11 for year T were those just produced using the grade progression method. The projection for grade 1 for year T was produced using the enrollment rate method, as outlined in steps 4 and 5 below.

The same procedure was used for the remaining years in the projections period.

Step 4. *For the last year of actual data, calculate enrollment rates for prekindergarten, kindergarten, grade 1, elementary special and ungraded, and secondary special and ungraded.* The first step in projecting prekindergarten, kindergarten, first-grade, elementary special and ungraded, and secondary special and ungraded enrollments using the enrollment rate method was to calculate enrollment rates for each enrollment category for the last year of actual data, $T-1$, where:

$$RN_{T-1} = N_{T-1}/P_{5,T-1}$$
$$RK_{T-1} = K_{T-1}/P_{5,T-1}$$
$$RG_{1,T-1} = G_{1,T-1}/P_{6,T-1}$$
$$RE_{T-1} = E_{T-1}/\Sigma_{i=5}^{13}P_{i,T-1}$$
$$RS_{T-1} = S_{T-1}/\Sigma_{i=14}^{17}P_{i,T-1}$$

These enrollment rates were then used as the projected enrollment rates for each year in the forecast period ($\widehat{RN}$, $\widehat{RK}$, $\widehat{RG_1}$, $\widehat{RE}$, and $\widehat{RS}$.).

Step 5. *Using the rates for the last year of actual data as the projected enrollment rates, calculate enrollment projections for prekindergarten through grade 1 and the ungraded categories.* For each year in the forecast period, the enrollment rates were then multiplied by the appropriate population projections from the U.S. Census Bureau ($\hat{P}_{i,t}$) to calculate enrollment projections for prekindergarten (nursery school) ($\hat{N}_t$), kindergarten ($\hat{K}_t$), first grade ($\hat{G}_{1,t}$), elementary ungraded ($\hat{E}_t$), and secondary ungraded ($\hat{S}_t$)

$$\hat{N}_t = \widehat{RN} \cdot \hat{P}_{5,t}$$
$$\hat{K}_t = \widehat{RK} \cdot \hat{P}_{5,t}$$
$$\hat{G}_{1,t} = \widehat{RG_1} \cdot \hat{P}_{5,t}$$
$$\hat{E}_t = \widehat{RE} \cdot (\sum_{i=5}^{13} \hat{P}_{i,t})$$
$$\hat{S}_t = \widehat{RS} \cdot (\sum_{i=14}^{17} \hat{P}_{i,t})$$

Step 6. *Calculate total elementary and secondary enrollments by summing the projections for each grade and the ungraded categories.* To obtain projections of total enrollment, projections of enrollments for the individual grades (prekindergarten through 12), elementary ungraded, and secondary ungraded were summed.

National Elementary and Secondary Enrollment Projection Model

This model was used to project national total, public, and private school enrollments by grade level and for ungraded elementary and ungraded secondary programs. National enrollment projections for public and private schools were developed separately, then added together to yield total elementary and secondary enrollment projections for the nation. To develop these projections, enrollment data from NCES were used, along with population estimates and projections from the U.S. Census Bureau. Below is information about the specific data used to develop the public school projections and the private school projections, as well as information about the grade progression rates and enrollment rates specific to public schools and private schools.

For details on procedures used to develop the projections, see "Procedures and equations used in all three elementary and secondary enrollment projection models," earlier in this section of appendix A.

Data used to develop national elementary and secondary enrollment projections

Public school enrollment data. Public school enrollment data from the NCES *Statistics of Public Elementary and Secondary School Systems* for 1972 to 1980 and the NCES Common Core of Data (CCD) for 1981 to 2012 were used to develop the national public school enrollment projections.

Private school enrollment data. Private school enrollment data from the NCES Private School Universe Survey (PSS) for 1989–90, 1991–92, 1993–94, 1995–96, 1997–98, 1999–2000, 2001–02, 2003–04, 2005–06, 2007–08, 2009–10, and 2011–12 were used to develop the national private school enrollment projections. Since the PSS is collected in the fall of odd-numbered years, data for even-numbered years without a PSS collection were estimated by interpolating grade-by-grade progression data from PSS.

Population estimates and projections used for public school enrollment projections. Population estimates for 1972 to 2013 and population projections for 2014 to 2024 from the U.S. Census Bureau were also used to develop the public school enrollment projections. The set of population projections used in this year's *Projections of Education Statistics* are the Census Bureau's 2012 National Population Projections by age and sex (December 2012), adjusted to line up with the most recent historical estimates. This was done through the use of ratio adjustments in which, for each combination of state, age, and sex, the population projections from 2014 to 2024 were multiplied by the ratio of the population estimate for 2013 to the population projection for 2013.

Population estimates and projections used for private school enrollment projections. Population estimates for 1989 to 2013 and population projections for 2014 to 2024 from the U.S. Census Bureau were used to develop the private school enrollment projections. The population projections were ratio-adjusted to line up with the most recent historical estimates.

Grade progression and enrollment rates for national elementary and secondary enrollment projections

Public school grade progression and enrollment rates. Table A-5 on page 82 shows the public school grade progression rates for 2012 and projections for 2013 through 2024. Table A-6 on page 82 shows the public school enrollment rates for 2012 and projections for 2013 through 2024.

Accuracy of national elementary and secondary enrollment projections

Mean absolute percentage errors (MAPEs) for projections of public school enrollment were calculated using the last 31 editions of *Projections of Education Statistics*, while MAPEs for projections of private school enrollment were calculated using the last 13 editions. Table A, below, shows MAPEs for both public and private school enrollment projections.

Table A.   Mean absolute percentage errors (MAPEs) of enrollment projections, by lead time, control of school, and grade in elementary and secondary schools: *Projections of Education Statistics to 1984–85* through *Projections of Education Statistics to 2023*

Statistic	Lead time (years)									
	1	2	3	4	5	6	7	8	9	10
Public elementary and secondary schools										
Prekindergarten–12 enrollment	0.3	0.5	0.8	1.0	1.3	1.5	1.7	1.9	2.1	2.4
Prekindergarten–8 enrollment	0.3	0.6	1.0	1.2	1.5	1.8	2.1	2.3	2.6	3.0
9–12 enrollment	0.4	0.6	0.9	1.1	1.2	1.4	1.7	2.0	2.3	2.5
Private elementary and secondary schools										
Prekindergarten–12 enrollment	2.2	5.5	3.7	8.4	8.3	11.7	12.1	15.1	16.2	15.2
Prekindergarten–8 enrollment	2.6	5.8	4.3	9.5	10.0	14.0	15.0	17.4	19.3	17.9
9–12 enrollment	2.7	4.2	2.5	4.5	3.0	4.6	4.0	7.8	6.2	6.6

NOTE: Mean absolute percentage error is the average value over past projections of the absolute values of errors expressed in percentage terms. MAPEs for public prekindergarten–12 enrollments were calculated using the last 31 editions of *Projections of Education Statistics*, from *Projections of Education Statistics to 1984–85* through *Projections of Education Statistics to 2023*. MAPEs for private prekindergarten–12 enrollments were calculated from the past 13 editions, from *Projections of Education Statistics to 2011* through *Projections of Education Statistics to 2023*. Calculations were made using unrounded numbers. Some data have been revised from previously published figures.
SOURCE: U.S. Department of Education, National Center for Education Statistics, *Projections of Education Statistics*, various issues. (This table was prepared March 2015.)

For more information about MAPEs, see Section A.0. Introduction, earlier in appendix A.

State Public Elementary and Secondary Enrollment Projection Model

This edition of *Projections of Education Statistics* contains projected trends in public elementary and secondary enrollment by grade level from 2013 to 2024 for each of the 50 states and the District of Columbia, as well as for each region of the country. The state enrollment projections were produced in two stages:

» first, an initial set of projections for each state was produced; and

» second, these initial projections were adjusted to sum to the national public enrollment totals produced by the National Elementary and Secondary Enrollment Projection Model.

For each region, the enrollment projections equaled the sum of enrollment projections for the states within that region. The states comprising each geographic region can be found in appendix F.

Initial set of state projections

The same methods used to produce the national enrollment projections—namely, the grade progression rate method and the enrollment rate method—were used to produce the initial sets of public school enrollment projections for each state and the District of Columbia. A separate smoothing constant, chosen to minimize the sum of squared forecast errors, was used to calculate the projected progression rate for each combination of jurisdiction and grade.

For details on the procedures used to develop the initial sets of projections, see "Procedures and equations used in all three elementary and secondary enrollment projection models," earlier in this section of appendix A.

Limitations of the grade progression method for state projections

The grade progression rate method assumes that past trends in factors affecting public school enrollments will continue over the forecast period. This assumption implies that all factors influencing enrollments will display future patterns consistent with past patterns. Therefore, this method has limitations when applied to states with unanticipated changes in migration rates. This method implicitly includes the net effect of such factors as migration, dropouts, deaths, nonpromotion, and transfers to and from private schools.

Adjustments to the state projections

The initial projections of state public school enrollments were adjusted to sum to the national projections of public school prekindergarten (preK)–12, preK–8, and 9–12 enrollments shown in table 1 on page 35. This was done through the use of ratio adjustments in which all the states' initial enrollment projections for each grade level were multiplied by the ratio of the national enrollment projection for that grade level to the sum of the state enrollment projections for that grade level.

Data used to develop state elementary and secondary enrollment projections

Public school enrollment data. Public school enrollment data from the NCES *Statistics of Public Elementary and Secondary School Systems* for 1980 and from the NCES Common Core of Data (CCD) for 1981 to 2012 were used to develop these projections.

Population estimates and projections. Population estimates for 1980 to 2013 and population projections for 2013 to 2024 from the U.S. Census Bureau were used to develop the state-level enrollment projections. The set of population projections used in this year's *Projections of Education Statistics* are the Census Bureau's set of Interim State Population Projections by age and sex (April 2005). In order for the state-level population projections to be consistent with the most recent historical estimates released by the Census Bureau, these projections were adjusted to line up with the most recent historical estimate for each state. This was done through the use of ratio adjustments in which, for each combination of state, age, and sex, the population projections from 2013 to 2024 were multiplied by the ratio of the population estimate for 2013 to the population projection for 2013.

Accuracy of state elementary and secondary enrollment projections

Mean absolute percentage errors (MAPEs) for projections of public school enrollment by state were calculated using the last 19 editions of *Projections of Education Statistics*. Tables A-7 through A-9 on pages 83–85 show MAPEs for preK–12, preK–8, and 9–12 enrollment in public elementary and secondary schools by state.

National Public Elementary and Secondary Enrollment by Race/Ethnicity Projection Model

This edition of *Projections of Education Statistics* contains projected trends in national public elementary and secondary enrollment by race/ethnicity from 2013 to 2024.

This is the second edition to include enrollment projections for students of Two or more races. As 2010 is the first year in which all 50 states and the District of Columbia reported enrollment data for students of Two or more races, enrollment projections for this category were produced using a different method than that used for the other five racial/ethnic groups.

Prior to 2008, there was a single category for students of Asian and/or Native Hawaiian or Other Pacific Islander origin. In 2008 and 2009, states could choose to either place these students in either the single category, Asian and/or Native Hawaiian or Other Pacific Islander, or in one of three categories, (1) Asian, (2) Hawaiian or Other Pacific Islander, and (3) Two or more races (for students of both Asian and Hawaiian or Other Pacific Islander origin). Beginning in 2010, the option of using the single category was eliminated and states were required to place students in one of those three categories. For students of Asian and/or Native Hawaiian or Other Pacific Islander origin, projections were calculated for a single category, Asian/Pacific Islander. For 2008 and 2009, the count of the Asian/Pacific Islander students included the total of the Asian and/or Native Hawaiian or Other Pacific Islander students for states reporting one category and the counts for Asian students and Native Hawaiian or Other Pacific Islander students for states reporting three categories. Beginning in 2010, the count of the Asian/Pacific Islander students was the sum of the counts Asian students and Native Hawaiian or Other Pacific Islander students.

The enrollment projections by race/ethnicity were produced in two stages:

» first, an initial set of projections by race/ethnicity was produced; and

» second, these initial projections were adjusted to sum to the national totals.

Initial set of projections by race/ethnicity

The same methods used to produce the national enrollment projections—namely, the grade progression rate method and the enrollment rate method—were used to produce initial sets of projections for each of the following five racial/ethnic groups: White, Black, Hispanic, Asian/Pacific Islander, and American Indian/Alaska Native. A separate smoothing constant, chosen to minimize the sum of squared forecast errors, was used to calculate the projected progression rate for each combination of race/ethnicity and grade.

For details on the procedures used to develop the initial sets of projections, see "Procedures and equations used in all three elementary and secondary enrollment models," earlier in this section of appendix A.

National enrollment projections for students of Two or more races by grade level were produced by taking the 2012 grade level enrollment numbers for students of Two or more races and applying the growth rates from 2013 to 2024 of the U.S. Census Bureau's age specific population projections for persons of Two or more races.

Adjustments to the projections by race/ethnicity

The initial projections of enrollments by race/ethnicity were adjusted to sum to the national projections of public school preK–12, preK–8, and 9–12 enrollments shown in table 1 on page 35. This was done through the use of ratio adjustments in which all the initial enrollment projections by race/ethnicity for each grade level were multiplied by the ratio of the national enrollment projection for that grade level to the sum of the initial enrollment projections by race/ethnicity for that grade level.

Data and imputations used to develop enrollment projections by race/ethnicity

Public school enrollment data. Public school enrollment data by grade level and race/ethnicity from the NCES Common Core of Data (CCD) for 1994 to 2012 were used to develop these projections. While projections by race/ethnicity were produced at the national level only, the national data used to develop these projections were constructed from state-level data on enrollment by grade level and race/ethnicity. In those instances where states did not report their enrollment data by grade level and race/ethnicity, the state-level data had to be examined and some imputations made in order to produce the national public school enrollment by grade level and race/ethnicity data. For example, in 1994, North Dakota did not report grade-level enrollment data by race/ethnicity. It did, however, report these numbers for 1995. So, to impute these numbers for 1994, North Dakota's 1994 grade-level enrollment data were multiplied by the state's 1995 racial/ethnic breakdowns at each grade level.

Population estimates and projections. Population estimates for 2000 to 2013 and population projections for 2014 to 2024 from the U.S. Census Bureau were used to develop the enrollment projections by race/ethnicity. The set of population projections used in this year's *Projections of Education Statistics* are the Census Bureau's 2012 National Population Projections by age, sex, and race/ethnicity (December 2012), ratio-adjusted to line up with the most recent historical estimates.

Accuracy of enrollment projections by race/ethnicity

Mean absolute percentage errors (MAPEs) for projections of public school enrollment by race/ethnicity were calculated using the last five editions of *Projections of Education Statistics*. Table B, below, shows MAPEs for public school enrollment by race/ethnicity projections.

Table B. Mean absolute percentage errors (MAPEs) of enrollment projections, by lead time and race/ethnicity: *Projections of Education Statistics to 1984–85* through *Projections of Education Statistics to 2023*

Statistic	Lead time (years)									
	1	2	3	4	5	6	7	8	9	10
Total enrollment	**0.3**	**0.5**	**0.8**	**1.0**	**1.3**	**1.5**	**1.7**	**1.9**	**2.1**	**2.4**
White	0.5	1.7	3.6	4.3	4.0	—	—	—	—	—
Black or African American	0.7	2.1	4.0	4.2	2.7	—	—	—	—	—
Hispanic or Latino	1.1	2.2	2.8	3.3	0.5	—	—	—	—	—
Asian/Hawaiian or other Pacific Islander	0.8	3.1	6.2	7.3	7.0	—	—	—	—	—
American Indian/Alaska Native	1.6	4.9	7.6	12.0	13.8	—	—	—	—	—

— Not available.
NOTE: Mean absolute percentage error is the average value over past projections of the absolute values of errors expressed in percentage terms. MAPEs for public prekindergarten–12 enrollments were calculated using the last 31 editions of *Projections of Education Statistics*, from *Projections of Education Statistics to 1984–85* through *Projections of Education Statistics to 2023*. MAPEs for public prekindergarten–12 enrollments by race/ethnicity were calculated using the last 5 editions of *Projections of Education Statistics*, from *Projections of Education Statistics to 2019* through *Projections of Education Statistics to 2023*. Calculations were made using unrounded numbers.
SOURCE: U.S. Department of Education, National Center for Education Statistics, *Projections of Education Statistics*, various issues. (This table was prepared March 2015.)

Table A-5. Actual and projected national public school grade progression rates: Fall 2012, and fall 2013 through fall 2024

Grade	Actual 2012	Projected 2013 through 2024
1	2	3
1 to 2...	98.9	98.9
2 to 3...	100.1	100.2
3 to 4...	99.6	100.0
4 to 5...	99.7	100.2
5 to 6...	100.2	100.6
6 to 7...	100.4	100.6
7 to 8...	100.1	100.1
8 to 9...	108.1	108.1
9 to 10...	93.6	94.3
10 to 11...	93.3	94.1
11 to 12...	97.6	98.1

NOTE: The progression rate for a particular grade in a year equals the enrollment in the grade for that year divided by the enrollment in the previous grade in the previous year all multiplied by 100. For example, the progression rate for third-graders in 2012 equals the enrollment of third-graders in 2012 divided by the enrollment of second-graders in 2011, all multiplied by 100.

SOURCE: U.S. Department of Education, National Center for Education Statistics, Common Core of Data (CCD), "State Nonfiscal Survey of Public Elementary/Secondary Education," 2012–13; and National Elementary and Secondary Enrollment Projection Model, 1972 through 2024. (This table was prepared March 2015.)

Table A-6. Actual and projected national enrollment rates in public schools, by grade level: Fall 2012, and fall 2013 through fall 2024

Grade level	Actual 2012	Projected 2013 through 2024
1	2	3
Prekindergarten	31.6	31.6
Kindergarten...	92.7	92.7
Grade 1...	93.3	93.3
Elementary ungraded	0.2	0.2
Secondary ungraded	0.2	0.2

NOTE: The enrollment rate for each grade level equals the enrollment at that grade level divided by the population of that grade's base age, all multiplied by 100. The base age for each grade level is as follows: kindergarten, 5 years old; grade 1, 6 years old; elementary ungraded, 5 to 13 years olds; and secondary ungraded, 14 to 17 years olds. Projected values for 2013 through 2024 were held constant at the actual values for 2012.

SOURCE: U.S. Department of Education, National Center for Education Statistics, Common Core of Data (CCD), "State Nonfiscal Survey of Public Elementary/Secondary Education," 2012–13; and National Elementary and Secondary Enrollment Projection Model, 1972 through 2024. (This table was prepared March 2015.)

Table A-7. Mean absolute percentage errors (MAPEs) for projected prekindergarten–12 enrollment in public elementary and secondary schools, by lead time, region, and state: *Projections of Education Statistics to 1984–85* through *Projections of Education Statistics to 2023*

Region and state	Lead time (years)									
	1	2	3	4	5	6	7	8	9	10
1	2	3	4	5	6	7	8	9	10	11
United States	**0.3**	**0.5**	**0.8**	**1.0**	**1.3**	**1.5**	**1.7**	**1.9**	**2.1**	**2.4**
Region										
Northeast	0.5	0.6	0.8	1.0	0.8	0.8	0.9	0.8	0.8	1.1
Midwest	0.2	0.4	0.5	0.7	0.8	0.9	1.2	1.4	1.4	1.5
South	0.4	0.9	1.3	1.7	2.1	2.6	2.9	3.3	3.8	4.8
West	0.5	0.9	1.3	1.6	1.9	2.1	2.2	2.0	1.9	2.0
State										
Alabama	0.6	0.8	1.0	1.4	2.0	2.8	3.6	4.5	5.3	5.9
Alaska	1.0	1.8	2.4	2.7	2.9	3.8	5.1	6.4	8.0	10.2
Arizona	2.2	3.5	5.2	6.5	8.1	9.0	9.2	8.8	10.1	10.6
Arkansas	0.5	1.0	1.7	2.2	3.0	3.9	4.5	4.7	5.2	5.9
California	0.6	1.0	1.5	2.0	2.5	3.0	3.3	3.4	3.7	4.4
Colorado	0.5	0.9	1.3	1.7	2.2	2.9	3.8	4.6	5.6	6.7
Connecticut........................	0.6	0.8	1.0	1.3	1.9	2.4	3.2	3.9	4.7	5.7
Delaware	0.7	1.2	1.8	2.3	3.1	3.8	4.9	6.0	7.2	8.4
District of Columbia.............	5.2	5.1	6.1	6.8	6.5	6.9	6.0	4.8	6.9	5.9
Florida................................	0.9	1.8	2.5	3.4	4.3	5.5	6.2	6.4	6.8	7.7
Georgia...............................	0.7	1.2	1.9	2.6	3.3	4.0	4.4	4.7	5.4	6.6
Hawaii	1.7	2.8	3.8	5.1	6.8	8.5	10.0	11.8	13.4	15.6
Idaho..................................	0.7	1.5	2.1	2.8	3.6	4.2	4.2	4.2	3.9	4.0
Illinois................................	0.6	0.8	1.0	1.1	1.3	1.6	1.8	2.1	2.3	2.7
Indiana...............................	0.3	0.6	0.9	1.2	1.6	2.1	2.5	2.7	2.9	3.2
Iowa...................................	0.6	0.9	1.2	1.5	1.8	1.8	1.8	2.2	3.0	3.6
Kansas...............................	0.7	1.1	1.5	1.7	1.9	2.1	2.3	2.3	2.6	2.7
Kentucky	1.4	1.5	2.1	2.2	2.2	2.9	3.1	3.4	4.0	4.9
Louisiana	1.8	3.1	3.9	4.9	5.8	6.6	7.1	5.7	6.7	7.9
Maine	0.9	1.2	1.4	1.7	2.0	1.9	1.8	2.0	2.4	2.7
Maryland.............................	0.5	0.9	1.3	1.7	2.1	2.0	2.0	2.1	2.1	2.2
Massachusetts....................	0.4	0.5	0.7	0.8	0.9	1.0	1.0	1.1	1.6	2.1
Michigan	0.6	1.5	2.1	2.5	3.1	4.0	4.7	5.2	5.4	5.2
Minnesota	0.4	0.5	0.7	0.9	1.1	1.2	1.5	1.6	1.7	2.0
Mississippi	0.5	0.9	1.2	1.4	1.7	2.0	2.4	2.8	3.0	3.4
Missouri	0.4	0.5	0.6	0.7	0.9	1.0	1.0	1.2	1.2	1.6
Montana	0.8	1.4	2.2	2.9	4.0	5.2	6.7	8.3	9.9	11.9
Nebraska	0.5	0.8	1.1	1.4	1.8	2.1	2.4	2.6	3.1	3.2
Nevada...............................	1.0	1.9	3.1	4.6	6.2	7.9	9.4	10.5	12.3	14.5
New Hampshire	0.6	0.8	0.9	1.2	1.4	2.0	2.5	3.1	3.1	3.6
New Jersey	0.9	1.1	1.7	1.8	2.2	2.7	3.2	4.0	4.7	5.3
New Mexico	1.3	2.2	3.1	3.9	5.1	6.6	8.1	9.3	10.5	11.6
New York............................	0.8	1.2	1.4	1.9	2.0	2.3	2.3	2.4	2.8	2.8
North Carolina	0.9	1.5	2.3	3.2	3.9	4.2	4.6	5.2	6.5	8.0
North Dakota	1.0	1.5	2.1	3.1	3.9	4.8	6.0	7.2	8.3	9.1
Ohio...................................	0.4	0.6	0.9	1.1	1.4	1.8	1.9	2.1	2.0	1.9
Oklahoma...........................	0.9	1.4	2.0	2.5	3.1	3.8	4.6	5.5	6.6	7.3
Oregon...............................	1.0	1.2	1.6	1.7	2.1	2.4	2.9	3.4	3.7	3.6
Pennsylvania......................	0.9	1.4	1.5	1.4	1.3	1.6	1.8	1.9	1.8	2.4
Rhode Island......................	1.0	1.6	2.5	3.1	3.4	3.3	3.3	3.2	3.7	4.0
South Carolina....................	0.7	1.2	1.6	2.1	2.6	3.2	3.8	4.6	5.4	6.0
South Dakota......................	1.4	2.2	3.3	4.4	5.8	6.7	7.0	7.5	8.0	8.9
Tennessee..........................	1.0	1.3	1.8	2.1	2.4	2.8	3.1	3.7	3.8	4.0
Texas.................................	0.7	1.4	2.0	2.5	3.1	3.9	4.7	5.4	6.6	8.1
Utah	1.5	2.0	2.0	2.9	3.9	4.1	5.1	6.2	7.4	7.5
Vermont	1.2	2.2	2.4	2.8	3.5	4.0	4.6	5.3	5.5	6.6
Virginia	0.4	0.6	0.9	1.2	1.6	1.9	2.5	3.0	3.4	4.1
Washington	0.5	0.8	1.1	1.5	1.7	2.0	2.4	2.9	3.0	3.0
West Virginia......................	0.5	0.7	1.0	1.5	2.1	2.6	3.4	4.1	5.0	5.5
Wisconsin	0.6	0.9	1.3	1.5	1.6	1.7	2.0	2.2	2.0	2.2
Wyoming	0.8	1.4	2.4	3.5	5.0	6.7	8.3	9.6	11.5	13.3

NOTE: Mean absolute percentage error (MAPE) is the average value over past projections of the absolute values of errors expressed in percentage terms. National MAPEs for public prekindergarten–12 enrollments were calculated using the last 31 editions of *Projections of Education Statistics*, from *Projections of Education Statistics to 1984–85* through *Projections of Education Statistics to 2023*. State MAPEs were calculated using the last 19 editions of *Projections of Education Statistics*, from *Projections of Education Statistics to 2005* through *Projections of Education Statistics to 2023*. Calculations were made using unrounded numbers. Some data have been revised from previously published figures.
SOURCE: U.S. Department of Education, National Center for Education Statistics, *Projections of Education Statistics*, various issues. (This table was prepared March 2015.)

Table A-8. Mean absolute percentage errors (MAPEs) for projected prekindergarten–8 enrollment in public elementary and secondary schools, by lead time, region, and state: *Projections of Education Statistics to 1984–85* through *Projections of Education Statistics to 2023*

Region and state	Lead time (years)									
	1	2	3	4	5	6	7	8	9	10
1	2	3	4	5	6	7	8	9	10	11
United States	**0.3**	**0.6**	**1.0**	**1.2**	**1.5**	**1.8**	**2.1**	**2.3**	**2.6**	**3.0**
Region										
Northeast	0.4	0.7	0.8	0.9	0.9	0.7	0.9	0.9	0.6	0.9
Midwest	0.2	0.4	0.6	0.7	0.8	0.9	1.1	1.2	1.1	1.3
South	0.5	1.1	1.7	2.1	2.7	3.2	3.5	3.8	4.3	5.3
West	0.6	1.1	1.6	1.9	2.2	2.5	2.5	2.3	2.4	2.6
State										
Alabama	0.7	1.0	1.6	1.9	2.6	3.5	4.1	4.8	5.5	6.1
Alaska	1.2	2.0	2.8	3.4	4.1	5.5	7.7	9.7	11.8	14.3
Arizona	2.1	3.3	5.0	6.2	7.4	8.8	8.6	8.6	9.7	10.4
Arkansas	0.7	1.2	2.1	2.7	3.7	4.8	5.4	5.6	6.1	6.7
California	0.8	1.5	2.0	2.6	3.2	3.9	4.2	4.2	4.7	5.8
Colorado	0.6	1.1	1.5	1.9	2.6	3.5	4.5	5.6	6.9	8.1
Connecticut	0.6	0.9	1.3	1.6	2.2	2.7	3.5	4.3	4.8	5.5
Delaware	0.9	1.5	2.0	2.7	3.4	4.3	5.5	6.7	8.1	9.6
District of Columbia	4.7	5.2	5.4	6.0	5.7	6.0	6.3	4.5	6.9	5.9
Florida	1.0	2.1	3.2	4.1	5.5	6.6	7.3	7.3	7.7	8.4
Georgia	0.9	1.6	2.5	3.2	4.1	4.7	5.2	5.4	6.0	7.1
Hawaii	1.8	3.1	4.3	5.8	8.1	10.4	12.5	15.1	16.9	19.2
Idaho	0.9	2.0	3.0	3.7	4.5	5.0	4.9	4.9	4.6	4.7
Illinois	0.7	0.9	1.1	1.3	1.5	2.0	2.1	2.3	2.4	2.8
Indiana	0.4	0.7	1.0	1.3	1.6	2.0	2.3	2.4	2.6	3.1
Iowa	0.8	1.2	1.6	2.1	2.6	2.8	2.9	3.2	4.2	4.7
Kansas	0.8	1.1	1.5	1.8	2.2	2.6	2.9	3.0	3.5	3.6
Kentucky	1.5	1.9	2.8	3.0	3.1	3.2	3.4	3.7	4.1	5.5
Louisiana	1.7	2.9	3.4	4.0	4.7	5.5	6.1	5.3	5.9	6.8
Maine	0.7	0.9	1.2	1.6	2.1	2.6	3.2	4.4	5.4	6.0
Maryland	0.5	0.9	1.4	2.0	2.4	2.6	2.8	3.4	3.7	3.9
Massachusetts	0.3	0.6	0.9	1.1	1.2	1.3	1.4	1.6	1.8	2.2
Michigan	0.6	1.4	2.0	2.6	3.1	3.9	4.6	5.4	5.3	5.0
Minnesota	0.4	0.6	0.8	1.0	1.2	1.2	1.3	1.2	1.2	1.5
Mississippi	0.6	1.2	1.6	2.0	2.5	2.8	3.1	3.5	3.5	3.6
Missouri	0.5	0.8	1.0	1.2	1.4	1.5	1.4	1.4	1.1	1.3
Montana	1.0	1.8	2.9	4.0	5.5	7.3	9.5	11.9	14.0	16.1
Nebraska	0.6	1.0	1.3	1.6	2.0	2.4	2.8	3.0	3.5	3.7
Nevada	1.2	2.7	4.7	6.6	8.7	10.7	12.6	14.3	16.3	18.5
New Hampshire	0.6	1.0	1.2	1.7	2.5	3.3	3.9	4.8	4.9	5.5
New Jersey	0.9	1.3	1.7	1.8	2.0	2.3	2.9	3.4	3.9	4.2
New Mexico	1.2	2.1	2.6	3.4	4.6	6.3	8.0	9.7	10.8	11.4
New York	0.6	1.0	1.4	1.8	2.1	2.0	2.3	2.5	2.8	2.9
North Carolina	1.1	2.0	3.0	4.0	4.8	5.3	5.6	6.5	7.9	9.7
North Dakota	1.3	2.1	2.9	4.0	5.0	6.3	7.8	9.4	10.5	11.0
Ohio	0.4	0.5	0.7	0.8	1.0	1.2	1.3	1.5	1.3	1.4
Oklahoma	1.2	1.9	2.6	3.3	3.9	4.9	5.8	6.8	8.0	8.9
Oregon	1.1	1.3	1.4	1.4	2.1	2.5	2.5	3.2	3.9	3.8
Pennsylvania	0.6	1.0	1.1	1.1	1.1	1.3	1.6	1.7	1.7	1.9
Rhode Island	1.3	1.8	2.6	3.3	3.7	3.9	4.2	4.2	4.9	5.6
South Carolina	0.9	1.4	1.8	2.4	2.8	3.6	4.2	5.0	5.9	6.7
South Dakota	1.5	2.3	3.2	4.7	6.5	7.9	8.4	9.8	10.7	11.3
Tennessee	0.9	1.3	2.0	2.3	2.4	2.7	2.6	3.0	3.1	3.3
Texas	0.9	1.7	2.6	3.2	3.9	4.6	5.3	5.9	7.0	8.7
Utah	1.4	2.0	2.2	2.9	3.9	4.5	5.7	6.9	8.1	8.0
Vermont	1.8	2.6	2.6	3.3	4.4	5.3	6.7	8.2	8.0	9.3
Virginia	0.5	0.8	1.0	1.3	1.7	2.2	2.8	3.3	3.6	4.2
Washington	0.5	0.8	1.1	1.5	1.8	2.2	2.5	3.0	3.0	2.9
West Virginia	0.6	0.7	1.0	1.4	2.0	2.6	3.4	4.2	5.0	5.6
Wisconsin	0.6	0.8	1.1	1.5	1.8	1.9	2.0	2.1	2.0	2.2
Wyoming	1.0	1.6	2.9	4.3	6.4	8.6	10.7	12.8	15.1	16.8

NOTE: Mean absolute percentage error (MAPE) is the average value over past projections of the absolute values of errors expressed in percentage terms. National MAPEs for public prekindergarten–8 enrollments were calculated using the last 31 editions of *Projections of Education Statistics*, from *Projections of Education Statistics to 1984–85* through *Projections of Education Statistics to 2023*. State MAPEs were calculated using the last 19 editions of *Projections of Education Statistics*, from *Projections of Education Statistics to 2005* through *Projections of Education Statistics to 2023*. Calculations were made using unrounded numbers. Some data have been revised from previously published figures.
SOURCE: U.S. Department of Education, National Center for Education Statistics, *Projections of Education Statistics*, various issues. (This table was prepared March 2015.)

Table A-9. Mean absolute percentage errors (MAPEs) for projected grades 9–12 enrollment in public schools, by lead time, region, and state: *Projections of Education Statistics to 1984–85* through *Projections of Education Statistics to 2023*

Region and state	Lead time (years)									
	1	2	3	4	5	6	7	8	9	10
1	2	3	4	5	6	7	8	9	10	11
United States	**0.4**	**0.6**	**0.9**	**1.1**	**1.2**	**1.4**	**1.7**	**2.0**	**2.3**	**2.5**
Region										
Northeast	1.0	1.2	1.1	1.3	1.4	1.3	1.3	1.2	1.3	1.8
Midwest	0.4	0.8	1.0	1.1	1.2	1.3	1.7	2.0	2.0	2.1
South	0.4	0.9	1.4	1.6	1.8	2.0	2.3	2.6	3.2	3.8
West	0.5	0.8	1.1	1.4	1.5	1.7	2.0	2.2	2.0	1.4
State										
Alabama	0.9	1.3	1.9	2.4	2.8	3.9	4.6	5.5	6.2	6.6
Alaska	1.1	2.3	3.1	3.2	3.5	3.5	3.7	3.8	3.5	3.7
Arizona	3.8	6.0	8.1	8.6	9.6	10.0	10.5	9.3	10.9	11.4
Arkansas	0.5	0.9	1.3	1.4	1.7	2.1	2.6	2.8	3.2	3.9
California	0.5	0.9	1.4	1.8	2.1	2.3	2.6	2.7	2.4	2.3
Colorado	0.6	1.3	1.9	2.2	2.7	3.0	3.1	3.0	3.2	3.7
Connecticut	0.7	1.0	1.0	1.3	1.9	2.6	3.4	4.4	5.5	7.3
Delaware	1.3	1.5	2.0	2.4	2.9	3.3	3.9	4.4	5.5	6.8
District of Columbia	7.0	8.1	11.3	13.6	15.6	16.5	13.8	14.2	16.2	16.1
Florida	0.8	1.3	1.6	2.1	2.0	3.0	4.3	5.2	5.4	6.0
Georgia	0.5	1.0	1.3	1.5	1.8	2.5	3.0	3.6	4.6	5.4
Hawaii	1.7	2.5	3.3	3.9	4.4	5.0	5.5	6.3	6.2	7.5
Idaho	0.7	1.1	1.5	2.0	2.8	3.2	3.8	4.2	3.9	3.7
Illinois	0.8	1.0	1.3	1.5	1.8	2.3	2.7	3.2	3.2	3.7
Indiana	0.5	0.9	1.5	1.9	2.3	2.7	3.2	3.7	4.2	4.6
Iowa	0.7	0.9	1.3	1.1	1.5	1.7	2.0	2.0	2.1	2.4
Kansas	1.1	1.7	2.3	2.5	2.3	2.0	1.7	1.6	1.6	1.1
Kentucky	1.6	2.0	2.1	2.0	2.0	3.3	4.0	4.3	5.3	5.2
Louisiana	2.7	4.1	5.6	7.1	8.8	9.9	10.3	7.9	9.5	11.2
Maine	1.6	3.0	3.8	4.7	5.4	6.7	7.5	8.4	9.0	8.9
Maryland	0.6	0.9	1.4	1.8	1.8	1.8	1.6	1.7	1.9	2.0
Massachusetts	0.6	1.0	1.5	1.9	2.4	2.8	3.0	2.7	2.8	2.9
Michigan	1.5	2.5	3.2	3.4	4.0	4.8	6.0	7.4	9.0	9.9
Minnesota	0.5	1.0	1.2	1.4	1.6	1.9	2.2	2.6	3.1	3.4
Mississippi	0.7	1.4	2.0	2.4	2.9	3.3	3.8	4.3	4.6	4.7
Missouri	0.4	0.8	1.0	1.4	1.6	1.6	1.7	1.8	2.1	2.3
Montana	0.5	1.0	1.4	1.8	2.4	3.0	3.5	3.9	3.5	3.5
Nebraska	0.4	0.8	1.2	1.5	1.7	2.0	2.4	2.8	3.3	3.3
Nevada	1.3	2.3	2.8	3.0	3.7	4.6	5.6	7.3	8.8	8.9
New Hampshire	0.6	1.1	1.5	1.8	1.9	2.2	2.8	3.8	4.6	5.0
New Jersey	0.9	1.4	2.1	2.1	2.7	3.9	4.8	5.8	7.0	7.9
New Mexico	2.4	4.3	5.9	6.8	8.3	9.2	10.2	11.3	11.8	13.2
New York	1.5	2.2	1.9	2.2	2.6	2.9	2.7	2.9	3.4	3.2
North Carolina	1.0	1.4	1.6	1.7	2.3	2.5	2.9	3.2	4.0	5.3
North Dakota	0.8	1.2	1.7	2.4	2.9	3.5	4.6	6.0	7.1	7.8
Ohio	1.0	1.7	2.3	2.6	2.8	3.3	3.7	3.8	3.6	2.9
Oklahoma	0.4	0.9	1.3	1.7	2.1	2.5	2.9	3.4	4.1	4.8
Oregon	1.1	1.7	2.4	2.8	3.0	3.5	4.3	4.9	5.0	4.8
Pennsylvania	1.7	2.2	2.3	2.4	2.3	2.7	2.4	2.4	2.0	3.5
Rhode Island	0.8	1.6	2.4	3.4	3.9	4.3	4.4	4.2	4.1	4.7
South Carolina	0.8	1.4	2.1	2.5	3.1	3.6	3.8	3.8	4.3	5.5
South Dakota	1.5	3.1	4.7	6.0	7.0	8.0	9.1	10.3	10.5	10.7
Tennessee	2.0	2.1	3.0	3.8	4.6	5.3	5.7	6.4	6.2	6.1
Texas	0.5	1.2	1.7	2.0	2.5	2.9	3.6	4.6	5.5	6.5
Utah	1.9	2.4	1.8	3.2	4.2	3.6	4.4	5.6	5.7	6.3
Vermont	1.1	2.4	3.0	3.6	3.8	4.1	4.3	4.5	4.4	4.1
Virginia	0.5	1.0	1.6	2.2	2.6	3.0	3.1	3.2	3.6	3.9
Washington	0.6	0.9	1.2	1.7	2.1	2.6	3.2	3.8	4.1	4.4
West Virginia	0.7	0.9	1.2	1.6	2.3	3.0	3.7	4.4	5.0	5.2
Wisconsin	0.8	1.2	1.5	1.6	1.9	2.1	2.3	2.7	2.0	2.1
Wyoming	0.8	1.2	2.1	3.0	4.1	5.4	6.9	8.3	8.9	8.9

NOTE: Mean absolute percentage error (MAPE) is the average value over past projections of the absolute values of errors expressed in percentage terms. National MAPEs for public 9–12 enrollments were calculated using the last 31 editions of *Projections of Education Statistics*, from *Projections of Education Statistics to 1984–85* through *Projections of Education Statistics to 2023*. State MAPEs were calculated using the last 19 editions of *Projections of Education Statistics*, from *Projections of Education Statistics to 2005* through *Projections of Education Statistics to 2023*. Calculations were made using unrounded numbers. Some data have been revised from previously published figures.
SOURCE: U.S. Department of Education, National Center for Education Statistics, *Projections of Education Statistics*, various issues. (This table was prepared March 2015.)

A.2. ELEMENTARY AND SECONDARY TEACHERS

Projections in this edition

This edition of *Projections of Education Statistics* presents projected trends in elementary and secondary teachers, pupil/teacher ratios, and new teacher hires from 2013 to 2024. These projections were made using two models:

» The *Elementary and Secondary Teacher Projection Model* was used to project the number of public school teachers, the number of private school teachers, and the total number of teachers for the nation. It was also used to project pupil/teacher ratios for public schools, private schools, and all elementary and secondary schools.

» The *New Teacher Hires Projection Model* was used to project the number of new teacher hires in public schools, private schools, and all schools.

Overview of approach

Approach for numbers of teachers and pupil/teacher ratios

Public schools. Multiple linear regression was used to produce initial projections of public school pupil/teacher ratios separately for elementary and secondary schools. The initial projections of elementary pupil/teacher ratios and secondary pupil/teacher ratios were applied to enrollment projections to project the numbers of elementary teachers and secondary teachers, which were summed to get the total number of public school teachers. Final projections of the overall public school pupil/teacher ratios were produced by dividing total projected public school enrollment by the total projected number of teachers.

Assumptions underlying this method

This method assumes that past relationships between the public school pupil/teacher ratio (the dependent variable) and the independent variables used in the regression analysis will continue throughout the forecast period. For more information about the independent variables, see "Elementary and Secondary Teacher Projection Model," later in this section of appendix A.

Private schools. Private school pupil/teacher ratios were projected by applying each year's projected annual percentage change in the overall public school pupil/teacher ratio to the previous year's private school pupil/teacher ratio. The projected private school pupil/teacher ratios were then applied to projected enrollments at private schools to produce projected numbers of private school teachers.

Assumptions underlying this method

This method assumes that the future pattern in the trend of private school pupil/teacher ratios will be the same as that for public school pupil/teacher ratios. The reader is cautioned that a number of factors could alter the assumption of consistent patterns of change in ratios over the forecast period.

Approach for new teacher hires

The following numbers were projected separately for public schools and for private schools:

» *The number of teachers needed to fill openings when there is an increase in the size of the teaching workforce from one year to the next and the decrease in the number of replacement teachers needed if there is a decrease in the size of the teaching workforce from one year to the next.* This number was estimated based on continuation rates of teachers by their age.

» *The number of teachers needed to fill openings due to an increase in the size of the teaching workforce from one year to the next.* This number was estimated by subtracting the projected number of teachers in one year from the projected number of teachers in the next year.

These two numbers were summed to yield the total number of "new teacher hires" for each control of school—that is, teachers who will be hired in a given year, but who did not teach in that control the previous year. A teacher who moves from one control to the other control (i.e. from a public to private school or from a private to a public school) is considered a new teacher hire, but a teacher who moves from one school to another school in the same control is not considered a new teacher hire.

Elementary and Secondary Teacher Projection Model

Projections for public schools were produced first. Projections for private schools were produced based partially on input from the public school projections. Finally, the public and private school projections were combined into total elementary and secondary school projections (not shown in the steps below).

Steps used to project numbers of teachers and pupil/teacher ratios

Public school teachers. The following steps were used for the public school projections:

Step 1. Produce projections of pupil/teacher ratios for public elementary schools and public secondary schools separately. Two separate equations were used—one for elementary schools and one for secondary schools. The equations for elementary and secondary schools included an AR(1) term for correcting for autocorrelation and the following independent variables:

» *Independent variables for public elementary school pupil/teacher ratios*—(1) average teacher wage relative to the overall economy-level wage, and (2) level of education revenue from state sources in constant dollars per public elementary student.

» *Independent variables for public secondary school pupil/teacher ratios*—(1) level of education revenue from state sources in constant dollars per public secondary student, and (2) the number of students enrolled in public secondary schools relative to the secondary school–age population.

To estimate the models, they were first transformed into nonlinear models and then the coefficients were estimated simultaneously by applying a Marquardt nonlinear least squares algorithm to the transformed equation.

For details on the equations, model statistics, and data used to project public school pupil/teacher ratios, see "Data and equations used for projections of teachers and pupil/teacher ratios," below.

Step 2. Produce projections of the number of teachers for public elementary schools and public secondary schools separately. The projections of the public elementary pupil/teacher ratio and public secondary pupil/teacher ratio were applied to projections of enrollments in elementary schools and secondary schools, respectively, to produce projections of public elementary teachers and public secondary teachers.

Step 3. Produce projections of the total number of teachers for public elementary and secondary schools combined. The projections of public elementary teachers and public secondary teachers were added together to produce the projections of the total number of public elementary and secondary teachers.

Step 4. Produce projections of the pupil/teacher ratio for public elementary and secondary schools combined. The projections of total enrollment in public elementary and secondary schools were divided by the projections of the total number of public elementary and secondary teachers to produce projections of the overall pupil/teacher ratio in public elementary and secondary schools.

Private school teachers. The following steps were used for the private school projections:

Step 1. Produce projections of the private school pupil/teacher ratio. First, the projection of the private school pupil/teacher ratio for 2012 was calculated by multiplying the private school pupil/teacher ratio for 2011 (the last year of actual data) by the percentage change from 2010 to 2011 in the public school pupil/teacher ratio. The same method was used to calculate the projections of the private school pupil/teacher ratio for 2012 through 2024. That is, each year's projected annual percentage change in the public school pupil/teacher ratio was applied to the previous year's private school pupil/teacher ratio.

Step 2. Produce projections of the number of private school teachers. The projected pupil/teacher ratios were applied to projected private school enrollments to produce projections of private school teachers from 2012 through 2024.

For information about the private school teacher and enrollment data used for the private school projections, see "Data and equations used for projections of teachers and pupil/teacher ratios," below.

Data and equations used for projections of teachers and pupil/teacher ratios

Public school data used in these projections were by organizational level (i.e., school level), not by grade level. Thus, secondary school enrollment is not the same as enrollment in grades 9 through 12 because many jurisdictions count some grade 7 and 8 enrollment as secondary. For example, some jurisdictions may have 6-year high schools with grades 7 through 12.

Data used to estimate the equation for public elementary school pupil/teacher ratios. The following data were used to estimate the equation:

» To compute the historical elementary school pupil/teacher ratios—Data on 1972–73 to 1980–81 enrollments in public elementary schools came from the NCES *Statistics of Public Elementary and Secondary Day Schools* and data on 1981–82 to 2012–13 enrollment came from the NCES Common Core of Data (CCD). The proportion of public school teachers who taught in elementary schools was taken from the National Education Association and then applied to the total number of public school teachers from the CCD to produce the number of teachers in elementary schools.

- » For 1973–74 and 1975–76, the education revenue from state sources data came from *Statistics of State School Systems*, published by NCES. For 1972–73, 1974–75, and 1976–77, the education revenue from state sources data came from *Revenues and Expenditures for Public Elementary and Secondary Education*, also published by NCES. For 1977–78 through 2011–12, these data came from the NCES Common Core of Data (CCD).

Estimated equation and model statistics for public elementary school pupil/teacher ratios. For the estimated equation and model statistics, see table A-10 on page 91. In the public elementary pupil/teacher ratio equation, the independent variables affect the dependent variable in the expected way:

- » As the average teacher wage relative to the overall economy-level wage increases, the pupil/teacher ratio increases; and

- » As the level of education revenue from state sources in constant dollars per public elementary student increases, the pupil/teacher ratio decreases.

Data used to project public elementary school pupil/teacher ratios. The estimated equation was run using projected values for teacher salaries and education revenues from state sources from 2012–13 through 2024–25. For more information, see Section A.0. Introduction, earlier in this appendix and Section A.4 Expenditures for Public Elementary and Secondary Education later in this appendix.

Data used to estimate the equation for public secondary school pupil/teacher ratios. The following data were used to estimate the equation:

- » To compute the historical secondary school pupil/teacher ratios—Data on 1972–73 to 1980–81 enrollments in public elementary schools came from the NCES *Statistics of Public Elementary and Secondary Day Schools* and data on 1981–82 to 2012–13 enrollment came from the NCES Common Core of Data (CCD). The proportion of public school teachers who taught in secondary schools was taken from the National Education Association and then applied to the total number of public school teachers from the CCD to produce the number of teachers in secondary schools.

- » For 1973–74 and 1975–76, the education revenue from state sources data came from *Statistics of State School Systems*, published by NCES. For 1972–73, 1974–75, and 1976–77, the education revenue from state sources data came from *Revenues and Expenditures for Public Elementary and Secondary Education*, also published by NCES. For 1977–78 through 2011–12, these data came from the NCES Common Core of Data (CCD).

- » To compute the historical secondary school enrollment rate—Data on the secondary school-age population from 1972–73 to 2012–13 came from the U.S. Census Bureau. Data on enrollments in public secondary schools during the same period came from the CCD, as noted above.

Estimated equation and model statistics for public secondary school pupil/teacher ratios. For the estimated equation and model statistics, see table A-10 on page 91. In the public secondary pupil/teacher ratio equation, the independent variables affect the dependent variable in the expected way:

- » As enrollment rates (number of enrolled students relative to the school-age population) increase, the pupil/teacher ratio increases; and

- » As the level of education revenue from state sources in constant dollars per public secondary student increases, the pupil/teacher ratio decreases.

Data used to project public secondary school pupil/teacher ratios. The estimated equation was run using projections for education revenues, public secondary enrollments, and secondary school–age populations from 2012–13 through 2024–25. Secondary enrollment projections were derived from the enrollment projections described in Section A.1. Elementary and Secondary Enrollment. Population projections were from the Census Bureau's 2012 National Population Projections by age and sex (December 2012), ratio-adjusted to line up with the most recent historical estimates.

Private school teacher and enrollment data. Private school data for 1989–90, 1991–92, 1993–94, 1995–96, 1997–98, 1999–2000, 2001–02, 2003–04, 2005–06, 2007–08, 2009–10, and 2011–12 came from the biennial NCES Private School Universe Survey (PSS). Since the PSS is collected in the fall of odd-numbered years, data for years without a PSS collection were estimated using data from the PSS.

Private school enrollment projections. Private school enrollments from 2011 to 2024 came from the projections described in Section A.1. Elementary and Secondary Enrollment, earlier in this appendix.

Accuracy of projections of numbers of teachers

Mean absolute percentage errors (MAPEs) for projections of public school teachers were calculated using the last 24 editions of *Projections of Education Statistics*. Table C, below, shows MAPEs for projections of the numbers of public school teachers. There was a change in the methodology for projecting private school teachers beginning with *Projections of Education Statistics to 2017*, and therefore there are too few years of data to present the MAPEs for private school teachers.

Table C. Mean absolute percentage errors (MAPEs) of projections of number of public elementary and secondary school teachers, by lead time: *Projections of Education Statistics to 1997–98* through *Projections of Education Statistics to 2023*

	Lead time (years)									
Statistic	1	2	3	4	5	6	7	8	9	10
Public elementary and secondary teachers	0.8	1.6	1.8	2.4	3.0	3.7	4.6	5.1	5.0	5.4

NOTE: MAPEs for teachers were calculated from the past 24 editions of *Projections of Education Statistics*, from *Projections of Education Statistics to 1997–98* through *Projections of Education Statistics to 2023*, excluding *Projections of Education Statistics to 2012* which did not include projections of teachers. Calculations were made using unrounded numbers. Some data have been revised from previously published figures. Number of teachers reported in full-time equivalents.
SOURCE: U.S. Department of Education, National Center for Education Statistics, *Projections of Education Statistics*, various issues. (This table was prepared February 2014.)

For more information about MAPEs, see Section A.0. Introduction, earlier in this appendix.

New Teacher Hires Projection Model

The New Teacher Hires Projection Model was estimated separately for public and private school teachers. The model produces projections of the number of teachers who were not teaching in the previous year, but who will be hired in a given year.

About new teacher hires

A teacher is considered to be a new teacher hire for a control of school (public or private) for a given year if the teacher teaches in that control that year but had not taught in that control in the previous year. Included among new teachers hires are: (1) teachers who are new to the profession; (2) teachers who had taught previously but had not been teaching the previous year; and (3) teachers who had been teaching in one control the previous year but have moved to the other control. Concerning the last category, if a teacher moves from one public school to a different public school, that teacher would not be counted as a new teacher hire for the purposes of this model. On the other hand, if a teacher moves from a public school to a private school, that teacher would be counted as a private school new teacher hire, since the teacher did not teach in a private school in the previous year.

The New Teacher Hires Projection Model measures the demand for teacher hires. Due to difficulties in defining and measuring the pool of potential teachers, no attempt was made to measure the supply of new teacher candidates.

Steps used to project numbers of new teacher hires

The steps outlined below provide a general summary of how the New Teacher Hires Projection Model was used to produce projections of the need for new teacher hires.

For more information about the New Teacher Hires Projection Model, see Hussar (1999).

First, the series of steps outlined below was used to produce projections of public school new teacher hires. Then, the same steps were used to produce projections of private school new hires. Finally, the public and private new teacher hires were combined to produce projections of total new teacher hires.

Step 1. *Estimate the age distribution of full-time-equivalent (FTE) teachers in 2011.* For this estimate, the age distribution of the headcount of school teachers (including both full-time and part-time teachers) in 2011 was applied to the national number of FTE teachers in the same year.

Step 2. *Project the number of new FTE teacher hires needed to replace those who left teaching between 2011 and 2012.* In this step

» Age-specific continuation rates for 2012 (due to data availability, 2008 continuation rates were used for private school new teacher hires) were applied to the FTE count of teachers by age for 2011, resulting in estimates of the number of FTE teachers who remained in teaching in 2012 by individual age.

» The FTE teachers who remained in teaching by individual age were summed across all ages to produce a projection of the total number of FTE teachers who remained teaching in 2012.

» The total projection of remaining FTE teachers in 2012 was subtracted from the total FTE teacher count for 2011 to produce the projected number of FTE teachers who left teaching.

Step 3. *Project the number of new FTE teacher hires needed due to the overall increase in the teacher workforce between 2011 and 2012.* The total number of FTE teachers in 2011 was subtracted from the total projected number of FTE teachers in 2012 to project the overall increase in the teaching workforce between 2011 and 2012.

Step 4. *Project the total number of new FTE teacher hires needed in 2012.* The number of FTE teachers who left teaching from step 2 was added to the projected net change in the number of FTE teachers from step 3 to project the total number of new FTE teacher hires needed in 2012.

Step 5. *Project the FTE count of teachers by age for 2012.* In this step

>> The age distribution for the headcount of newly hired teachers in 2011 was applied to the projected total number of new FTE teacher hires in 2012, resulting in the projected number of new FTE teacher hires by age.

>> For each individual age, the projected number of new FTE teacher hires was added to the projected number of remaining FTE teachers (from step 2, first bullet) to produce the projected FTE count of teachers by age for 2012.

Step 6. *Repeat steps 2 to 5 for each year from 2013 through 2024.*

>> In step 2

• For public school teachers ages 22 through 66 and private school teachers ages 21 through 65, projections of age-specific continuation rates were used. A separate smoothing constant, chosen to minimize the sum of squared forecast errors, was used to calculate the projected progression rate for each age. (For a general description of the exponential smoothing technique, see Section A.0. Introduction, earlier in this appendix.)

• For all other ages, the age-specific continuation rates for 2012 for public school teachers and 2008 for private school teachers (the last year of actual data) were used.

>> In step 3, projections of the numbers of FTE teachers were used for all years in which there were no actual teacher numbers. The projections of FTE teachers are described under "Elementary and Secondary Teacher Projection Model," earlier in this section of appendix A.

Assumptions underlying this method

A number of assumptions are made in order to make these projections. They include that (1) the age distribution of FTE teachers in 2011 was similar to that of full-time and part-time teachers in that year (step 1); (2) the age-specific continuation rates for FTE teachers for each year from 2012 through 2024 are similar to either the projections produced using single exponential smoothing or the values for 2012, depending on the age of the teachers (step 2); (3) the age distribution for newly hired FTE teachers from 2012 through 2024 is similar to that of newly hired full-time and part-time teachers in 2011 (step 3); (4) the actual numbers of FTE teachers for each year from 2013 through 2024 are similar to projections of FTE teachers shown in table 8 on page 48; and (5) no economic or political changes further affect the size of the teaching force.

Data used for projections of new teacher hires

Data on numbers of public school teachers. The number of FTE teachers for 2012 came from the NCES Common Core of Data (CCD).

Data on numbers of private school teachers. Private school data on the numbers of FTE teachers in 2003–04, 2005–06, 2007–08, 2009–10, and 2011–12 came from the biennial NCES Private School Universe Survey (PSS). Since the PSS is collected in the fall of odd-numbered years, data for years without a PSS collection were estimated using data from the PSS.

Data on the age distribution of public and private school teachers. Data on the age distribution of full-time and part-time public and private school teachers came from the 2011–12 NCES Schools and Staffing Survey (SASS). These data and their standard errors are shown in table A-11 on page 91.

Data on the age distribution of public and private new teacher hires. Data on the age distribution of newly hired full-time and part-time public and private school teachers came from the 2011–12 NCES Schools and Staffing Survey (SASS). These data and their standard errors are shown in table A-12 on page 91.

Data on and projections of age-specific continuation rates of public and private school teachers. The 2008 continuation rates came from the 2008–09 NCES Teacher Follow-Up Survey (TFS) and the 2012 continuation rates came from the 2012–13 TFS. Data from the 1994–95, 2000–01, and 2004-05 TFS were also used in the projection of age-specific continuation rates. The actual data, their standard errors, and the projections are shown in table A-13 on page 92.

Projections of the numbers of public and private elementary and secondary school teachers. These projections are described under "Elementary and Secondary Teacher Projection Model," earlier in this section of appendix A.

Accuracy of projections of new teacher hires

No MAPEs are presented for new teacher hires as there has only been two additional years of historical data for this statistic since it was first included in *Projections of Education Statistics to 2018.*

Table A-10. Estimated equations and model statistics for public elementary and secondary teachers based on data from 1972 through 2012

Dependent variable	Equation[1]	R^2	Breusch-Godfrey Serial Correlation LM test statistic[2]	Time period
1	2	3	4	5
Elementary	ln (RELENRTCH) = 3.91 + 0.05 ln (RSALARY) - 0.25 ln (RSGRNTELENR) (30.964) (3.052) (-8.737)	0.99	15.37 (0.001)	1972 to 2012
Secondary	ln (RSCENRTCH) = 4.15 - 0.23 ln (RSGRNTSCENR) + 0.57 ln (RSCENRPU) + .48 AR (1) (48.958) (-20.885) (5.052) (3.204)	0.98	2.26 (0.323)	1973 to 2012

[1]AR(1) indicates that the model was estimated using least squares with the AR(1) process for correcting for first-order autocorrelation. To estimate the model, it was first transformed into a nonlinear model and then the coefficients were estimated simultaneously by applying a Marquardt nonlinear least squares algorithm to the transformed equation. For a general discussion of the problem of autocorrelation, and the method used to forecast in the presence of autocorrelation, see Judge, G., Hill, W., Griffiths, R., Lutkepohl, H., and Lee, T. (1985). *The Theory and Practice of Econometrics*. New York: John Wiley and Sons, pp. 315–318. Numbers in parentheses are *t*-statistics.

[2]The number in parentheses is the probability of the Chi-Square associated with the Breusch-Godfrey Serial Correlation LM Test. A *p* value greater that 0.05 implies that we do not reject the null hypothesis of no autocorrelation at the 5 percent significance level for a two-tailed test and 10 percent significance level for a one-tailed test (i.e., there is no autocorrelation present). For an explanation of the Breusch-Godfrey Serial Correlation LM test statistic, see Greene, W. (2000). *Econometric Analysis*. New Jersey: Prentice-Hall.
NOTE: R^2 indicates the coefficient of determination.

RELENRTCH = Ratio of public elementary school enrollment to classroom teachers (i.e., pupil/teacher ratio).
RSCENRTCH = Ratio of public secondary school enrollment to classroom teachers (i.e., pupil/teacher ratio).
RSALARY = Average annual teacher salary relative to the overall economy wage in 2000 dollars.
RSGRNTELENR = Ratio of education revenue receipts from state sources per capita to public elementary school enrollment in 2000 dollars.
RSGRNTSCENR = Ratio of education revenue receipts from state sources per capita to public secondary school enrollment in 2000 dollars.
RSCENRPU = Ln of the ratio of enrollment in public secondary schools to the 11- to 18-year-old population.
SOURCE: U.S. Department of Education, National Center for Education Statistics, Elementary and Secondary Teacher Projection Model, 1972 through 2024. (This table was prepared March 2015.)

Table A-11. Percentage distribution of full-time and part-time school teachers, by age, control of school, and teaching status: School year 2011–12

Control of school and teaching status	Percent of total	Total	Age distribution						
			Less than 25 years	25–29 years	30–39 years	40–49 years	50–59 years	60–64 years	65 years or more
1	2	3	4	5	6	7	8	9	10
Public	**100.0** (†)	**100.0**	2.8 (0.24)	12.5 (0.58)	28.9 (0.79)	25.1 (0.75)	23.1 (0.72)	6.1 (0.45)	1.4 (0.20)
Full-time	93.1 (0.46)	100.0	2.9 (0.25)	12.8 (0.60)	29.3 (0.85)	24.9 (0.81)	22.8 (0.76)	6.0 (0.48)	1.3 (0.21)
Part-time	6.9 (0.46)	100.0	1.9 (0.59)	8.7 (2.04)	23.4 (2.92)	27.5 (3.22)	27.0 (2.58)	8.7 (1.80)	2.9 (0.99)
Private	**100.0** (†)	**100.0**	4.6 (1.35)	12.2 (1.26)	24.0 (1.58)	23.8 (1.57)	21.3 (1.57)	9.6 (0.97)	4.6 (0.93)
Full-time	79.4 (2.04)	100.0	4.7 (1.30)	12.5 (1.25)	25.6 (1.82)	23.8 (1.75)	21.1 (1.66)	9.0 (1.07)	3.3 (0.94)
Part-time	20.6 (2.04)	100.0	4.0 (1.90)	10.9 (3.14)	18.2 (4.31)	23.5 (3.39)	22.2 (3.15)	11.8 (3.09)	9.4 (2.60)

† Not applicable.
NOTE: Detail may not sum to totals because of rounding. Standard errors appear in parentheses. The 2011–12 data are the most recent data available.

SOURCE: U.S. Department of Education, National Center for Education Statistics, Schools and Staffing Survey (SASS), "Public School Teacher Questionnaire," 2011–12 and "Private School Teacher Questionnaire," 2011–12; and unpublished tabulations. (This table was prepared February 2014.)

Table A-12. Percentage distribution of full-time and part-time newly hired teachers, by age and control of school: Selected school years, 1987–88 through 2011–12

Control of school and school year	Total	Age distribution						
		Less than 25 years	25–29 years	30–39 years	40–49 years	50–59 years	60–64 years	65 years or more
1	2	3	4	5	6	7	8	9
Public								
1987–88	100.0	17.7 (0.79)	23.7 (1.19)	33.0 (1.43)	21.2 (0.80)	4.0 (0.51)	0.3 ! (0.11)	‡ (†)
1990–91	100.0	17.5 (1.06)	24.0 (1.35)	30.6 (1.33)	21.4 (1.28)	5.6 (0.65)	0.6 (0.18)	‡ (†)
1993–94	100.0	16.2 (0.91)	28.7 (1.15)	24.9 (1.04)	24.6 (1.16)	5.0 (0.63)	0.5 (0.13)	0.2 ! (0.09)
1999–2000	100.0	23.6 (1.28)	22.5 (0.97)	22.2 (1.10)	19.2 (0.90)	11.1 (0.88)	0.9 (0.23)	0.6 ! (0.26)
2003–04	100.0	24.4 (1.21)	19.0 (1.23)	24.6 (1.10)	16.5 (1.18)	13.3 (0.93)	1.5 (0.29)	0.7 ! (0.29)
2007–08	100.0	23.8 (1.75)	24.3 (1.79)	20.4 (1.56)	15.1 (0.94)	13.6 (1.22)	2.3 (0.39)	0.5 ! (0.22)
2011–12	100.0	21.9 (2.46)	23.0 (2.93)	24.1 (2.79)	15.9 (2.79)	10.9 (2.58)	3.5 ! (1.35)	‡ (†)
Private								
1987–88	100.0	17.0 (1.27)	22.8 (1.68)	32.5 (2.17)	17.9 (1.61)	5.3 (1.09)	‡ (†)	1.8 ! (0.77)
1990–91	100.0	15.8 (1.47)	26.3 (1.83)	29.1 (1.86)	21.1 (1.67)	5.6 (0.88)	1.1 ! (0.40)	1.0 ! (0.42)
1993–94	100.0	19.3 (1.13)	24.4 (1.19)	24.9 (1.49)	22.6 (1.18)	7.3 (0.85)	0.9 (0.20)	0.6 ! (0.23)
1999–2000	100.0	18.5 (0.89)	17.2 (0.87)	24.1 (1.24)	22.1 (1.19)	14.0 (1.01)	2.6 (0.39)	1.5 (0.38)
2003–04	100.0	17.1 (1.59)	16.0 (2.13)	23.0 (2.19)	22.8 (3.32)	15.3 (1.77)	3.6 (0.83)	2.1 (0.58)
2007–08	100.0	14.3 (1.26)	18.2 (1.36)	23.2 (1.97)	23.6 (1.92)	14.4 (1.49)	4.2 (0.84)	2.1 ! (0.69)
2011–12	100.0	14.9 ! (5.78)	20.7 (4.29)	27.5 (4.62)	17.4 (4.74)	10.8 (2.51)	5.3 ! (2.32)	‡ (†)

† Not applicable.
! Interpret with caution. The coefficient of variation (CV) for this estimate is between 30 and 50 percent.
‡ Reporting standards not met. The coeffiecient of variation (CV) for this estimate is 50 percent or greater.

NOTE: Detail may not sum to totals because of rounding. Standard errors appear in parentheses. The 2011–12 data are the most recent data available.
SOURCE: U.S. Department of Education, National Center for Education Statistics, Schools and Staffing Survey (SASS), "Public School Teacher Questionnaire," 1987–88 through 2011–12 and "Private School Teacher Questionnaire," 1987–88 through 2011–12; and unpublished tabulations. (This table was prepared February 2014.)

Table A-13. Actual and projected continuation rates of full-time and part-time school teachers, by age and control of school: Selected school years, 1993–94 to 1994–95 through 2024–25 to 2025–26

Control of school and school year	Total		Less than 25 years		25–29 years		30–39 years		40–49 years		50–59 years		60–64 years		65 years or more	
1	2		3		4		5		6		7		8		9	
Public actual																
1993–94 to 1994–95	93.4	(0.36)	96.2	(1.09)	90.0	(1.22)	93.3	(1.03)	96.1	(0.54)	93.7	(0.77)	69.5	(4.79)	65.9	(8.81)
1999–2000 to 2000–01	92.4	(0.38)	95.8	(0.98)	89.3	(7.38)	93.2	(2.76)	94.5	(0.61)	92.9	(4.58)	76.8 !	(29.18)	(‡)	(†)
2003–04 to 2004–05	91.4	(0.55)	94.9	(1.79)	90.1	(1.71)	92.6	(0.93)	94.5	(0.78)	90.8	(0.81)	77.2	(3.00)	70.3	(9.40)
2007–08 to 2008–09	91.8	(0.45)	92.2	(1.95)	89.0	(2.33)	92.4	(1.29)	95.1	(1.06)	92.3	(1.23)	82.8	(3.97)	88.9	(4.26)
2011–12 to 2012–13	92.1	(0.65)	83.1	(9.79)	92.3	(1.39)	94.2	(1.14)	96.7	(0.53)	90.2	(1.38)	81.9	(3.11)	70.2	(12.44)
Public projected																
2012–13 to 2013–14	92.3	(†)	90.1	(†)	91.8	(†)	94.0	(†)	96.7	(†)	90.3	(†)	81.4	(†)	69.6	(†)
2013–14 to 2014–15	92.3	(†)	89.9	(†)	91.8	(†)	93.9	(†)	96.8	(†)	90.2	(†)	81.7	(†)	69.8	(†)
2014–15 to 2015–16	92.2	(†)	89.9	(†)	91.8	(†)	93.9	(†)	96.8	(†)	90.2	(†)	81.5	(†)	68.6	(†)
2015–16 to 2016–17	92.3	(†)	89.9	(†)	91.8	(†)	93.8	(†)	96.7	(†)	90.3	(†)	81.8	(†)	69.5	(†)
2016–17 to 2017–18	92.3	(†)	89.9	(†)	91.8	(†)	93.8	(†)	96.7	(†)	90.3	(†)	81.6	(†)	70.4	(†)
2017–18 to 2018–19	92.3	(†)	90.0	(†)	91.8	(†)	93.9	(†)	96.7	(†)	90.3	(†)	81.5	(†)	70.3	(†)
2018–19 to 2019–20	92.4	(†)	89.9	(†)	91.8	(†)	93.9	(†)	96.6	(†)	90.4	(†)	81.6	(†)	70.8	(†)
2019–20 to 2020–21	92.4	(†)	89.9	(†)	91.8	(†)	94.0	(†)	96.6	(†)	90.4	(†)	81.6	(†)	70.8	(†)
2020–21 to 2021–22	92.5	(†)	89.9	(†)	91.8	(†)	94.0	(†)	96.6	(†)	90.4	(†)	81.6	(†)	71.4	(†)
2021–22 to 2022–23	92.5	(†)	89.9	(†)	91.8	(†)	94.0	(†)	96.6	(†)	90.5	(†)	81.5	(†)	71.1	(†)
2022–23 to 2023–24	92.5	(†)	89.9	(†)	91.8	(†)	94.0	(†)	96.6	(†)	90.5	(†)	81.6	(†)	70.9	(†)
2023–24 to 2024–25	92.5	(†)	89.9	(†)	91.8	(†)	94.0	(†)	96.6	(†)	90.5	(†)	81.6	(†)	70.9	(†)
2024–25 to 2025–26	92.5	(†)	89.9	(†)	91.8	(†)	93.9	(†)	96.6	(†)	90.5	(†)	81.5	(†)	70.5	(†)
Private actual																
1993–94 to 1994–95	88.1	(0.74)	80.0	(4.42)	86.9	(1.64)	85.1	(1.70)	91.3	(1.14)	91.8	(1.52)	86.9	(2.74)	58.1	(8.67)
1999–2000 to 2000–01	83.0	(0.72)	61.7	(4.90)	72.2	(2.76)	80.2	(1.57)	86.1	(1.47)	92.3	(1.00)	78.8	(4.79)	75.2	(5.17)
2003–04 to 2004–05	83.3	(2.06)	75.4	(5.97)	71.7	(3.62)	82.2	(2.30)	86.8	(2.28)	89.2	(9.17)	80.1	(4.15)	79.5	(6.07)
2007–08 to 2008–09	82.2	(1.69)	77.7	(8.33)	71.7	(6.44)	79.1	(3.43)	86.1	(2.92)	86.8	(2.17)	85.2	(4.21)	77.3	(8.23)
Private projected																
2012–13 to 2013–14	81.6	(†)	69.3	(†)	73.2	(†)	80.2	(†)	86.0	(†)	88.1	(†)	80.1	(†)	75.9	(†)
2013–14 to 2014–15	81.5	(†)	69.3	(†)	73.3	(†)	80.2	(†)	86.1	(†)	87.6	(†)	80.0	(†)	75.4	(†)
2014–15 to 2015–16	81.6	(†)	69.4	(†)	73.4	(†)	80.3	(†)	86.0	(†)	87.5	(†)	79.3	(†)	77.8	(†)
2015–16 to 2016–17	81.6	(†)	69.2	(†)	73.4	(†)	80.2	(†)	86.2	(†)	87.9	(†)	80.1	(†)	76.7	(†)
2016–17 to 2017–18	81.5	(†)	69.2	(†)	73.3	(†)	80.1	(†)	85.8	(†)	87.8	(†)	80.4	(†)	76.0	(†)
2017–18 to 2018–19	81.4	(†)	69.1	(†)	73.3	(†)	80.2	(†)	85.9	(†)	87.6	(†)	79.4	(†)	77.4	(†)
2018–19 to 2019–20	81.3	(†)	69.2	(†)	73.2	(†)	80.1	(†)	86.0	(†)	87.7	(†)	79.4	(†)	77.1	(†)
2019–20 to 2020–21	81.3	(†)	69.2	(†)	73.2	(†)	80.2	(†)	86.0	(†)	87.8	(†)	79.9	(†)	76.2	(†)
2020–21 to 2021–22	81.3	(†)	69.2	(†)	73.2	(†)	80.2	(†)	85.9	(†)	87.7	(†)	79.8	(†)	76.9	(†)
2021–22 to 2022–23	81.3	(†)	69.2	(†)	73.2	(†)	80.2	(†)	86.0	(†)	87.6	(†)	79.8	(†)	75.9	(†)
2022–23 to 2023–24	81.2	(†)	69.2	(†)	73.2	(†)	80.2	(†)	85.9	(†)	87.7	(†)	80.1	(†)	75.3	(†)
2023–24 to 2024–25	81.3	(†)	69.2	(†)	73.2	(†)	80.2	(†)	85.9	(†)	87.7	(†)	80.1	(†)	76.0	(†)
2024–25 to 2025–26	81.2	(†)	69.2	(†)	73.2	(†)	80.2	(†)	86.0	(†)	87.7	(†)	79.6	(†)	76.0	(†)

† Not applicable.
! Interpret with caution. The coefficient of variation (CV) for this estimate is between 30 and 50 percent.
‡ Reporting standards not met. The coefficient of variation (CV) for this estimate is 50 percent or greater.
NOTE: The continuation rate for teachers for each control of school (public schools and private schools) is the percentage of teachers in that control who continued teaching in the same control from one year to the next. Standard errors appear in parentheses. The 2012–13 data are the most recent data available for public school teachers and the 2008–09 data are the most recent data available for private school teachers.
SOURCE: U.S. Department of Education, National Center for Education Statistics, Teacher Follow up Survey (TFS), "Public School Teacher Questionnaire," 1994–95 through 2008–09 and "Private School Teacher Questionnaire," 1994–95 through 2012–13; and unpublished tabulations. (This tables was prepared March 2015.)

A.3. HIGH SCHOOL GRADUATES

Projections in this edition

This edition of *Projections of Education Statistics* presents projected trends in the number of high school graduates from 2012–13 to 2024–25. These projections were made using three models:

» The *National High School Graduates Projection Model* was used to project the number of public high school graduates, the number of private high school graduates, and the total number of high school graduates for the nation.

» The *State Public High School Graduates Projection Model* was used to project the number of public high school graduates for individual states and regions.

» The *National Public High School Graduates by Race/Ethnicity Projection Model* was used to project the number of public high school graduates for the nation by race/ethnicity.

Overview of approach

All the high school graduates models first calculated the number of high school graduates as a percentage of grade 12 enrollment based on historical data. Single exponential smoothing was used to project this percentage. The projected percentage was then applied to projections of grade 12 enrollment.

Assumptions underlying this approach

The percentage of 12th-graders who graduate was assumed to remain constant at levels consistent with the most recent rates. This methodology assumes that past trends in factors affecting graduation rates, such as dropouts, migration, and public or private transfers, will continue over the forecast period. No specific assumptions were made regarding the dropout rate, retention rate, or the rate at which alternative credentials are awarded. The combined effect of these proportions is reflected implicitly in the graduate proportion. In addition to student behaviors, the projected number of graduates could be affected by changes in graduation requirements, but this is not considered in the projections in this report.

Procedures used in all three high school graduates projection models

The following steps were used to project the numbers of high school graduates:

Step 1. *For each year in the historic period, express the number of high school graduates as a percentage of grade 12 enrollment.* This value represents the approximate percentage of 12th graders who graduate. For information about the specific historical data and analysis periods used for the National High School Graduates Model, the State Public High School Graduates Model, and the National Public High School Graduates by Race/Ethnicity Model, see the description of the appropriate model, later in this section of appendix A.

Step 2. *Project the percentage of 12th-graders who graduate from step 1.* This percentage was projected using single exponential smoothing with a smoothing constant chosen to minimize the sum of squared forecast errors. Because single exponential smoothing produces a single forecast for all years in the forecast period, the same projected percentage of grade 12 enrollment was used for each year in the forecast period.

Step 3. *Calculate projections of the numbers of high school graduates.* For each year in the forecast period, the projected percentage from step 2 was applied to projections of grade 12 enrollment to yield projections of high school graduates.

National High School Graduates Projection Model

This model was used to project the number of public high school graduates, the number of private high school graduates, and the total number of high school graduates for the nation. Public and private high school graduates were projected separately. The public and private projections were then summed to yield projections of the total number of high school graduates for the nation.

For details of the procedures used to develop the projections, see "Procedures used in all three high school graduates projection models," above.

Data used in the National High School Graduates Projection Model

Public school data on graduates and grade 12 enrollment. Data on public school 12th-grade enrollments and high school graduates from the NCES *Statistics of Public Elementary and Secondary School Systems* for 1972–73 to 1980–81 and the NCES Common Core of Data (CCD) for 1981–82 through 2005–06 were used to develop national projections of public high school. Also, for 2006–07 through 2011–12, data on public school 12th-grade enrollments from the CCD and data on high school graduate from the "State Dropout and Completion Data File" were used.

Private school data on graduates and grade 12 enrollment. Data on private school 12th-grade enrollments for 1989–90 through 2010–11 and high school graduates for 1988–89 through 2009–10 were used to develop national projections of private high school graduates. The data were from the biennial NCES Private School Universe Survey (PSS) from 1989–90 to 2011–12 with data for 12th grade enrollment the same as the year of the survey and the data for high school graduates for the preceding year (i.e. the 2011–12 PSS presents high school graduates for 2010–11). Since the PSS is collected in the fall of odd-numbered years, data for missing years were estimated using data from the PSS. For 12th grade enrollment, estimates for missing years were linear interpolations of the prior year's and succeeding year's actual values. For high school graduates, estimates for the missing years were the interpolations of the high school graduates to estimated 12th grade enrollment percentages for the prior and succeeding years multiplied by the estimated enrollments for the current year.

Public and private school enrollment projections for grade 12. Projections of grade 12 enrollment in public schools and in private schools were used to develop projections of public high school graduates and private high school graduates, respectively. The grade 12 enrollment projections were made using the grade progression method. For more information, see Section A.1. Elementary and Secondary Enrollment, earlier in this appendix.

Accuracy of national high school graduates projections

Mean absolute percentage errors (MAPEs) for projections of graduates from public high schools were calculated using the last 24 editions of *Projections of Education Statistics*, while MAPEs for projections of graduates from private high schools were calculated using the last 13 editions. Table D, below, shows MAPEs for both public and private school graduation projections.

Table D. Mean absolute percentage errors (MAPEs) of projections of high school graduates, by lead time and control of school: *Projections of Education Statistics to 2000* through *Projections of Education Statistics to 2023*

Statistic	Lead time (years)									
	1	2	3	4	5	6	7	8	9	10
Public high school graduates	1.0	1.1	1.8	2.3	2.2	2.6	3.2	4.1	4.7	5.0
Private high school graduates	0.9	1.2	1.6	2.8	4.1	5.2	3.3	5.6	4.6	4.9

NOTE: MAPEs for public high school graduates were calculated from the past 24 editions of *Projections of Education Statistics*, from *Projections of Education Statistics to 2000* through *Projections of Education Statistics to 2023*. MAPEs for private high school graduates were calculated from the past 13 editions of *Projections of Education Statistics*, from *Projections of Education Statistics to 2011* through *Projections of Education Statistics to 2023*. Calculations were made using unrounded numbers. Some data have been revised from previously published figures.
SOURCE: U.S. Department of Education, National Center for Education Statistics, *Projections of Education Statistics*, various issues. (This table was prepared April 2015.)

For more information about MAPEs, see Section A.0. Introduction, earlier in appendix A.

State Public High School Graduates Projection Model

This edition of *Projections of Education Statistics* contains projections of public high school graduates from 2012–13 to 2024–25 for each of the 50 states and the District of Columbia, as well as for each region of the country. The state projections of high school graduates were produced in two stages:

» first, an initial set of projections for each state was produced; and

» second, these initial projections were adjusted to sum to the national public school totals produced by the National High School Graduates Projection Model.

For each region, the high school graduate projections equaled the sum of high school graduate projections for the states within that region.

Initial set of state projections

The same steps used to produce the national projections of high school graduates were used to produce an initial set of projections for each state and the District of Columbia. A separate smoothing constant, chosen to minimize the sum of squared forecast errors, was used to calculate the projected percentage of 12th grade enrollment for each jurisdiction.

For details on the steps used to develop the initial sets of projections, see "Procedures used in all three high school graduate projection models," earlier in this section of appendix A.

Adjustments to the state projections

The initial projections of state public high school graduates were adjusted to sum to the national projections of public high school graduates shown in table 9 on page 49. This was done through the use of ratio adjustments in which all the states' high school graduate projections were multiplied by the ratio of the national public high school graduate projection to the sum of the state public high school graduate projections.

Data used in the State Public High School Graduates Projection Model

Public school data on graduates and grade 12 enrollment at the state level. State-level data on public school 12th-grade enrollments and high school graduates from the NCES *Statistics of Public Elementary and Secondary School Systems* for 1972–73 to 1980–81 and the NCES Common Core of Data (CCD) for 1981–82 through 2005–06 were used to develop stat-level projections of public high school. Also, for 2006–07 through 2011–12, state-level data on public school 12th-grade enrollments from the CCD and state-level data on high school graduate from the "State Dropout and Completion Data File" were used.

Public school projections for grade 12 enrollment at the state level. State-level projections of grade 12 enrollment in public schools were used to develop the state-level projections of public high school graduates. The grade 12 enrollment projections were made using the grade progression method. For more information, see Section A.1. Elementary and Secondary Enrollment, earlier in this appendix.

Accuracy of state public high school graduate projections

Mean absolute percentage errors (MAPEs) for projections of the number of public high school graduates by state were calculated using the last 19 editions of *Projections of Education Statistics*. Table A-14 on page 97 shows MAPEs for the number of high school graduates by state.

National Public High School Graduates by Race/Ethnicity Projection Model

The projections of public high school graduates by race/ethnicity were produced in two stages:

>» first, an initial set of projections for each racial/ethnic group was produced; and

>» second, these initial projections were adjusted to sum to the national public school totals produced by the National High School Graduates Projection Model.

Initial set of projections by race/ethnicity

The same steps used to produce the national projections of high school graduates were used to produce an initial set of projections for each of the following five racial/ethnic groups: White, Black, Hispanic, Asian/Pacific Islander, and American Indian/Alaska Native. For example, the number of White public high school graduates was projected as a percentage of White grade 12 enrollment in public schools. A separate smoothing constant, chosen to minimize the sum of squared forecast errors, was used to calculate the projected percentage of 12th-grade enrollment for each racial/ethnic group. This is the second edition of *Projections of Education Statistics* to include projections for high school graduates of Two or more races. To produce an initial set of projections for this racial/ethnic group, the 2011–12 ratio of 12th-grade enrollment to high school graduates of the group were multiplied by the 12th-grade enrollment projections of the group from table 6.

Adjustments to the projections by race/ethnicity

The projections of public high school graduates by race/ethnicity were adjusted to sum to the national projections of public high school graduates shown in table 9 on page 49. This was done through the use of ratio adjustments in which all high school graduate projections by race/ethnicity were multiplied by the ratio of the national high school graduate projection to the sum of the high school projections by race/ethnicity.

Data and imputations used in the Public High School Graduates by Race/Ethnicity Projection Model

Public school data on graduates and grade 12 enrollment by race/ethnicity. Data on public school 12th-grade enrollments and high school graduates by race/ethnicity from the NCES *Statistics of Public Elementary and Secondary School Systems* for 1972–73 to 1980–81 and the NCES Common Core of Data (CCD) for 1981–82 through 2005–06 were used to develop national projections of public high school. Also, for 2006–07 through 2011–12, data on public school 12th-grade enrollments by race/ethnicity from the CCD and data on high school graduate by race/ethnicity from the "State Dropout and Completion Data File" were used. In those instances where states did not report their high school graduate data by race/ethnicity, the state-level data had to be examined and some imputations made. For example, in 1994, Arizona did not report high school graduate data by race/ethnicity. It did, however, report grade 12 enrollment numbers by race/ethnicity for that year. So, to impute the high school graduate numbers by race/ethnicity for that year, Arizona's total number of high school graduates for 1994 was multiplied by the state's 1994 racial/ethnic distribution for grade 12 enrollment.

Public enrollment projections for grade 12 by race/ethnicity. Projections of grade 12 enrollment in public schools by race/ethnicity were used to develop the projections of public high school graduates by race/ethnicity. The grade 12 enrollment projections were made using the grade progression method. For more information, see Section A.1. Elementary and Secondary Enrollment, earlier in this appendix.

Accuracy of enrollment projections by race/ethnicity

Mean absolute percentage errors (MAPEs) for projections of the number of public high school graduates by race/ethnicity were calculated using the last five editions of *Projections of Education Statistic*. Table E, below, shows MAPEs for public high school graduates by race/ethnicity projections.

Table E. Mean absolute percentage errors (MAPEs) of projections of public high school graduates, by lead time and race/ethnicity: *Projections of Education Statistics to 2000* through *Projections of Education Statistics to 2023*

Statistic	Lead time (years)									
	1	2	3	4	5	6	7	8	9	10
Total high school graduates	**1.0**	**1.1**	**1.8**	**2.3**	**2.2**	**2.6**	**3.2**	**4.1**	**4.7**	**5.0**
White	1.2	0.5	1.0	1.6	2.9	—	—	—	—	—
Black or African American	2.7	3.1	5.6	5.5	7.6	—	—	—	—	—
Hispanic or Latino	4.1	4.7	10.4	15.3	14.4	—	—	—	—	—
Asian/Hawaiian or other Pacific Islander	1.7	2.6	1.7	2.2	0.7	—	—	—	—	—
American Indian/Alaska Native	2.3	1.7	4.9	8.9	10.6	—	—	—	—	—

— Not available.
NOTE: MAPEs for public high school graduates were calculated from the past 24 editions of *Projections of Education Statistics*, from *Projections of Education Statistics to 2000* through *Projections of Education Statistics to 2023*. MAPEs for public high school graduates by race/ethnicity were calculated using the last 5 editions of *Projections of Education Statistics*, from *Projections of Education Statistics to 2019* through *Projections of Education Statistics to 2023*. Calculations were made using unrounded numbers. Some data have been revised from previously published figures.
SOURCE: U.S. Department of Education, National Center for Education Statistics, *Projections of Education Statistics*, various issues. (This table was prepared April 2015.)

Table A-14. Mean absolute percentage errors (MAPEs) for the projected number of high school graduates in public schools, by lead time, region, and state: *Projections of Education Statistics to 2000* through *Projections of Education Statistics to 2023*

Region and state	Lead time (years)									
	1	2	3	4	5	6	7	8	9	10
1	2	3	4	5	6	7	8	9	10	11
United States	**1.0**	**1.1**	**1.8**	**2.3**	**2.2**	**2.6**	**3.2**	**4.1**	**4.7**	**5.0**
Region										
Northeast	1.2	1.6	1.8	2.4	2.6	3.1	3.5	3.9	4.9	5.2
Midwest	1.2	1.1	1.5	1.7	2.2	2.6	2.5	2.8	3.1	3.0
South	1.2	1.6	2.7	3.2	3.3	4.1	4.5	5.7	6.7	7.6
West	1.8	2.0	2.9	3.7	3.1	3.2	2.6	2.5	3.1	3.4
State										
Alabama	3.4	3.2	2.9	5.4	5.9	7.0	7.8	8.0	8.8	9.5
Alaska	2.8	2.2	2.9	4.6	5.1	6.2	7.1	7.3	7.2	7.2
Arizona	7.8	8.2	11.0	13.3	11.8	12.0	14.1	9.9	11.2	10.8
Arkansas	1.4	1.6	2.1	2.5	2.7	2.2	2.3	2.9	2.9	3.7
California	2.5	2.6	3.6	4.4	4.6	4.8	4.8	4.0	4.7	5.0
Colorado	1.8	2.3	2.8	2.1	2.6	2.5	2.8	3.6	4.4	4.2
Connecticut	2.9	2.6	2.4	3.1	3.4	3.7	4.4	4.0	5.2	4.9
Delaware	2.2	2.6	3.5	4.7	3.9	4.6	4.9	5.9	6.8	7.5
District of Columbia	7.1	8.5	11.7	13.7	12.9	15.4	14.6	17.1	17.5	19.6
Florida	2.1	4.1	5.6	4.7	4.4	4.7	5.7	7.0	8.6	7.9
Georgia	2.1	2.8	3.9	5.8	7.2	8.2	8.9	9.4	9.9	9.7
Hawaii	3.6	4.0	4.8	5.6	8.5	9.2	11.2	12.3	14.0	15.2
Idaho	1.0	1.3	1.6	1.9	2.2	2.8	3.2	4.1	5.2	5.8
Illinois	2.7	2.3	3.2	3.7	3.9	3.5	5.4	4.3	5.2	6.4
Indiana	1.6	1.9	1.9	2.4	2.4	2.9	3.6	4.1	4.5	4.8
Iowa	1.5	1.3	2.0	2.1	2.6	2.7	2.6	2.5	2.5	2.8
Kansas	1.3	1.9	2.5	3.1	4.1	5.0	5.6	5.9	6.5	6.4
Kentucky	2.4	3.4	3.6	4.6	5.3	6.4	7.4	7.8	7.4	9.4
Louisiana	2.1	3.0	4.7	6.2	7.1	6.1	5.6	3.8	3.4	5.2
Maine	2.8	3.9	4.1	5.1	5.8	7.1	8.1	8.9	10.5	11.9
Maryland	1.4	1.3	1.8	1.8	2.3	2.3	2.7	2.9	3.3	4.4
Massachusetts	1.0	1.6	2.4	3.0	3.3	3.5	3.9	3.5	3.4	3.4
Michigan	3.2	3.8	5.0	5.8	5.7	5.9	7.2	8.3	9.1	10.4
Minnesota	2.1	1.2	1.5	1.8	2.1	2.2	2.8	3.5	4.1	4.4
Mississippi	1.7	1.7	2.3	2.6	3.4	4.1	4.2	4.7	5.2	5.1
Missouri	1.0	1.4	2.5	3.0	3.4	4.1	4.7	5.3	6.2	6.4
Montana	0.9	1.0	1.5	1.6	2.5	3.6	4.5	6.0	7.3	8.6
Nebraska	2.2	2.8	2.7	2.6	2.9	2.9	2.5	2.5	2.5	2.8
Nevada	5.6	7.6	9.5	9.7	8.5	9.1	8.7	10.2	11.8	12.8
New Hampshire	1.2	2.1	2.5	3.1	3.7	4.6	5.3	6.4	7.0	7.0
New Jersey	2.1	3.7	4.3	4.1	4.4	5.5	6.5	7.8	8.5	9.4
New Mexico	3.2	3.1	4.6	4.7	6.5	6.5	6.9	7.7	9.7	10.0
New York	1.9	3.0	3.5	5.0	5.9	6.9	7.6	8.4	9.5	9.6
North Carolina	2.3	2.7	3.7	4.1	4.9	5.2	5.3	6.5	7.5	9.6
North Dakota	1.3	1.8	2.3	2.9	2.9	3.1	3.7	4.0	5.1	6.9
Ohio	3.3	3.1	3.6	3.1	3.4	3.5	3.1	3.7	4.2	5.8
Oklahoma	1.2	1.4	1.8	1.6	2.2	2.8	3.3	3.4	3.8	4.1
Oregon	1.8	2.1	2.9	4.1	4.6	5.3	6.0	6.8	7.4	6.8
Pennsylvania	1.6	2.7	3.3	3.3	2.7	2.4	2.5	3.1	3.7	3.9
Rhode Island	1.3	1.4	2.3	1.8	2.0	3.0	4.1	5.3	5.7	5.6
South Carolina	1.8	3.5	3.2	5.3	6.4	7.6	7.8	8.1	8.4	8.7
South Dakota	2.5	3.0	3.4	5.2	5.2	7.6	8.6	9.8	11.0	12.5	14.1
Tennessee	4.5	6.2	8.6	11.7	14.0	15.5	16.0	16.3	15.8	14.6
Texas	2.7	3.6	5.0	6.2	6.1	7.0	8.1	9.9	11.3	13.1
Utah	4.7	5.6	5.7	6.2	5.3	4.7	5.0	5.0	3.3	2.1
Vermont	2.0	2.4	3.8	5.0	6.7	6.9	7.5	8.4	9.5	10.0
Virginia	1.5	2.1	2.9	4.1	4.6	4.5	3.8	3.4	3.9	4.5
Washington	1.9	2.0	3.0	2.7	2.9	3.5	3.7	4.1	5.1	5.2
West Virginia	0.7	1.1	1.8	1.9	2.2	3.2	3.5	4.8	5.3	5.6
Wisconsin	1.3	1.5	2.5	2.9	3.2	3.9	4.4	5.2	5.3	5.4
Wyoming	1.6	2.0	2.6	3.1	4.1	5.7	7.5	8.5	10.0	10.8

NOTE: Mean absolute percentage error (MAPE) is the average value over past projections of the absolute values of errors expressed in percentage terms. National MAPEs for public high school graduates were calculated using the last 24 editions of *Projections of Education Statistics*, from *Projections of Education Statistics to 2000* through *Projections of Education Statistics to 2023*. State MAPEs were calculated using the last 19 editions of *Projections of Education Statistics*, from *Projections of Education Statistics to 2005* through *Projections of Education Statistics to 2023*. Calculations were made using unrounded numbers. Some data have been revised from previously published figures.

SOURCE: U.S. Department of Education, National Center for Education Statistics, *Projections of Education Statistics*, various issues. (This table was prepared March 2015.)

A.4. EXPENDITURES FOR PUBLIC ELEMENTARY AND SECONDARY EDUCATION

Projections in this edition

This edition of *Projections of Education Statistics* presents projections of total current expenditures for public elementary and secondary education, current expenditures per pupil in fall enrollment, and current expenditures per pupil in average daily attendance for 2012–13 through 2024–25.

As the source of the elementary and secondary private school data, the NCES Private School Universe Survey, does not collect data for current expenditures, there are no projections for private school current expenditures.

Overview of approach

Theoretical and empirical background

The Public Elementary and Secondary Education Current Expenditure Projection Model used in this report is based on the theoretical and empirical literature on the demand for local public services such as education.[1] Specifically, it is based on a type of model that has been called a median voter model. In brief, a median voter model posits that spending for each public good in the community (in this case, spending for education) reflects the preferences of the "median voter" in the community. This individual is identified as the voter in the community with the median income and median property value. The amount of spending in the community reflects the price of education facing the voter with the median income, as well as his income and tastes. There are competing models in which the level of spending reflects the choices of others in the community, such as government officials.

In a median voter model, the demand for education expenditures is typically linked to four different types of independent variables: (1) measures of the income of the median voter; (2) measures of intergovernmental aid for education going indirectly to the median voter; (3) measures of the price to the median voter of providing one more dollar of education expenditures per pupil; and (4) any other variables that may affect one's tastes for education. The Public Elementary and Secondary Education Current Expenditure Projection Model contains independent variables of the first two types. It uses multiple linear regression analysis to define the relationships between these independent variables and current expenditures (the dependent variable).

Elementary and Secondary Education Current Expenditure Projection Model

Projections for current expenditures per pupil in fall enrollment were produced first. These projections were then used in calculating total expenditures and expenditures per pupil in average daily attendance.

Steps used to project current expenditures for public elementary and secondary education

Step 1. *Produce projections of education revenue from state sources.* The equation for education revenue included an AR(1) term for correcting for autocorrelation and the following independent variables:

» disposable income per capita in constant dollars; and

» the ratio of fall enrollment to the population.

To estimate the model, it was first transformed into a nonlinear model and then the coefficients were estimated simultaneously by applying a Marquardt nonlinear least squares algorithm to the transformed equation.

Step 2. *Produce projections of current expenditures per pupil in fall enrollment.* The equation for current expenditures per pupil for fall enrollment included an AR(1) term for correcting for autocorrelation and the following independent variables:

» disposable income per capita in constant dollars; and

» education revenue from state sources per capita in constant dollars. This variable was projected in step 1.

---

[1] For a discussion of the theory together with a review of some of the older literature, see Inman (1979). More recent empirical work includes Gamkhar and Oates (1996) and Mitias and Turnbull (2001).

To estimate the models, they were first transformed into nonlinear models and then the coefficients were estimated simultaneously by applying a Marquardt nonlinear least squares algorithm to the transformed equation.

For details on the equations used in steps 1 and 2, the data used to estimate these equations, and their results, see "Data and equations used for projections of current expenditures for public elementary and secondary education," below.

Step 3. *Produce projections of total current expenditures.* Projections of total current expenditures were made by multiplying the projections for current expenditures per pupil in fall enrollment by projections for fall enrollment.

Step 4. *Produce projections of current expenditures per pupil in average daily attendance.* The projections for total current expenditures were divided by projections for average daily attendance to produce projections of current expenditures per pupil in average daily attendance.

All the projections were developed in 1982–84 dollars and then placed in 2013–14 dollars using the projections of the Consumer Price Index. Current-dollar projections were produced by multiplying the constant-dollar projections by projections for the Consumer Price Index. The Consumer Price Index and the other economic variables used in calculating the projections presented in this report were placed in school year terms rather than calendar year terms.

Data and equations used for projections of current expenditures for public elementary and secondary education

Data used to estimate the equations for revenue from state sources and current expenditures per pupil. The following data for the period from 1973–74 to 2010–11 were used to estimate the equations:

» Current expenditures and revenues from state sources—For 1973–74 and 1975–76, the current expenditures data came from *Statistics of State School Systems*, published by NCES. For 1974–75 and 1976–77, the current expenditures data came from *Revenues and Expenditures for Public Elementary and Secondary Education*, also published by NCES. For 1977–78 through 2011–12, these data came from the NCES Common Core of Data (CCD) and unpublished data. For most years, the sources for the past values of revenue from state sources were identical to the sources for current expenditures.

» Disposable personal income per capita—Disposable personal income data from the Bureau of Economic Analysis were divided by population data from the U.S. Census Bureau.

» The ratio of fall enrollment to population data—Fall enrollment data from the CCD were divided by population data from the U.S. Census Bureau.

Estimated equations and model statistics for revenue from state sources and current expenditures per pupil. For the results of the equations, see table A-15 on page 101. In each equation, the independent variables affect the dependent variable in the expected way. In the revenues from state sources equation:

» All other things being equal, as disposable income per capita increases so does local governments' education revenue from state sources per capita; and

» As enrollment increases relative to the population, so does the local governments' education revenue from state sources per capita.

» In the current expenditures per pupil equation: All other things being equal, as disposable income per capita increases, so does current expenditures per pupil; and

» As local governments' education revenue from state sources per capita increases, so does current expenditures per pupil.

Projections for economic variables. Projections for economic variables, including disposable income and the Consumer Price Index, were from the "U.S. Quarterly Model: 1st Quarter 2015 Short-Term Baseline Projections" from the economic consulting firm, IHS Global Inc. (see supplemental table B-6). This set of projections was IHS Global Inc.'s most recent set at the time the education projections in this report were produced. The values of all the variables from IHS Global Inc. were placed in school-year terms. The school-year numbers were calculated by taking the average of the last two quarters of one year and the first two quarters of the next year.

Projections for fall enrollment. The projections for fall enrollment are those presented in section 1 of this publication. The methodology for these projections is presented in Section A.1. Elementary and Secondary Enrollment, earlier in this appendix.

Projections for population. Population estimates for 1973 to 2013 and population projections for 2014 to 2024 from the U.S. Census Bureau were used to develop the public school current expenditure projections. The set of population projections used in this year's *Projections of Education Statistics* are the Census Bureau's 2012 National Population Projections (December 2012).

Historical data for average daily attendance. For 1973–74 and 1975–76, these data came from *Statistics of State School Systems*, published by NCES. For 1974–75 and 1976–77, the current expenditures data came from *Revenues and Expenditures for Public Elementary and Secondary Education*, also published by NCES. For 1977–78 through 2011–12, these data came from the CCD and unpublished NCES data.

Projections for average daily attendance. These projections were made by multiplying the projections for enrollment by the average value of the ratios of average daily attendance to enrollment from 1993–94 to 2011–12; this average value was approximately 0.93.

Accuracy of projections

Mean absolute percentage errors (MAPEs) for projections of current expenditures for public elementary and secondary education were calculated using the last 24 editions of *Projections of Education Statistics*. Table F, below, shows the MAPEs for projections of current expenditures.

Table F. Mean absolute percentage errors (MAPEs) of projections for total and per pupil current expenditures for public elementary and secondary education, by lead time: *Projections of Education Statistics to 1984–85* **through** *Projections of Education Statistics to 2023*

	Lead time (years)									
Statistic	1	2	3	4	5	6	7	8	9	10
Total current expenditures	1.6	2.4	2.2	2.1	2.5	3.9	4.9	5.0	4.7	4.5
Current expenditures per pupil in fall enrollment	1.6	2.3	2.2	2.1	2.6	3.8	4.9	5.3	5.7	5.7

NOTE: Expenditures were in constant dollars based on the Consumer Price Index for all urban consumers, Bureau of Labor Statistics, U.S. Department of Labor. MAPEs for current expenditures were calculated using projections from the last 24 editions of *Projections of Education Statistics*, from *Projections of Education Statistics to 1997–98* through *Projections of Education Statistics to 2023*, excluding *Projections of Education Statistics to 2012* which did not include projections of current expenditures. Calculations were made using unrounded numbers. Some data have been revised from previously published figures.
SOURCE: U.S. Department of Education, National Center for Education Statistics, *Projections of Education Statistics*, various issues. (This table was prepared April 2015.)

For more information about MAPEs, see Section A.0. Introduction, earlier in this appendix.

Table A-15. Estimated equations and model statistics for current expenditures per pupil in fall enrollment for public elementary and secondary schools, and education revenue from state sources per capita based on data from 1973–74 to 2011–12

Dependent variable	Equation[1]				R^2	Breusch-Godfrey Serial Correlation LM test statistic[2]	Time period
1	2				3	4	5
Current expenditures per pupil..................	ln(CUREXP) =	1.95 + (0.996)	0.52ln(PCI) + (2.503)	0.18ln(SGRANT) + (1.951)	0.94AR(1) (24.407)	0.996	5.75 (0.057)	1973–74 to 2011–12
Education revenue from state sources per capita...	ln(SGRNT) =	7.03 + (1.729)	0.97ln(PCI) + (7.158)	1.28ln(ENRPOP) + (2.892)	0.81AR(1) (10.265)	0.985	1.31 (0.520)	1973–74 to 2011–12

[1]AR(1) indicates that the model was estimated using least squares with the AR(1) process for correcting for first-order autocorrelation. To estimate the model, it was first transformed into a nonlinear model and then the coefficients were estimated simultaneously by applying a Marquardt nonlinear least squares algorithm to the transformed equation. For a general discussion of the problem of autocorrelation, and the method used to forecast in the presence of autocorrelation, see Judge, G., Hill, W., Griffiths, R., Lutkepohl, H., and Lee, T. (1985). *The Theory and Practice of Econometrics*. New York: John Wiley and Sons, pp. 315–318. Numbers in parentheses are *t*-statistics.

[2]The number in parentheses is the probability of the Chi-Square associated with the Breusch-Godfrey Serial Correlation LM Test. A *p* value greater that 0.05 implies that we do not reject the null hypothesis of no autocorrelation at the 5 percent significance level for a two-tailed test and 10 percent significance level for a one-tailed test (i.e., there is no autocorrelation present). For an explanation of the Breusch-Godfrey Serial Correlation LM test statistic, see Greene, W. (2000). *Econometric Analysis*. New Jersey: Prentice-Hall.

NOTE: R^2 indicates the coefficient of determination.

CUREXP = Current expenditures of public elementary and secondary schools per pupil in fall enrollment in constant 1982–84 dollars.

SGRANT = Local governments' education revenue from state sources, per capita, in constant 1982–84 dollars.

PCI = Disposable income per capita in constant 2000 chained dollars.

ENRPOP = Ratio of fall enrollment to the population.

SOURCE: U.S. Department of Education, National Center for Education Statistics, Public Elementary and Secondary Education Current Expenditure Projection Model, 1973–74 through 2024–25. (This table was prepared March 2015.)

A.5. ENROLLMENT IN DEGREE-GRANTING POSTSECONDARY INSTITUTIONS

Projections in this edition

This edition of *Projections of Education Statistics* presents projections of enrollment in degree-granting postsecondary institutions for fall 2014 through fall 2024. Three different models were used to produce these enrollment projections:

» The *Enrollment in Degree-Granting Institutions Projection Model* produced projections of enrollments by attendance status, level of student, level of institution, control of institution, sex, and age. It also produced projections of full-time-equivalent enrollments by level of student, level of institution, and control of institution.

» The *Enrollment in Degree-Granting Institutions by Race/Ethnicity Projection Model* produced projections of enrollments by race/ethnicity.

» The *First-Time Freshmen Projection Model* produced projections of enrollments of first-time freshmen by sex.

Overview of approach

Basic features of the three degree-granting enrollment projection models

The Enrollment in Degree-Granting Institutions Projection Model is the primary model for projecting enrollment in degree-granting postsecondary institutions. For this model, enrollment rates by attendance status and sex are projected for various age categories using either the pooled seemingly unrelated regression method or the pooled seemingly unrelated regression method with a first-order autocorrelation correction. These rates are applied to projections of populations of the same sex and age to produce projections of enrollment by attendance status, sex, and age. To project enrollments by level of student, level of institution, and control of institution, rates for these characteristics are projected using single exponential smoothing and applied to enrollment projections previously produced by the model.

The Enrollment in Degree-Granting Institutions by Race/Ethnicity Projection Model takes an approach similar to that of the Enrollment in Degree-Granting Institutions Projection Model. Enrollment rates by attendance status, sex, and race/ethnicity are projected for the age categories using either the pooled seemingly unrelated regression method or the pooled seemingly unrelated regression method with a first-order autocorrelation correction. The resulting rates are iteratively corrected to ensure consistency with those projected by the Enrollment in Degree-Granting Institutions Projection Model. The adjusted rates are then applied to projections of populations of the same sex, age, and race/ethnicity.

The First-Time Freshmen Enrollment in Degree-Granting Institutions Projection Model uses single exponential smoothing to project the ratio of freshmen enrollment to undergraduate enrollment separately for males and for females. It then applies the projected ratios to the projections of undergraduate enrollment by sex that were produced by the Enrollment in Degree-Granting Institutions Projection Model.

The Enrollment in Degree-Granting Institutions Projection Model

The Enrollment in Degree-Granting Institutions Projection Model produces projections of enrollment counts by six levels of detail, as well as projections of full-time-equivalent enrollments by level of student, level of institution, and control of institution.

Steps used in the Enrollment in Degree-Granting Institutions Projection Model

Step 1. *Adjust age-specific enrollment counts from the U.S. Census Bureau to make them agree with the more highly aggregated NCES enrollment counts that do not include age.* The Enrollment in Degree-Granting Institutions Projection Model projects enrollments by six levels of detail: attendance status, level of student, level of institution, control of institution, sex, and age. While NCES does produce enrollment counts by the first five levels of detail, it does not produce data by the sixth level of detail, age, every year. However, the U.S. Census Bureau does produce annual age-specific enrollment counts.

In step 1, the age distributions from the Census Bureau counts for 1980 to 2013 were applied to the NCES counts to produce a set of enrollment data that breaks enrollments down by age while being consistent with NCES counts. Specifically, the most detailed level of Census Bureau data (by attendance status, level of student, level of institution, control of institution, sex, and age) was iteratively changed using proportions based on the more highly aggregated NCES enrollment numbers to ensure that all sums across this most detailed level of Census enrollment data equaled the more highly aggregated NCES enrollment totals that did not include age.

Step 2. *Calculate enrollment rates by attendance status, sex, and age category.* The enrollment data were broken up into 14 age categories, with separate age categories for individual ages 14 through 24 as well as for the age groups 25 to 29, 30 to 34, and 35 and over. For each of the 14 age categories, 4 enrollment rates were calculated—part-time male, full-time male, part-time female, and full-time female—resulting in a total of 56 enrollment rates. Each of the 56 enrollment rates was calculated by dividing the enrollment count for that combination of attendance status, sex, and age category by the total population for the corresponding combination of sex and age category. For each combination of attendance and sex, the enrollment rate for the oldest age category was calculated by dividing the enrollment count for those 35 and over by the total population for those 35 to 44.

Step 3. *Produce projections of enrollment rates by attendance status, sex, and age category.* Enrollment rates for most of the age groups were projected using multiple linear regression. However, because enrollment in degree-granting postsecondary institutions is negligible for ages 14, 15, and 16, these ages were not included in the multiple linear regression models. Instead, projections for individual ages 14, 15, and 16 were produced by double exponential smoothing.

The following 11 age categories were modeled: individual ages 17 through 24 and age groups 25 to 29, 30 to 34, and 35 and over. For each of these age categories, enrollment rates by attendance status and sex were produced using four pooled time-series models—one for each combination of attendance status and sex. Each model was pooled across age categories. Each equation contained two independent variables, which were measures of

» disposable income; and

» the unemployment rate.

Either the pooled seemingly unrelated regression method or the pooled seemingly unrelated regression method with a first-order autocorrelation correction was used to estimate each equation.

For more details on the equations used in step 3, the data used to estimate these equations, and their results, see tables A-16 through A-18 on pages 109–111.

Step 4. *Produce projections of enrollments by attendance status, sex, and age category.* For each combination of attendance status, sex, and age category, enrollment projections were produced by multiplying the projected enrollment rate for that combination by projections of the total population with the corresponding combination of sex and age category.

Step 5. *Add two additional levels of detail—level of student and level of institution—to the projected enrollments by attendance status, sex, and age category.* For this step, the 14 age categories used in the previous steps were collapsed into the following 8 categories: ages 14 to 16, 17, 18 and 19, 20 and 21, 22 to 24, 25 to 29, 30 to 34, and 35 and over. Step 5 can be broken into three parts:

First, the historic data were used to calculate the percentage distribution of enrollment by level of student and level of institution for each combination of attendance status, sex, and age category. Because it was assumed that there was no enrollment in 2-year institutions at the postbaccalaureate level, three combinations of student level and institution type were used: undergraduates at 4-year institutions, undergraduates at 2-year institutions, and postbaccalaureate students at 4-year institutions.

Second, for each combination of attendance status, sex, and age category, the percentage distribution by level of student and level of institution was projected using single exponential smoothing. A separate smoothing constant, chosen to minimize the sum of squared forecast errors, was used in each case. The percentages were then adjusted so the sum of the categories by attendance status, level of student, level of institution, sex, and age category would equal 100 percent.

For the projected percentage distributions from step 5 and the actual 2013 distributions, see tables A-19 and A-20 on pages 112 and 113.

Third, the projected distributions by level of student and type of institution were applied to the projected enrollments by attendance status, sex, and age category from step 4 to obtain the enrollment projections by attendance status, level of student, level of institution, sex, and age category.

Step 6. *Add the sixth level of detail—control of institutions—to the projected enrollments in degree-granting postsecondary institutions.* In this step, the data on enrollment by age category were not used. Control of institutions was added in the following manner:

First, the historic data were used to calculate the percentage of enrollment in public institutions for each combination of attendance status, level of student, level of institution, and sex.

Second, the percentages of enrollment in public institutions were projected using single exponential smoothing. A separate smoothing constant, chosen to minimize the sum of squared forecast errors, was used for each percentage.

For the projected percentages from step 6 and the actual 2013 percentages, see table A-21 on page 114.

Third, the projected percentages were applied to the projected enrollments in each corresponding enrollment combination to obtain projections for public institutions by attendance status, level of student, level of institution, and sex.

Fourth, the projected enrollments for public institutions were subtracted from the total to produce the projected enrollments for private institutions.

Step 7. *Produce projections of full-time-equivalent enrollment by level of student, level of institution, and control of institution.* Full-time-equivalent enrollment represents total full-time and part-time enrollment as if it were enrollment on a full-time basis. It equals the sum of full-time enrollment plus the full-time-equivalent of part-time enrollment. Full-time-equivalent enrollment projections were produced in the following manner:

First, for each combination of level of student, level of institution, and control of institution, the historic data were used to calculate the full-time-equivalent of part-time enrollment as a percentage of part-time enrollment.

Second, for each combination of level of student, level of institution, and control of institution, the full-time equivalent of part-time enrollment as a percentage of part-time enrollment was projected using single exponential smoothing. A separate smoothing constant, chosen to minimize the sum of squared forecast errors, was used for each percentage.

Third, for each combination of level of student, level of institution, and control of institution, the projected percentages were applied to the projections of part-time enrollment to project the full-time equivalent of the part-time enrollment.

Fourth, the projections of full-time equivalents of part-time enrollment were added to projections of full-time enrollment to obtain projections of full-time-equivalent enrollment.

Data and equation results for the Enrollment in Degree-Granting Institutions Projection Model

Enrollment data for degree-granting postsecondary institutions. Enrollment data for 1981 to 2013 by attendance status, level of student, level of institution, control of institution, and sex came from the NCES Integrated Postsecondary Education Data System (IPEDS). These are universe counts. The U.S. Census Bureau was the source for enrollment estimates for 1981 to 2013 by the characteristics listed above, as well as age of student.

Population data and projections. Population counts for 1980 to 2013 came from the U.S. Census Bureau. Population projections for 2014 to 2024 are the Census Bureau's 2012 National Population Projections of the population by sex and age (December 2012), ratio-adjusted to line up with the most recent historical estimates. For more information, see Section A.0. Introduction, earlier in this appendix.

Projections for economic variables. The economic variables used in developing these projections were from the "U.S. Quarterly Model: 1st Quarter 2015 Short-Term Baseline Projections" from the economic consulting firm, IHS Global Inc. This set of projections was IHS Global Inc.'s most recent set at the time the education projections in this report were produced.

Data and results for the equations. The following details for the equations are shown on pages 109–114:

» Table A-16 shows enrollment rates by sex, attendance status, and age for fall 2013 and projected enrollment rates for fall 2019 and fall 2024.

» Table A-17 shows the estimated equations and model statistics used to project enrollments for men by attendance status, and table A-18 shows the estimated equations and model statistics used to project enrollment rates for women by attendance status. The particular equations shown were selected on the basis of their statistical properties, such as coefficients of determination (R^2s), the *t*-statistics of the coefficients, the Durbin-Watson statistic, the Breusch-Godfrey Serial Correlation LM test statistic, and residual plots.

» Table A-19 shows actual and projected percentage distributions of full-time students, and table A-20 shows actual and projected percentage distributions of part-time students.

» Table A-21 shows actual and projected data for enrollment in public degree-granting institutions as a percentage of total enrollment by sex, attendance status, student level, and level of institution.

Accuracy of projections for the Enrollment in Degree-Granting Institutions Projection Model

Mean absolute percentage errors (MAPEs) for enrollment in degree-granting institutions were calculated using the last 17 editions of *Projections of Education Statistics*. Table G, below, shows MAPEs for key projections of the Enrollment in Degree-Granting Institutions Model.

Table G. **Mean absolute percentage errors (MAPEs) of projected enrollment in degree-granting postsecondary institutions, by lead time, sex, and level of institution:** *Projections of Education Statistics to 2007* through *Projections of Education Statistics to 2023*

Statistic	Lead time (years)									
	1	2	3	4	5	6	7	8	9	10
Total enrollment	**1.6**	**2.6**	**3.8**	**4.7**	**5.4**	**6.3**	**7.4**	**8.5**	**10.7**	**12.4**
Males	1.6	3.0	4.1	5.2	6.3	7.3	8.5	9.7	11.5	13.0
Females	1.7	2.7	4.0	4.5	4.8	5.5	6.7	7.7	10.1	11.9
4-year institutions	1.5	2.9	4.1	5.4	6.5	7.6	9.0	10.3	12.6	14.5
2-year institutions	2.5	3.5	5.0	5.0	4.9	4.6	5.1	6.0	8.1	9.0

NOTE: MAPEs for degree-granting postsecondary enrollment were calculated using the last 17 editions of *Projections of Education Statistics*, from *Projections of Education Statistics to 2007* through *Projections of Education Statistics to 2023*. Some data have been revised from previously published figures.
SOURCE: U.S. Department of Education, National Center for Education Statistics, *Projections of Education Statistics*, various issues. (This table was prepared April 2015.)

For more information about MAPEs, see Section A.0. Introduction, earlier in this appendix.

The Enrollment in Degree-Granting Institutions by Race/Ethnicity Projection Model

The Enrollment in Degree-Granting Institutions by Race/Ethnicity Projection Model projects enrollments in degree-granting institutions by attendance status, sex, age, and race/ethnicity. The following groups are projected in this model:

- » White;
- » Black;
- » Hispanic;
- » Asian/Pacific Islander;
- » American Indian/Alaska Native; and
- » nonresident alien.

See the glossary for definitions of the five racial/ethnic categories and the nonresident alien category. (The race/ethnicity of nonresident aliens is unknown, but they are considered a separate group for purposes of this analysis.)

Steps used in the Degree-Granting Institutions by Race/Ethnicity Projection Model

Step 1. Adjust U.S. Census Bureau enrollment counts by attendance status, sex, age, and race/ethnicity to make them sum to NCES enrollment counts by attendance status, sex, and race/ethnicity. For 1981 to 2013, the most detailed levels of Census Bureau enrollment data (by enrollment status, sex, age, and race/ethnicity) were iteratively changed using proportions that were based on the more highly aggregated NCES enrollment numbers to ensure that the sums across these most detailed levels of enrollment data equaled the more highly aggregated NCES enrollment numbers that did not include age.

Step 2. Calculate enrollment rates by attendance status, sex, age category, and race/ethnicity. The enrollment data were broken up into 14 age categories, with separate age categories for individual ages 14 through 24 as well as for the age groups 25 to 29, 30 to 34, and 35 and over. For each of the 14 age categories, enrollment rates were calculated for each combination of attendance status, sex, and the six racial/ethnic groups, resulting in a total of 336 enrollment rates. Each of the 336 enrollment rates was calculated by dividing the enrollment count for that combination of attendance status, sex, age category, and race/ethnicity by the total population for the corresponding combination of sex, age category, and race/ethnicity. For each combination of attendance status, sex and racial/ethnic group, the enrollment rate for the oldest age category was calculated by dividing the enrollment count for those 35 and over by the total population for those 35 to 44.

Step 3. *Produce projections of enrollment rates by attendance status, sex, age category, and race/ethnicity.* Enrollment rates for most of the age groups and racial/ethnic groups were projected using multiple linear regression. However, there were several exceptions:

>> Due to negligible enrollments for ages 14, 15, and 16, these ages were not included in the multiple linear regression models. Instead, projections of enrollment rates for individual ages 14, 15, and 16 were produced by single exponential smoothing.

>> Due to the relatively large fluctuations in the historical enrollment rates resulting from small sample sizes, American Indian/Alaska Native enrollments were projected using single exponential smoothing.

>> Since there were no applicable population counts to compute enrollment rates for nonresident aliens, their enrollments were projected using patterns in recent historical growth.

Four racial/ethnic groups were modeled: White, Black, Hispanic, and Asian/Pacific Islander. Eleven age categories were modeled: individual ages 17 through 24 and age groups 25 to 29, 30 to 34, and 35 to 44. For each of the age categories, projected enrollment rates by attendance status, sex, and race/ethnicity were produced using 16 pooled time-series models—one for each combination of attendance status, sex, and the four racial/ethnic groups. Each equation included variables measuring

>> recent trends;

>> economic conditions (such as disposable income); and

>> demographic changes.

For more information on the equations used to project enrollment rates for the combinations of attendance status, sex, and race/ethnicity, see tables A-22 through A-29, under "Data and equations used for the Enrollment in Degree-Granting Institutions by Race/Ethnicity Projection Model," below.

The final set of projected rates by attendance status, sex, age, and race/ethnicity were controlled to enrollment rates by attendance status, sex, and age produced by the Enrollment in Degree-Granting Institutions Projection Model to ensure consistency across models.

Step 4. *Produce projections of enrollments by attendance status, sex, age category, and race/ethnicity.* For each combination of attendance status, sex, age category, and race/ethnicity, enrollment projections were produced by multiplying the projected enrollment rate for that combination by projections of the total population with the corresponding combination of sex, age category, and race/ethnicity.

Data and equations used for the Enrollment in Degree-Granting Institutions by Race/Ethnicity Projection Model

Enrollment data for degree-granting institutions by race/ethnicity. Enrollment data for 1981 to 2013 by attendance status, sex, and race/ethnicity came from the NCES Integrated Postsecondary Education Data System (IPEDS). These are universe counts. The U.S. Census Bureau, Current Population Survey was the source for enrollment estimates for 1981 to 2013 by the characteristics listed above, as well as age of student.

Population data and projections by race/ethnicity. Population counts for 1981 to 2013 came from the U.S. Census Bureau, Population Estimates series. Population projections for 2014 to 2024 are the Census Bureau's 2012 National Population Projections of the population by sex, age and race/ethnicity (December 2012), ratio-adjusted to line up with most recent historical estimates.

Projections for economic variables. The economic variables used in developing these projections were from the "U.S. Quarterly Model: 1st Quarter 2015 Short-Term Baseline Projections" from the economic consulting firm, IHS Global Inc. This set of projections was IHS Global Inc.'s most recent set at the time the education projections in this report were produced.

Estimated equations and model statistics. Tables A-22 through A-29 show the estimated equations and model statistics used to project enrollment rates for the various combinations of attendance status, sex, and race/ethnicity.

Accuracy of projections for the Degree-Granting Institutions by Race/Ethnicity Projection Model

Mean absolute percentage errors (MAPEs) for enrollment in degree-granting institutions by race/ethnicity were calculated using the last nine editions of *Projections of Education Statistics*. Table H, below, shows MAPEs for key projections of the Enrollment in Degree-Granting Institutions by Race/Ethnicity Projection Model.

Table H. Mean absolute percentage errors (MAPEs) of projected enrollment in degree-granting postsecondary institutions, by lead time and race/ethnicity: *Projections of Education Statistics to 2015* through *Projections of Education Statistics to 2023*

Statistic	Lead time (years)									
	1	2	3	4	5	6	7	8	9	10
Total enrollment	**1.6**	**2.6**	**3.8**	**4.7**	**5.4**	**6.3**	**7.4**	**8.5**	**10.7**	**12.4**
White	2.3	4.0	4.7	4.7	4.8	3.4	3.0	3.2	4.3	—
Black	3.3	8.1	11.0	12.8	13.2	14.0	13.0	10.2	8.2	—
Hispanic	3.7	6.9	10.4	14.9	18.6	20.5	21.2	21.2	22.3	—
Asian/Pacific Islander	3.2	6.1	7.4	8.1	6.7	5.2	4.7	6.9	6.6	—
American Indian/Alaska Native	6.1	8.2	10.2	11.6	13.9	21.3	24.4	30.7	35.8	—

— Not available.
NOTE: MAPEs for total postsecondary degree-granting institution enrollments were calculated using the last 17 editions of *Projections of Education Statistics*, from *Projections of Education Statistics to 2007* through *Projections of Education Statistics to 2023*. MAPEs for degree-granting postsecondary institution enrollment by race/ethnicity were calculated using the last nine editions of *Projections of Education Statistics*, from *Projections of Education Statistics to 2015* through *Projections of Education Statistics to 2023*. Calculations were made using unrounded numbers. Some data have been revised from previously published figures.
SOURCE: U.S. Department of Education, National Center for Education Statistics, *Projections of Education Statistics*, various issues. (This table was prepared April 2015.)

The First-Time Freshmen Enrollment in Degree-Granting Institutions Projection Model

The First-Time Freshmen Enrollment in Degree-Granting Institutions Projection Model produced projections of first-time freshmen enrollment in degree-granting institutions by sex.

Steps used in the First-Time Freshmen Enrollment in Degree-Granting Institutions Projection Model

The projections were produced in the following manner:

Step 1. Calculate the ratio of first-time freshmen enrollment to undergraduate enrollment. For 1975 to 2013, the ratio of first-time freshmen enrollment to undergraduate enrollment was calculated for males and females.

Step 2. Project the ratio of first-time freshmen enrollment to undergraduate enrollment. The percentages of undergraduate enrollment for both males and females were projected using single exponential smoothing. A separate smoothing constant, chosen to minimize the sum of squared forecast errors, was used for each percentage.

Step 3. Apply the projected ratio to projected undergraduate enrollment. The projected ratios were applied to projections of undergraduate enrollment by sex from the Enrollment in Degree-Granting Institutions Model to yield projections of first-time freshmen enrollment.

Assumptions underlying this method

This method assumes that the future pattern in the trend of first-time freshmen enrollment will be the same as that for undergraduate enrollment.

Data used in the First-Time Freshmen Enrollment in Degree-Granting Institutions Projection Model

Undergraduate and freshmen enrollment data for degree-granting institutions. Undergraduate and freshmen enrollment data by sex for 1975 to 2013 came from the NCES Integrated Postsecondary Education Data System (IPEDS).

Projections of undergraduate enrollment. Projections of undergraduate enrollment by sex came from the Enrollment in Degree-Granting Institutions Model, discussed earlier in this section of appendix A.

Accuracy of projections for the First-Time Freshmen Enrollment Projection Model

Mean absolute percentage errors (MAPEs) for enrollment in degree-granting institutions by race/ethnicity were calculated using the last five editions of *Projections of Education Statistics*. Table I, below, shows MAPEs for key projections of the First-Time Freshmen Enrollment in Degree-Granting Institutions Model.

Table I. Mean absolute percentage errors (MAPEs) of projected first-time freshmen enrollment in degree-granting postsecondary institutions, by lead time and sex: *Projections of Education Statistics to 2018* through *Projections of Education Statistics to 2023*

Statistic	Lead time (years)									
	1	2	3	4	5	6	7	8	9	10
Total first-time freshmen enrollment	**3.6**	**6.3**	**6.6**	**5.1**	**1.9**	**0.3**	—	—	—	—
Males	3.7	6.3	6.6	4.9	2.3	2.6	—	—	—	—
Females	3.6	6.2	6.6	5.3	2.5	2.8	—	—	—	—

— Not available.
NOTE: MAPEs for first-time freshmen enrollment in postsecondary degree-granting institutions were calculated using the last 6 editions of *Projections of Education Statistics*, from *Projections of Education Statistics to 2018* through *Projections of Education Statistics to 2023*. Calculations were made using unrounded numbers. Some data have been revised from previously published figures.
SOURCE: U.S. Department of Education, National Center for Education Statistics, *Projections of Education Statistics*, various issues. (This table was prepared April 2015.)

Table A-16. Actual and projected enrollment rates of all students at degree-granting postsecondary institutions, by sex, attendance status, and age: Fall 2013, fall 2019, and fall 2024

Sex, attendance status, and age	Actual 2013	Projected 2019	Projected 2024
1	2	3	4
Men			
Full-time			
16 years old	1.0	0.6	0.6
17 years old	3.5	3.9	4.2
18 years old	28.4	30.1	31.7
19 years old	36.3	38.4	40.0
20 years old	32.5	34.3	35.8
21 years old	33.8	35.7	37.2
22 years old	22.7	24.2	25.5
23 years old	16.2	17.4	18.4
24 years old	14.6	15.7	16.7
25 to 29 years old	6.5	7.0	7.5
30 to 34 years old	2.5	2.7	2.9
35 to 44 years old	1.6	1.8	1.9
Part-time			
16 years old	0.2	0.1	0.1
17 years old	0.8	0.8	0.9
18 years old	5.2	5.2	5.4
19 years old	8.2	8.1	8.4
20 years old	11.0	10.9	11.3
21 years old	11.0	10.9	11.3
22 years old	9.3	9.3	9.8
23 years old	11.1	11.1	11.7
24 years old	7.1	7.1	7.6
25 to 29 years old	5.2	5.3	5.6
30 to 34 years old	3.1	3.1	3.3
35 to 44 years old	3.9	4.0	4.3
Women			
Full-time			
16 years old	0.9	0.8	0.8
17 years old	4.3	5.1	5.9
18 years old	37.7	41.7	44.7
19 years old	45.3	49.0	51.7
20 years old	43.0	46.6	49.4
21 years old	43.7	47.3	50.0
22 years old	24.4	27.4	29.7
23 years old	20.5	23.3	25.6
24 years old	14.7	16.8	18.6
25 to 29 years old	7.0	7.8	8.3
30 to 34 years old	3.9	4.3	4.5
35 to 44 years old	3.2	3.4	3.6
Part-time			
16 years old	0.4	0.2	0.2
17 years old	0.8	0.9	1.0
18 years old	7.3	7.8	8.1
19 years old	13.2	13.7	14.1
20 years old	12.0	12.6	13.0
21 years old	13.2	13.8	14.2
22 years old	12.9	14.0	14.8
23 years old	9.2	10.1	10.8
24 years old	10.8	12.0	12.9
25 to 29 years old	8.7	9.4	9.9
30 to 34 years old	4.6	4.9	5.2
35 to 44 years old	7.1	7.2	7.6

SOURCE: U.S. Department of Education, National Center for Education Statistics, Integrated Postsecondary Education Data System, Spring 2013; Enrollment in Degree-Granting Institutions Projection Model, 1980 through 2024; and U.S. Department of Commerce, Census Bureau, Current Population Reports, "Social and Economic Characteristics of Students," 2013. (This table was prepared March 2015.)

Table A-17. Estimated equations and model statistics for full-time and part-time enrollment rates of males at degree-granting postsecondary institutions based on data from 1981 to 2013

Independent variable	Coefficient	Standard error	t-statistic	R^2	D.W. statistic
1	2	3	4	5	6
Full-time					
Intercept term for 17-year-olds..........................	-7.12	0.180	-39.56	1.00	2.14*
Intercept term for 18-year-olds..........................	-4.41	0.220	-20.08		
Intercept term for 19-year-olds..........................	-4.03	0.127	-31.78		
Intercept term for 20-year-olds..........................	-4.07	0.131	-31.01		
Intercept term for 21-year-olds..........................	-4.21	0.130	-32.40		
Intercept term for 22-year-olds..........................	-4.65	0.130	-35.77		
Intercept term for 23-year-olds..........................	-5.14	0.130	-39.65		
Intercept term for 24-year-olds..........................	-5.46	0.151	-36.13		
Intercept term for 25- to 29-year-olds	-6.14	0.137	-44.87		
Intercept term for 30- to 34-year-olds	-7.10	0.150	-47.30		
Intercept term for 35- to 44-year-olds	-7.63	0.163	-46.93		
Log of three-period weighted average of per capita disposable income in 2000 dollars, using the present period and the previous two periods.....	0.65	0.021	31.09		
Log age-specific unemployment rate for men	0.24	0.020	12.11		
Autocorrelation coefficient for 17-year-olds..............	0.62	0.094	6.67		
Autocorrelation coefficient for 18-year-olds..............	0.88	0.064	13.83		
Autocorrelation coefficient for 19-year-olds..............	-0.06	0.134	-0.46		
Autocorrelation coefficient for 20-year-olds..............	0.46	0.124	3.69		
Autocorrelation coefficient for 21-year-olds..............	0.21	0.149	1.44		
Autocorrelation coefficient for 22-year-olds..............	0.10	0.139	0.73		
Autocorrelation coefficient for 23-year-olds..............	-0.10	0.145	-0.68		
Autocorrelation coefficient for 24-year-olds..............	0.74	0.124	5.92		
Autocorrelation coefficient for 25- to 29-year-olds ...	0.49	0.130	3.77		
Autocorrelation coefficient for 30- to 34-year-olds ...	0.71	0.114	6.17		
Autocorrelation coefficient for 35- to 44-year-olds ...	0.75	0.098	7.65		
Part-time					
Intercept term for 17-year-olds..........................	-6.49	0.812	-7.99	0.95	2.13*
Intercept term for 18-year-olds..........................	-3.61	0.501	-7.20		
Intercept term for 19-year-olds..........................	-3.13	0.540	-5.80		
Intercept term for 20-year-olds..........................	-3.05	0.513	-5.93		
Intercept term for 21-year-olds..........................	-3.12	0.503	-6.20		
Intercept term for 22-year-olds..........................	-3.35	0.506	-6.63		
Intercept term for 23-year-olds..........................	-3.36	0.506	-6.65		
Intercept term for 24-year-olds..........................	-3.47	0.497	-6.98		
Intercept term for 25- to 29-year-olds	-3.82	0.493	-7.74		
Intercept term for 30- to 34-year-olds	-4.29	0.507	-8.47		
Intercept term for 35- to 44-year-olds	-4.27	0.503	-8.49		
Log of three-period weighted average of per capita disposable income in 2000 dollars, using the present period and the previous two periods.....	0.07	0.073	0.95		
Log unemployment rate	0.31	0.067	4.53		
Autocorrelation coefficient for 17-year-olds..............	0.14	0.131	1.06		
Autocorrelation coefficient for 18-year-olds..............	0.54	0.123	4.42		
Autocorrelation coefficient for 19-year-olds..............	0.79	0.089	8.93		
Autocorrelation coefficient for 20-year-olds..............	0.74	0.090	8.20		
Autocorrelation coefficient for 21-year-olds..............	0.70	0.086	8.14		
Autocorrelation coefficient for 22-year-olds..............	0.56	0.129	4.35		
Autocorrelation coefficient for 23-year-olds..............	0.64	0.138	4.64		
Autocorrelation coefficient for 24-year-olds..............	0.35	0.171	2.03		
Autocorrelation coefficient for 25- to 29-year-olds ...	0.20	0.191	1.04		
Autocorrelation coefficient for 30- to 34-year-olds ...	0.77	0.126	6.14		
Autocorrelation coefficient for 35- to 44-year-olds ...	0.74	0.104	7.16		

* $p < .05$.
NOTE: R^2 = Coefficient of determination. D.W. statistic = Durbin-Watson statistic, a test for autocorrelation among regression residuals. For more details see Johnston, J., and Dinardo, J. (1996). *Econometric Methods*. New York: McGraw-Hill. The regression method used to estimate the full-time and part-time equations was the pooled seemingly unrelated regression method with a first-order autocorrelation correction. The time period used to estimate both equations is from 1981 to 2013, and the number of observations is 363 after the correction for autocorrelation. For additional information, see Intriligator, M.D. (1978). *Econometric Models, Techniques, & Applications*. New Jersey: Prentice-Hall, Inc., pp. 165–173.
SOURCE: U.S. Department of Education, National Center for Education Statistics, Enrollment in Degree-Granting Institutions Projection Model, 1980 through 2024. (This table was prepared March 2015.)

Table A-18. Estimated equations and model statistics for full-time and part-time enrollment rates of females at degree-granting postsecondary institutions based on data from 1980 to 2013

Independent variable	Coefficient	Standard error	t-statistic	R^2	D.W. statistic
1	2	3	4	5	6
Full-time					
Intercept term for 17-year-olds..............................	-9.51	0.168	-56.54	1.00	1.66*
Intercept term for 18-year-olds..............................	-6.68	0.152	-44.06		
Intercept term for 19-year-olds..............................	-6.52	0.147	-44.44		
Intercept term for 20-year-olds..............................	-6.57	0.150	-43.87		
Intercept term for 21-year-olds..............................	-6.78	0.150	-45.18		
Intercept term for 22-year-olds..............................	-7.45	0.151	-49.26		
Intercept term for 23-year-olds..............................	-7.93	0.153	-51.79		
Intercept term for 24-year-olds..............................	-8.31	0.154	-54.02		
Intercept term for 25- to 29-year-olds	-8.85	0.159	-55.51		
Intercept term for 30- to 34-year-olds	-9.55	0.159	-60.25		
Intercept term for 35- to 44-year-olds	-9.77	0.159	-61.62		
Log of three-period weighted average of per capita disposable income in 2000 dollars, using the present period and the previous two periods	1.17	0.025	46.22		
Log age-specific unemployment rate for women	0.37	0.036	10.33		
Part-time					
Intercept term for 17-year-olds..............................	-11.68	0.389	-30.00	0.96	2.08*
Intercept term for 18-year-olds..............................	-9.03	0.283	-31.98		
Intercept term for 19-year-olds..............................	-8.55	0.280	-30.54		
Intercept term for 20-year-olds..............................	-8.66	0.274	-31.66		
Intercept term for 21-year-olds..............................	-8.65	0.277	-31.25		
Intercept term for 22-year-olds..............................	-8.86	0.272	-32.60		
Intercept term for 23-year-olds..............................	-8.94	0.273	-32.76		
Intercept term for 24-year-olds..............................	-8.98	0.274	-32.75		
Intercept term for 25- to 29-year-olds	-9.38	0.281	-33.43		
Intercept term for 30- to 34-year-olds	-9.91	0.323	-30.66		
Intercept term for 35- to 44-year-olds	-9.58	0.318	-30.10		
Log of three-period weighted average of per capita disposable income in 2000 dollars, using the present period and the previous two periods	1.07	0.043	24.72		
Log unemployment rate	0.21	0.024	8.88		
Autocorrelation coefficient for 17-year-olds..............	0.68	0.098	6.95		
Autocorrelation coefficient for 18-year-olds..............	0.48	0.115	4.15		
Autocorrelation coefficient for 19-year-olds..............	0.52	0.106	4.89		
Autocorrelation coefficient for 20-year-olds..............	0.21	0.128	1.63		
Autocorrelation coefficient for 21-year-olds..............	0.52	0.150	3.48		
Autocorrelation coefficient for 22-year-olds..............	-0.02	0.137	-0.12		
Autocorrelation coefficient for 23-year-olds..............	0.07	0.130	0.50		
Autocorrelation coefficient for 24-year-olds..............	0.44	0.101	4.32		
Autocorrelation coefficient for 25- to 29-year-olds ...	0.81	0.051	15.83		
Autocorrelation coefficient for 30- to 34-year-olds ...	0.88	0.039	22.55		
Autocorrelation coefficient for 35- to 44-year-olds ...	0.90	0.034	25.97		

* $p < .05$.
~ Inconclusive
NOTE: R^2 = Coefficient of determination. D.W. statistic = Durbin-Watson statistic, a test for autocorrelation among regression residuals. For more details see Johnston, J., and Dinardo, J. (1996). *Econometric Methods*. New York: McGraw-Hill. The regression method used to estimate the full-time and part-time equations was the pooled seemingly unrelated regression method with a first-order autocorrelation correction. The time period used to estimate the full-time equation was from 1980 to 2013 and that for the part-time equation was from 1981 to

2013. The number of observations for the full-time equation is 374 and the number of observations for the part-time equation, after the correction for autocorrelation, is 363. For additional information, see Intriligator, M.D. (1978). *Econometric Models, Techniques, & Applications*. New Jersey: Prentice-Hall, Inc., pp. 165–173.
SOURCE: U.S. Department of Education, National Center for Education Statistics, Enrollment in Degree-Granting Institutions Projection Model, 1980 through 2024. (This table was prepared March 2015.)

Table A-19. Actual and projected percentages of full-time students at degree-granting postsecondary institutions, by sex, age group, student level, and level of institution: Fall 2013, and fall 2014 through fall 2024

Age group, student level, and institution level	Males		Females	
	Actual 2013	Projected 2014 through 2024	Actual 2013	Projected 2014 through 2024
1	2	3	4	5
18 and 19 years old				
Undergraduate, 4-year institutions	68.3	67.4	72.0	70.1
Undergraduate, 2-year institutions	31.0	31.9	27.8	28.6
Postbaccalaureate, 4-year institutions	0.7	0.7	0.2	1.3
20 and 21 years old				
Undergraduate, 4-year institutions	75.8	76.4	80.4	79.9
Undergraduate, 2-year institutions	20.8	21.4	17.6	18.1
Postbaccalaureate, 4-year institutions	3.3	2.2	2.0	1.9
22 to 24 years old				
Undergraduate, 4-year institutions	66.0	64.3	59.1	60.8
Undergraduate, 2-year institutions	15.4	16.0	18.5	17.7
Postbaccalaureate, 4-year institutions	18.5	19.7	22.4	21.5
25 to 29 years old				
Undergraduate, 4-year institutions	48.8	42.7	43.4	43.5
Undergraduate, 2-year institutions	18.1	18.5	20.4	21.5
Postbaccalaureate, 4-year institutions	33.0	38.8	36.2	35.0
30 to 34 years old				
Undergraduate, 4-year institutions	51.1	46.2	44.6	44.8
Undergraduate, 2-year institutions	20.2	21.3	28.4	30.2
Postbaccalaureate, 4-year institutions	28.7	32.5	27.0	24.9
35 years and over				
Undergraduate, 4-year institutions	37.2	41.1	41.2	42.3
Undergraduate, 2-year institutions	28.4	27.7	28.9	30.7
Postbaccalaureate, 4-year institutions	34.5	31.2	29.9	27.0

NOTE: Detail may not sum to totals because of rounding.
SOURCE: U.S. Department of Education, National Center for Education Statistics, Integrated Postsecondary Education Data System, Spring 2014; Enrollment in Degree-Granting Institutions Projection Model, 1980 through 2024; and U.S. Department of Commerce, Census Bureau, Current Population Reports, "Social and Economic Characteristics of Students," 2013. (This table was prepared March 2015.)

Table A-20. Actual and projected percentages of part-time students at degree-granting postsecondary institutions, by sex, age group, student level, and level of institution: Fall 2013, and fall 2014 through fall 2024

Age, student level, and level of institution	Males		Females	
	Actual 2013	Projected 2014 through 2024	Actual 2013	Projected 2014 through 2024
1	2	3	4	5
18 and 19 years old				
Undergraduate, 4-year institutions	24.7	24.2	18.0	18.0
Undergraduate, 2-year institutions	75.0	73.9	79.9	80.4
Postbaccalaureate, 4-year institutions	0.3	1.9	2.1	1.6
20 and 21 years old				
Undergraduate, 4-year institutions	27.6	27.3	32.4	28.2
Undergraduate, 2-year institutions	71.4	70.5	64.3	69.3
Postbaccalaureate, 4-year institutions	1.0	2.1	3.4	2.4
22 to 24 years old				
Undergraduate, 4-year institutions	35.5	32.6	38.5	37.2
Undergraduate, 2-year institutions	57.7	57.0	50.8	50.6
Postbaccalaureate, 4-year institutions	6.9	10.5	10.7	12.2
25 to 29 years old				
Undergraduate, 4-year institutions	31.7	30.7	28.4	28.1
Undergraduate, 2-year institutions	50.1	49.7	54.2	51.3
Postbaccalaureate, 4-year institutions	18.2	19.6	17.3	20.5
30 to 34 years old				
Undergraduate, 4-year institutions	32.4	32.4	32.1	32.5
Undergraduate, 2-year institutions	42.2	45.1	40.8	43.7
Postbaccalaureate, 4-year institutions	25.4	22.5	27.1	23.8
35 years and over				
Undergraduate, 4-year institutions	32.0	32.3	30.9	29.9
Undergraduate, 2-year institutions	39.2	39.7	43.3	45.5
Postbaccalaureate, 4-year institutions	28.8	28.0	25.8	24.6

NOTE: Detail may not sum to totals because of rounding. Some data have been revised from previously published figures.
SOURCE: U.S. Department of Education, National Center for Education Statistics, Integrated Postsecondary Education Data System, Spring 2013; Enrollment in Degree-Granting Institutions Projection Model, 1980 through 2024; and U.S. Department of Commerce, Census Bureau, Current Population Reports, "Social and Economic Characteristics of Students," 2013. (This table was prepared March 2015.)

Table A-21. Actual and projected enrollment in public degree-granting postsecondary institutions as a percentage of total postsecondary enrollment, by sex, attendance status, student level, and level of institution: Fall 2013, and fall 2014 through fall 2024

Attendance status, student level, and level of institution	Males		Females	
	Actual 2013	Projected 2014 through 2024	Actual 2013	Projected 2014 through 2024
Full-time, undergraduate, 4-year institutions...............	65.7	65.7	61.8	61.8
Part-time, undergraduate, 4-year institutions..............	67.8	67.7	63.5	63.5
Full-time, undergraduate, 2-year institutions...............	92.1	92.1	87.0	87.0
Part-time, undergraduate, 2-year institutions..............	99.4	99.3	98.8	98.7
Full-time, postbaccalaureate, 4-year institutions	49.0	49.0	45.4	45.4
Part-time, postbaccalaureate, 4-year institutions.........	51.2	51.2	49.0	49.0

SOURCE: U.S. Department of Education, National Center for Education Statistics, Integrated Postsecondary Education Data System, Spring 2014; and Enrollment in Degree-Granting Institutions Projection Model, 1980 through 2024. (This table was prepared March 2015.)

Table A-22. Estimated equations and model statistics for full-time and part-time enrollment rates of White males at degree-granting postsecondary institutions based on data from 1980 to 2013

Independent variable	Coefficient	Standard error	t-statistic	R^2	D.W. statistic
1	2	3	4	5	6
Full-time					
Intercept term for 17-year-olds.................................	-9.80	0.242	-40.43	0.99	1.56*
Intercept term for 18-year-olds.................................	-6.79	0.230	-29.56		
Intercept term for 19-year-olds.................................	-6.53	0.227	-28.82		
Intercept term for 20-year-olds.................................	-6.71	0.227	-29.57		
Intercept term for 21-year-olds.................................	-6.84	0.227	-30.13		
Intercept term for 22-year-olds.................................	-7.33	0.227	-32.26		
Intercept term for 23-year-olds.................................	-7.89	0.227	-34.73		
Intercept term for 24-year-olds.................................	-8.28	0.229	-36.12		
Intercept term for 25- to 29-year-olds	-9.14	0.228	-40.14		
Intercept term for 30- to 34-year-olds	-10.17	0.230	-44.29		
Intercept term for 35- to 44-year-olds	-10.79	0.230	-46.86		
Log of White per capita disposable income in current dollars	0.32	0.012	27.19		
Part-time					
Intercept term for 17-year-olds.................................	-5.09	0.533	-9.54	0.91	1.61*
Intercept term for 18-year-olds.................................	-1.49	0.121	-12.36		
Intercept term for 19-year-olds.................................	-1.06	0.129	-8.21		
Intercept term for 20-year-olds.................................	-1.02	0.122	-8.41		
Intercept term for 21-year-olds.................................	-1.04	0.124	-8.40		
Intercept term for 22-year-olds.................................	-1.25	0.123	-10.17		
Intercept term for 23-year-olds.................................	-1.30	0.119	-10.94		
Intercept term for 24-year-olds.................................	-1.31	0.117	-11.18		
Intercept term for 25- to 29-year-olds	-1.64	0.117	-14.07		
Intercept term for 30- to 34-year-olds	-2.11	0.119	-17.73		
Intercept term for 35- to 44-year-olds	-2.14	0.116	-18.49		
Log of real total private compensation employment cost index	1.49	0.153	9.77		

* $p < .05$.
NOTE: R^2 = Coefficient of determination. D.W. statistic = Durbin-Watson statistic, a test for autocorrelation among regression residuals. For more details see Johnston, J., and Dinardo, J. (1996). *Econometric Methods.* New York: McGraw-Hill. The regression method used to estimate the full-time and part-time equations was the pooled seemingly unrelated regression method. The time period used to estimate the equations is from 1980 to 2013. The number of observations is 374. For additional information, see Intriligator, M.D. (1978). *Econometric Models, Techniques, & Applications.* New Jersey: Prentice-Hall, Inc., pp. 165–173. Race categories exclude persons of Hispanic ethnicity.
SOURCE: U.S. Department of Education, National Center for Education Statistics, Enrollment in Degree-Granting Institutions by Race/Ethnicity Projection Model, 1980 through 2024. (This table was prepared April 2015.)

Table A-23. Estimated equations and model statistics for full-time and part-time enrollment rates of White females at degree-granting postsecondary institutions based on data from 1980 to 2013

Independent variable	Coefficient	Standard error	t-statistic	R^2	D.W. statistic
1	2	3	4	5	6
Full-time					
Intercept term for 17-year-olds................................	-14.31	0.288	-49.63	0.99	1.64*
Intercept term for 18-year-olds................................	-11.33	0.275	-41.14		
Intercept term for 19-year-olds................................	-11.17	0.273	-40.98		
Intercept term for 20-year-olds................................	-11.39	0.273	-41.81		
Intercept term for 21-year-olds................................	-11.63	0.273	-42.55		
Intercept term for 22-year-olds................................	-12.38	0.273	-45.30		
Intercept term for 23-year-olds................................	-12.94	0.274	-47.17		
Intercept term for 24-year-olds................................	-13.33	0.275	-48.57		
Intercept term for 25- to 29-year-olds	-14.13	0.274	-51.60		
Intercept term for 30- to 34-year-olds	-14.87	0.274	-54.35		
Intercept term for 35- to 44-year-olds	-15.04	0.274	-54.93		
Log of White per capita disposable income in current dollars	0.57	0.014	40.83		
Part-time					
Intercept term for 17-year-olds................................	-10.11	0.387	-26.11	0.76	1.64*
Intercept term for 18-year-olds................................	-6.84	0.350	-19.53		
Intercept term for 19-year-olds................................	-6.36	0.352	-18.09		
Intercept term for 20-year-olds................................	-6.43	0.351	-18.31		
Intercept term for 21-year-olds................................	-6.50	0.351	-18.53		
Intercept term for 22-year-olds................................	-6.72	0.349	-19.26		
Intercept term for 23-year-olds................................	-6.79	0.349	-19.44		
Intercept term for 24-year-olds................................	-6.81	0.348	-19.54		
Intercept term for 25- to 29-year-olds	-7.12	0.348	-20.45		
Intercept term for 30- to 34-year-olds	-7.49	0.349	-21.43		
Intercept term for 35- to 44-year-olds	-7.15	0.348	-20.56		
Log of real total private compensation employment cost index	0.24	0.018	13.24		

* $p < .05$.
NOTE: R^2 = Coefficient of determination. D.W. statistic = Durbin-Watson statistic, a test for autocorrelation among regression residuals. For more details see Johnston, J., and Dinardo, J. (1996). *Econometric Methods*. New York: McGraw-Hill. The regression method used to estimate the full-time and part-time equations was the pooled seemingly unrelated regression method. The time period used to estimate the equations is from 1980 to 2013. The number of observations is 374. For additional information, see Intriligator, M.D. (1978). *Econometric Models, Techniques, & Applications*. New Jersey: Prentice-Hall, Inc., pp. 165–173. Race categories exclude persons of Hispanic ethnicity.
SOURCE: U.S. Department of Education, National Center for Education Statistics, Enrollment in Degree-Granting Institutions by Race/Ethnicity Projection Model, 1980 through 2024. (This table was prepared April 2015.)

Table A-24. Estimated equations and model statistics for full-time and part-time enrollment rates of Black males at degree-granting postsecondary institutions based on data from 1980 to 2013

Independent variable	Coefficient	Standard error	t-statistic	R^2	D.W. statistic
1	2	3	4	5	6
Full-time					
Intercept term for 17-year-olds...............................	-11.55	0.679	-17.00	0.96	1.84*
Intercept term for 18-year-olds...............................	-9.26	0.673	-13.75		
Intercept term for 19-year-olds...............................	-8.98	0.673	-13.35		
Intercept term for 20-year-olds...............................	-9.04	0.673	-13.43		
Intercept term for 21-year-olds...............................	-9.27	0.674	-13.75		
Intercept term for 22-year-olds...............................	-9.51	0.674	-14.12		
Intercept term for 23-year-olds...............................	-9.96	0.676	-14.72		
Intercept term for 24-year-olds...............................	-10.25	0.674	-15.20		
Intercept term for 25- to 29-year-olds	-11.03	0.674	-16.35		
Intercept term for 30- to 34-year-olds	-11.80	0.677	-17.43		
Intercept term for 35- to 44-year-olds	-12.16	0.676	-17.99		
Log of Black per capita disposable income in current dollars	0.41	0.036	11.43		
Part-time					
Intercept term for 17-year-olds...............................	-12.53	0.768	-16.32	0.48	1.89*
Intercept term for 18-year-olds...............................	-10.99	0.600	-18.32		
Intercept term for 19-year-olds...............................	-10.21	0.591	-17.28		
Intercept term for 20-year-olds...............................	-10.21	0.592	-17.26		
Intercept term for 21-year-olds...............................	-10.15	0.585	-17.34		
Intercept term for 22-year-olds...............................	-10.15	0.592	-17.14		
Intercept term for 23-year-olds...............................	-10.33	0.598	-17.29		
Intercept term for 24-year-olds...............................	-10.45	0.596	-17.53		
Intercept term for 25- to 29-year-olds	-10.52	0.584	-18.01		
Intercept term for 30- to 34-year-olds	-10.77	0.583	-18.48		
Intercept term for 35- to 44-year-olds	-10.81	0.581	-18.60		
Log of Black per capita disposable income in current dollars	0.39	0.031	12.59		

* $p < .05$.

NOTE: R^2 = Coefficient of determination. D.W. statistic = Durbin-Watson statistic, a test for autocorrelation among regression residuals. For more details see Johnston, J., and Dinardo, J. (1996). *Econometric Methods*. New York: McGraw-Hill. The regression method used to estimate the full-time and part-time equations was the pooled seemingly unrelated regression method. The time period used to estimate the equations is from 1980 to 2013. The number of observations is 374. For additional information, see Intriligator, M.D. (1978). *Econometric Models, Techniques, & Applications*. New Jersey: Prentice-Hall, Inc., pp. 165–173. Race categories exclude persons of Hispanic ethnicity.

SOURCE: U.S. Department of Education, National Center for Education Statistics, Enrollment in Degree-Granting Institutions by Race/Ethnicity Projection Model, 1980 through 2024. (This table was prepared April 2015.)

Table A-25. Estimated equations and model statistics for full-time and part-time enrollment rates of Black females at degree-granting postsecondary institutions based on data from 1980 to 2013

Independent variable	Coefficient	Standard error	t-statistic	R^2	D.W. statistic
1	2	3	4	5	6
Full-time					
Intercept term for 17-year-olds............................	-16.04	0.601	-26.67	0.97	1.76*
Intercept term for 18-year-olds............................	-13.74	0.593	-23.17		
Intercept term for 19-year-olds............................	-13.51	0.592	-22.82		
Intercept term for 20-year-olds............................	-13.74	0.593	-23.18		
Intercept term for 21-year-olds............................	-13.94	0.592	-23.55		
Intercept term for 22-year-olds............................	-14.37	0.592	-24.26		
Intercept term for 23-year-olds............................	-14.65	0.593	-24.70		
Intercept term for 24-year-olds............................	-15.00	0.594	-25.26		
Intercept term for 25- to 29-year-olds	-15.77	0.594	-26.55		
Intercept term for 30- to 34-year-olds	-16.22	0.593	-27.33		
Intercept term for 35- to 44-year-olds	-16.56	0.595	-27.84		
Log of Black per capita disposable income in current dollars	0.69	0.032	21.68		
Part-time					
Intercept term for 17-year-olds............................	-14.98	0.658	-22.78	0.57	1.77*
Intercept term for 18-year-olds............................	-13.22	0.649	-20.36		
Intercept term for 19-year-olds............................	-12.74	0.649	-19.63		
Intercept term for 20-year-olds............................	-12.80	0.649	-19.73		
Intercept term for 21-year-olds............................	-12.72	0.648	-19.64		
Intercept term for 22-year-olds............................	-12.73	0.648	-19.65		
Intercept term for 23-year-olds............................	-12.76	0.648	-19.70		
Intercept term for 24-year-olds............................	-12.89	0.648	-19.89		
Intercept term for 25- to 29-year-olds	-13.05	0.644	-20.26		
Intercept term for 30- to 34-year-olds	-13.21	0.644	-20.51		
Intercept term for 35- to 44-year-olds	-13.05	0.644	-20.26		
Log of Black per capita disposable income in current dollars	0.56	0.035	16.14		

* $p < .05$.
NOTE: R^2 = Coefficient of determination. D.W. statistic = Durbin-Watson statistic, a test for autocorrelation among regression residuals. For more details see Johnston, J., and Dinardo, J. (1996). *Econometric Methods*. New York: McGraw-Hill. The regression method used to estimate the full-time and part-time equations was the pooled seemingly unrelated regression method. The time period used to estimate the equations is from 1980 to 2013. The number of observations is 374. For additional information, see Intriligator, M.D. (1978). *Econometric Models, Techniques, & Applications*. New Jersey: Prentice-Hall, Inc., pp. 165–173. Race categories exclude persons of Hispanic ethnicity.
SOURCE: U.S. Department of Education, National Center for Education Statistics, Enrollment in Degree-Granting Institutions by Race/Ethnicity Projection Model, 1980 through 2024. (This table was prepared April 2015.)

Table A-26. Estimated equations and model statistics for full-time and part-time enrollment rates of Hispanic males at degree-granting postsecondary institutions based on data from 1980 to 2013

Independent variable	Coefficient	Standard error	t-statistic	R^2	D.W. statistic
1	2	3	4	5	6
Full-time					
Intercept term for 17-year-olds.............................	-12.51	0.870	-14.37	0.93	1.89*
Intercept term for 18-year-olds.............................	-10.44	0.866	-12.06		
Intercept term for 19-year-olds.............................	-10.20	0.866	-11.78		
Intercept term for 20-year-olds.............................	-10.41	0.866	-12.02		
Intercept term for 21-year-olds.............................	-10.62	0.868	-12.24		
Intercept term for 22-year-olds.............................	-11.09	0.867	-12.80		
Intercept term for 23-year-olds.............................	-11.39	0.868	-13.13		
Intercept term for 24-year-olds.............................	-11.57	0.867	-13.34		
Intercept term for 25- to 29-year-olds	-12.40	0.867	-14.30		
Intercept term for 30- to 34-year-olds	-13.23	0.868	-15.24		
Intercept term for 35- to 44-year-olds	-13.69	0.869	-15.75		
Log of Hispanic per capita disposable income in current dollars	0.47	0.047	9.88		
Part-time					
Intercept term for 17-year-olds.............................	-12.03	0.775	-15.52	0.61	1.70*
Intercept term for 18-year-olds.............................	-10.04	0.593	-16.94		
Intercept term for 19-year-olds.............................	-9.71	0.595	-16.30		
Intercept term for 20-year-olds.............................	-9.58	0.592	-16.18		
Intercept term for 21-year-olds.............................	-9.62	0.592	-16.25		
Intercept term for 22-year-olds.............................	-10.02	0.590	-16.97		
Intercept term for 23-year-olds.............................	-9.95	0.596	-16.70		
Intercept term for 24-year-olds.............................	-10.13	0.592	-17.12		
Intercept term for 25- to 29-year-olds	-10.45	0.585	-17.85		
Intercept term for 30- to 34-year-olds	-10.92	0.586	-18.62		
Intercept term for 35- to 44-year-olds	-10.93	0.585	-18.69		
Log of Hispanic per capita disposable income in current dollars	0.38	0.032	12.08		

* $p < .05$.
NOTE: R^2 = Coefficient of determination. D.W. statistic = Durbin-Watson statistic, a test for autocorrelation among regression residuals. For more details see Johnston, J., and Dinardo, J. (1996). *Econometric Methods*. New York: McGraw-Hill. The regression method used to estimate the full-time and part-time equations was the pooled seemingly unrelated regression method. The time period used to estimate the equations is from 1980 to 2013. The number of observations is 374. For additional information, see Intriligator, M.D. (1978). *Econometric Models, Techniques, & Applications*. New Jersey: Prentice-Hall, Inc., pp. 165–173.
SOURCE: U.S. Department of Education, National Center for Education Statistics, Enrollment in Degree-Granting Institutions by Race/Ethnicity Projection Model, 1980 through 2024. (This table was prepared April 2015.)

Table A-27. Estimated equations and model statistics for full-time and part-time enrollment rates of Hispanic females at degree-granting postsecondary institutions based on data from 1980 to 2013

Independent variable	Coefficient	Standard error	t-statistic	R^2	D.W. statistic
1	2	3	4	5	6
Full-time					
Intercept term for 17-year-olds..............................	-19.11	0.710	-26.91	0.93	1.82*
Intercept term for 18-year-olds..............................	-16.57	0.700	-23.68		
Intercept term for 19-year-olds..............................	-16.44	0.698	-23.55		
Intercept term for 20-year-olds..............................	-16.75	0.699	-23.97		
Intercept term for 21-year-olds..............................	-16.88	0.699	-24.13		
Intercept term for 22-year-olds..............................	-17.46	0.700	-24.93		
Intercept term for 23-year-olds..............................	-17.77	0.700	-25.40		
Intercept term for 24-year-olds..............................	-18.25	0.702	-25.98		
Intercept term for 25- to 29-year-olds	-18.89	0.698	-27.07		
Intercept term for 30- to 34-year-olds	-19.56	0.700	-27.92		
Intercept term for 35- to 44-year-olds	-19.92	0.701	-28.41		
Log of Hispanic per capita disposable income in current dollars	0.83	0.038	21.93		
Part-time					
Intercept term for 17-year-olds..............................	-16.05	0.567	-28.30	0.69	1.91*
Intercept term for 18-year-olds..............................	-13.95	0.559	-24.96		
Intercept term for 19-year-olds..............................	-13.56	0.556	-24.38		
Intercept term for 20-year-olds..............................	-13.83	0.560	-24.68		
Intercept term for 21-year-olds..............................	-13.68	0.560	-24.44		
Intercept term for 22-year-olds..............................	-13.97	0.562	-24.87		
Intercept term for 23-year-olds..............................	-13.89	0.557	-24.96		
Intercept term for 24-year-olds..............................	-14.15	0.559	-25.33		
Intercept term for 25- to 29-year-olds	-14.47	0.552	-26.23		
Intercept term for 30- to 34-year-olds	-14.85	0.552	-26.91		
Intercept term for 35- to 44-year-olds	-14.74	0.552	-26.71		
Log of Hispanic per capita disposable income in current dollars	0.63	0.030	20.85		

* $p < .05$.
NOTE: R^2 = Coefficient of determination. D.W. statistic = Durbin-Watson statistic, a test for autocorrelation among regression residuals. For more details see Johnston, J., and Dinardo, J. (1996). *Econometric Methods*. New York: McGraw-Hill. The regression method used to estimate the full-time and part-time equations was the pooled seemingly unrelated regression method. The time period used to estimate the equations is from 1980 to 2013. The number of observations is 374. For additional information, see Intriligator, M.D. (1978). *Econometric Models, Techniques, & Applications*. New Jersey: Prentice-Hall, Inc., pp. 165–173.
SOURCE: U.S. Department of Education, National Center for Education Statistics, Enrollment in Degree-Granting Institutions by Race/Ethnicity Projection Model, 1980 through 2024. (This table was prepared April 2015.)

Table A-28. Estimated equations and model statistics for full-time and part-time enrollment rates of Asian/Pacific Islander males at degree-granting postsecondary institutions based on data from 1989 to 2013

Independent variable	Coefficient	Standard error	t-statistic	R^2	D.W. statistic
1	2	3	4	5	6
Full-time					
Intercept term for 17-year-olds...............................	-5.76	0.589	-14.87	0.94	1.99*
Intercept term for 18-year-olds...............................	-3.05	0.575	-10.11		
Intercept term for 19-year-olds...............................	-2.79	0.577	-9.69		
Intercept term for 20-year-olds...............................	-2.94	0.576	-9.94		
Intercept term for 21-year-olds...............................	-2.91	0.576	-9.87		
Intercept term for 22-year-olds...............................	-3.28	0.577	-10.48		
Intercept term for 23-year-olds...............................	-3.53	0.578	-10.88		
Intercept term for 24-year-olds...............................	-3.88	0.579	-11.46		
Intercept term for 25- to 29-year-olds	-4.73	0.576	-13.19		
Intercept term for 30- to 34-year-olds	-5.74	0.577	-14.98		
Intercept term for 35- to 44-year-olds	-6.53	0.576	-16.47		
Log of Asian/Pacific Islander per capita disposable income in current dollars...................................	0.15	0.028	5.25		
Log unemployment rate for Asian/Pacific Islanders .	0.09	0.049	1.79		
Part-time					
Intercept term for 17-year-olds...............................	-2.64	1.053	-2.51	0.63	1.90*
Intercept term for 18-year-olds...............................	-1.10	0.821	-1.34		
Intercept term for 19-year-olds...............................	-0.23	0.813	-0.28		
Intercept term for 20-year-olds...............................	-0.36	0.819	-0.43		
Intercept term for 21-year-olds...............................	-0.46	0.820	-0.56		
Intercept term for 22-year-olds...............................	-0.56	0.825	-0.68		
Intercept term for 23-year-olds...............................	-0.58	0.813	-0.72		
Intercept term for 24-year-olds...............................	-0.72	0.812	-0.89		
Intercept term for 25- to 29-year-olds	-1.13	0.804	-1.40		
Intercept term for 30- to 34-year-olds	-1.79	0.806	-2.22		
Intercept term for 35- to 44-year-olds	-2.07	0.803	-2.58		
Log of Asian/Pacific Islander level of educational attainment per household	0.08	0.051	1.53		

* $p < .05$.
NOTE: R^2 = Coefficient of determination. D.W. statistic = Durbin-Watson statistic, a test for autocorrelation among regression residuals. For more details see Johnston, J., and Dinardo, J. (1996). *Econometric Methods*. New York: McGraw-Hill. The regression method used to estimate the full-time and part-time equations was the pooled seemingly unrelated regression method. The time period used to estimate the part-time equation is from 1989 to 2013.

The number of observations equal to 275. For additional information, see Intriligator, M.D. (1978). *Econometric Models, Techniques, & Applications*. New Jersey: Prentice-Hall, Inc., pp. 165–173. Race categories exclude persons of Hispanic ethnicity.
SOURCE: U.S. Department of Education, National Center for Education Statistics, Enrollment in Degree-Granting Institutions by Race/Ethnicity Projection Model, 1989 through 2023. (This table was prepared April 2015.)

Table A-29. Estimated equations and model statistics for full-time and part-time enrollment rates of Asian/Pacific Islander females at degree-granting postsecondary institutions based on data from 1989 to 2013

Independent variable	Coefficient	Standard error	t-statistic	R^2	D.W. statistic
1	2	3	4	5	6
Full-time					
Intercept term for 17-year-olds..............................	-8.74	0.546	-16.01	0.98	1.82*
Intercept term for 18-year-olds..............................	-6.28	0.529	-11.89		
Intercept term for 19-year-olds..............................	-5.77	0.534	-10.81		
Intercept term for 20-year-olds..............................	-6.08	0.531	-11.45		
Intercept term for 21-year-olds..............................	-6.06	0.529	-11.45		
Intercept term for 22-year-olds..............................	-6.59	0.531	-12.41		
Intercept term for 23-year-olds..............................	-6.91	0.530	-13.05		
Intercept term for 24-year-olds..............................	-7.44	0.540	-13.77		
Intercept term for 25- to 29-year-olds	-8.37	0.527	-15.88		
Intercept term for 30- to 34-year-olds	-9.61	0.531	-18.12		
Intercept term for 35- to 44-year-olds	-10.17	0.532	-19.13		
Log of Asian/Pacific Islander per capita disposable income in current dollars....................................	0.32	0.027	11.60		
Part-time					
Intercept term for 17-year-olds..............................	-6.39	0.696	-9.18	0.74	1.93*
Intercept term for 18-year-olds..............................	-4.69	0.692	-6.77		
Intercept term for 19-year-olds..............................	-4.07	0.717	-5.68		
Intercept term for 20-year-olds..............................	-4.44	0.705	-6.30		
Intercept term for 21-year-olds..............................	-3.87	0.696	-5.56		
Intercept term for 22-year-olds..............................	-4.15	0.697	-5.95		
Intercept term for 23-year-olds..............................	-4.40	0.692	-6.35		
Intercept term for 24-year-olds..............................	-4.49	0.698	-6.43		
Intercept term for 25- to 29-year-olds	-5.04	0.684	-7.37		
Intercept term for 30- to 34-year-olds	-5.62	0.685	-8.20		
Intercept term for 35- to 44-year-olds	-5.50	0.682	-8.06		
Log of Asian/Pacific Islander per capita disposable income in current dollars....................................	0.14	0.035	3.91		

* $p < .05$.
NOTE: R^2 = Coefficient of determination. D.W. statistic = Durbin-Watson statistic, a test for autocorrelation among regression residuals. For more details see Johnston, J., and Dinardo, J. (1996). *Econometric Methods*. New York: McGraw-Hill. The regression method used to estimate the full-time and part-time equations was the pooled seemingly unrelated regression method. The time period used to estimate the equations is from 1989 to 2013.

The number of observations is 275. For additional information, see Intriligator, M.D. (1978). *Econometric Models, Techniques, & Applications*. New Jersey: Prentice-Hall, Inc., pp. 165–173. Race categories exclude persons of Hispanic ethnicity.
SOURCE: U.S. Department of Education, National Center for Education Statistics, Enrollment in Degree-Granting Institutions by Race/Ethnicity Model, 1989–2012. (This table was prepared April 2015.)

A.6. POSTSECONDARY DEGREES CONFERRED

Projections in this edition

This edition of *Projections of Education Statistics* presents projections of postsecondary degrees conferred by level of degree and sex of recipient for 2013–14 through 2024–25.

Overview of approach

Basic approach

Projections of associate's, bachelor's, master's, and doctor's degrees for males and females were produced using forecasting equations that relate degrees conferred to full-time enrollment in degree-granting institutions by sex, student level (undergraduate or postbaccalaureate), and institution level (2-year or 4-year).

Degrees Conferred Projection Model

Procedures used to project degrees

For all degree levels, projections of degrees conferred were made separately for males and for females. The projections for males and females were then summed to get projections of the total number of degrees.

Multiple linear regression was used to project associate's, bachelor's, master's, and doctor's degrees based on enrollment variables for males and females. The enrollment variables used for the different levels of degrees are briefly described below.

For details and results of the regression analyses used to project associate's, bachelor's, master's, and doctor's degrees, see table A-30, under "Data and equations used to project degrees," later in this section.

Associate's degrees. *Projections were based on full-time undergraduate enrollment in 2-year institutions by sex.* Males' projections of associate's degrees were based on current full-time enrollment and full-time enrollment lagged 2 years. Females' projections of associate's degrees were based on current full-time enrollment and full-time enrollment lagged 1 and 2 years.

Bachelor's degrees. *Projections were based on full-time undergraduate enrollment in 4-year institutions by sex.* For males and for females, bachelor's degree projections were based on current full-time enrollment and full-time enrollment lagged 2 years.

Master's degrees. *Projections were based on full-time postbaccalaureate enrollment by sex.* Males' projections of master's degrees were based on current full-time enrollment and full-time enrollment lagged 1 year. Females' projections of master's degrees were based on current full-time enrollment.

Doctor's degrees. *Projections were based on full-time postbaccalaureate enrollment by sex.* For males and for females, doctor's degree projections were based on current full-time postbaccalaureate enrollment and full-time postbaccalaureate enrollment lagged 1 and 2 years.

Data and equations used to project degrees

Enrollment data and projections for degree-granting institutions. Historical enrollment data by sex, level of student, and level of institution came from the NCES Integrated Postsecondary Education Data System (IPEDS). For the time period used for each level of degree, see table A-30 on page 124. The enrollment projections used are those produced for this edition of *Projections of Education Statistics*. For more information about the enrollment projections, see Section A.5. Enrollment in Degree-granting postsecondary Institutions, earlier in this appendix.

Data on degrees awarded at all levels. Historical data by level of degree and sex of recipient came from the NCES Integrated Postsecondary Education Data System (IPEDS). All degrees were projected using data for 1970–71 to 2012–13.

Estimated equations and model statistics. For details on the equations used to project associate's, bachelor's, master's, and doctor's degrees, see table A-30 on page 124. The equations shown were selected on the basis of their statistical properties, such as coefficients of determination (R^2s), the *t*-statistics of the coefficients, the Durbin-Watson statistic, the Breusch-Godfrey Serial Correlation LM test statistic, and residual plots.

Accuracy of projections

Mean absolute percentage errors (MAPEs) for associate's and bachelor's degrees conferred by degree-granting institutions were calculated using the last six editions of *Projections of Education Statistics*. Table J, below, shows MAPEs projections of associate's and bachelor's degrees conferred. No MAPEs were calculated for master's and doctor's degrees as currently defined because the current models have only been used for three other editions.

Table J. **Mean absolute percentage errors (MAPEs) of projected associate's and bachelor's degrees conferred by degree-granting postsecondary institutions, by lead time: *Projections of Education Statistics to 2018* through *Projections of Education Statistics to 2023***

Statistic	Lead time (years)									
	1	2	3	4	5	6	7	8	9	10
Associate's degrees	2.7	6.1	10.2	14.9	18.3	18.3	—	—	—	—
Bachelor's degrees	0.7	0.4	0.9	3.1	5.0	6.6	—	—	—	—

— Not available.
NOTE: MAPEs for associate's and bachelor's degrees conferred were calculated using the last six editions of *Projections of Education Statistics*, from *Projections of Education Statistics to 2018* through *Projections of Education Statistics to 2023*. No MAPEs were calculated for master's and doctor's degrees as currently defined because the current models have only been used for three other editions. Calculations were made using unrounded numbers.
SOURCE: U.S. Department of Education, National Center for Education Statistics, *Projections of Education Statistics*, various issues. (This table was prepared April 2015.)

For more information about MAPEs, see Section A.0. Introduction, earlier in this appendix.

Table A-30. Estimated equations and model statistics for degrees conferred, by degree type and sex based on data from 1970–71 to 2012–2013

Dependent variable	Equation[1]				R^2	Breusch-Godfrey Serial Correlation LM test statistic[2]		Time period
1	2				3	4		5
Associate's degrees, men	DASSOCM =	266.2 + (2.09)	87.0DUGFT2M + (4.53)	105.7DUGFT2ML2 (5.23)	0.53	1.81	(0.404)	1970–71 to 2012–13
Associate's degrees, women	DLOGASSOCW =	# † +	0.9DLOGUGFT2WS3 + (8.63)	.5MA(1) (4.16)	0.81	3.65	(0.161)	1970–71 to 2012–13
Bachelor's degrees, men	DBACHM =	323.0 + (0.27)	58.8DUGFT4M + (3.20)	151.3DUGFT4ML2 (8.61)	0.75	0.50	(0.779)	1970–71 to 2012–13
Bachelor's degrees, women	DBACHW =	3644.4 + (1.95)	35.2DUGFT4W + (1.74)	153.2DUGFT4WL2 (7.28)	0.65	1.43	(0.489)	1970–71 to 2012–13
Master's degrees, men	PCHMASTM =	# † +	0.6PCHPBFTM + (4.29)	0.5PCHPBFTML1 (3.24)	0.66	1.01	(0.602)	1970–71 to 2012–13
Master's degrees, women	PCHMASTW =	# † +	0.4PCHPBFTW + (2.27)	0.6AR(1) (4.40)	0.56	3.71	(0.157)	1970–71 to 2012–13
Doctor's degrees, men	DDOCM =	-365.4 + (-1.56)	55.4DPBFTML1 + (2.60)	60.5DPBFTML2 (2.50)	0.53	1.18	(0.556)	1970–71 to 2012–13
Doctor's degrees, women	DDOCW =	487.1 + (1.58)	25.1DPBFTWL1 + (2.08)	45.1DPBFTWL2 (3.74)	0.50	0.40	(0.820)	1970–71 to 2012–13

† Not applicable.

Rounds to zero.

[1]AR(1) indicates that the model was estimated to account for first-order autocorrelation. To estimate the model, it was first transformed into a nonlinear model and then the coefficients were estimated simultaneously by applying a Marquardt nonlinear least squares algorithm to the transformed equation. MA(1) indicates that the model was estimated to incorporate moving average of the residual into model fit. For a general discussion of the problem of autocorrelation, and the method used to forecast in the presence of autocorrelation, see Judge, G., Hill, W., Griffiths, R., Lutkepohl, H., and Lee, T. (1985). *The Theory and Practice of Econometrics*. New York: John Wiley and Sons, pp. 315–318. Numbers in parentheses are *t*-statistics.

[2]The number in parentheses is the probability of the Chi-Square associated with the Breusch-Godfrey Serial Correlation LM Test. A *p* value greater that 0.05 implies that we do not reject the null hypothesis of no autocorrelation at the 5 percent significance level for a two-tailed test or 10 percent significance level for a one-tailed test (i.e., there is no autocorrelation present). For an explanation of the Breusch-Godfrey Serial Correlation LM test statistic, see Greene, W. (2000). *Econometric Analysis*. New Jersey: Prentice-Hall.

NOTE: R^2 is the coefficient of determination.

DASSOCM = First difference of associate's degrees awarded to males.
DLOGASSOCW = First difference of the log of associate's degrees awarded to females.
DBACHM = First difference of bachelor's degrees awarded to males.
DBACHW = First difference of bachelor's degrees awarded to females.
PCHMASTM = Percentage change in master's degrees awarded to males.
PCHMASTW = Percentage change in master's degrees awarded to females.

DDOCM = First difference of doctor's degrees awarded to males.
DDOCW = First difference of doctor's degrees awarded to females.
DUGFT2M = First difference of full-time male undergraduate enrollment in 2-year institutions.
DUGFT2ML2 = First difference of full-time male undergraduate enrollment in 2-year institutions, lagged two periods.
DLOGUGFT2WS3= First difference of the sum of the full-time female undergraduate enrollment in 2-year institutions over the present year and the previous 2 years.
DUGFT4M = First difference of full-time male undergraduate enrollment in 4-year institutions.
DUGFT4ML2 = First difference of full-time male undergraduate enrollment in 4-year institutions, lagged two periods.
DUGFT4W = First difference of full-time female undergraduate enrollment in 4-year institutions.
DUGFT4WL2 = First difference of full-time female undergraduate enrollment in 4-year institutions, lagged two periods.
PCHPBFTM = Percentage change in full-time male postbaccalaureate enrollment.
PCHPBFTML1 = Percentage change in full-time male postbaccalaureate enrollment lagged 1 year.
PCHPBFTW = Percentage change in full-time female postbaccalaureate enrollment.
DPBFTML1 = First difference of full-time male postbaccalaureate enrollment lagged 1 year.
DPBFTML2 = First difference of full-time male postbaccalaureate enrollment lagged 2 years.
DPBFTWL1 = First difference of full-time female postbaccalaureate enrollment lagged 1 year.
DPBFTWL2 = First difference of full-time female postbaccalaureate enrollment lagged 2 years.
SOURCE: U.S. Department of Education, National Center for Education Statistics, Degrees Conferred Projection Model, 1970–71 through 2024–25. (This table was prepared March 2015.)

Appendix B
Supplementary Tables

Table B-1. Annual number of births: 1946 through 2013

Calendar year	Number of births, in thousands	Calendar year	Number of births, in thousands
1	2	1	2
1946	3,426	1980	3,612
1947	3,834	1981	3,629
1948	3,655	1982	3,681
1949	3,667	1983	3,639
1950	3,645	1984	3,669
1951	3,845	1985	3,761
1952	3,933	1986	3,757
1953	3,989	1987	3,809
1954	4,102	1988	3,910
1955	4,128	1989	4,041
1956	4,244	1990	4,158
1957	4,332	1991	4,111
1958	4,279	1992	4,065
1959	4,313	1993	4,000
1960	4,307	1994	3,953
1961	4,317	1995	3,900
1962	4,213	1996	3,891
1963	4,142	1997	3,881
1964	4,070	1998	3,942
1965	3,801	1999	3,959
1966	3,642	2000	4,059
1967	3,555	2001	4,026
1968	3,535	2002	4,022
1969	3,626	2003	4,090
1970	3,739	2004	4,112
1971	3,556	2005	4,138
1972	3,258	2006	4,266
1973	3,137	2007	4,317
1974	3,160	2008	4,248
1975	3,144	2009	4,131
1976	3,168	2010	3,999
1977	3,327	2011	3,954
1978	3,333	2012	3,953
1979	3,494	2013	3,932

NOTE: Some data have been revised from previously published figures.
SOURCE: U.S. Department of Health and Human Services, National Center for Health Statistics (NCHS), *National Vital Statistics Reports*, various years. (This table was prepared March 2015.)

Table B-2. Actual and projected prekindergarten- and kindergarten-age populations, by age: 1999 through 2024

[In thousands]

Year (July 1)	3- to 5-year-olds	3-year-olds	4-year-olds	5-year-olds
1	2	3	4	5
Actual				
1999	11,768	3,827	3,946	3,996
2000	11,691	3,821	3,902	3,968
2001	11,540	3,803	3,827	3,910
2002	11,454	3,804	3,813	3,837
2003	11,501	3,861	3,817	3,824
2004	11,714	4,008	3,877	3,830
2005	11,866	3,943	4,030	3,893
2006	11,987	3,966	3,971	4,051
2007	11,996	4,004	3,998	3,993
2008	12,058	3,992	4,041	4,024
2009	12,129	4,026	4,033	4,070
2010	12,254	4,112	4,078	4,065
2011	12,311	4,102	4,122	4,088
2012	12,225	3,982	4,112	4,132
2013	12,103	3,990	3,992	4,122
Projected				
2014	12,031	4,028	4,001	4,002
2015	12,278	4,226	4,040	4,012
2016	12,546	4,257	4,238	4,051
2017	12,805	4,285	4,270	4,250
2018	12,892	4,311	4,298	4,282
2019	12,971	4,335	4,325	4,311
2020	13,044	4,357	4,349	4,337
2021	13,111	4,377	4,371	4,362
2022	13,172	4,395	4,392	4,385
2023	13,226	4,410	4,410	4,405
2024	13,272	4,423	4,425	4,424

NOTE: Some data have been revised from previously published figures. Detail may not sum to totals because of rounding. As the Census Bureau projections were not updated to reflect the most recent 2013 Census Bureau population estimates, the Census Bureau age-specific population projections for each year were adjusted by multiplying the ratio of the total Census Bureau estimate for 2013 to the total Census Bureau projection for 2013.

SOURCE: U.S. Department of Commerce, Census Bureau, Population Estimates, retrieved January 5, 2015 from http://www.census.gov/popest/data/index.html; and Population Projections, retrieved January 5, 2015, from http://www.census.gov/population/projections/data/national/2012.html. (This table was prepared March 2015.)

Table B-3. Actual and projected school-age populations, by selected ages: 1999 through 2024

[In thousands]

Year (July 1)	5-year-olds	6-year-olds	5- to 13-year-olds	14- to 17-year-olds
1	2	3	4	5
Actual				
1999..	3,996	4,045	36,804	16,007
2000..	3,968	4,004	37,054	16,144
2001..	3,910	3,973	37,093	16,280
2002..	3,837	3,913	37,001	16,506
2003..	3,824	3,838	36,814	16,694
2004..	3,830	3,822	36,458	17,054
2005..	3,893	3,828	36,248	17,358
2006..	4,051	3,891	36,269	17,549
2007..	3,993	4,046	36,296	17,597
2008..	4,024	3,988	36,438	17,395
2009..	4,070	4,018	36,657	17,232
2010..	4,065	4,073	36,867	17,064
2011..	4,088	4,075	36,915	16,865
2012..	4,132	4,098	37,004	16,714
2013..	4,122	4,142	37,074	16,644
Projected				
2014..	4,002	4,132	36,921	16,710
2015..	4,012	4,012	36,835	16,742
2016..	4,051	4,022	36,883	16,683
2017..	4,250	4,062	37,107	16,642
2018..	4,282	4,261	37,326	16,562
2019..	4,311	4,293	37,577	16,538
2020..	4,337	4,322	37,833	16,629
2021..	4,362	4,349	38,073	16,738
2022..	4,385	4,374	38,345	16,801
2023..	4,405	4,397	38,758	16,746
2024..	4,424	4,418	39,180	16,680

NOTE: Some data have been revised from previously published figures. Detail may not sum to totals because of rounding. As the Census Bureau projections were not updated to reflect the most recent 2013 Census Bureau population estimates, the Census Bureau age-specific population projections for each year were adjusted by multiplying the ratio of the total Census Bureau estimate for 2013 to the total Census Bureau projection for 2013.

SOURCE: U.S. Department of Commerce, Census Bureau, Population Estimates, retrieved January 5, 2015 from http://www.census.gov/popest/data/index.html; and Population Projections, retrieved January 5, 2015, from http://www.census.gov/population/projections/data/national/2012.html. (This table was prepared March 2015.)

Table B-4. Actual and projected college-age populations, by selected ages: 1999 through 2024

[In thousands]

Year (July 1)	18-year-olds	18- to 24-year-olds	25- to 29-year-olds	30- to 34-year-olds	35- to 44-year-olds
1	2	3	4	5	6
Actual					
1999	3,993	26,780	19,632	20,647	45,130
2000	4,082	27,390	19,328	20,560	45,217
2001	4,106	28,081	18,866	20,689	45,101
2002	4,087	28,598	18,752	20,705	44,706
2003	4,206	29,121	18,872	20,545	44,251
2004	4,218	29,474	19,193	20,220	43,881
2005	4,228	29,609	19,629	19,787	43,594
2006	4,303	29,758	20,200	19,343	43,325
2007	4,397	29,973	20,640	19,231	42,879
2008	4,590	30,355	21,003	19,365	42,275
2009	4,537	30,687	21,184	19,708	41,573
2010	4,492	30,914	21,248	20,131	41,062
2011	4,399	31,216	21,387	20,577	40,715
2012	4,354	31,470	21,476	20,961	40,580
2013	4,287	31,560	21,656	21,315	40,511
Projected					
2014	4,209	31,456	22,025	21,540	40,459
2015	4,190	31,130	22,453	21,643	40,468
2016	4,191	30,780	22,934	21,810	40,466
2017	4,202	30,500	23,362	21,926	40,765
2018	4,281	30,399	23,602	22,130	41,261
2019	4,229	30,293	23,674	22,517	41,770
2020	4,139	30,170	23,472	22,963	42,315
2021	4,168	30,152	23,168	23,462	42,965
2022	4,208	30,194	22,905	23,908	43,503
2023	4,211	30,238	22,742	24,167	44,100
2024	4,237	30,296	22,637	24,259	44,743

NOTE: Some data have been revised from previously published figures. Detail may not sum to totals because of rounding. As the Census Bureau projections were not updated to reflect the most recent 2013 Census Bureau population estimates, the Census Bureau age-specific population projections for each year were adjusted by multiplying the ratio of the total Census Bureau estimate for 2013 to the total Census Bureau projection for 2013.

SOURCE: U.S. Department of Commerce, Census Bureau, Population Estimates, retrieved January 5, 2015 from http://www.census.gov/popest/data/index.html; and Population Projections, retrieved January 5, 2015, from http://www.census.gov/population/projections/data/national/2012.html. (This table was prepared March 2015.)

Table B-5. Actual and projected fall enrollment in public elementary and secondary schools, change in fall enrollment from previous year, resident population, and fall enrollment as a ratio of the population: School years 1999–2000 through 2024–25

School year	Fall enrollment (in thousands)	Change in fall enrollment from previous year (in thousands)	Resident population (in millions)	Fall enrollment as a ratio of the population
1	2	3	4	5
Actual				
1999–2000	46,857	319	279.3	0.168
2000–01	47,204	346	282.4	0.167
2001–02	47,672	468	285.2	0.167
2002–03	48,183	511	287.9	0.167
2003–04	48,540	357	290.6	0.167
2004–05	48,795	255	293.2	0.166
2005–06	49,113	318	296.0	0.166
2006–07	49,316	203	298.8	0.165
2007–08	49,293	-23	301.7	0.163
2008–09	49,266	-27	304.5	0.162
2009–10	49,361	95	307.2	0.161
2010–11	49,484	123	309.7	0.160
2011–12	49,522	37	312.0	0.159
2012–13	49,771	249	314.2	0.158
Projected				
2013–14	49,942	171	316.4	0.158
2014–15	49,986	44	318.9	0.157
2015–16	50,094	109	321.4	0.156
2016–17	50,229	135	323.8	0.155
2017–18	50,584	355	326.3	0.155
2018–19	50,871	287	328.9	0.155
2019–20	51,183	312	331.4	0.154
2020–21	51,547	365	333.9	0.154
2021–22	51,910	363	336.4	0.154
2022–23	52,260	350	338.9	0.154
2023–24	52,601	341	341.4	0.154
2024–25	52,920	318	343.9	0.154

NOTE: Resident population includes civilian population and armed forces personnel residing with the United States; it excludes armed forces personnel overseas. Calculations were made using unrounded numbers. Some data have been revised from previously published figures. Detail may not sum to totals because of rounding. As the Census Bureau projections were not updated to reflect the most recent 2013 Census Bureau population estimates, the Census Bureau age-specific population projections for each year were adjusted by multiplying the ratio of the total Census Bureau estimate for 2012 to the total Census Bureau projection for 2013.

SOURCE: U.S. Department of Commerce, Census Bureau, Population Estimates, retrieved January 5, 2015 from http://www.census.gov/popest/data/index.html; and Population Projections, retrieved January 5, 2015, from http://www.census.gov/population/projections/data/national/2012.html. U.S. Department of Education, National Center for Education Statistics, Common Core of Data (CCD), "State Nonfiscal Survey of Public Elementary/Secondary Education," 1996–97 through 2012–13; and National Elementary and Secondary Enrollment Projection Model, 1972 through 2024. (This table was prepared March 2015.)

Table B-6. Actual and projected macroeconomic measures of the economy: School years 1999–2000 through 2024–25

School year	Disposable income per capita in constant 2013–14 dollars[1]	Education revenue receipts from state sources per capita in constant 2013–14 dollars[2]	Consumer Price Index[3]
1	2	3	4
Actual			
1999–2000	$33,589	$917	0.720
2000–01	34,550	949	0.745
2001–02	35,313	955	0.758
2002–03	35,684	960	0.775
2003–04	36,752	944	0.792
2004–05	37,296	955	0.816
2005–06	37,971	966	0.847
2006–07	38,786	1,016	0.869
2007–08	39,196	1,040	0.901
2008–09	38,896	994	0.914
2009–10	38,467	913	0.923
2010–11	39,146	915	0.941
2011–12	39,729	898	0.969
2012–13[4]	40,172	869	0.985
2013–14[4]	40,236	875	1.000
Projected			
2014–15	41,140	894	1.006
2015–16	41,950	911	1.021
2016–17	43,027	933	1.045
2017–18	44,160	960	1.070
2018–19	45,070	980	1.097
2019–20	46,086	1,002	1.123
2020–21	46,972	1,023	1.151
2021–22	47,774	1,041	1.177
2022–23	48,594	1,059	1.203
2023–24	49,433	1,077	1.231
2024–25	49,939	1,087	1.251

[1]Based on the price deflator for personal consumption expenditures, Bureau of Labor Statistics, U.S. Department of Labor.
[2]Based on the Consumer Price Index for all urban consumers, Bureau of Labor Statistics, U.S. Department of Labor.
[3]Consumer Price Index adjusted to a school-year basis (July through June).
[4]Education revenue receipts from state sources per capita is a projection.

NOTE: Calculations were made using unrounded numbers. Some data have been revised from previously published figures.
SOURCE: U.S. Department of Education, National Center for Education Statistics, Common Core of Data (CCD), "National Public Education Financial Survey," 1997–98 through 2011–12; Revenue Receipts From State Sources Projections Model, 1971–72 through 2024–25; and IHS Global Inc., "U.S. Quarterly Macroeconomic Model, 1st Quarter 2015 Short-Term Baseline Projections." (This table was prepared March 2015.)

This page intentionally left blank.

Appendix C
Data Sources

SOURCES AND COMPARABILITY OF DATA

The information in this report was obtained from many sources, including federal and state agencies, private research organizations, and professional associations. The data were collected by many methods, including surveys of a universe (such as all colleges) or of a sample, and compilations of administrative records. Care should be used when comparing data from different sources. Differences in procedures, such as timing, phrasing of questions, and interviewer training, mean that the results from the different sources are not strictly comparable. More extensive documentation of one survey's procedures than of another's does not imply more problems with the data, only that more information is available on the survey.

ACCURACY OF DATA

The accuracy of any statistic is determined by the joint effects of "sampling" and "nonsampling" errors. Estimates based on a sample will differ from the figures that would have been obtained if a complete census had been taken using the same survey instruments, instructions, and procedures. Besides sampling errors, both types of the surveys, universe and sample, are subject to errors of design, reporting, and processing, and errors due to nonresponse. To the extent possible, these nonsampling errors are kept to a minimum by methods built into the survey procedures. In general, however, the effects of nonsampling errors are more difficult to gauge than those produced by sampling variability.

SAMPLING ERRORS

The standard error is the primary measure of the sampling variability of an estimate. Standard errors can be used to produce confidence intervals. For example, from table A-12, an estimated 91.8 percent of public school teachers reported that they worked full time in 2007–08. This figure has an estimated standard error of 0.29 percent. Therefore, the estimated 95 percent confidence interval for this statistic is approximately 91.27 to 92.41 percent (91.8 ± 1.96 (0.29)). That is, if the processes of selecting a sample, collecting the data, and constructing the confidence interval were repeated, it would be expected that in 95 out of 100 samples from the same population, the confidence interval would contain the true full-time working rate.

Analysis of standard errors can help assess how valid a comparison between two estimates might be. The *standard error of a difference* between two independent sample estimates is equal to the square root of the sum of the squared standard errors of the estimates. The standard error (*se*) of the difference between independent sample estimates *a* and *b* is

$$SE_{A-B} = (se_a^2 + se_b^2)^{1/2}$$

Note that some of the standard errors in the original documents are approximations. That is, a number of approximations were required in order to derive estimates of standard errors that would be applicable to a wide variety of items and could be prepared at moderate costs. As a result, most of the standard errors presented provide a general order of magnitude rather than the exact standard error for any specific item.

NONSAMPLING ERRORS

Both universe and sample surveys are subject to nonsampling errors. Nonsampling errors are of two kinds—random and nonrandom. Random nonsampling errors may arise when respondents or interviewers interpret questions differently, when respondents must estimate values, or when coders, keyers, and other processors handle answers differently. Nonrandom nonsampling errors result from total nonresponse (no usable data obtained for a sampled unit), partial or item nonresponse (only a portion of a response may be usable), inability or unwillingness on the part of respondents to provide information, difficulty interpreting questions, mistakes in recording or keying data, errors of collection or processing, and overcoverage or undercoverage of the target universe. Random nonresponse errors usually, but not always, result in an understatement of sampling errors and thus an overstatement of the precision of survey estimates. Because estimating the magnitude of nonsampling errors would require special experiments or access to independent data, these magnitudes are seldom available.

To compensate for suspected nonrandom errors, adjustments of the sample estimates are often made. For example, adjustments are frequently made for nonresponse, both total and partial. Imputations are usually made separately within various groups of sample members that have similar survey characteristics. Imputation for item nonresponse is usually made by substituting for a missing item the response to that item by another respondent having characteristics similar to those of the respondent.

Although the magnitude of nonsampling errors in the data used in *Projections of Education Statistics* is frequently unknown, idiosyncrasies that have been identified are noted on the appropriate tables.

FEDERAL AGENCY SOURCES

National Center for Education Statistics (NCES)

Common Core of Data

The Common Core of Data (CCD) is NCES's primary database on public elementary and secondary education in the United States. It is a comprehensive, annual, national statistical database of all public elementary and secondary schools and school districts containing data designed to be comparable across all states. This database can be used to select samples for other NCES surveys and provide basic information and descriptive statistics on public elementary and secondary schools and schooling in general.

The CCD collects statistical information annually from approximately 100,000 public elementary and secondary schools and approximately 18,000 public school districts (including supervisory unions and regional education service agencies) in the 50 states, the District of Columbia, Department of Defense (DoD) dependents schools, the Bureau of Indian Education, Puerto Rico, American Samoa, Guam, the Northern Mariana Islands, and the U.S. Virgin Islands. Three categories of information are collected in the CCD survey: general descriptive information on schools and school districts; data on students and staff; and fiscal data. The general descriptive information includes name, address, phone number, and type of locale; the data on students and staff include selected demographic characteristics; and the fiscal data pertain to revenues and current expenditures.

The ED*Facts* data collection system is the primary collection tool for the CCD. NCES works collaboratively with the Department of Education's Performance Information Management Service to develop the CCD collection procedures and data definitions. Coordinators from State Education Agencies (SEAs) submit the CCD data at different levels (school, agency, and state) to the ED*Facts* collection system. Prior to submitting CCD files to ED*Facts*, SEAs must collect and compile information from their respective Local Education Agencies (LEAs) through established administrative records systems within their state or jurisdiction.

Once SEAs have completed their submissions, the CCD survey staff analyzes and verifies the data for quality assurance. Even though the CCD is a universe collection and thus not subject to sampling errors, nonsampling errors can occur. The two potential sources of nonsampling errors are nonresponse and inaccurate reporting. NCES attempts to minimize nonsampling errors through the use of annual training of SEA coordinators, extensive quality reviews, and survey editing procedures. In addition, each year, SEAs are given the opportunity to revise their state-level aggregates from the previous survey cycle.

The CCD survey consists of six components: The Public Elementary/Secondary School Universe Survey, the Local Education Agency (School District) Universe Survey, the State Nonfiscal Survey of Public Elementary/Secondary Education, the National Public Education Financial Survey (NPEFS), the School District Fiscal Data Survey (F-33), and the Teacher Compensation Survey. The following sections describe the CCD surveys that were used in preparing this report.

State Nonfiscal Survey of Public Elementary/Secondary Education

The State Nonfiscal Survey of Public Elementary/Secondary Education for the 2011–12 school year provides state-level, aggregate information about students and staff in public elementary and secondary education. It includes data from the 50 states, the District of Columbia, Puerto Rico, the U.S. Virgin Islands, the Commonwealth of the Northern Mariana Islands, and Guam. The DoD dependents schools (overseas and domestic), the Bureau of Indian Education, and American Samoa did not report data for the 2011–12 school year. This survey covers public school student membership by grade, race/ethnicity, and state or jurisdiction and covers number of staff in public schools by category and state or jurisdiction. Beginning with the 2006–07 school year, the number of diploma recipients and other high school completers are no longer included in the State Nonfiscal Survey of Public Elementary/Secondary Education file. These data are now collected through the Local Education Agency (School District) Universe Survey and published in the public-use Common Core of Data State Dropout and Completion Data File.

National Public Education Financial Survey

The purpose of the National Public Education Financial Survey (NPEFS) is to provide district, state, and federal policymakers, researchers, and other interested users with descriptive information about revenues and expenditures for public elementary and secondary education. The data collected are useful to (1) chief officers of state education agencies; (2) policymakers in the executive and legislative branches of federal and state governments; (3) education policy and public policy researchers; and (4) the public, journalists, and others.

Data for NPEFS are collected from SEAs in the 50 states, the District of Columbia, Puerto Rico, and four other jurisdictions (American Samoa, Guam, the Commonwealth of the Northern Mariana Islands, and the U.S. Virgin Islands). The data file is organized by state or jurisdiction and contains revenue data by funding source; expenditure data by function (the activity being supported by the expenditure) and object (the category of expenditure); average daily attendance data; and total student membership data from the CCD State Nonfiscal Survey of Public Elementary/Secondary Education.

Further information on the nonfiscal CCD data may be obtained from

Patrick Keaton
Administrative Data Division
Elementary and Secondary Branch
National Center for Education Statistics
Potomac Center Plaza
550 12th Street SW
Washington, DC 20202
patrick.keaton@ed.gov
http://nces.ed.gov/ccd

Further information on the fiscal CCD data may be obtained from

Stephen Cornman
Administrative Data Division
Elementary and Secondary Branch
National Center for Education Statistics
Potomac Center Plaza
550 12th Street SW
Washington, DC 20202
stephen.cornman@ed.gov
http://nces.ed.gov/ccd

Integrated Postsecondary Education Data System

The Integrated Postsecondary Education Data System (IPEDS) surveys approximately 7,500 postsecondary institutions, including universities and colleges, as well as institutions offering technical and vocational education beyond the high school level. IPEDS, an annual universe collection that began in 1986, replaced the Higher Education General Information Survey (HEGIS).

IPEDS consists of interrelated survey components that provide information on postsecondary institutions, student enrollment, programs offered, degrees and certificates conferred, and both the human and financial resources involved in the provision of institutionally based postsecondary education. Prior to 2000, the IPEDS survey had the following subject-matter components: Graduation Rates; Fall Enrollment; Institutional Characteristics; Completions; Salaries, Tenure, and Fringe Benefits of Full-Time Faculty; Fall Staff; Finance; and Academic Libraries (in 2000, the Academic Libraries component became a survey separate from IPEDS). Since 2000, IPEDS survey components occurring in a particular collection year have been organized into three seasonal collection periods: fall, winter, and spring. The Institutional Characteristics and Completions components first took place during the fall 2000 collection; the Employees by Assigned Position (EAP), Salaries, and Fall Staff components first took place during the winter 2001–02 collection; and the Enrollment, Student Financial Aid, Finance, and Graduation Rates components first took place during the spring 2001 collection. In the winter 2005–06 data collection, the Employees by Assigned Position, Fall Staff, and Salaries components were merged into the Human Resources component. During the 2007–08 collection year, the Enrollment component was broken into two separate components: 12-Month Enrollment (taking place in the fall collection) and Fall Enrollment (taking place in the spring collection). In the 2011–12 IPEDS data collection year, the Student Financial Aid component was moved to the winter data collection to aid in the timing of the net price of attendance calculations displayed on the College Navigator (http://nces.ed.gov/collegenavigator). In the 2012–13 IPEDS data collection year, the Human Resources component was moved to the spring data collection.

Beginning in 2008–09, the first-professional degree category was combined with the doctor's degree category. However, some degrees formerly identified as first-professional that take more than two full-time-equivalent academic years to complete, such as those in Theology (M.Div, M.H.L./Rav), are included in the Master's degree category. Doctor's degrees were broken out into three distinct categories: research/scholarship, professional practice, and other doctor's degrees.

IPEDS race/ethnicity data collection also changed in 2008–09. The "Asian" race category is now separate from a "Native Hawaiian or Other Pacific Islander" category. Survey takers also have the option of identifying themselves as being of "Two or more races." To reflect the recognition that "Hispanic" refers to ethnicity, not race, the new Hispanic category reads "Hispanics of any race."

The degree-granting institutions portion of IPEDS is a census of colleges that award associate's or higher degrees and are eligible to participate in Title IV financial aid programs. Prior to 1993, data from technical and vocational institutions were collected through a sample survey. Beginning in 1993, all data are gathered in a census of all postsecondary institutions. Beginning in 1997, the survey was restricted to institutions participating in Title IV programs.

The classification of institutions offering college and university education changed as of 1996. Prior to 1996, institutions that had courses leading to an associate's or higher degree or that had courses accepted for credit toward those degrees were considered higher education institutions. Higher education institutions were accredited by an agency or association that was recognized by the U.S. Department of Education or were recognized directly by the Secretary of Education. The newer standard includes institutions that award associate's or higher degrees and that are eligible to participate in Title IV federal financial aid programs. Tables that contain any data according to this standard are titled "degree-granting" institutions. Time-series tables may contain data from both series, and they are noted accordingly. The impact of this change on data collected in 1996 was not large. The largest impact was on private 2-year college enrollment. In contrast, most of the data on public 4-year colleges were affected to a minimal extent. The impact on enrollment in public 2-year colleges was noticeable in certain states, such as Arizona, Arkansas, Georgia, Louisiana, and Washington, but was relatively small at the national level. Overall, total enrollment for all institutions was about one-half of a percent higher in 1996 for degree-granting institutions than for higher education institutions.

Prior to the establishment of IPEDS in 1986, HEGIS acquired and maintained statistical data on the characteristics and operations of institutions of higher education. Implemented in 1966, HEGIS was an annual universe survey of institutions accredited at the college level by an agency recognized by the Secretary of the U.S. Department of Education. These institutions were listed in NCES's *Education Directory, Colleges and Universities*.

HEGIS surveys collected information on institutional characteristics, faculty salaries, finances, enrollment, and degrees. Since these surveys, like IPEDS, were distributed to all higher education institutions, the data presented are not subject to sampling error. However, they are subject to nonsampling error, the sources of which varied with the survey instrument.

The NCES Taskforce for IPEDS Redesign recognized that there were issues related to the consistency of data definitions as well as the accuracy, reliability, and validity of other quality measures within and across surveys. The IPEDS redesign in 2000 provided institution-specific web-based data forms. While the new system shortened data processing time and provided better data consistency, it did not address the accuracy of the data provided by institutions.

Beginning in 2003–04 with the Prior Year Data Revision System, prior-year data have been available to institutions entering current data. This allows institutions to make changes to their prior-year entries either by adjusting the data or by providing missing data. These revisions allow the evaluation of the data's accuracy by looking at the changes made.

NCES conducted a study (NCES 2005-175) of the 2002–03 data that were revised in 2003–04 to determine the accuracy of the imputations, track the institutions that submitted revised data, and analyze the revised data they submitted. When institutions made changes to their data, it was assumed that the revised data were the "true" data. The data were analyzed for the number and type of institutions making changes, the type of changes, the magnitude of the changes, and the impact on published data.

Because NCES imputes for missing data, imputation procedures were also addressed by the Redesign Taskforce. For the 2003–04 assessment, differences between revised values and values that were imputed in the original files were compared (i.e., revised value minus imputed value). These differences were then used to provide an assessment of the effectiveness of imputation procedures. The size of the differences also provides an indication of the accuracy of imputation procedures. To assess the overall impact of changes on aggregate IPEDS estimates, published tables for each component were reconstructed using the revised 2002–03 data. These reconstructed tables were then compared to the published tables to determine the magnitude of aggregate bias and the direction of this bias.

The fall 2011 and spring 2012 data collections were entirely web-based. Data were provided by "keyholders," institutional representatives appointed by campus chief executives, who were responsible for ensuring that survey data submitted by the institution were correct and complete. Because Title IV institutions are the primary focus of IPEDS and because these institutions are required to respond to the survey, response rates for Title IV institutions in the fall 2011 IPEDS collection were high. The Institutional Characteristics (IC) component response rate among all Title IV entities was 100.0 percent (all 7,479 Title IV entities responded). In addition, the response rates for the Completions and 12-Month Enrollment components were also 100.0 percent. More details on the accuracy and reliability of IPEDS data can be found in the *Integrated Postsecondary Education Data System Data Quality Study* (NCES 2005-175).

Further information on IPEDS may be obtained from

Richard Reeves
Administrative Data Division
Postsecondary Branch
National Center for Education Statistics
Potomac Center Plaza
550 12th Street SW
Washington, DC 20202
richard.reeves@ed.gov
http://nces.ed.gov/ipeds

Fall (12-Month Enrollment)

Data on 12-month enrollment are collected for award levels ranging from postsecondary certificates of less than 1 year to doctoral degrees. The 12-month period during which data are collected is July 1 through June 30. Data are collected by race/ethnicity and gender and include unduplicated headcounts and instructional activity (contact or credit hours). These data are also used to calculate a full-time-equivalent (FTE) enrollment based on instructional activity. FTE enrollment is useful for gauging the size of the educational enterprise at the institution. Prior to the 2007–08 IPEDS data collection, the data collected in the 12-Month Enrollment component were part of the Fall Enrollment component, which is conducted during the spring data collection period. However, to improve the timeliness of the data, a separate 12-Month Enrollment survey component was developed in 2007. These data are now collected in the fall for the previous academic year. Of the 7,407 Title IV entities that were expected to respond to the 12-Month Enrollment component of the fall 2012 data collection, 7,403 responded, for an approximate response rate of 100.0 percent.

Further information on the IPEDS 12-Month Enrollment component may be obtained from

IPEDS Staff
Administrative Data Division
Postsecondary Branch
National Center for Education Statistics
Potomac Center Plaza
550 12th Street SW
Washington, DC 20202
http://nces.ed.gov/ncestaff/SurvDetl.asp?surveyID=010

Fall (Completions)

This survey was part of the HEGIS series throughout its existence. However, the degree classification taxonomy was revised in 1970–71, 1982–83, 1991–92, 2002–03, and 2009–10. Collection of degree data has been maintained through IPEDS.

Degrees-conferred trend tables arranged by the 2009–10 classification are included in the *Projections of Education Statistics* to provide consistent data from 1970–71 through the most recent year. Data in this edition on associate's degree, by field of study, cannot be made comparable with figures from years prior to 1982–83. The nonresponse rate does not appear to be a significant source of nonsampling error for this survey. The response rate over the years has been high; for the fall 2012 Completions component, it was about 100.0 percent. Because of the high response rate, there was no need to conduct a nonresponse bias analysis. Imputation methods for the fall 2012 Completions component are discussed in *Postsecondary Institutions and Cost of Attendance in 2012–13; Degrees and Other Awards Conferred, 2011–12; and 12-Month Enrollment, 2011–12* (NCES 2013-289rev). The *Integrated Postsecondary Education Data System Data Quality Study* (NCES 2005-175) indicated that most Title IV institutions supplying revised data on completions in 2003–04 were able to supply missing data for the prior year. The small differences between imputed data for the prior year and the revised actual data supplied by the institution indicated that the imputed values produced by NCES were acceptable.

Further information on the IPEDS Completions component may be obtained from

IPEDS Staff
Administrative Data Division
Postsecondary Branch
National Center for Education Statistics
Potomac Center Plaza
550 12th Street SW
Washington, DC 20202
http://nces.ed.gov/ncestaff/SurvDetl.asp?surveyID=010

Spring (Fall Enrollment)

This survey has been part of the HEGIS and IPEDS series since 1966. Response rates for this survey have been relatively high, generally exceeding 85 percent. Beginning in 2000, with web-based data collection, higher response rates were attained. In the spring 2013 data collection, where the Fall Enrollment component covered fall 2012, the response rate was 99.9 percent. Data collection procedures for the Fall Enrollment component of the spring 2013 data collection are presented in *Enrollment in Postsecondary Institutions, Fall 2012; Financial Statistics, Fiscal Year 2012; Graduation Rates, Selected Cohorts, 2004–09; and Employees in Postsecondary Institutions, Fall 2012* (NCES 2013-183).

Beginning with the fall 1986 survey and the introduction of IPEDS (see above), the survey was redesigned. The survey allows (in alternating years) for the collection of age and residence data. Beginning in 2000, the survey collected instructional activity and unduplicated headcount data, which are needed to compute a standardized, full-time-equivalent (FTE) enrollment statistic for the entire academic year. As of 2007–08, the timeliness of the instructional activity data has been improved by collecting these data in the fall as part of the 12-Month-Enrollment component instead of in the spring as part of the Fall Enrollment component.

The *Integrated Postsecondary Education Data System Data Quality Study* (NCES 2005-175) showed that public institutions made the majority of changes to enrollment data during the 2004 revision period. The majority of changes were made to unduplicated headcount data, with the net differences between the original data and the revised data at about 1 percent. Part-time students in general and enrollment in private not-for-profit institutions were often underestimated. The fewest changes by institutions were to Classification of Instructional Programs (CIP) code data. (The CIP is a taxonomic coding scheme that contains titles and descriptions of primarily postsecondary instructional programs.)

Further information on the IPEDS Fall Enrollment component may be obtained from

IPEDS Staff
Administrative Data Division
Postsecondary Branch
National Center for Education Statistics
Potomac Center Plaza
550 12th Street SW
Washington, DC 20202
http://nces.ed.gov/ncestaff/SurvDetl.asp?surveyID=010

Private School Universe Survey

The purposes of the Private School Universe Survey (PSS) data collection activities are (1) to build an accurate and complete list of private schools to serve as a sampling frame for NCES sample surveys of private schools and (2) to report data on the total number of private schools, teachers, and students in the survey universe. Begun in 1989 under the U.S. Census Bureau, the PSS has been conducted every 2 years, and data for the 1989–90, 1991–92, 1993–94, 1995–96, 1997–98, 1999–2000, 2001–02, 2003–04, 2005–06, 2007–08, and 2009–10 school years have been released. A First Look report of the 2011–12 PSS data, *Characteristics of Private Schools in the United States: Results From the 2011–12 Private School Universe Survey* (NCES 2013-316) was published in July 2013.

The PSS produces data similar to that of the CCD for public schools, and can be used for public-private comparisons. The data are useful for a variety of policy- and research-relevant issues, such as the growth of religiously affiliated schools, the number of private high school graduates, the length of the school year for various private schools, and the number of private school students and teachers.

The target population for this universe survey is all private schools in the United States that meet the PSS criteria of a private school (i.e., the private school is an institution that provides instruction for any of grades K through 12, has one or more teachers to give instruction, is not administered by a public agency, and is not operated in a private home).

The survey universe is composed of schools identified from a variety of sources. The main source is a list frame initially developed for the 1989–90 PSS. The list is updated regularly by matching it with lists provided by nationwide private school associations, state departments of education, and other national guides and sources that list private schools. The other source is an area frame search in approximately 124 geographic areas, conducted by the U.S. Census Bureau.

Of the 40,302 schools included in the 2009–10 sample, 10,229 were found ineligible for the survey. Those not responding numbered 1,856, and those responding numbered 28,217. The unweighted response rate for the 2009–10 PSS survey was 93.8 percent.

Of the 39,325 schools included in the 2011–12 sample, 10,030 cases were considered as out-of-scope (not eligible for the PSS). A total of 26,983 private schools completed a PSS interview (15.8 percent completed online), while 2,312 schools refused to participate, resulting in an unweighted response rate of 92.1 percent.

Further information on the PSS may be obtained from

Steve Broughman
Sample Surveys Division
Cross-Sectional Surveys Branch
National Center for Education Statistics
Potomac Center Plaza
550 12th Street SW
Washington, DC 20202
stephen.broughman@ed.gov
http://nces.ed.gov/surveys/pss

Schools and Staffing Survey

The Schools and Staffing Survey (SASS) is a set of related questionnaires that collect descriptive data on the context of public and private elementary and secondary education. Data reported by districts, schools, principals, and teachers provide a variety of statistics on the condition of education in the United States that may be used by policymakers and the general public. The SASS system covers a wide range of topics, including teacher demand, teacher and principal characteristics, teachers' and principals' perceptions of school climate and problems in their schools, teacher and principal compensation, district hiring and retention practices, general conditions in schools, and basic characteristics of the student population.

SASS data are collected through a mail questionnaire with telephone and in-person field follow-up. SASS has been conducted by the Census Bureau for NCES since the first administration of the survey, which was conducted during the 1987–88 school year. Subsequent SASS administrations were conducted in 1990–91, 1993–94, 1999–2000, 2003–04, 2007–08, and 2011–12.

SASS is designed to produce national, regional, and state estimates for public elementary and secondary schools, school districts, principals, teachers, and school library media centers and national and regional estimates for public charter schools, as well as principals, teachers, and school library media centers within these schools. For private schools, the sample supports national, regional, and affiliation estimates for schools, principals, and teachers.

From its inception, SASS has had four core components: school questionnaires, teacher questionnaires, principal questionnaires, and school district (prior to 1999–2000, "teacher demand and shortage") questionnaires. A fifth component, school library media center questionnaires, was introduced in the 1993–94 administration and has been included in every subsequent administration of SASS. School library data were also collected in the 1990–91 administration of the survey through the school and principal questionnaires.

School questionnaires used in SASS include the Public and Private School Questionnaires; teacher questionnaires include the Public and Private School Teacher Questionnaires; principal questionnaires include the Public and Private School Principal (or School Administrator) Questionnaires; and school district questionnaires include the School District (or Teacher Demand and Shortage) Questionnaires.

Although the four core questionnaires and the school library media questionnaires have remained relatively stable over the various administrations of SASS, the survey has changed to accommodate emerging issues in elementary and secondary education. Some items have been added, some have been deleted, and some questionnaire items have been reworded.

During the 1990–91 SASS cycle, NCES worked with the Office of Indian Education to add an Indian School Questionnaire to SASS, and it remained a part of SASS through 2007–08. The Indian School Questionnaire explores the same school-level issues that the Public and Private School Questionnaires explore, allowing comparisons among the three types of schools. The 1990–91, 1993–94, 1999–2000, 2003–04, and 2007–08 administrations of SASS obtained data on Bureau of Indian Education (BIE) schools (schools funded or operated by the BIE), but the 2011–12 administration did not obtain BIE data. SASS estimates for all survey years presented in this report exclude BIE schools, and as a result, estimates in this report may differ from those in previously published reports.

The SASS teacher surveys collect information on the characteristics of teachers, such as their age, race/ethnicity, years of teaching experience, average number of hours per week spent on teaching activities, base salary, average class size, and highest degree earned. These teacher-reported data may be combined with related information on their school's characteristics, such as school type (e.g., public traditional, public charter, Catholic, private other religious, and private nonsectarian), community type, and school enrollment size. The teacher questionnaires also ask for information on teacher opinions regarding the school and teaching environment. In 1993–94, about 53,000 public school teachers and 10,400 private school teachers were sampled. In 1999–2000, about 56,300 public school teachers, 4,400 public charter school teachers, and 10,800 private school teachers were sampled. In 2003–04, about 52,500 public school teachers and 10,000 private school teachers were sampled. In 2007–08, about 48,400 public school teachers and 8,200 private school teachers were sampled. In 2011–12, about 51,100 public school teachers and 7,100 private school teachers were sampled. Weighted overall response rates in 2011–12 were 61.8 percent for public school teachers and 50.1 percent for private school teachers.

The SASS 2011–12 sample of schools was confined to the 50 states and the District of Columbia and excludes the other jurisdictions, the Department of Defense overseas schools, the BIE schools, and schools that do not offer teacher-provided classroom instruction in grades 1–12 or the ungraded equivalent. The SASS 2011–12 sample included 10,250 traditional public schools, 750 public charter schools, and 3,000 private schools.

The public school sample for the 2011–12 SASS was based on an adjusted public school universe file from the 2009–10 Common Core of Data (CCD), a database of all the nation's public school districts and public schools. The private school sample for the 2011–12 SASS was selected from the 2009–10 Private School Universe Survey (PSS), as updated for the 2011–12 PSS. This update collected membership lists from private school associations and religious denominations, as well as private school lists from state education departments. The 2011–12 SASS private school frame was further augmented by the inclusion of additional schools that were identified through the 2009–10 PSS area frame data collection.

Additional resources available regarding SASS include the methodology report *Quality Profile for SASS, Rounds 1–3: 1987–1995, Aspects of the Quality of Data in the Schools and Staffing Surveys (SASS)* (NCES 2000-308), as well as these reports: *Survey Documentation for the 2011–12 Schools and Staffing Survey* and *User's Manual for the 2011–12 Schools and Staffing Survey, Volumes 1–6* (Goldring et al. 2013) (NCES 2013-330 through 2013-335).

Further information on SASS may be obtained from

Chelsea Hickey
Sample Surveys Division
Cross-Sectional Surveys Branch
National Center for Education Statistics
Potomac Center Plaza
550 12th Street SW
Washington, DC 20202
chelsea.hickey@ed.gov
http://nces.ed.gov/surveys/sass

Teacher Follow-Up Survey

The Teacher Follow-Up Survey (TFS) is a SASS survey whose purpose is to determine how many teachers remain at the same school, move to another school, or leave the profession in the year following a SASS administration. It is administered to elementary and secondary teachers in the 50 states and the District of Columbia. The TFS uses two questionnaires, one for teachers who left teaching since the previous SASS administration and another for those who are still teaching either in the same school as last year or in a different school. The objective of the TFS is to focus on the characteristics of each group in order to answer questions about teacher mobility and attrition.

The 2008–09 TFS is different from any previous TFS administration in that it also serves as the second wave of a longitudinal study of first-year teachers. Because of this, the 2008–09 TFS consists of four questionnaires. Two are for respondents who were first-year public school teachers in the 2007–08 SASS and two are for the remainder of the sample.

Further information on the TFS may be obtained from

Chelsea Hickey
Sample Surveys Division
Cross-Sectional Surveys Branch
National Center for Education Statistics
Potomac Center Plaza
550 12th Street SW
Washington, DC 20202
chelsea.hickey@ed.gov
http://nces.ed.gov/surveys/sass

Bureau of Economic Analysis

National Income and Product Accounts (NIPAs)

The National Income and Product Accounts (NIPAs), produced by the Bureau of Economic Analysis, represent measures of economic activity in the United States, including production, income distribution, and personal savings. NIPAs also include data on employee compensation and wages. These estimations were first calculated in the early 1930s to help the government design economic policies to combat the Great Depression. Most of the NIPA series are published quarterly, with annual reviews of estimates from the three most recent years conducted in the summer.

Revisions to the NIPAs have been made over the years to create a more comprehensive economic picture of the United States. For example, in 1976, consumption of fixed capital (CFC) estimates shifted to a current-cost basis. In 1991, NIPAs began to use gross domestic product (GDP), instead of gross national product (GNP), as the primary measure of U.S. production. (At that time, virtually all other countries were already using GDP as their primary measure of production.) In the 2003 comprehensive revision, a more complete and accurate measure of insurance services was adopted. The incorporation of a new classification system for personal consumption expenditures (PCE) was among the changes contained in the 2009 comprehensive revision. The comprehensive revision of 2013 included the treatment of research and development expenditures by business, government, and nonprofit institutions serving households as fixed investment.

NIPA is slowly being integrated with other federal account systems, such as the federal account system of the Bureau of Labor Statistics.

Further information on NIPAs may be obtained from

U.S. Department of Commerce
Bureau of Economic Analysis
http://www.bea.gov

Bureau of Labor Statistics

Consumer Price Indexes

The Consumer Price Index (CPI) represents changes in prices of all goods and services purchased for consumption by urban households. Indexes are available for two population groups: a CPI for All Urban Consumers (CPI-U) and a CPI for Urban Wage Earners and Clerical Workers (CPI-W). Unless otherwise specified, data are adjusted for inflation using the CPI-U. These values are generally adjusted to a school-year basis by averaging the July through June figures. Price indexes are available for the United States, the four Census regions, size of city, cross-classifications of regions and size classes, and 26 local areas. The major uses of the CPI include as an economic indicator, as a deflator of other economic series, and as a means of adjusting income.

Also available is the Consumer Price Index research series using current methods (CPI-U-RS), which presents an estimate of the CPI-U from 1978 to the present that incorporates most of the improvements that the Bureau of Labor Statistics has made over that time span into the entire series. The historical price index series of the CPI-U does not reflect these changes, though these changes do make the present and future CPI more accurate. The limitations of the CPI-U-RS include considerable uncertainty surrounding the magnitude of the adjustments and the several improvements in the CPI that have not been incorporated into the CPI-U-RS for various reasons. Nonetheless, the CPI-U-RS can serve as a valuable proxy for researchers needing a historical estimate of inflation using current methods. This series has not been used in this report.

Further information on consumer price indexes may be obtained from

Bureau of Labor Statistics
U.S. Department of Labor
2 Massachusetts Avenue NE
Washington, DC 20212
http://www.bls.gov/cpi

Employment and Unemployment Surveys

Statistics on the employment and unemployment status of the population and related data are compiled by the Bureau of Labor Statistics (BLS) using data from the Current Population Survey (CPS) (see below) and other surveys. The Current Population Survey, a monthly household survey conducted by the U.S. Census Bureau for the Bureau of Labor Statistics, provides a comprehensive body of information on the employment and unemployment experience of the nation's population, classified by age, sex, race, and various other characteristics.

Further information on unemployment surveys may be obtained from

Bureau of Labor Statistics
U.S. Department of Labor
2 Massachusetts Avenue NE
Washington, DC 20212
cpsinfo@bls.gov
http://www.bls.gov/bls/employment.htm

Census Bureau

Current Population Survey

The Current Population Survey (CPS) is a monthly survey of about 60,000 households conducted by the U.S. Census Bureau for the Bureau of Labor Statistics. The CPS is the primary source of information of labor force statistics for the U.S. noninstitutionalized population (e.g., it excludes military personnel and their families living on bases and inmates of correctional institutions). In addition, supplemental questionnaires are used to provide further information about the U.S. population. Specifically, in October, detailed questions regarding school enrollment and school characteristics are asked. In March, detailed questions regarding income are asked.

The current sample design, introduced in July 2001, includes about 72,000 households. Each month about 58,900 of the 72,000 households are eligible for interview, and of those, 7 to 10 percent are not interviewed because of temporary absence or unavailability. Information is obtained each month from those in the household who are 15 years of age and older, and demographic data are collected for children 0–14 years of age. In addition, supplemental questions regarding school enrollment are asked about eligible household members ages 3 and older in the October survey. Prior to July 2001, data were collected in the CPS from about 50,000 dwelling units. The samples are initially selected based on the decennial census files and are periodically updated to reflect new housing construction.

A major redesign of the CPS was implemented in January 1994 to improve the quality of the data collected. Survey questions were revised, new questions were added, and computer-assisted interviewing methods were used for the survey data collection. Further information about the redesign is available in *Current Population Survey, October 1995: (School Enrollment Supplement) Technical Documentation* at http://www.census.gov/prod/techdoc/cps/cpsoct95.pdf.

Caution should be used when comparing data from 1994 through 2001 with data from 1993 and earlier. Data from 1994 through 2001 reflect 1990 census-based population controls, while data from 1993 and earlier reflect 1980 or earlier census-based population controls. Caution should also be used when comparing data from 1994 through 2001 with data from 2002 onward, as data from 2002 reflect 2000 census-based controls. Changes in population controls generally have relatively little impact on summary measures such as means, medians, and percentage distributions. They can have a significant impact on population counts. For example, use of the 1990 census-based population controls resulted in about a 1 percent increase in the civilian noninstitutional population and in the number of families and households. Thus, estimates of levels for data collected in 1994 and later years will differ from those for earlier years by more than what could be attributed to actual changes in the population. These differences could be disproportionately greater for certain subpopulation groups than for the total population.

Beginning in 2003, race/ethnicity questions expanded to include information on people of Two or more races. Native Hawaiian/Pacific Islander data are collected separately from Asian data. The questions have also been worded to make it clear that self-reported data on race/ethnicity should reflect the race/ethnicity with which the responder identifies, rather than what may be written in official documentation.

The estimation procedure employed for monthly CPS data involves inflating weighted sample results to independent estimates of characteristics of the civilian noninstitutional population in the United States by age, sex, and race. These independent estimates are based on statistics from decennial censuses; statistics on births, deaths, immigration, and emigration; and statistics on the population in the armed services. Generalized standard error tables are provided in the Current Population Reports; methods for deriving standard errors can be found within the CPS technical documentation at http://www.census.gov/cps/methodology/techdocs.html. The CPS data are subject to both nonsampling and sampling errors.

Prior to 2009, standard errors were estimated using the generalized variance function. The generalized variance function is a simple model that expresses the variance as a function of the expected value of a survey estimate. Beginning with March 2009 CPS data, standard errors were estimated using replicate weight methodology. Those interested in using CPS household-level supplement replicate weights to calculate variances may refer to *Estimating Current Population Survey (CPS) Household-Level Supplement Variances Using Replicate Weights* at http://thedataweb.rm.census.gov/pub/cps/supps/HH-level_Use_of_the_Public_Use_Replicate_Weight_File.doc.

Further information on CPS may be obtained from

Education and Social Stratification Branch
Population Division
Census Bureau
U.S. Department of Commerce
4600 Silver Hill Road
Washington, DC 20233
http://www.census.gov/cps

Dropouts

Each October, the Current Population Survey (CPS) includes supplemental questions on the enrollment status of the population ages 3 years and over as part of the monthly basic survey on labor force participation. In addition to gathering the information on school enrollment, with the limitations on accuracy as noted below under "School Enrollment," the survey data permit calculations of dropout rates. Both status and event dropout rates are tabulated from the October CPS. Event rates describe the proportion of students who leave school each year without completing a high school program. Status rates provide cumulative data on dropouts among all young adults within a specified age range. Status rates are higher than event rates because they include all dropouts ages 16 through 24, regardless of when they last attended school.

In addition to other survey limitations, dropout rates may be affected by survey coverage and exclusion of the institutionalized population. The incarcerated population has grown more rapidly and has a higher dropout rate than the general population. Dropout rates for the total population might be higher than those for the noninstitutionalized population if the prison and jail populations were included in the dropout rate calculations. On the other hand, if military personnel, who tend to be high school graduates, were included, it might offset some or all of the impact from the theoretical inclusion of the jail and prison population.

Another area of concern with tabulations involving young people in household surveys is the relatively low coverage ratio compared to older age groups. CPS undercoverage results from missed housing units and missed people within sample households. Overall CPS undercoverage for October 2012 is estimated to be about 14 percent. CPS coverage varies with age, sex, and race. Generally, coverage is larger for females than for males and larger for non-Blacks than for Blacks. For example, in October 2012 the coverage ratio for Black 20- to 24-year-old males was 63 percent. The CPS weighting procedure partially corrects for the bias due to undercoverage. Further information on CPS methodology may be obtained from http://www.census.gov/cps.

Further information on the calculation of dropouts and dropout rates may be obtained from *Trends in High School Dropout and Completion Rates in the United States: 1972–2009* (NCES 2012-006) at http://nces.ed.gov/pubsearch/pubsinfo.asp?pubid=2012006 or by contacting

Joel McFarland
Annual Reports and Information Staff
National Center for Education Statistics
Potomac Center Plaza
550 12th Street SW
Washington, DC 20202
joel.mcfarland@ed.gov

School Enrollment

Each October, the Current Population Survey (CPS) includes supplemental questions on the enrollment status of the population ages 3 years and over. Prior to 2001, the October supplement consisted of approximately 47,000 interviewed households. Beginning with the October 2001 supplement, the sample was expanded by 9,000 to a total of approximately 56,000 interviewed households. The main sources of nonsampling variability in the responses to the supplement are those inherent in the survey instrument. The question of current enrollment may not be answered accurately for various reasons. Some respondents may not know current grade information for every student in the household, a problem especially prevalent for households with members in college or in nursery school. Confusion over college credits or hours taken by a student may make it difficult to determine the year in which the student is enrolled. Problems may occur with the definition of nursery school (a group or class organized to provide educational experiences for children) where respondents' interpretations of "educational experiences" vary.

For the October 2012 basic CPS, the household-level nonresponse rate was 9.6 percent. The person-level nonresponse rate for the school enrollment supplement was an additional 9.2 percent. Since the basic CPS nonresponse rate is a household-level rate and the school enrollment supplement nonresponse rate is a person-level rate, these rates cannot be combined to derive an overall nonresponse rate. Nonresponding households may have fewer persons than interviewed ones, so combining these rates may lead to an overestimate of the true overall nonresponse rate for persons for the school enrollment supplement.

Further information on CPS methodology may be obtained from http://www.census.gov/cps.

Further information on the CPS School Enrollment Supplement may be obtained from

Education and Social Stratification Branch
Census Bureau
U.S. Department of Commerce
4600 Silver Hill Road
Washington, DC 20233
http://www.census.gov/hhes/school/index.html

Decennial Census, Population Estimates, and Population Projections

The Decennial Census is a universe survey mandated by the U.S. Constitution. It is a questionnaire sent to every household in the country, and it is composed of seven questions about the household and its members (name, sex, age, relationship, Hispanic origin, race, and whether the housing unit is owned or rented). The Census Bureau also produces annual estimates of the resident population by demographic characteristics (age, sex, race, and Hispanic origin) for the nation, states, and counties, as well as national and state projections for the resident population. The reference date for population estimates is July 1 of the given year. With each new issue of July 1 estimates, the Census Bureau revises estimates for each year back to the last census. Previously published estimates are superseded and archived.

Further information on the Decennial Census may be obtained from http://www.census.gov.

National Population Projections

The 2012 National Population Projections, the first based on the 2010 Census, provide projections of resident population and projections of the United States resident population by age, sex, race, and Hispanic origin from 2012 through 2060. The following is a general description of the methods used to produce the 2012 National Population Projections.

The projections were produced using a cohort-component method beginning with an estimated base population for July 1, 2011. First, components of population change (mortality, fertility, and net international migration) were projected. Next, for each passing year, the population is advanced one year of age and the new age categories are updated using the projected survival rates and levels of net international migration for that year. A new birth cohort is then added to form the population under one year of age by applying projected age-specific fertility rates to the average female population aged 10 to 54 years and updating the new cohort for the effects of mortality and net international migration.

The assumptions for the components of change were based on time series analysis. Initially, demographic models were used to summarize historical trends. Further information on the methodologies used to produce the 2012 National Population Projections may be obtained from http://www.census.gov/population/projections/methodology/.

State Population Projections

These state population projections were prepared using a cohort-component method by which each component of population change—births, deaths, state-to-state migration flows, international in-migration, and international out-migration—was projected separately for each birth cohort by sex, race, and Hispanic origin. The basic framework was the same as in past Census Bureau projections.

Detailed components necessary to create the projections were obtained from vital statistics, administrative records, census data, and national projections. The cohort-component method is based on the traditional demographic accounting system:

$$P_1 = P_0 + B - D + DIM - DOM + IIM - IOM$$

where:

P_1 = population at the end of the period

P_0 = population at the beginning of the period

B = births during the period

D = deaths during the period

DIM = domestic in-migration during the period

DOM = domestic out-migration during the period

IIM = international in-migration during the period

IOM = international out-migration during the period.

To generate population projections with this model, the Census Bureau created separate datasets for each of these components. In general, the assumptions concerning the future levels of fertility, mortality, and international migration are consistent with the assumptions developed for the national population projections of the Census Bureau.

Once the data for each component were developed the cohort-component method was applied to produce the projections. For each projection year, the base population for each state was disaggregated into eight race and Hispanic categories (non-Hispanic White; non-Hispanic Black; non-Hispanic American Indian, Eskimo, and Aleut; non-Hispanic Asian and Pacific

Islander; Hispanic White; Hispanic Black; Hispanic American Indian, Eskimo, and Aleut; and Hispanic Asian and Pacific Islander), by sex, and single year of age (ages 0 to 85+). The next step was to survive each age-sex-race-ethnic group forward 1 year using the pertinent survival rate. The internal redistribution of the population was accomplished by applying the appropriate state-to-state migration rates to the survived population in each state. The projected out-migrants were subtracted from the state of origin and added to the state of destination (as in-migrants). Next, the appropriate number of immigrants from abroad was added to each group. The population under age 1 was created by applying the appropriate age-race-ethnic-specific birth rates to females of childbearing age (ages 15 to 49). The number of births by sex and race/ethnicity were survived forward and exposed to the appropriate migration rate to yield the population under age 1. The final results of the projection process were proportionally adjusted to be consistent with the national population projections by single years of age, sex, race, and Hispanic origin. The entire process was then repeated for each year of the projection.

More information on Census Bureau projections may be obtained from

Population Division
Census Bureau
U.S. Department of Commerce
Washington, DC 20233
http://www.census.gov

OTHER SOURCES

IHS Global Inc.

IHS Global Inc. provides an information system that includes databases of economic and financial information; simulation and planning models; regular publications and special studies; data retrieval and management systems; and access to experts on economic, financial, industrial, and market activities. One service is the IHS Global Inc. Model of the U.S. Economy, which contains annual projections of U.S. economic and financial conditions, including forecasts for the federal government, incomes, population, prices and wages, and state and local governments, over a long-term (10- to 25-year) forecast period.

Additional information is available from

IHS Global Inc.
1000 Winter Street
Suite 4300N
Waltham, MA 02451-124
http://www.ihsglobalinsight.com

Appendix D
References

Broughman, S.P., and Swaim, N.L. (2013). *Characteristics of Private Schools in the United States: Results From the 2011–12 Private School Universe Survey* (NCES 2013-316). National Center for Education Statistics, Institute of Education Sciences, U.S Department of Education. Washington, DC.

Chapman, C., Laird, J., Ifill, N., and KewalRamani, A. (2011). *Trends in High School Dropout and Completion Rates in the United States: 1972–2009* (NCES 2012-006). National Center for Education Statistics, Institute of Education Sciences, U.S. Department of Education. Washington, DC.

Gamkhar, S., and Oates, W. (1996). Asymmetries in the Response to Increases and Decreases in Intergovernmental Grants: Some Empirical Findings. *National Tax Journal, 49*(3): 501–512.

Ginder, S.A., and Kelly-Reid, J.E. (2013). *Enrollment in Postsecondary Institutions, Fall 2012; Financial Statistics, Fiscal Year 2012; Graduation Rates, Selected Cohorts, 2004–09; and Employees in Postsecondary Institutions, Fall 2012* (NCES 2013-183). National Center for Education Statistics, Institute of Education Sciences, U.S. Department of Education. Washington, DC.

Goldring, R., Taie, S., Rizzo, L., Colby, D., and Fraser, A. (2013). *User's Manual for the 2011–12 Schools and Staffing Survey, Volume 1: Overview* (NCES 2013-330). National Center for Education Statistics, Institute of Education Sciences, U.S. Department of Education. Washington, DC.

Goldring, R., Taie, S., Rizzo, L., Colby, D., and Fraser, A. (2013). *User's Manual for the 2011–12 Schools and Staffing Survey Volume 2: Public and Private School Data Files* (NCES 2013-331). National Center for Education Statistics, Institute of Education Sciences, U.S. Department of Education. Washington, DC.

Goldring, R., Taie, S., Rizzo, L., Colby, D., and Fraser, A. (2013). *User's Manual for the 2011–12 Schools and Staffing Survey Volume 3: Public School District Data File* (NCES 2013-332). National Center for Education Statistics, Institute of Education Sciences, U.S. Department of Education. Washington, DC.

Goldring, R., Taie, S., Rizzo, L., Colby, D., and Fraser, A. (2013). *User's Manual for the 2011–12 Schools and Staffing Survey Volume 4: Public and Private School Principal Data Files* (NCES 2013-333). National Center for Education Statistics, Institute of Education Sciences, U.S. Department of Education. Washington, DC.

Goldring, R., Taie, S., Rizzo, L., Colby, D., and Fraser, A. (2013). *User's Manual for the 2011–12 Schools and Staffing Survey Volume 5: Library Media Center Data File* (NCES 2013-334). National Center for Education Statistics, Institute of Education Sciences, U.S. Department of Education. Washington, DC.

Goldring, R., Taie, S., Rizzo, L., Colby, D., and Fraser, A. (2013). *User's Manual for the 2011–12 Schools and Staffing Survey Volume 6: Public and Private School Teacher Data Files* (NCES 2013-335). National Center for Education Statistics, Institute of Education Sciences, U.S. Department of Education. Washington, DC.

Greene, W. (2000). *Econometric Analysis.* New Jersey: Prentice-Hall.

Hussar, W.J. (1999). *Predicting the Need for Newly Hired Teachers in the United States to 2008–09* (NCES 99-026). National Center for Education Statistics, U.S. Department of Education. Washington, DC.

IHS Global Inc., "U.S. Quarterly Macroeconomic Model, 1st Quarter 2015 Short-Term Baseline Projections."

Inman, R.P. (1979). The Fiscal Performance of Local Governments: An Interpretive Review. In P. Mieszkowski and M. Straszheim (Eds.), *Current Issues in Urban Economics,* (pp. 270–321). Baltimore: Johns Hopkins Press.

Intriligator, M.D. (1978). *Econometric Models, Techniques, & Applications.* New Jersey: Prentice-Hall, Inc.

Jackson, K.W., Jang, D., Sukasih, A., and Peeckson, S. (2005). *Integrated Postsecondary Education Data System Data Quality Study* (NCES 2005-175). National Center for Education Statistics, Institute of Education Sciences, U.S. Department of Education. Washington, DC.

Johnston, J., and Dinardo, J. (1996). *Econometric Methods.* New York: McGraw-Hill.

Judge, G., Hill, W., Griffiths, R., Lutkepohl, H., and Lee, T. (1985). *The Theory and Practice of Econometrics.* New York: John Wiley and Sons.

Kalton, G., Winglee, M., Krawchuk, S., and Levine, D. (2000). *Quality Profile for SASS, Rounds 1–3: 1987–1995, Aspects of the Quality of Data in the Schools and Staffing Surveys (SASS)* (NCES 2000-308). National Center for Education Statistics, Institute of Education Sciences, U.S. Department of Education. Washington, DC.

Knapp, L.G., Kelly-Reid, J.E., and Ginder, S.A. (2011). *Postsecondary Institutions and Price of Attendance in the United States: 2011–12, Degrees and Other Awards Conferred: 2010–11, and 12-Month Enrollment: 2010–11* (NCES 2012-289rev). National Center for Education Statistics, Institute of Education Sciences, U.S. Department of Education. Washington, DC.

Mitias, P., and Turnbull, G. (2001). Grant Illusion, Tax Illusion, and Local Government Spending. *Public Finance Review, 29*(5): 347–368.

U.S. Department of Commerce, Census Bureau, 2012 National Population Projections, retrieved January 5, 2015, from http://www.census.gov/popest/data/index.html.

U.S. Department of Commerce, Census Bureau, Current Population Reports, "Social and Economic Characteristics of Students," 2013.

U.S. Department of Commerce, Census Bureau, Population Estimates, retrieved January 5, 2015, from http://www.census.gov/popest/data/index.html.

U.S. Department of Commerce, Census Bureau, 2005 Interim State Population Projections, retrieved November 2, 2008, from http://www.census.gov/population/projections/data/state/projectionsagesex.html.

Appendix E
List of Abbreviations

ADA	Average daily attendance
CCD	Common Core of Data
CPI	Consumer Price Index
CPS	Current Population Survey
CV	Coefficient of Variation
D.W. statistic	Durbin-Watson statistic
FTE	Full-time-equivalent
HEGIS	Higher Education General Information Survey
IPEDS	Integrated Postsecondary Education Data System
IPEDS-C	Integrated Postsecondary Education Data System, Completions Survey
IPEDS-EF	Integrated Postsecondary Education Data System, Fall Enrollment Survey
MAPE	Mean absolute percentage error
NCES	National Center for Education Statistics
PreK	Prekindergarten
PreK–8	Prekindergarten through grade 8
PreK–12	Prekindergarten through grade 12
PSS	Private School Survey
SASS	Schools and Staffing Survey

This page intentionally left blank.

Appendix F
Glossary

A

Associate's degree A degree granted for the successful completion of a sub-baccalaureate program of studies, usually requiring at least 2 years (or equivalent) of full-time college-level study. This includes degrees granted in a cooperative or work-study program.

Autocorrelation Correlation of the error terms from different observations of the same variable. Also called Serial correlation.

Average daily attendance (ADA) The aggregate attendance of a school during a reporting period (normally a school year) divided by the number of days school is in session during this period. Only days on which the pupils are under the guidance and direction of teachers should be considered days in session.

Average daily membership (ADM) The aggregate membership of a school during a reporting period (normally a school year) divided by the number of days school is in session during this period. Only days on which the pupils are under the guidance and direction of teachers should be considered as days in session. The average daily membership for groups of schools having varying lengths of terms is the average of the average daily memberships obtained for the individual schools. Membership includes all pupils who are enrolled, even if they do not actually attend.

B

Bachelor's degree A degree granted for the successful completion of a baccalaureate program of studies, usually requiring at least 4 years (or equivalent) of full-time college-level study. This includes degrees granted in a cooperative or work-study program.

Breusch-Godfrey serial correlation LM test A statistic testing the independence of errors in least-squares regression against alternatives of first-order and higher degrees of serial correlation. The test belongs to a class of asymptotic tests known as the Lagrange multiplier (LM) tests.

C

Capital outlay Funds for the acquisition of land and buildings; building construction, remodeling, and additions; the initial installation or extension of service systems and other built-in equipment; and site improvement. The category also encompasses architectural and engineering services including the development of blueprints.

Classroom teacher A staff member assigned the professional activities of instructing pupils in self-contained classes or courses, or in classroom situations; usually expressed in full-time equivalents.

Coefficient of variation (CV) Represents the ratio of the standard error to the estimate. For example, a CV of 30 percent indicates that the standard error of the estimate is equal to 30 percent of the estimate's value. The CV is used to compare the amount of variation relative to the magnitude of the estimate. A CV of 30 percent or greater indicates that an estimate should be interpreted with caution. For a discussion of standard errors, see Appendix C: Data Sources.

Cohort A group of individuals that have a statistical factor in common, for example, year of birth.

Cohort-component method A method for estimating and projecting a population that is distinguished by its ability to preserve knowledge of an age distribution of a population (which may be of a single sex, race, and Hispanic origin) over time.

College A postsecondary school that offers general or liberal arts education, usually leading to an associate's, bachelor's, master's, or doctor's degree. Junior colleges and community colleges are included under this terminology.

Constant dollars Dollar amounts that have been adjusted by means of price and cost indexes to eliminate inflationary factors and allow direct comparison across years.

Consumer Price Index (CPI) This price index measures the average change in the cost of a fixed market basket of goods and services purchased by consumers. Indexes vary for specific areas or regions, periods of time, major groups of consumer expenditures, and population groups. The CPI reflects spending patterns for two population groups: (1) all urban consumers and urban wage earners and (2) clerical workers. CPIs are calculated for both the calendar year and the school year using the U.S. All Items CPI for All Urban Consumers (CPI-U). The calendar year CPI is the same as the annual CPI-U. The school year CPI is calculated by adding the monthly CPI-U figures, beginning with July of the first year and ending with June of the following year, and then dividing that figure by 12.

Control of institutions A classification of institutions of elementary/secondary or postsecondary education by whether the institution is operated by publicly elected or appointed officials and derives its primary support from public funds (public control) or is operated by privately elected or appointed officials and derives its major source of funds from private sources (private control).

Current dollars Dollar amounts that have not been adjusted to compensate for inflation.

Current expenditures (elementary/secondary) The expenditures for operating local public schools, excluding capital outlay and interest on school debt. These expenditures include such items as salaries for school personnel, benefits, student transportation, school books and materials, and energy costs. Beginning in 1980–81, expenditures for state administration are excluded.

> **Instruction expenditures** Includes expenditures for activities related to the interaction between teacher and students. Includes salaries and benefits for teachers and instructional aides, textbooks, supplies, and purchased services such as instruction via television. Also included are tuition expenditures to other local education agencies.

> **Administration expenditures** Includes expenditures for school administration (i.e., the office of the principal, full-time department chairpersons, and graduation expenses), general administration (the superintendent and board of education and their immediate staff), and other support services expenditures.

> **Transportation** Includes expenditures for vehicle operation, monitoring, and vehicle servicing and maintenance.

> **Food services** Includes all expenditures associated with providing food to students and staff in a school or school district. The services include preparing and serving regular and incidental meals or snacks in connection with school activities, as well as the delivery of food to schools.

> **Enterprise operations** Includes expenditures for activities that are financed, at least in part, by user charges, similar to a private business. These include operations funded by sales of products or services, together with amounts for direct program support made by state education agencies for local school districts.

Current expenditures per pupil in average daily attendance Current expenditures for the regular school term divided by the average daily attendance of full-time pupils (or full-time equivalency of pupils) during the term. See also Current expenditures and Average daily attendance.

D

Degree An award conferred by a college, university, or other postsecondary education institution as official recognition for the successful completion of a program of studies. Refers specifically to associate's or higher degrees conferred by degree-granting institutions. See also Associate's degree, Bachelor's degree, Master's degree, and Doctor's degree.

Degree-granting institutions Postsecondary institutions that are eligible for Title IV federal financial aid programs and grant an associate's or higher degree. For an institution to be eligible to participate in Title IV financial aid programs it must offer a program of at least 300 clock hours in length, have accreditation recognized by the U.S. Department of Education, have been in business for at least 2 years, and have signed a participation agreement with the Department.

Degrees of freedom The number of free or linearly independent sample observations used in the calculation of a statistic. In a time series regression with t time periods and k independent variables including a constant term, there would be t minus k degrees of freedom.

Department of Defense (DoD) dependents schools Schools that are operated by the Department of Defense Education Activity (a civilian agency of the U.S. Department of Defense) and provide comprehensive prekindergarten through 12th-grade educational programs on military installations both within the United States and overseas.

Dependent variable A mathematical variable whose value is determined by that of one or more other variables in a function. In regression analysis, when a random variable, y, is expressed as a function of variables $x1, x2, ... xk$, plus a stochastic term, then y is known as the "dependent variable."

Disposable personal income Current income received by people less their contributions for social insurance, personal tax, and nontax payments. It is the income available to people for spending and saving. Nontax payments include passport fees, fines and penalties, donations, and tuitions and fees paid to schools and hospitals operated mainly by the government. See also Personal income.

Doctor's degree The highest award a student can earn for graduate study. Includes such degrees as the Doctor of Education (Ed.D.); the Doctor of Juridical Science (S.J.D.); the Doctor of Public Health (Dr.P.H.); and the Doctor of Philosophy (Ph.D.) in any field, such as agronomy, food technology, education, engineering, public administration, ophthalmology, or radiology. The doctor's degree classification encompasses three main subcategories—research/scholarship degrees, professional practice degrees, and other degrees—which are described below.

> **Doctor's degree—research/scholarship** A Ph.D. or other doctor's degree that requires advanced work beyond the master's level, including the preparation and defense of a dissertation based on original research, or the planning and execution of an original project demonstrating substantial artistic or scholarly achievement. Examples of this type of degree may include the following and others, as designated by the awarding institution: the Ed.D. (in education), D.M.A. (in musical arts), D.B.A. (in business administration), D.Sc. (in science), D.A. (in arts), or D.M (in medicine).

Doctor's degree—professional practice A doctor's degree that is conferred upon completion of a program providing the knowledge and skills for the recognition, credential, or license required for professional practice. The degree is awarded after a period of study such that the total time to the degree, including both preprofessional and professional preparation, equals at least 6 full-time-equivalent academic years. Some doctor's degrees of this type were formerly classified as first-professional degrees. Examples of this type of degree may include the following and others, as designated by the awarding institution: the D.C. or D.C.M. (in chiropractic); D.D.S. or D.M.D. (in dentistry); L.L.B. or J.D. (in law); M.D. (in medicine); O.D. (in optometry); D.O. (in osteopathic medicine); Pharm.D. (in pharmacy); D.P.M., Pod.D., or D.P. (in podiatry); or D.V.M. (in veterinary medicine).

Doctor's degree—other A doctor's degree that does not meet the definition of either a doctor's degree—research/scholarship or a doctor's degree—professional practice.

Double exponential smoothing A method that takes a single smoothed average component of demand and smoothes it a second time to allow for estimation of a trend effect.

Durbin-Watson statistic A statistic testing the independence of errors in least squares regression against the alternative of first-order serial correlation. The statistic is a simple linear transformation of the first-order serial correlation of residuals and, although its distribution is unknown, it is tested by bounding statistics that follow R. L. Anderson's distribution.

E

Econometrics The quantitative examination of economic trends and relationships using statistical techniques, and the development, examination, and refinement of those techniques.

Elementary school A school classified as elementary by state and local practice and composed of any span of grades not above grade 8.

Elementary/secondary school Includes only schools that are part of state and local school systems, and also most nonprofit private elementary/secondary schools, both religiously affiliated and nonsectarian. Includes regular, alternative, vocational, and special education schools. U.S. totals exclude federal schools for American Indians, and federal schools on military posts and other federal installations.

Enrollment The total number of students registered in a given school unit at a given time, generally in the fall of a year.

Estimate A numerical value obtained from a statistical sample and assigned to a population parameter. The particular value yielded by an estimator in a given set of circumstances or the rule by which such particular values are calculated.

Estimating equation An equation involving observed quantities and an unknown that serves to estimate the latter.

Estimation Estimation is concerned with inference about the numerical value of unknown population values from incomplete data, such as a sample. If a single figure is calculated for each unknown parameter, the process is called point estimation. If an interval is calculated within which the parameter is likely, in some sense, to lie, the process is called interval estimation.

Expenditures, Total For elementary/secondary schools, these include all charges for current outlays plus capital outlays and interest on school debt. For degree-granting institutions, these include current outlays plus capital outlays. For government, these include charges net of recoveries and other correcting transactions other than for retirement of debt, investment in securities, extension of credit, or as agency transactions. Government expenditures include only external transactions, such as the provision of perquisites or other payments in kind. Aggregates for groups of governments exclude intergovernmental transactions among the governments.

Expenditures per pupil Charges incurred for a particular period of time divided by a student unit of measure, such as average daily attendance or fall enrollment.

Exponential smoothing A method used in time series analysis to smooth or to predict a series. There are various forms, but all are based on the supposition that more remote history has less importance than more recent history.

F

First-order serial correlation When errors in one time period are correlated directly with errors in the ensuing time period.

First-professional degree NCES no longer uses this classification. Most degrees formerly classified as first-professional (such as M.D., D.D.S., Pharm.D., D.V.M., and J.D.) are now classified as doctor's degrees—professional practice. However, master's of divinity degrees are now classified as master's degrees.

First-time student (undergraduate) A student who has no prior postsecondary experience (except as noted below) attending any institution for the first time at the undergraduate level. Includes students enrolled in the fall term who attended college for the first time in the prior summer term, and students who entered with advanced standing (college credits earned before graduation from high school).

Fiscal year A period of 12 months for which accounting records are compiled. Institutions and states may designate their own accounting period, though most states use a July 1 through June 30 accounting year. The yearly accounting period for the federal government begins on October 1 and ends on the following September 30. The fiscal year is designated by the calendar year in which it ends; e.g., fiscal year 2006 begins on October 1, 2005, and ends on September 30, 2006. (From fiscal year 1844 to fiscal year 1976, the federal fiscal year began on July 1 and ended on the following June 30.)

Forecast An estimate of the future based on rational study and analysis of available pertinent data, as opposed to subjective prediction.

Forecasting Assessing the magnitude that a quantity will assume at some future point in time, as distinct from "estimation," which attempts to assess the magnitude of an already existent quantity.

For-profit institution A private institution in which the individual(s) or agency in control receives compensation other than wages, rent, or other expenses for the assumption of risk.

Full-time enrollment The number of students enrolled in postsecondary education courses with total credit load equal to at least 75 percent of the normal full-time course load. At the undergraduate level, full-time enrollment typically includes students who have a credit load of 12 or more semester or quarter credits. At the postbaccalaureate level, full-time enrollment includes students who typically have a credit load of 9 or more semester or quarter credits, as well as other students who are considered full time by their institutions.

Full-time-equivalent (FTE) enrollment For postsecondary institutions, enrollment of full-time students, plus the full-time equivalent of part-time students. The full-time equivalent of the part-time students is estimated using different factors depending on the type and control of institution and level of student.

FTE teacher See Instructional staff.

Function A mathematical correspondence that assigns exactly one element of one set to each element of the same or another set. A variable that depends on and varies with another.

Functional form A mathematical statement of the relationship among the variables in a model.

G

Geographic region One of the four regions of the United States used by the U.S. Census Bureau, as follows:

Northeast	Midwest
Connecticut (CT)	Illinois (IL)
Maine (ME)	Indiana (IN)
Massachusetts (MA)	Iowa (IA)
New Hampshire (NH)	Kansas (KS)
New Jersey (NJ)	Michigan (MI)
New York (NY)	Minnesota (MN)
Pennsylvania (PA)	Missouri (MO)
Rhode Island (RI)	Nebraska (NE)
Vermont (VT)	North Dakota (ND)
	Ohio (OH)
	South Dakota (SD)
	Wisconsin (WI)

South	West
Alabama (AL)	Alaska (AK)
Arkansas (AR)	Arizona (AZ)
Delaware (DE)	California (CA)
District of Columbia (DC)	Colorado (CO)
Florida (FL)	Hawaii (HI)
Georgia (GA)	Idaho (ID)
Kentucky (KY)	Montana (MT)
Louisiana (LA)	Nevada (NV)
Maryland (MD)	New Mexico (NM)
Mississippi (MS)	Oregon (OR)
North Carolina (NC)	Utah (UT)
Oklahoma (OK)	Washington (WA)
South Carolina (SC)	Wyoming (WY)
Tennessee (TN)	
Texas (TX)	
Virginia (VA)	
West Virginia (WV)	

Graduate An individual who has received formal recognition for the successful completion of a prescribed program of studies.

H

High school A secondary school offering the final years of high school work necessary for graduation, usually includes grades 10, 11, 12 (in a 6-3-3 plan) or grades 9, 10, 11, and 12 (in a 6-2-4 plan).

High school completer An individual who has been awarded a high school diploma or an equivalent credential, including a General Educational Development (GED) certificate.

High school diploma A formal document regulated by the state certifying the successful completion of a prescribed secondary school program of studies. In some states or communities, high school diplomas are differentiated by type, such as an academic diploma, a general diploma, or a vocational diploma.

High school equivalency certificate A formal document certifying that an individual has met the state requirements for high school graduation equivalency by obtaining satisfactory scores on an approved examination and meeting other performance requirements (if any) set by a state education agency or other appropriate body. One particular version of this certificate is the General Educational Development (GED) test. The GED test is a comprehensive test used primarily to appraise the educational development of students who have not completed their formal high school education and who may earn a high school equivalency certificate by achieving satisfactory scores. GEDs are awarded by the states or other agencies, and the test is developed and distributed by the GED Testing Service (a joint venture of the American Council on Education and Pearson).

Higher education Study beyond secondary school at an institution that offers programs terminating in an associate's, bachelor's, or higher degree.

I

Income tax Taxes levied on net income, that is, on gross income less certain deductions permitted by law. These taxes can be levied on individuals or on corporations or unincorporated businesses where the income is taxed distinctly from individual income.

Independent variable In regression analysis, a random variable, *y*, is expressed as a function of variables *x1, x2, ... xk*, plus a stochastic term; the *x*'s are known as "independent variables."

Inflation A rise in the general level of prices of goods and services in an economy over a period of time, which generally corresponds to a decline in the real value of money or a loss of purchasing power. See also Constant dollars.

Instruction (elementary and secondary) Instruction encompasses all activities dealing directly with the interaction between teachers and students. Teaching may be provided for students in a school classroom, in another location such as a home or hospital, and in other learning situations such as those involving co-curricular activities. Instruction may be provided through some other approved medium, such as the Internet, television, radio, telephone, and correspondence.

Instructional staff Full-time-equivalent number of positions, not the number of different individuals occupying the positions during the school year. In local schools, includes all public elementary and secondary (junior and senior high) day-school positions that are in the nature of teaching or in the improvement of the teaching-learning situation; includes consultants or supervisors of instruction, principals, teachers, guidance personnel, librarians, psychological personnel, and other instructional staff, and excludes administrative staff, attendance personnel, clerical personnel, and junior college staff.

Interest on debt Includes expenditures for long-term debt service interest payments (i.e., those longer than 1 year).

Interpolation See Linear interpolation.

L

Lag An event occurring at time *t* + *k* (*k* > 0) is said to lag behind an event occurring at time *t*, the extent of the lag being *k*. An event occurring *k* time periods before another may be regarded as having a negative lag.

Lead time When forecasting a statistic, the number of time periods since the last time period of actual data for that statistic used in producing the forecast.

Level of school A classification of elementary/secondary schools by instructional level. Includes elementary schools, secondary schools, and combined elementary and secondary schools.

Linear interpolation A method that allows the prediction of an unknown value if any two particular values on the same scale are known and the rate of change is assumed constant.

Local education agency (LEA) See School district.

M

Master's degree A degree awarded for successful completion of a program generally requiring 1 or 2 years of full-time college-level study beyond the bachelor's degree. One type of master's degree, including the Master of Arts degree, or M.A., and the Master of Science degree, or M.S., is awarded in the liberal arts and sciences for advanced scholarship in a subject field or discipline and demonstrated ability to perform scholarly research. A second type of master's degree is awarded for the completion of a professionally oriented program, for example, an M.Ed. in education, an M.B.A. in business administration, an M.F.A. in fine arts, an M.M. in music, an M.S.W. in social work, and an M.P.A. in public administration. Some master's degrees—such as divinity degrees (M.Div. or M.H.L./Rav), which were formerly classified as "first-professional"—may require more than 2 years of full-time study beyond the bachelor's degree.

Mean absolute percentage error (MAPE) The average value of the absolute value of errors expressed in percentage terms.

Migration Geographic mobility involving a change of usual residence between clearly defined geographic units, that is, between counties, states, or regions.

Model A system of postulates, data, and inferences presented as a mathematical description of a phenomenon, such as an actual system or process. The actual phenomenon is represented by the model in order to explain, predict, and control it.

N

Non-degree-granting institutions Postsecondary institutions that participate in Title IV federal financial aid programs but do not offer accredited 4-year or 2-year degree programs. Includes some institutions transitioning to higher level program offerings, though still classified at a lower level.

Nonresident alien A person who is not a citizen of the United States and who is in this country on a temporary basis and does not have the right to remain indefinitely.

Nursery school An instructional program for groups of children during the year or years preceding kindergarten, which provides educational experiences under the direction of teachers. See also Prekindergarten and Preschool.

O

Ordinary least squares (OLS) The estimator that minimizes the sum of squared residuals.

P

Parameter A quantity that describes a statistical population.

Part-time enrollment The number of students enrolled in postsecondary education courses with a total credit load less than 75 percent of the normal full-time credit load. At the undergraduate level, part-time enrollment typically includes students who have a credit load of less than 12 semester or quarter credits. At the postbaccalaureate level, part-time enrollment typically includes students who have a credit load of less than 9 semester or quarter credits.

Personal income Current income received by people from all sources, minus their personal contributions for social insurance. Classified as "people" are individuals (including owners of unincorporated firms), nonprofit institutions serving individuals, private trust funds, and private noninsured welfare funds. Personal income includes transfers (payments not resulting from current production) from government and business such as social security benefits and military pensions, but excludes transfers among people.

Postbaccalaureate enrollment The number of students working towards advanced degrees and of students enrolled in graduate-level classes but not enrolled in degree programs.

Postsecondary education The provision of formal instructional programs with a curriculum designed primarily for students who have completed the requirements for a high school diploma or equivalent. This includes programs of an academic, vocational, and continuing professional education purpose, and excludes avocational and adult basic education programs.

Postsecondary institutions (basic classification by level)

4-year institution An institution offering at least a 4-year program of college-level studies wholly or principally creditable toward a baccalaureate degree.

2-year institution An institution offering at least a 2-year program of college-level studies which terminates in an associate degree or is principally creditable toward a baccalaureate degree. Data prior to 1996 include some institutions that have a less-than-2-year program, but were designated as institutions of higher education in the Higher Education General Information Survey.

Less-than-2-year institution An institution that offers programs of less than 2 years' duration below the baccalaureate level. Includes occupational and vocational schools with programs that do not exceed 1,800 contact hours.

Prekindergarten Preprimary education for children typically ages 3–4 who have not entered kindergarten. It may offer a program of general education or special education and may be part of a collaborative effort with Head Start.

Preschool An instructional program enrolling children generally younger than 5 years of age and organized to provide children with educational experiences under professionally qualified teachers during the year or years immediately preceding kindergarten (or prior to entry into elementary school when there is no kindergarten). See also Nursery school and Prekindergarten.

Primary school A school with at least one grade lower than 5 and no grade higher than 8.

Private institution An institution that is controlled by an individual or agency other than a state, a subdivision of a state, or the federal government, which is usually supported primarily by other than public funds, and the operation of whose program rests with other than publicly elected or appointed officials.

Private nonprofit institution An institution in which the individual(s) or agency in control receives no compensation other than wages, rent, or other expenses for the assumption of risk. These include both independent nonprofit institutions and those affiliated with a religious organization.

Private for-profit institution An institution in which the individual(s) or agency in control receives compensation other than wages, rent, or other expenses for the assumption of risk (e.g., proprietary schools).

Private school Private elementary/secondary schools surveyed by the Private School Universe Survey (PSS) are assigned to one of three major categories (Catholic, other religious, or nonsectarian) and, within each major category, one of three subcategories based on the school's religious affiliation provided by respondents.

Catholic Schools categorized according to governance, provided by Catholic school respondents, into parochial, diocesan, and private schools.

Other religious Schools that have a religious orientation or purpose but are not Roman Catholic. Other religious schools are categorized according to religious association membership, provided by respondents, into Conservative Christian, other affiliated, and unaffiliated schools. Conservative Christian schools are those "Other religious" schools with membership in at least one of four associations: Accelerated Christian Education, American Association of Christian Schools, Association of Christian Schools International, and Oral Roberts University Education Fellowship. Affiliated schools are those "Other religious" schools not classified as Conservative Christian with membership in at least 1 of 11 associations— Association of Christian Teachers and Schools, Christian Schools International, Evangelical Lutheran Education Association, Friends Council on Education, General Conference of the Seventh-Day Adventist Church, Islamic School League of America, National Association of Episcopal Schools, National Christian School Association,

National Society for Hebrew Day Schools, Solomon Schechter Day Schools, and Southern Baptist Association of Christian Schools—or indicating membership in "other religious school associations." Unaffiliated schools are those "Other religious" schools that have a religious orientation or purpose but are not classified as Conservative Christian or affiliated.

Nonsectarian Schools that do not have a religious orientation or purpose and are categorized according to program emphasis, provided by respondents, into regular, special emphasis, and special education schools. Regular schools are those that have a regular elementary/secondary or early childhood program emphasis. Special emphasis schools are those that have a Montessori, vocational/technical, alternative, or special program emphasis. Special education schools are those that have a special education program emphasis.

Projection In relation to a time series, an estimate of future values based on a current trend.

Public school or institution A school or institution controlled and operated by publicly elected or appointed officials and deriving its primary support from public funds.

Pupil/teacher ratio The enrollment of pupils at a given period of time, divided by the full-time-equivalent number of classroom teachers serving these pupils during the same period.

R

R² The coefficient of determination; the square of the correlation coefficient between the dependent variable and its ordinary least squares (OLS) estimate.

Racial/ethnic group Classification indicating general racial or ethnic heritage. Race/ethnicity data are based on the *Hispanic* ethnic category and the race categories listed below (five single-race categories, plus the *Two or more races* category). Race categories exclude persons of Hispanic ethnicity unless otherwise noted.

> ***White*** A person having origins in any of the original peoples of Europe, the Middle East, or North Africa.

> ***Black or African American*** A person having origins in any of the black racial groups of Africa. Used interchangeably with the shortened term *Black*.

> ***Hispanic or Latino*** A person of Cuban, Mexican, Puerto Rican, South or Central American, or other Spanish culture or origin, regardless of race. Used interchangeably with the shortened term *Hispanic*.

> ***Asian*** A person having origins in any of the original peoples of the Far East, Southeast Asia, or the Indian subcontinent, including, for example, Cambodia, China, India, Japan, Korea, Malaysia, Pakistan, the Philippine Islands, Thailand, and Vietnam. Prior to 2010–11, the Common Core of Data (CCD) combined Asian and Pacific Islander categories.

> ***Native Hawaiian or Other Pacific Islander*** A person having origins in any of the original peoples of Hawaii, Guam, Samoa, or other Pacific Islands. Prior to 2010–11, the Common Core of Data (CCD) combined Asian and Pacific Islander categories. Used interchangeably with the shortened term *Pacific Islander*.

> ***American Indian or Alaska Native*** A person having origins in any of the original peoples of North and South America (including Central America), and who maintains tribal affiliation or community attachment.

> ***Two or more races*** A person identifying himself or herself as of two or more of the following race groups: White, Black, Asian, Native Hawaiian or Other Pacific Islander, or American Indian or Alaska Native. Some, but not all, reporting districts use this category. "Two or more races" was introduced in the 2000 Census and became a regular category for data collection in the Current Population Survey (CPS) in 2003. The category is sometimes excluded from a historical series of data with constant categories. It is sometimes included within the category "Other."

Region See Geographic region.

Regression analysis A statistical technique for investigating and modeling the relationship between variables.

Regular school A public elementary/secondary or charter school providing instruction and education services that does not focus primarily on special education, vocational/technical education, or alternative education.

Resident population Includes civilian population and armed forces personnel residing within the United States; excludes armed forces personnel residing overseas.

Revenue All funds received from external sources, net of refunds, and correcting transactions. Noncash transactions, such as receipt of services, commodities, or other receipts in kind are excluded, as are funds received from the issuance of debt, liquidation of investments, and nonroutine sale of property.

Revenue receipts Additions to assets that do not incur an obligation that must be met at some future date and do not represent exchanges of property for money. Assets must be available for expenditures.

Rho A measure of the correlation coefficient between errors in time period t and time period t minus 1.

S

Salary The total amount regularly paid or stipulated to be paid to an individual, before deductions, for personal services rendered while on the payroll of a business or organization.

School A division of the school system consisting of students in one or more grades or other identifiable groups and organized to give instruction of a defined type. One school may share a building with another school or one school may be housed in several buildings. Excludes schools that have closed or are planned for the future.

An education agency at the local level that ... to operate public schools or to contract ... services. Synonyms are "local basic ... unit" and "local education agency."

...ndary enrollment The total number of students registered in a school beginning with the next grade following an elementary or middle school (usually 7, 8, or 9) and ending with or below grade 12 at a given time.

Senior high school A secondary school offering the final years of high school work necessary for graduation.

Serial correlation Correlation of the error terms from different observations of the same variable. Also called Autocorrelation.

Standard error of estimate An expression for the standard deviation of the observed values about a regression line. An estimate of the variation likely to be encountered in making predictions from the regression equation.

Student An individual for whom instruction is provided in an educational program under the jurisdiction of a school, school system, or other education institution. No distinction is made between the terms "student" and "pupil," though "student" may refer to one receiving instruction at any level while "pupil" refers only to one attending school at the elementary or secondary level. A student may receive instruction in a school facility or in another location, such as at home or in a hospital. Instruction may be provided by direct student-teacher interaction or by some other approved medium such as television, radio, telephone, and correspondence.

Student membership Student membership is an annual headcount of students enrolled in school on October 1 or the school day closest to that date. The Common Core of Data (CCD) allows a student to be reported for only a single school or agency. For example, a vocational school (identified as a "shared time" school) may provide classes for students from a number of districts and show no membership.

T

Teacher see Instructional staff.

Time series A set of ordered observations on a quantitative characteristic of an individual or collective phenomenon taken at different points in time. Usually the observations are successive and equally spaced in time.

Time series analysis The branch of quantitative forecasting in which data for one variable are examined for patterns of trend, seasonality, and cycle.

Type of school A classification of public elementary and secondary schools that includes the following categories: regular schools, special education schools, vocational schools, and alternative schools.

U

Unadjusted dollars See Current dollars.

Undergraduate students Students registered at an institution of postsecondary education who are working in a baccalaureate degree program or other formal program below the baccalaureate, such as an associate's degree, vocational, or technical program.

Ungraded student (elementary/secondary) A student who has been assigned to a school or program that does not have standard grade designations.

V

Variable A quantity that may assume any one of a set of values.

Y

Years out In forecasting by year, the number of years since the last year of actual data for that statistic used in producing the forecast.

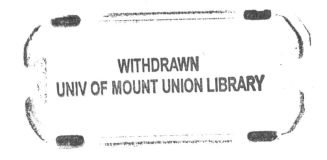